c·o·m·a·n·c·h·e · c·o·d·e · t·a·l·k·e·r·s

WILLIAM C. MEADOWS

The

c·o·m·a·n·c·h·e
c·o·d·e
t·a·l·k·e·r·s

of World War II

UNIVERSITY OF TEXAS PRESS, AUSTIN

The material in appendixes C and D originally appeared in Shelby L. Stanton's book *Order of Battle: U.S. Army, World War II* (Novato, California: Presidio Press, 1984). Used with permission of the publisher.

First edition, 2002

Requests for permission to reproduce material from this work should be sent to Permissions, University of Texas Press, Box 7819, Austin, TX 78713-7819.

♾ The paper used in this book meets the minimum requirements of ANSI/NISO Z39.48-1992 (R1997) (Permanence of Paper).

Library of Congress Cataloging-in-Publication Data

Meadows, William C., 1966–
    The Comanche code talkers of World War II / William C. Meadows.
        p.   cm.
    Includes bibliographical references and index.
        ISBN 0-292-75263-6 (cloth : alk. paper)—
    ISBN 0-292-75274-1 (pbk. : alk. paper)
        1. World War, 1939–1945—Cryptography.   2. World War, 1939–1945—Participation, Indian.   3. Comanche Indians. 4. World War, 1939–1945—France—Normandy.   I. Title.
        D810.C88 M43   2003
        940.54'03—dc21
                                            2002006779

c·o·n·t·e·n·t·s

t·a·b·l·e·s

p·r·e·f·a·c·e

On June 6, 1944, D-Day, thirteen Comanches in the Fourth Infantry Division, Fourth Signal Company, made an amphibious landing with thousands of Allied troops along the Utah Beachhead on the Normandy coast of France. While under German fire, they immediately began to lay wire for communications transmission lines and began to send their messages in a form never before heard in Europe, in coded Comanche. During the next eleven months, this small, select group of Native Americans—the Comanche Code Talkers—would play a contributing role in the Allied war effort. They would transmit coded orders and messages in a form that the Germans, Italians, and even other Comanches not trained as code talkers could not understand. The Germans remained perplexed about this code, a form they were never able to break, for many years following the war. The Comanche Code Talkers were a small group of Comanche men who were specially recruited and trained in communications skills and used their native Comanche language to communicate critical messages during World War II.

THE N̶U̶M̶U̶N̶U̶U̶

Of all of the Plains tribes, the N̶u̶m̶u̶n̶u̶u̶, meaning "People" or "The People" (often spelled by Anglos as "Numina," and popularly known as the Comanches), are one of the most well known by name (Richardson 1933; Wallace and Hoebel 1952; Kavanagh 1996), but have long been one of the least understood in terms of actual cultural content. Originally a part of the Numic-speaking Shoshone from Wyoming, the N̶u̶m̶u̶n̶u̶u̶, or Comanches, separated and migrated southward in the mid- to late seventeenth century. By the early to mid-eighteenth century, the Co-

XII manches had gained firm control of much of Texas, southwestern Oklahoma, and portions of eastern New Mexico. The seminal role played by the Comanches in the military and political development of Texas, New Mexico, and Mexico during 1706–1875 was enormously significant. During this period, the Comanches were integrally involved in the evolving competition for trade with the Spanish, French, and, later, Mexicans and Americans. Economically, the Comanche language had long been of great importance as a trade language in the Southern Plains. Throughout much of the 1700s and 1800s, the Comanche language served as a *lingua franca* for much of the intertribal and Indian-Anglo trade in the region. A mobile hunting-gathering population, the Comanches possessed a strong warrior ethos, and for men the means to social status were largely acquired through a war record (Meadows 1999). In prereservation times, the Comanches are better viewed as a number of linguistically and culturally related tribes (generally described as divisions), as they never comprised a single political or geographically centralized entity until after their entrance onto a reservation (Kavanagh 1996). After more than 150 years of warfare, competition with numerous other tribes and Anglo nations, and disease, the last remaining autonomous bands of Comanches were forced onto the collective Kiowa, Comanche, and Apache Reservation in Southwestern Oklahoma in 1875. What followed were decades of status as governmental wards, forced reduction of their lands, inadequate food, mandatory boarding schools, denial of citizenship and civil rights, continual broken treaties and legal agreements, forced allotment of their remaining lands, and an Anglo-based assimilationist war against their culture, religion, and language.

Sixty-five years later the United States Army came seeking the aid of the Comanches and their language in preparation for World War II. The Comanches had numerous reasons to resent the Taiboo' (Anglos). But in spite of all of the past experiences and the often paternalistic treatment of the Comanches by the government, when the call of duty came, they, like other Native American populations, patriotically joined in the defense of America. Prior to their recruitment, the Comanches had no idea of the ultimately unique role that they and their language would play in the outcome of that war. There was no way they could have known that they would be selected to carry out highly specialized communications service that would be unique in the European campaign. The Comanches represent a population whose loyalty to their people and the American country was unswerving in its devotion, and they were unhesitant in their decision to make the necessary sacrifices called for in the Second World War.

While many works have focused upon the broad impacts that World War II held for Native Americans, few works have focused on individual communities or topics, and even fewer have included accounts from Native Americans themselves. One of the best works on Native Americans in World War II (Bernstein 1991) is strictly based on Anglo archival materials and demonstrates no input from Native American veterans. Most studies concerning the role of Native American Code Talkers in World War II focus only upon the Navajo; however, several other tribes participated in similar fashion.

This book traces the development and history of Native American code talking, beginning with the Oklahoma Choctaws in World War I. I then focus on the United States armed forces' decision to use Native American code talkers in World War II, examining the development of the Comanche and Navajo Code Talker programs. The Comanche Code Talkers who served as communications operators in the European theater of World War II were the first organized native code-talking unit in World War II. As cryptology, World Wars I and II, and United States military communications are all enormous topics, this work does not attempt to provide a comprehensive account of these subjects, only a general background for understanding the role of Native American code talkers in World Wars I and II and those events in which the Comanche Code Talkers were involved and for which documentation exists. Because the Comanche Code Talkers were only involved in the operations extending from France through Germany, I do not address the North African and Sicilian campaigns. While select aspects of the European theater are discussed, they are largely in relation to the regions in which the Comanches served. Some of the ins and outs of signals/intelligence work during World War II, and the experiences collected from the emic perspective of the code talkers who remain alive—what they experienced, what they thought was important about their service, and how they felt about their experiences—form the content upon which much of this work focuses. This work is the story of a number of young Choctaw and Comanche men, their experiences as code talkers, and their unique contribution in military service in World Wars I and II, and how their experiences relate to Comanche and larger Native American service in the U.S. military. For more comprehensive accounts of the European theater of World War II, the reader may refer to other works, such as Kahn (1967), MacDonald (1969), Weigley (1981), and Stetson Conn's (1963) nine-volume *United States Army in World War II: The History of the European Theater of Operations.* For a thorough history of the U.S. Army Signal Corps Branch, see Raines (1996).

CONTEXT AND THEORY

This work is interdisciplinary, emphasizing historical and firsthand ethnographic data, while addressing theoretical concerns of dependency theory, the Native American martial ethos, processes behind Native American militarization and armed forces service, Native American military syncretism, and United States armed forces attitudes toward Indian servicemen as communications operators. Most authors attempting studies of Native Americans in World War II have essentially explained Indian entrance into the military as an attempt to legitimize themselves as American citizens. This work demonstrates clearly that this process of militarization is far more complex than most Native American scholars realize. As it affected the Comanche Code Talkers, the militarization context is a reflection of the larger regional processes that I have found regarding service in World Wars I and II for most Kiowa, Comanche, and Apache veterans and their traditional military society structures (Meadows 1995), and that Tom Holm (1996) has found for Native American Vietnam veterans collectively.

Theoretically, the Comanche Code Talkers serve as a case study which demonstrates that Native American motivations for enlisting in World War II and many other conflicts take complex, multifaceted, yet largely culturally based forms rather than the primarily assimilationist forms proposed in prior historical works relying on dependency theory. Native Americans did not join the armed forces in World Wars I and II solely to prove or to legitimize themselves as American citizens; many already knew that they held dual citizenship as members of their respective tribes and as American citizens via the allotment process, the 1924 Indian Citizenship Act, and the 1936 Oklahoma Indian Welfare Act. As this work will point out, most joined for a complex combination of: (1) traditional sociocultural influences (warrior-based themes), (2) acculturative influences (boarding school), (3) contemporary economic factors (employment), and (4) patriotism for the defense of their own lands, peoples, and the United States. The opportunity to (5) use their unique linguistic skills and to (6) remain in a select Native American unit with fellow Comanche kinsmen provided two additional incentives for these men during World War II. As with other Native Americans in United States military service, the Comanche Code Talkers demonstrate how a group of individuals syncretized native concepts with military service in a basically foreign institution while maintaining a strong sense of their own ethnic identity—a uniquely Comanche sense of identity. In doing so, they gave service in the United States military a meaning far beyond that of simply legitimizing themselves as American citizens.

This work also provides historical documentation that will more clearly convey the temporal developments and historical dimensions involving the Choctaw, Comanche, Navajo, and other Native American code talkers. This work distinguishes two distinct types of Native American code talking and clarifies many of the larger developments of Native American code talkers as a whole. I also demonstrate that the full potential for using Native American code talkers in World War II was unrecognized at the logistical levels of the United States armed forces and therefore underutilized.

These were but a few Comanche men participating in an amphibious landing of seven thousand ships transporting 250,000 troops of American, British, Canadian, Free French, Polish, Norwegian, and other nationalities who began their advance on five strategic beachheads. In a war in which millions of men and women served, one might ask, what is so significant about a small group of, originally seventeen and later thirteen, soldiers? What makes the contributions of such a small number of men significant given the massive scope of the war? Although these soldiers underwent much of the same military training as their peers, and performed many of the same duties, they were uniquely different from most Anglo soldiers. In addition to their contrasting cultural background and upbringing, these men brought a rare and special skill to be used as a weapon in their military service—their native language. By using their native language in a coded form, thirteen Comanche Code Talkers were able to send communications throughout their division that were faster than any of the then-existing Anglo coded forms and that were never broken by the Axis forces. In addition, the Comanches represent one of at least nineteen Native American groups known to have used various coded and noncoded forms of their native language for United States armed forces military communications in World Wars I and II. As will be demonstrated, only the conservative policies of the upper echelons of the United States Army regarding the ability of Native Americans as communications operators prevented the Comanches and other tribal groups in the European theater from contributing to the degree that the Navajos in the Marine Corps did in the Pacific theater of operations. In examining the development of Native American code talkers in the United States armed forces, I provide data demonstrating that Native Americans as code talkers held greater potential in terms of available numbers, diversity of languages, and possibility for rotation than was either realized or used in the war. Excepting select aspects of their respective backgrounds, the primary differences between the experiences of the Comanche and Navajo Code Talkers in World War II were those of military policy, unit size, and the extent of their use.

Three factors of a personal nature led me toward this study. First, coming from a family containing many veterans, I grew up hearing of their experiences in World War II, Korea, and Vietnam, and have always had an interest in military topics and veterans. Second, my early exposure to and participation in Native American dance, the evolution of the contemporary Plains Indian powwow from earlier military societies, and the associated honoring of veterans in these activities only strengthened my interest. Third, upon becoming familiar with this topic and discovering that only a few of the code talkers remained alive, I realized the urgency of time if this project were ever to be undertaken.

During research for my doctoral dissertation (Meadows 1995), I conducted ethnographic fieldwork on nineteenth- and twentieth-century military societies and veterans' issues among the Kiowa, Apache, and Comanche of southwestern Oklahoma. During my research I was fortunate to meet Mr. Forrest Kassanavoid, an extremely knowledgeable elder, a fluent Comanche speaker, a head man of the Comanche War Dance Society, and a World War II veteran. During one interview, Forrest told me he had served as a "Comanche Code Talker" during the war, and he proceeded to discuss this topic for the next hour. During subsequent visits with Forrest he began to relate to me the detailed history of the Comanche Code Talkers from their formation in late 1940 to the present. As I began to learn more of the code talkers' experiences, I realized that they were a largely unrecognized and undocumented subject. Although I was busy with the research for my dissertation, I realized that this was a subject that deserved serious attention. Considering the small number of remaining code talkers, their ages, and the almost total lack of documentation available on the subject, I felt the situation was urgent and decided to make the time to record their experiences. When I suggested to Forrest that we continue to document the group's history for a possible publication, he responded favorably and encouraged me to "work up" some material on them. Interviews with the other surviving members provided additional materials. Although several small grant requests to fund this research were turned down, I considered the personal expense justified and more than worthwhile and managed to give some monetary compensation to the members as the work progressed.

SOURCES

The research for this work combines anthropological and historical methodologies. The material for this work was very interdisciplinary, involving firsthand ethnographic fieldwork with the basic information obtained from the actual Comanche Code Talkers themselves and archival materials from Native American history, United States military records, United States Army organizational and signals intelligence data, newspapers, and appropriate secondary literature sources to test pertinent ideas and hypotheses. Archival research produced many vital, but highly fragmentary, sources, often in the form of newspaper articles and brief military-based publications. Most published sources on Native American code talkers focus only on the Navajo; the Comanches are generally either mentioned in passing or, more often than not, not at all. Some sources even incorrectly and unsupportedly state that the Comanches did not serve as code talkers. Indeed, the only formal sources on the Comanche Code Talkers are by one of the unit's own members, the late Roderick Red Elk (1991, 1992), who published brief accounts both of his personal experiences and those of the group. Inquiry and correspondence with army and Marine Corps military archives provided prompt, but minimal, material. No prior comprehensive account of the Comanche Code Talkers' experiences exists. To achieve a thorough account of this group, an ethnohistorical approach combining elements of anthropological fieldwork and archival research was necessary. Whereas most definitions of ethnohistory focus on combining archival and library research with the insights gained from using an anthropological concept of culture, my approach differs. My ethnohistorical methodology emphasizes significant firsthand ethnographic and linguistic fieldwork and extensive archival research to obtain as thorough and holistic an approach to a subject as possible.

The greatest hindrance encountered in this project was time. Only five of the original seventeen Comanche Code Talkers and their commanding training officer were living at the time I began my research. The vast majority of the information contained in this study was obtained from my fieldwork in the form of audio and video tape-recorded interviews with the three surviving members who saw combat action (Forrest Kassanavoid, Roderick Red Elk, and Charles Chibitty), and through correspondence with their training officer, Major General Hugh F. Foster Jr., U.S. Army (Retired). An interview with Albert Nahquaddy Jr. (one of two surviving members who were trained as code talkers but discharged prior to service overseas) provided additional information about the period from the group's origin through their stateside training. Anthony Tabbytite could not be reached (and has since passed away). Finally, an audio recorded archival interview with the late Mr. Haddon Codynah, another of the code talkers who saw combat action, added a sixth voice to the work. Although six of eighteen consultants is statistically a good sample and their accounts clearly address most of the group's experiences, the ability to have worked with other, **XVII**

XVIII now deceased members would only have enriched this material further. To have waited any longer would have resulted in losing much of the remaining knowledge concerning the code talkers. In hindsight this decision proved sound, as three of the four remaining members passed away before this manuscript came to print.

Indian support and encouragement, both from Comanches and other tribes, were very positive during this project. Sharp criticism by two earlier non-Indian reviewers was also very beneficial. After reading the manuscript one military historian nearly accused me of making up the entire account, responding that he did not believe the Comanches ever served as code talkers, and strenuously criticizing my assertion that sufficient numbers of fluent Native Americans in many tribes existed at the time of World War II to have formed other code-talking units. This response led me to provide additional quantitative data to complement my qualitative data, and became the majority of Chapter 2. One Anglo historian stated that after all of the harsh past treatment Indians had received, she found it a "striking irony" that Native Americans found themselves in a position to be useful in wartime communications and would enlist for military service for the reasons I propose. However, as explained by the code talkers themselves, these reasons are supported. Even more ironic is the fact that while this individual writes about Native American veterans, her work shows no evidence of having conducted any firsthand research with them. These criticisms, while largely the result of not working with Native Americans, only allowed me to further improve and enhance this manuscript.

By the spring of 1996, what was intended as an article had grown to a book-length manuscript. One of my personal tenets in conducting anthropological and Native American research is to allow my consultants to read and discuss drafts of my manuscripts prior to their publication. That summer I sent drafts of the manuscript to Mr. Kassanavoid, Mr. Red Elk, Mr. Chibitty, Mrs. Judy Allen, and Major General Foster, who provided constructive reviews and comments. Their responses were favorable. I had already decided to dedicate the book to the seventeen Comanche Code Talkers. Because Forrest Kassanavoid had played such an instrumental role in participating in and encouraging my research on the Comanche Code Talkers, I had also decided to include a special dedication of the work to him. On September 20, 1996, I received a phone call from Major General Foster informing me that Forrest was gravely ill. Forrest was undergoing cancer treatments when I last visited him the previous July. Later that afternoon after my classes, I called to check on him, planning to inform him of the dedication. However, before I could tell him, his wife Marian informed me that he had died at home in Indiahoma, Oklahoma, less than two hours earlier that afternoon. Everyone who knew Forrest lost a wonderful and cherished friend. Forrest was a tremendous friend to many people, Indian and non-Indian alike, and an extremely knowledgeable elder. During this project he always declined to accept any money I offered for his help. He was enthusiastic just to see the research undertaken and to contribute to it. I have therefore included a special dedication to him to recognize and honor his friendship, enthusiasm, and the tremendous input upon which this work so heavily rests.

FORMAT AND CONTENT

My goal is to convey an overview of the experiences, throughout their lives, of a small group of Native American veterans who performed a unique form of service in a divisional-level communications system in the European theater during World War II. It is an inspiring and little-known piece of history. I have tried to detail the human experience of these men and relate it to the larger significance of the duties they undertook as code talkers. An additional goal is to honor and give recognition and historical clarity to these gracious men who, having made such a unique contribution to the United States armed forces, were only recently recognized for their dedication and sacrifice. Another focus of this work is historical clarity regarding the actual development of Native American code talkers in World Wars I and II, which in earlier works has often been presented inaccurately.

The format of this work is largely chronological. Chapter 1 introduces the origin of codes, military code formation, prior studies of Native American military literature and code talking, native motivations for service in World War I, the development of the first Native American code talkers (the Choctaws) in World War I, and other native groups that provided coded and noncoded military communications in their native languages during World War I. This chapter concludes by offering the first formal definition of the two distinct forms of Native American code talking. Chapter 2 explores a national-level debate among the branches of the United States armed forces concerning the possibility and potential for using Native American code talkers in World War II. Linguistic and demographic data indicate that the potential for using Native American code talkers was not fully recognized and was underutilized by the United States armed forces at this time. An examination of the distribution of Native American code talkers in World War II concludes this chapter. Chapter 3 covers the prewar experiences of the Comanches: their recruitment, basic training, communications training, assignments, code formation, and athletic and cultural activities. Chapter 4 briefly describes the communications role the Comanche Code **XIX**

Talkers performed in relation to the larger army military structure and organization from 1940 to 1945. Chapter 5 relates the code talkers' actual combat experiences and use of the code from D-Day, June 6, 1944, to the end of the European war in May 1945. Chapter 6 concludes by focusing upon the postwar experiences of the code talkers, including their educational, professional, and cultural pursuits; public acknowledgment; and the Comanche Code Talkers' own reflections on their military service and the importance of native linguistic retention. It also includes the first extensive comparison between two units of Native American code talkers (Comanche and Navajo).

While numerous sources have been written on the Navajo Code Talkers, only a relatively small amount of this material conveys the Navajos' own thoughts, reflections, and interpretations of the events surrounding their military role. In an attempt to improve upon this approach, and because only a few of the members remained alive at the time I began my research, I chose a broader, more interdisciplinary, and dialogical method for this work. I have used extensive interview materials and direct quotes to bring forth the participants' own explanations, assessments, and reflections about various portions of their experiences as code talkers. While much of the military history surrounding code talkers has focused on the more serious and strictly "historical" developments of their experiences, such accounts have often left out many of the more day-to-day and even humorous, dangerous, and compelling experiences that were a part of the larger story. I have chosen to include a variety of these materials to provide a more well-rounded, realistic, and accurate account of the code talkers' experiences. I wish to show the Comanche Code Talkers as they were then and are now, and as they remembered their experiences. They were a group of young men who underwent a wide range of human experiences and emotions and remain quite modest, yet forthright, in their recollections. Thus, in an effort to make this a more dialogical work, a large amount of quoted materials from personal interviews and correspondence—focusing on the subjects stressed by the remaining code talkers—is used to allow the actual participants to tell much of their own stories themselves.

Although initially choosing to quote the Comanche Code Talkers verbatim from my interviews with them, I later chose to lightly edit these quoted materials for several reasons. Because most humans do not speak extemporaneously in a fluid, cohesive, and nonrepetitive fashion, spoken prose may sound wonderful, but it usually looks terrible in print. Repetitious use of the same words and ideas and frequent interjections detract from the fluidity of the speaking and, more importantly, from the meaning of the code talkers' statements. I have edited verbatim texts as lightly as possible to reduce them to clear, straightforward statements, eliminating repetitions of the same words and ideas in the same situation while retaining the basic ideas as well as the style of the speaker. I have cited sources as thoroughly as possible to identify them for future scholars. Some materials and citations have been kept anonymous for reasons of privacy.

This work is directed toward a wide audience including those interested in Choctaw and Comanche history, twentieth-century Native American history, World Wars I and II, Native American military and veterans' studies, military history, and signals intelligence. I have tried to find the right balance among a broad multidisciplinary approach, scholarly objectivity, and a deep and abiding respect for the life experiences of my friends and consultants. Because much of the recognition for the Comanche Code Talkers came after the majority of the members had passed on, this work is directed at documenting and honoring their service. It is my hope that the families of the Comanche Code Talkers and future generations of Comanches will find this work worthwhile.

a·c·k·n·o·w·l·e·d·g·m·e·n·t·s

Several individuals contributed in various ways to the completion of this work. First and foremost, I would like to thank Forrest Kassanavoid, Roderick Red Elk, Charles Chibitty, Albert Nahquaddy Jr., and Major General (Retired) Hugh F. Foster for time spent conducting audio- and videotaped interviews, and for sharing various photographs, newspaper clippings, and other related sources of information. This project would have been a meager and somewhat historically bland article, instead of a book, without their direct involvement. I would also like to recognize Major General Foster for his willingness to provide information through a most helpful correspondence, and for sharing several of his photographs of the Comanche Code Talkers from their training at Ft. Benning, Georgia. Mr. Ernest Stahlberg, T/5 (the assigned combat partner of Comanche Code Talker Simmons Parker), and Mr. John Eckert, both of the Fourth Division Signal Company, provided very useful reflections of their service with the Comanches and of the non-Indian soldiers' attitudes toward the Comanches. Mr. George Stahlberg provided important assistance in obtaining information and photos from his father, and archival footage of the Fourth Infantry Division.

Towana Spivey, Judith Crowder, and Anne H. Davies of the Ft. Sill Museum archives in Lawton, Oklahoma, provided various periodicals containing related information. Rodger G. Harris and Joe Todd of the Archive and Manuscripts Division of the Oklahoma Historical Society, and Joe Hays, formerly of the Museum of the Great Plains at Lawton, Oklahoma, all helped in locating oral and written materials on the Comanche Code Talkers in their respective institutions' collections. Z. Frank Hanner, Director of the National Infantry Museum at Ft. Benning, Georgia;

XXIV Carol E. Stokes, Command Historian, U.S. Army Signal Corps, Ft. Gordon, Georgia; Mike Wright of Norman, Oklahoma; Mitchell A. Yockelson, Archives I Reference Branch, Textual Reference Division, National Archives; and Michael E. Gonzales, Curator, Forty-fifth Infantry Division Museum, Oklahoma City, Oklahoma, also provided related materials. I offer my sincere appreciation to Judy Allen (Choctaw), editor of the Choctaw Nation newspaper *Bishinik*, for numerous archival materials on the Choctaw Code Talkers in both world wars. Allen has actively researched the Choctaw Code Talkers since 1987 and played a significant part in preparing information needed for the posthumous 1989 honoring of the World War I Choctaw Code Talkers at the Oklahoma State Capitol. Allen graciously supplied me with copies of published and unpublished materials, news clippings, individual members' military records and discharge papers, and correspondence with family members of the Choctaw Code Talkers, and she even sent me one of the Choctaw tribal Medals of Valor to photograph. I would also like to offer my thanks to my friend Andrea Page (Standing Rock Lakota) for sharing information from her research on Lakota and other Northern Plains Indian code talkers. Her future publication on the Lakota Code Talkers will be a valuable and anticipated work.

I would like to thank the late Forrest Kassanavoid and Roderick Red Elk, Major General (Retired) Hugh F. Foster, Judy Allen (Choctaw), Tom Holm (Cherokee-Creek), Mike Davis, Alison Bernstein, and other, anonymous readers for providing valuable comments on drafts of this work and taking an active role in various portions of its creation. I am especially grateful to Tom Holm and Mike Davis for the stimulating commentary and encouragement they provided. General Foster patiently clarified and supplemented my lay knowledge of World War II–era military terminology and organization. One of my research methodologies emphasizes the ongoing need to integrate the study of linguistics in the writing of American Indian ethnography and history (cf. Parks 1988). In an exemplary collaboration, Comanche linguist Dr. Jean O. Charney greatly raised the quality of this work by enthusiastically providing orthographic aid with all Comanche vocabulary (see Charney 1993). Finally I offer my thanks to Theresa J. May, Rachel Chance, Allison Faust, and Lynne F. Chapman of the University of Texas Press in Austin, and to Paul Spragens for his thorough assistance in copyediting.

NOTES ON THE COMANCHE SOUND SYSTEM
Jean O. Charney

The Comanche language has many of the same sounds as English, and a few sounds that are different. This overall similarity has made it possible for many of the Comanche names and terms in this book to be transposed into an orthography that is fairly close to the actual sounds of Comanche. When both a good written representation and a more or less accurate translation of a form exist, we have often, but not always, been able to analyze that form.

The consonants of Comanche are much like their English equivalents—*p, t, k, m, n, w, y, s,* and *h* are much as in English. When it occurs between vowels, *p* sometimes is heard as a sound we are writing with *v*. This sound ranges from its English counterpart to a sound more like *b*. Similarly, a *t* between vowels is sometimes heard as the tap *r* found in words like ri̲der. In addition to the above, Comanche has consonants we represent with the letters *kw* and *ts*. These stand for sounds that English has—*kw* is like *qu* in words like 'quit'; *ts* occurs within words, as in 'cats'. English does not have *ts* at the beginning of words, but many readers will be familiar with the sound from words such as *'tsar'*. Finally, Comanche has the glottal stop, represented with an apostrophe ('), in which the air leaving the lungs is stopped momentarily deep in the throat. English speakers use a glottal stop in words like 'uh-oh'.

The vowels of Comanche and English are in most cases similar, although English equivalents of the linguists' rendering of these vowels do not correspond one-to-one with the way the vowels are written in English. The vowels *i, e, u, o,* and *a* are the same as English vowels in this way: *i* stands for the vowels in a word like 'beet'; *e* stands for the vowel in a word like 'pay'; *u* stands for the vowel in a word like 'fool'; *o* stands

XXVI for the first vowel in a word like 'sofa'; and *a* stands for the vowel in a word like 'mall'.

Comanche also has a vowel that does not exist as a "real" vowel in English, although the sound is often heard in unstressed English vowels. The vowel is ʉ, and it sounds like the "uh" sound in words like 'number'.

An underlined vowel represents a voiceless vowel—a vowel that is expressed with a puff of air (but if one watches the speaker's lips one can often see the shape of the vowel). Voiceless vowels become regular vowels when they are stressed. We have not marked stress, because the main stress in a Comanche word almost always falls on the first syllable of the word.

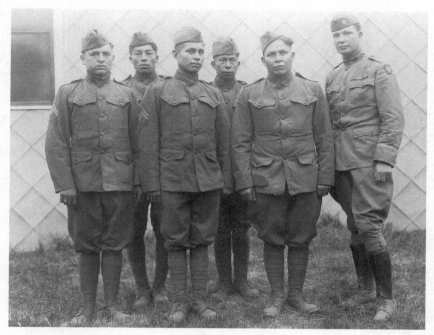

Choctaw "Telephone Squad," at Camp Devons, Massachusetts. Wanamaker Collection W6451, William Hammond Mathers Museum, Indiana University. Left to right: Taylor Lewis, Mitchell Bobb, James Edwards, Calvin Wilson, James Davenport, and Captain E. H. Horner.

Left to right: John Golombie; Czarina Colbert Conlan; Joel Joseph Oklahombi, wearing the Croix de Guerre medal, at Oklahombi's house, May 12, 1921. Photo by W. Hopkins, Idabel, Oklahoma. Archive & Manuscripts Division of the Oklahoma Historical Society. Photo number 4122.

Schlicht Billy, World War II Choctaw Communications Operator, and Choctaw Dancers. Photo courtesy of Judy Allen, editor, *Bishinik*, Choctaw tribal newspaper, Durant, Oklahoma.

Choctaw Medal of Honor awarded to the families of the World War I Choctaw Code Talkers. Medal courtesy of Judy Allen, editor, *Bishinik*, Choctaw tribal newspaper, Durant, Oklahoma. Author's photo.

The Comanche Code Talkers at Ft. Benning, Georgia, 1941. Front row, left to right: Roderick Red Elk, Simmons Parker, Larry Saupitty, Melvin Permansu, Willie Yackeschi, Charles Chibitty, and Wellington Mihecoby. Back row, left to right: Morris Sunrise, Perry Noyabad, Ralph Wahnee, Haddon Codynah, Robert Holder, Edward Nahquaddy, Clifford Otitivo, and Forrest Kassanavoid. Photo courtesy of Forrest Kassanavoid.

The Comanche Code Talkers at Ft. Benning, Georgia, 1941. Back row, left to right: Clifford Otitivo, Edward Nahquaddy, Haddon Codynah, Ralph Wahnee, Willie Yackeschi, Wellington Mihecoby. Front row, left to right: Simmons Parker, Forrest Kassanavoid, Charles Chibitty, Larry Saupitty, Roderick Red Elk. Photo courtesy of Major General (Ret.) Hugh F. Foster.

Major General (Ret.) Hugh F. Foster Jr. Photo courtesy of Major General (Ret.) Hugh F. Foster Jr.

Private Haddon Codynah installing a guy wire on a telephone pole to keep it from falling over due to the strain of the telephone lines added by the Fourth Signal Company, Camp Gordon, Georgia, 1941. Photo courtesy of Major General (Ret.) Hugh F. Foster Jr.

Private Wellington Mihecoby beside a BD-71 twelve-line manual telephone switchboard, the type normally used at Regimental and Division Artillery Headquarters, Ft. Benning, Georgia, 1941. Photo courtesy of Major General (Ret.) Hugh F. Foster Jr.

Ernest Stahlberg (standing) and camp barber by Fourth Signal Company sign. Augusta, Georgia, 1943. Photo courtesy of Ernest Stahlberg.

Forrest Kassanavoid displaying a Nazi flag he captured at Cherbourg, France, in June 1944. Author's photo, Indiahoma, Oklahoma, January 11, 1996.

Charles Chibitty (left) and Roderick Red Elk at the University of Oklahoma, August 4, 1995. Author's photo.

Forrest and Marian Kassanavoid at the Oklahoma State Capitol, Oklahoma City, Oklahoma, November 3, 1989. Photo by Joe Hayes, courtesy of Museum of the Great Plains, Lawton, Oklahoma.

Forrest Kassanavoid and Major General (Ret.) Hugh F. Foster Jr.,
at Comanche dance, Lawton, Oklahoma, ca. 1990. Photo courtesy of Forrest and Marian Kassanavoid.

Code talkers performing Victory Dance at Comanche Code Talkers Ceremony. Oklahoma State Capitol Building, Oklahoma City, Oklahoma, November 3, 1989. Left to right: Charles Chibitty, Major General (Ret.) Hugh F. Foster Jr., Forrest Kassanavoid, and Roderick Red Elk. Photo courtesy of Museum of the Great Plains, Lawton, Oklahoma.

Code Talker "Reunion," Left to right: Charles Chibitty, Roderick Red Elk, Major General (Ret.) Hugh F. Foster Jr. Albert Nahquaddy, Forrest Kassanavoid. Lawton, Oklahoma, 1990. Photo courtesy of Major General (Ret.) Hugh F. Foster Jr.

Code Talker Recognition Ceremony. Oklahoma State Capitol, Oklahoma City, Oklahoma, November 3, 1989. Left to right: Roderick Red Elk, Major General (Ret.) Hugh F. Foster Jr., Forrest Kassanavoid, Charles Chibitty. Photo by Joe Hayes, courtesy of Museum of the Great Plains, Lawton, Oklahoma.

Comanche Tuhwi (Black Knife) Society dance in honor of Comanche and Choctaw Code Talkers. Code Talker Recognition Ceremony, Oklahoma State Capitol, Oklahoma City, Oklahoma, November 3, 1989. Photo by Joe Hayes, courtesy of Museum of the Great Plains, Lawton, Oklahoma.

Comanche Code Talker Simmons Parker, ca. 1950. Photo courtesy of Ernest Stahlberg.

Cpl. Henry Blake Jr. (left) and PFC George H. Kirk, Navajo Code Talkers operating a portable radio set in a clearing they have cut in the dense jungle behind front lines. Bougainville, December 1943. Photo courtesy of National Archives (U.S. Marine Corps photograph USMC 69889-A, National Archives #127-GR-137-69889-A).

Roderick Red Elk (left) and his cousin Elgin Red Elk (right) practice sending telegraph messages at Fort Benning, Georgia. Photo courtesy of *Columbus Ledger-Enquirer*, Columbus, Georgia, c. 1941.

The Comanche Code Talkers in their barracks, Fort Benning, Georgia. Front row, left to right: Charles Chibitty, Robert Holder, Haddon Codynah, Willie Yackeschi, Elgin Red Elk, Simmons Parker. Back row, left to right: Roderick Red Elk, Clifton Otitivo, Wellington Mihecoby, and Morris Sunrise. Photo courtesy of *Columbus Ledger-Enquirer*, Columbus, Georgia, c. 1941.

Simmons Parker (left) and Charles Chibitty (right) dancing in Fancy-Feather dance attire to entertain fellow soldiers at Fort Benning, Georgia. Photo courtesy of *Columbus Ledger-Enquirer*, Columbus, Georgia, c. 1941.

Comanche Code Talkers at Fort Benning, Georgia. Photo courtesy of National Archives, Washington, D.C.

c·h·a·p·t·e·r · o·n·e

THE ORIGINS OF NATIVE AMERICAN CODE TALKING

I am bringing a distant nation against you.
An ancient and enduring nation.
A people whose language you do not know.
Whose speech you do not understand.

JEREMIAH 5:15

Developing and using high-level military intelligence are complex endeavors. In military operations secure communications are as important as weapons and troops. In order to be effective, communications must be rapid, but perhaps more importantly, they must be secure. To ensure success, those in charge of planning military strategy and tactics require up-to-the-minute action reports from the front lines. To coordinate joint actions with other units, constant communications must exist with those in combat. If any level of the process of friendly communications transmission falls into enemy hands, the enemy can make plans to counter one's actions. The side that can send secure messages more quickly and efficiently holds an enormous advantage over its opponent, and any advantage that can be gained through the communication of secret messages can make the difference between winning and losing a battle or even a war. Although communications intelligence makes no decisions itself, it does provide one of many forms of information that military commanders use in making decisions. The transmission of messages that the enemy cannot decode is a vital military factor in any engagement, especially in situations where combat units are operating over a wide area in which communications must be maintained by radio.

In World War I American forces were plagued by the Germans' ability to intercept and break coded communications transmissions until a virtually unbreakable and secure code was developed barely more than a month before the end of the war. Near the beginning of World War II

American intelligence units were able to break Japan's foremost diplomatic code that was generated by an electromechanical machine called Purple by the United States. The Purple Code was based on a machine that enciphered messages on the sending end and deciphered them at the receiving end. The intelligence resulting from breaking the Purple Code was code-named MAGIC. Although this was not of much aid in the Pacific theater of combat, it proved beneficial in the European theater. Because Baron Oshima Hiroshi, the Japanese ambassador to Berlin, sent back nearly 1,500 messages relating to German military affairs in Europe, some as long as thirty single-spaced typed pages, the United States learned much about the so-called Atlantic Wall from reading Oshima's messages. Despite problems in translating double veils of sophisticated ciphers and the complexity of numerous Japanese homonyms, the United States continued to read this code until V-J Day (Maslowski 1995:69–70). Based on American navy code-breakers partially solving the Japanese navy's primary code, JN25b, just before the Battle of the Coral Sea, "ULTRA" intelligence (the code name for intelligence gained from breaking military and not diplomatic codes used by Japan's army and navy) in the Pacific, and later in Europe, was able to provide timely information in some, but by no means all, cases (Maslowski 1995: 70–81). Despite enormously mathematically complex and frequent changing of codes and coding machines, Japan also enjoyed the same advantage through its code-breaking efforts. One way in which this balance was changed, however, involved American forces devising linguistic and coded voice transmission in forms never before heard by German or Japanese military forces. One form that the Germans and Japanese were eventually unprepared for, and in both instances unable to counter, was the use of voice-coded Native American languages.

Cryptography, from the Greek *kryptos* (secret) and *graphos* (writing), is the science of secret communications writing (Bruce 1973:13) and includes secret code and cipher making or writing: forming, sending, and rendering secure signals and extracting information from them. Including cryptography, cryptanalysis (the process of breaking or deciphering code and cipher systems without possessing the key with which to decipher the system), and the development of secret and coded communications, cryptology (the science and study of cryptography or secret communications) has a history of at least four thousand years (Kahn 1967, 1983; Bruce 1973; Van Der Rhoer 1978; Maslowski 1995:52).

Throughout the history of warfare, military leaders have sought the perfect code—one that no enemy could break down, regardless of the ability of its intelligence staff. For centuries a great number of clever codes have been developed by political and military personnel to disguise their messages. The two most common forms involved in sending secret messages are codes and ciphers. Codes are systems of symbols used to represent an understood meaning among those familiar with the code formation. Codes use symbols to represent a message's true meaning and make sense only to someone familiar with the code and agreed-upon associated meanings. Thus they reveal little to an enemy if intercepted, unless the enemy is able to break the code system and figure out the true context behind the symbols. Ciphers are systems of substitution or equivalents in which a standardized list of equivalents is used to transform regular symbols, such as letters, to represent others. In a cipher system, the letter A might represent the letter F, the letter B represent the letter G, and so on, or a more complex arrangement might prevail (Kahn 1967; Bruce 1973; Van Der Rhoer 1978). The struggle to break unknown codes and ciphers has long challenged humans and provides much of the drama surrounding cryptography and cryptology (Bruce 1973:14).

Written codes have been used for various political, military, and religious purposes. The earliest known use of cryptograms, or coded messages, began nearly four thousand years ago among political leaders in Egypt. In ancient Babylonia and Assyria a rare and unusual type of cuneiform was used in signing and dating clay tablets. The use of secret messages is mentioned among the Greeks by the ancient historian Herodotus. At least three forms of letter substitutions are known to have existed in Hebrew literature. The use of cryptic scripts for various political purposes also existed in Mesopotamia, India, Persia, Scandinavia, Anglo-Saxon Britain, and portions of Arabia. The Yezidis of northern Iraq developed and employed a cryptic script in their holy books from fear of religious persecution, and Tibetans have used cryptic scripts since the 1300s (Kahn 1967:71–105).

Cryptography has contributed to the political and military demise of some of the world's greatest armies, empires, and historical figures, including the Persian and Roman empires; Elizabethan England; Mary, Queen of Scots; Alexander II of Russia; Admiral Yamamoto of Japan; and the defeated in the First and Second World Wars (Bruce 1973). The first known system of military cryptography was used by the Spartan General Lysander in 405 B.C. against the Persians, through a device known as a "skytale." This device consisted of a strip of papyrus, parchment, or leather wrapped tightly around a staff of wood. A secret message was written on the parchment down the length of the staff, unwrapped, and then sent. Once unwrapped, the disconnected letters made no sense until they were repositioned by rewrapping them around another pole of equal diameter, thereby positioning the words into coherent messages. Julius Caesar himself made use of cryptographic messages in the Gallic Wars (Kahn 1967:1–105; Bruce 1973:15). In Western Europe the

3

4   rise of political cryptology emerged during the Middle Ages and has developed continuously to the present (Kahn 1967:106), becoming increasingly complex with the development of voice radio and telephone communication.

Between the Civil War and World War II, military intelligence, like warfare itself, shifted from being human-centered, personalized, and qualitative to being increasingly technological, bureaucratized, and quantitative. During the Civil War most operational military intelligence was human intelligence (humint), consisting of human-centered activities including spying, reconnaissance, observation, captured enemy documents, and interrogation. During the Civil War the need to communicate rapidly over long distances by sending signals led to the development of signal intelligence (sigint) and included forms such as flags, flares, and eventually the telegraph. The emergence of the telegraph naturally led to enemy wiretapping and the development of encryption, or coded messages. Although all humint sources (including modifications such as aerial and photo reconnaissance) present in the Civil War were also present in World War II, they had declined in overall importance. In contrast, sigint, which had been relatively unimportant in the Civil War, had evolved so dramatically that it comprised the majority of military communications by World War II and constituted an intelligence revolution. Centering on radio, sigint had become essential for efficient military operations at both tactical and strategic levels, and since radio waves were free for the taking, complex enciphering of messages became a necessity (Maslowski 1995:52–69). The level of communications systems involved in a war as large and complex as World War II is staggering. Sophisticated mathematics, systems of coding and decoding, frequent code changing, code-machine formation, and restructuring to statistically increase code complexity are only a few of the many aspects involved in these enormously complex communications systems. Virtually thousands of individuals participated in efforts to break a single major enemy code (Maslowski 1995). David Kahn (1983) provides a solid account of much of the cryptanalytic development of the twentieth century including the achievements of the various cryptanalytic agencies in World War II. Yet despite changes in warfare, technology, and communications transmission, the basic purpose of military intelligence has remained unchanged. Sending and breaking intelligence, of course, are different matters.

Most codes are based on the coder's native language, and if the language is a widely used one, it will also be familiar to one's enemy, and, regardless of how good your code may be, the enemy will eventually master it. However, the use of "hidden" languages, or those which (1) are little known by non-native members of the group and (2) have no written form, can be very effective for the communications transmissions of a second group. The use of obscure languages for military communication in wartime predates World War I, as the British, for example, used Latin to confuse their adversaries in the Boer War of 1899–1901. During World Wars I and II, many Native American languages existed and can be classified as hidden languages. It is precisely because of these factors that Native Americans and their languages were able to make a unique contribution in American military communications during World Wars I and II.

NATIVE AMERICAN MILITARY LITERATURE AND CODE TALKING

Native American contributions in World War I have generally been dismissed by Anglo military historians as too peripheral or insignificant to merit extensive recognition. Only recently (Britten 1997) has the first comprehensive general account of Native American participation in World War I been compiled. Although a greater body of literature focusing on Native American participation in World War II has been written, serious oversights remain. Most of these works focus on studies of national policy and postwar social, economic, and political changes, providing little insight concerning the effects of the war on individual Native American communities beyond a general overview (Collier 1942; Johnson 1977; Bernstein 1991; Parman 1994:59–70; Townsend 2000). Of these, Franco (1999) and Townsend (2000) are by far the most readable, providing more in-depth discussions of the impact of the Second World War for several native communities, while exploring several new topical areas largely unaddressed by previous scholars writing on the subject of Native Americans and World War II. Other works have focused more upon the collective role and experiences of Native American veterans (White 1979; Haynie 1984; Holm 1985, 1992, 1996; Tate 1986; Hale 1982, 1992; Meadows 1991, 1995). Regarding the war's impacts upon individual Native American communities and their veterans, only the activities of the Navajo, Pueblo, Zuni, and Chippewa (Ojibwa) have been documented in any detail (Ritzenthaler 1943; Adair 1947, 1948; Adair and Vogt 1949; Vogt 1948, 1949, 1951), and only Hale (1992) and the author (Meadows 1991, 1995, 1999) have focused at length upon the military contributions of Native Americans of Oklahoma.

Until recently little has been published about military codes, due to national and military security concerns. Furthermore, little of a comprehensive nature has been published concerning the subject of Native American code talkers. White (1976:22) and Hale (1982) briefly mention the service of Native American telephone operators in World War I. Walker (1980, 1983) provides a brief account of the use of Navajo and

6   Muskogee Creek in World War II and compiled a brief account of Native American code talking in both world wars from limited press releases. Yet even primary sources, such as the seminal works on the U.S. Signal Corps in World War II by the armed forces (Terrett 1956; Thompson et al. 1957; Thompson and Harris 1966), do not contain a single reference to Native American code talkers or their respective programs and service in either world war. Subsequent volumes on both the European and Pacific theaters of the same series *(U.S. Army in World War II)* are similar. The absence of any mention of Native Americans, and especially of Native American code talkers, reflects the U.S. government's concern and emphasis on keeping the code talkers' existence secret during the late 1950s and early 1960s. Native American code talkers were often instructed not to discuss their communications training and experiences following World Wars I and II, resulting in the overall secrecy of their role for decades following their service. Of the major independent nongovernmental sources on military codes and code breaking (Kahn 1967; Bruce 1973; Van Der Rhoer 1978), only Kahn's voluminous work briefly mentions Native American contributions (1967:549–550).

Regarding Native American code talking, the role of the Navajo Code Talkers in World War II is the best known to date. Despite several inaccuracies concerning the origins of Native American code talking and its use among other tribes, Paul's (1973) work remains the primary and most thorough account of the Navajo Code Talkers. Indeed, the vast majority of publications on Native American code talkers focus solely on the Navajo and their role in World War II. In addition to archival documents and numerous newspaper and journal articles, at least forty-four major sources (ten books, including four children's books, twenty-five articles, seven archival sources, and two documentary films) contain information about or focus solely on the Navajo Code Talkers.[1] During the summer of 2000 in Hawaii, MGM Studios began filming *Windtalkers*, a movie on the Navajo Code Talkers' experiences in World War II. Directed by action-film director John Woo, the film stars Adam Beach (Saulteaux) as fictional Navajo Code Talker Carl Yahzee and Nicolas Cage as John Enders, his Anglo bodyguard. The film was released on June 14, 2002. Aside from McClain's (1994) work, which offers some refreshing new materials and interviews, Paul's (1973) initial work has unquestionably served as the source upon which most subsequent brief accounts are based, the latter differing largely in the content of personal veterans' experiences.

Several other works of a more general nature include brief discussions of Native American contributions as code talkers (Johnson 1977; Haynie 1984; Iverson 1990; Bernstein 1991; Hale 1992). However, these works again generally focus on the Navajo, and only Paul (1973:7), White (1979:

18), Bernstein (1991:46), Hale (1992:416), Bixler (1992:42), McClain (1994), Holm (1996:105), and Townsend (2000:144, 150) even mention the Comanches as code talkers in the Second World War. In these passages some data are incorrect, and in some instances are continually and uncritically cited. Likewise Daily (1995:50–52) provides a brief account of the Comanche Code Talkers, but includes several factual errors. Only two brief sources, one written by one of the Comanche Code Talkers (Red Elk 1991:113–114, 1992:1–9) and the other by Gawne (1998:264), provide more than a brief mention of the unit's existence during the Second World War. The Navajo are often popularly believed to be the first Native American group to serve as code talkers (Paul 1973:7). While the Navajo Code Talkers are undeniably the most numerous and best-known Native American code talkers, they were not the first in either world war. Paul (1973:7) confuses the origins of, and the nature of code use by, the Choctaw Code Talkers in World War I, which developed during active combat service, and the Comanche Code Talkers in World War II, who were trained nearly three years prior to active combat duty, in 1941 at Ft. Benning, Georgia. The first platoon of Navajos was not recruited until April 1942 and completed training late in the summer of 1942 (Paul 1973; Tully 1995). While cryptography (the encoding and decoding of messages) and codes (systems of secret message transmission) have long been used in military intelligence to ensure secure communications transmissions and gain advantages in information and in warfare, Native American service in military communications operations, particularly as code talkers, has a more recent history.

WORLD WAR I AND NATIVE AMERICAN ENLISTMENT

On May 18, 1917, Congress passed the Selective Service Act. On June 5, 1917, the federal government enacted the first call to register for the draft, requiring all men between the ages of twenty-one and thirty-one to register. Native American males in this age range were required to register, but only those currently holding United States citizenship (a little less than two-thirds of all Native Americans in 1917) were subject to the draft. Despite their legal status, many Native Americans without U.S. citizenship waived their exemption from military service and enlisted (Britten 1997:57–58). By the end of September 1918, over 17,000 Native American men had registered for the draft in the First World War (Britten 1997:51–52). Eventually some 12,000 to 12,500 Native American men served in the American Expeditionary Force (AEF) in the world war, with nearly 1,000 in the navy (Britten 1997:83–84; Franco 1999: 60). This represents about 25 percent of the then-existing adult male Indian population (the number inducted after the September call is un-

7

known). Indians volunteered and were inducted at a rate nearly twice that of the rest of the American population. Holm (1996:99) reports that nearly two-thirds of all Native American veterans were volunteers, while Britten (1997:73) reports over 6,500 draftees. Nevertheless, the ratio of the number of Native American volunteers to draftees was significantly high (Britten 1997:59, 73, 84).[2] Although American involvement in World War I lasted only nineteen months, it held enduring effects for Native Americans concerning citizenship, economics, cultural retention, and political changes. Prior to the war, a series of American and Canadian national debates occurred concerning: (1) whether to integrate Indians into the United States and Canadian military; (2) attempts to determine their loyalty and reliability; and (3) whether or not to form separate all-Indian military units (Hale 1982; Dempsey 1983; Tate 1986; Parman 1994:60–61). By 1897, official military policy set the precedent of declining to segregate Native American soldiers into distinct racial units and henceforth integrated them into white units (Britten 1997:25). Thus, unlike blacks, who fought in segregated units in World Wars I and II, there were no "officially recognized" Indian regiments. Nevertheless, several native leaders made attempts to raise all-Indian regiments for service in France.[3] Early in the war, Secretary of War Newton D. Baker rejected the possibility of forming any separate Indian units, a position he maintained throughout the war.

The existing legislation determined United States citizenship for Native Americans at the time. Anyone allotted (having received an allotment, or trust-status land, on a reservation) prior to the 1906 Burke Act, or who had taken up separate nonreservation residence, was eligible for conscription, including children of citizens, individuals who received fee patents after 1906, and anyone declared a citizen by legislation. Noncitizens were those Indians who were not allotted or who had received allotments after 1906 and remained under federal trust status. However, as nearly one-third to one-half of all Native Americans remained as noncitizens of the United States, many were therefore not legally subject to the draft (Parman 1994:60). The passing of the Selective Service Act caused great confusion for some Native Americans, as many of those who were not citizens thought that draft registration meant instant conscription. Nevertheless, when the United States entered the war in 1917, thousands of Native Americans entered the armed forces regardless of their individual legal positions at the time. Refusing to take advantage of their draft exemptions, many took the military oath to defend the Constitution of the United States without possessing citizenship or any rights under it. Despite a popular nationwide media promotion that publicized a positive native response to the war, tribes and individuals reacted differently to registration and the draft. Many of the more isolated reservation communities of the Southwest and Great Basin regions generally resisted draft registration. These largely noncitizen and less-acculturated groups took little interest in the war and were far more suspicious of Anglo motivations. Greater participation and support were found among Plains, Southeastern, and Great Lakes populations, which had longer contact and greater assimilation with the Anglo majority. Some four thousand servicemen from the Southeastern "Five Civilized Tribes" reflected a high enlistment rate, with some six hundred serving in the Thirty-sixth Division, an activated Oklahoma National Guard unit. In reality there was no typical Indian serviceman; diversity existed to varying degrees through factors of tribal culture, acculturation, and education (Parman 1994:63).

Native Motivations for Military Service

In light of the previous 425 years of interactions with Anglos, why would thousands of Native Americans voluntarily enlist in 1917 to participate in the First World War? Most authors who have attempted studies of Native Americans in World Wars I and II have essentially explained the large-scale Indian entrance into the military as an attempt to legitimize themselves as American citizens (Bernstein 1991:22–42; Parman 1994:107–111; Rawles 1996:5). These authors explain increased Native American military service by emphasizing factors of Indians becoming subject to the draft, attempts to share in American democracy, increased prewar employment and urban migrations, increased military and war industries, and ensured employment, status, income, and a taste of the white world. Unquestionably, economic opportunity, job security, travel, adventure, escape from reservation conditions, citizenship status, patriotism, a desire to defend their homeland, devotion to tribal and American ideals of freedom and democracy, cultural differences, geography, demographics, levels of education, boarding school and paramilitary training experiences, vocational skills, levels of acculturation, individual and tribal relationships with the federal government, and levels of influence from the Bureau of Indian Affairs (BIA) and Indian-reform agencies were all significant factors. However, these influences were not experienced in the same combination or to the same degree by every native soldier, or, for those factors that applied, by Anglos. Although a correlation does exist between Native American populations possessing strong warrior traditions and the incentives presented by economic hardship to form economic and military alliances through military enlistments in Anglo military forces (Britten 1997:20), such developments are simply too complex to reduce to a single cause.

First, it must be recognized that Indian responses to the draft in World

9

10   War I were highly diverse and that no single "Indian response" accurately represents the motivations and decisions of all Indian volunteers (Britten 1997:60, 130). The same applies to later wars. Most prior works provide little attention to Native American cultural motivations for enlisting, associated cultural practices, and veterans' returns home. While increased interactions with non-Indians clearly fostered acculturation to some degree, they simultaneously served to intensify ethnic identity and revitalize numerous native traditions. The process of Native American militarization is far more complex than most scholars and general readers of American history realize (Meadows 1995; Holm 1996:100–102, 117–128), and has been largely overlooked by many authors relying on archival documents and not on interviews with Native American veterans themselves.

As best discussed by Holm (1996:100–101), it has often been assumed that Native American participation in the United States military is ultimately and adequately explained with dependency theory. That is, Indians have joined the military to legitimize themselves as American allies and then as American citizens. It has long been assumed that Native Americans, in doing so, have internalized colonization, lost their autonomy, and been deprived of political experience, and are presently seeking entrance into the larger American polity. As Holm states:

> From the viewpoint of dependency analysis, American political and military elites have accepted Indians as being politically reliable because they have supposedly adopted the same basic value system as whites in order to gain greater benefits from the state— either in terms of limited economic opportunity or a degree of social, cultural, and/or political autonomy. The militarization of Native Americans can be seen as the result of a continual process. (1996:100–101)

While American military and governmental leaders promoted integrated military service as a means of increasing acculturation, an explanation using dependency theory is far too simplistic, and correlates neither with existing American nor Native American data. Native American participation was clearly not solely draft-oriented, as an estimated 50 to 85 percent of all Native Americans in World War I were volunteers.[4] Enlistment was also not motivated strictly from a desire to assimilate into mainstream American society. If dependency and the desire to assimilate were sufficient explanations, then there should not have been the dramatically increased post–World War I tribal ceremonialism that rekindled past traditions and continues to the present day (Parman 1994:60, 63; Meadows 1995:407–409; Britten 1997:84,

149–151). Furthermore, although the Bureau of Indian Affairs and the Board of Indian Commissioners initially attempted to limit and prohibit such celebrations, implying that they were acts of disloyalty and attempts to subvert the will of the government, Commissioner Cato Sells later acquiesced amidst the nationwide cultural revivals held for returning native servicemen (Holm 1978:208; ARCIA 1918–1920:12).

Native Americans did not join the armed forces in World Wars I and II solely to legitimize themselves as American citizens. The majority who enlisted were already allotted citizens and, despite existing inequalities, many already knew that they were both members of their respective tribes and American citizens. Most World War I and II Native servicemen joined the armed forces for a complex combination of (1) traditional cultural motivations (warrior-based themes), (2) acculturative influences (such as boarding school), (3) contemporaneous economic factors (employment), and (4) a patriotic ideology regarding the defense of their own lands and peoples, and now the United States, of which they were a part. All of these factors were in turn blended into a uniquely Native American cultural process. In fact, many nineteenth-century tribal treaties with the United States contained obligatory clauses that Indians "would lay down their arms forever," or "war no more against the white man except in self-defense." The Onondaga and several other traditional tribal governments declared war on Germany independently of the United States, viewing military service as part of their own treaty obligations to the United States (Holm 1992:346). Militarization as it affected Native American code talkers is but a reflection of the larger regional processes I found regarding service in World Wars I and II for most Kiowa, Comanche, and Apache veterans and their traditional military sodality structures (Meadows 1999).

TRADITIONAL CULTURAL MOTIVATIONS   Traditional Native American motives for engaging in warfare include factors of alliance, geography, economics, politics, social status, and patriotism. While little firsthand autobiographical data exist concerning native motivations for enlisting in World War I, examination of the larger cultural patterns and data from both pre–World War I and –World War II periods suggests the development of a unique syncretic pattern. Reservation-era service as cavalry scouts served to provide younger men lacking war records access to a semblance of martial service, material culture, and status in a period when traditional martial roles were severely curtailed (Meadows 1995:400–403). Scouting service also provided an outlet for the restlessness of young men in reservation contexts (Dunlay 1982:48, 200) who combined two diverse military systems during a period of immense sociocultural and economic change. Comanches had already proven them-

12 selves in prereservation-era warfare (Richardson 1933), and later demonstrated their military worth and allegiance through service as peacetime Indian Scouts in Troop L at Ft. Sill, Oklahoma, from 1892 to 1897.

Native American servicemen have proven their allegiance in every major English, French, Spanish, and American conflict in the New World (Holm 1996; Britten 1997:10–17). As early as 1778, General George Washington observed, "I think they [Indians] can be made of excellent use, as scouts and light troops" (Bucholz et al. 1996:1). Documented cases in which Native Americans have fought alongside European powers include: King Phillip's War (1675–1676), the French and Indian War (1756–1763), the Revolutionary War (1776–1783), the War of 1812, and in large numbers as auxiliary troops on both sides in the Civil War. Recognizing Native American skills in scouting, the U.S. Army established the Indian Scouts in 1866, wherein members of various Plains and Southwestern tribes (Crow, Pawnee, Apache) served as scouts and auxiliaries in various Plains and Southwest campaigns, as members of Theodore Roosevelt's Rough Riders in the Spanish-American War in Cuba in 1898 (including members of the then-defunct Troop L, Seventh Cavalry), in the Philippine Insurrection of 1899–1902, in the Boxer Rebellion of 1899–1900, and in General John Pershing's expedition into Mexico against Pancho Villa in 1916. The Indian Scouts were formally deactivated with the retirement of the last member at Ft. Huachuca, Arizona, in 1947 (Dunlay 1982; Tate 1986:418–421; Bucholz et al. 1996:1). Later conflicts would include significant Native American participation: over 12,000 men in World War I; more than 44,000 from a total population of under 350,000 in World War II; some 29,700 in Korea; over 42,000 in Vietnam, including 90 percent volunteer enlistment; and service in Grenada, Panama, Somalia, the Persian Gulf, and Afghanistan.

Many Native American veterans of prior conflicts believed that it was only a matter of time until the United States would become involved in World War I. In addition, Native Americans felt that military service would gain them respect in their tribal communities and from other Native Americans, enable them to protect their land and people according to their traditional value systems, and link them to their traditional family and tribal male cultural roles and heritage as warriors. United States military service became a modern and obtainable substitute for past means of gaining prestige through individual valor. Native Americans had syncretized United States military service with their own tribal customs and value systems and were enlisting largely as a result of factors related to their own social and cultural backgrounds, and not due to the preconceptions and stereotypes of the larger American society (Meadows 1995; Holm 1996). Many veterans saw military service as traditionally protecting their land and their people, as well as the United

States, exactly what their forebears had been honored for doing. Many Native American veterans emphasized their desire to join in the common defense of tribal lands and America, and statements by veterans indicate that they were clearly fighting for "their" country and saw any enemy attack on the United States as an assault on them as well. This is nothing short of patriotism for their respective tribes, traditional homelands, and the United States.

Military service provided not only a contemporary link to past warrior roles and prominent social status, but also a link to the maintenance and subsequent postwar revival of many other tribal cultural forms, including song, dance, ceremony, economic redistribution, religion, and naming customs (Meadows 1995, 1999; Holm 1996). There are clear indications that some World War I servicemen enlisted for travel and adventure, and showed a clear preference for remaining together with other Indians in combat (LaBarre n.d.; Parman 1994:64) and for maintaining traditional concepts associated with prereservation ideologies involving kinship, war party, warrior sodality, and group cohesiveness (Meadows 1995). The motivations of World War I veterans were clearly culturally based, as reflected in the maintenance of a strong military ethos and by the revival of many cultural practices that were still technically prohibited by Bureau of Indian Affairs efforts that failed to suppress them. Thus a blending of two previously distinct military traditions developed into a new form that allowed for the continuation of traditional martial values and culture in a manner more conducive to modern United States military service.

ACCULTURATION AND ECONOMIC FACTORS   The acculturationist aspects of the boarding school experience preconditioned many Native Americans to military-style regimented daily activities. Army life posed few problems for Native American boarding school students, who were intimately familiar with regimented military discipline, uniforms, drills, and time schedules. This training was in turn syncretized with traditional martial-based themes that prepared Native American soldiers to renew and regain their position as veterans by combining traditional values with the modern U.S. military structure. Several cases of the influence of boarding schools in (1) preconditioning Native Americans of various tribal origins to military service and (2) later serving as recruiting centers are recorded (Hale 1982; Tate 1986; Parman 1994:63, 64; Holm 1992, 1996:99). Indian Commissioner Cato Sells turned all BIA programs toward ensuring victory in the war cause and fervently urged Indians to enter military service as a means to capitalize on their opportunity to assimilate. The reasons behind the extremely significant number of Native Americans in United States military forces for several **13**

14 generations become obvious, as Indians have been heavily recruited, have been consciously and rigidly conscripted, and have demonstrated a high rate of volunteerism (Holm 1992:345–346). Government control over reservations and the availability of annual tribal censuses allowed for an acceleration in promoting Native American enlistments and registration. Secretary of War Baker allowed Indian agencies to act as recruiting and induction centers. While the drafting of Indians was handled by local draft boards, the recruitment of volunteers was supported by agency and school officials, and Indian Service employees were required to serve as registrars and as members of registration boards (Hale 1982:39–40; Holm 1996:99). The First World War also provided new military and economic opportunities on a much larger scale (Parman 1994:64–76). Economic motivations provided additional incentives and increased urban relocations for jobs in wartime industries. This pattern set the stage for the larger-scale off-reservation exodus during and after World War II.

THE ORIGIN OF NATIVE AMERICAN CODE TALKERS: THE OKLAHOMA CHOCTAWS

During World War I, several thousand Native Americans from some sixty tribes served throughout twenty American divisions (Hale 1982: 40). Despite a policy of integrating Native Americans into Anglo regiments, the army inadvertently established a few units, mostly on the company level, in which the majority or all members were Native Americans. At various times during World War I, between 600 and 1,000 Native Americans from fourteen tribes were stationed in the Thirty-sixth Division at Camp Bowie, Texas. At Camp Travis near San Antonio, Texas, nearly 1,000 Oklahoma Indians, mainly from the Choctaw, Chickasaw, and Creek tribes, were in the Ninetieth Division, a National Army draft division, of which the 358th Infantry Regiment was composed mostly of Indians. One newspaper estimated that there were some 1,500 Indian soldiers stationed in four Texas camps. Many Native Americans in the Arizona National Guard were eventually transferred to a predominantly Indian company in the 158th Infantry Regiment, Fortieth Division. In addition, companies of the Second and Third Battalions of the Forty-second "Rainbow" Division were made up largely of Native Americans. The Canadian Army also had between 3,000 and 4,000 Indian troops throughout its forces as well as Asian-American and African-American troops (Hale 1982:40; Britten 1997:74–75, 116; White 1996:22, 58).

Among the nearly 1,000 Indians in the Thirty-sixth Division were some twenty-six Native American languages and dialects, of which only four or five had ever been written.[5] The men of the Thirty-sixth were mostly from the Southeastern, or "Five Civilized," tribes, and from the Plains and Prairie tribes, most of whom had been forcibly removed to Indian Territory, now Oklahoma. Prior to the war over half had served in the Texas-Oklahoma National Guard, the "Panther" or Thirty-sixth Division, which had trained at Camp Bowie at Fort Worth, Texas, under Major General Edwin St. John Greble (White 1978, 1996:71). Like the majority of Native Americans in the Ninetieth Division, the majority of those in the Thirty-sixth had attended government-run Indian boarding schools. While most appear to have had a good command of English, some were so deficient that they had to be placed beside other, bilingual members who could translate orders for them (White 1996:71).

The enlisted men of Company E of the 142d Infantry Regiment, Thirty-sixth Division (some 208 men from fourteen tribes) were exclusively Native Americans from Oklahoma. For those stationed at Camp Bowie in Fort Worth, Texas, the membership roster for November 17, 1917, lists 89 Choctaws, 68 Cherokees, 15 Chickasaws, 7 Osages, 7 Creeks, 6 Seminoles, 5 Delawares, 2 Shawnees, 2 Quapaws, 2 Poncas, 2 Caddos, 1 Peoria, 1 Arapaho, and 1 Cheyenne.[6] While several members of the 142d could not speak any English at the time of their induction, others were highly educated and were noted for their penmanship and typing abilities. Several had attended either Carlisle or Haskell Indian Schools, or various other military schools throughout the country. Their experiences in boarding schools and National Guard units had already familiarized many Native Americans with military procedure. Although these are the only known primarily Indian units, neither was formally recognized as such by the United States military.

America entered the First World War on April 6, 1917. Native American troops were among the first American troops to reach France, arriving in the last week of June 1917, and fought in every major engagement from Chateau-Thierry in May 1918 to the Meuse-Argonne offensive in September 1918 (Britten 1997:75). Hale (1982) demonstrates that while dozens of Native American servicemen were awarded decorations of valor, including the French War Cross (Croix de Guerre), their contributions were largely negated in two ways. First, news coverage on the role of Native Americans in the war was extremely limited; Stars and Stripes ran only four articles on the role of Indians in the war. Second, with the exception of accounts of General Pershing's use of Apache scouts, what coverage there was on Native Americans was almost inevitably filled with racist terms and overtones. One such article on the role of Choctaw communications operators in Stars and Stripes was entitled "Yank Indian Was Big Help in Winning the War." Another article about Native American veteran Walter Snow, who had received the Croix de

15

16 Guerre and had been decorated in every major campaign in which the Americans fought, was entitled "Redskin Hero of Verdun Can't Stalk Ivories as He Did Huns" (Hale 1982:39–41).

While the contributions of Native American soldiers were largely ignored by the American military forces, they did not go unnoticed by the French and British officers. Field Marshall Lord Haig praised the Indian soldiers highly. Ferdinand Foch, Marshall of France, wrote, "I cannot forget the brilliant services which the valorous Indian soldiers of the American armies have rendered to the common cause and the energy as well as the courage which they have shown to bring about victory—decisive victory—by attack" (Hale 1982:41).

Of the many accounts which originated from the First World War, those of Native American telephone talkers and their undecipherable code became one of the most enduring genres of battlefield legends (Stallings 1963:281, 288; White 1979:17–18; Tate 1986:432). Information on the first Native American code talkers, the Choctaws, has recently become public, largely through features in the Choctaw tribal newspaper *Bishinik* (1986a, 1986b, 1987a, 1987b, 1989, 1992a, 1992b, 1994a, 1994b, 1996) and various local newspapers in southeastern Oklahoma.

After success at St. Mihiel, the AEF undertook its final major offensive against Germany, the Meuse-Argonne campaign of 1918, a large-scale Allied (American, French, British, and Belgian) offensive that began in late September along the Western Front. The American objective was to break westward through the German forces known as the "Hindenburg Line," a concentration comprising the twenty miles between the Meuse River and the Argonne Forest. Characterized by heavy growth and steep ravines, the terrain was strategically defensive, and offensively problematic (Britten 1997:79). In the closing days of World War I fifteen members of the Choctaw tribe in the U.S. Army's Thirty-sixth Division were instrumental in helping the American Expeditionary Force win several key battles, including the Battle of St. Etienne, during the Meuse-Argonne campaign. This campaign helped set the stage for the signing of the Armistice in November 1918. During August 1918, the 142d Infantry Regiment, American Thirty-sixth Division, was moved to France for additional training. However, this training was cut short, as the regiment was desperately needed on the front lines. In October of 1918 elements of the 142d were among those sent to capture a German stronghold at Forest Ferme in France.[7] Included in this group were eight Choctaw Indians from Oklahoma. These eight men would lay the groundwork for a unique means of military communications—Native American code talking.

Up to this point, American forces' communications were highly ineffective. The Americans were aware that Germans were tapping into their radio circuits and telephone lines near St. Mihiel and St. Etienne, and that the Germans were intercepting intradivisional transmissions and had broken the Allies' codes. In addition, approximately one out of four messengers who served as runners between the various companies on the battle line were being captured (*Bishinik* 1986b). The American forces were searching for a more secure means of communication. Reaching the front lines on October 7, 1918, the Thirty-sixth Division was told that it would go over the top the next morning.[8] Based on military documentation of the Thirty-sixth's movements, this account (Imon 1977:86–87) refers to the attack by the Thirty-sixth Division's 142d Regiment down the northern slope of Blanc Mont toward and along the sunken road to Saint-Etienne-a-Arnes (Franks 1984:118–119; Stallings 1963:280–289). Imon (1977:87) and Stallings (1963:288) report the use and immediate result of the Choctaw communicators. James Edwards was placed at the field artillery and Solomon Louis at division headquarters. Shortly thereafter, James Edwards advised Louis in Choctaw that the Germans were preparing to go over the top of their trenches in a frontal assault, most likely to occur the following morning, reportedly at 7:00 A.M. Other Choctaws reported additional information from their respective posts, all of which gave indications of the Germans' preparations. Ben Carterby reported stiff resistance from a concentration of crack German troops (who he reported to be Prussian Guards). Upon receiving this information Colonel Brewer (probably Bloor) issued orders for a field artillery barrage to begin at 5:55 A.M. the next morning and for division troops to go over the top and attack the Germans at 6:00 A.M. This was prior to the designated time the Germans had planned to begin their advance. As a direct result of the information gathered and transmitted by the Choctaws, the Americans and Allies advanced, catching the Germans unprepared. German losses were heavy, and the Allies were able to take five hundred enemy prisoners in thirty minutes before the sun had fully risen, while "German dead literally littered the field of combat." Choctaw Code Talker Joseph Oklahombi distinguished himself by escorting prisoners back to a French detention camp in the reserve lines (Imon 1977:87).[9]

While credit is generally given to Regimental Commander Colonel Alfred W. Bloor (White 1979:17–18) and Captain E. W. Horner (Kahn 1967:55; Imon 1977:87) for conceiving the idea of using the Choctaw language for communications transmission, information obtained from an interview with Solomon Louis, the last surviving World War I Choctaw Code Talker, indicates that the idea was initially created by a Captain Lawrence (*Bishinik* 1986b).[10] According to Louis's account, Captain Lawrence, the commander of one of the American companies, was walking through the company area one day when he happened to overhear

18   Solomon Louis and Mitchell Bobb conversing in their native Choctaw
language. Captain Lawrence realized the immediate possibilities for a
communications advantage. After listening to them for a few minutes,
Lawrence called Louis aside and asked, "Corporal, how many of you
Choctaw boys do we have in this battalion?" After conferring with Bobb,
Louis reported to Captain Lawrence, "We have eight men who speak
fluent Choctaw in the battalion, Sir." "Are any of them over in headquarters company?" Lawrence asked. "I think Carterby and Maytubby
are over there," Louis replied. "You fellows wait right here," instructed
the captain. Lawrence got onto a field telephone and discovered that Ben
Carterby and Pete Maytubby were indeed attached to the headquarters
company. Lawrence told his commanding officer, Regimental Commander Colonel Alfred W. Bloor, "Get them and have them stand by, I've got
an idea that just might get these Heinies [Germans] off our backs." Calling Louis and Bobb together, Lawrence told them, "Look I'm going to
give you a message to call in to headquarters. I want you to give them a
message in your language. There will be somebody there who can understand it" (*Bishinik* 1986b).

The message was given to Private First Class Mitchell Bobb, who
used the field telephone to deliver the first Choctaw code message to fellow Choctaw Ben Carterby, who then translated it back into English for
the battalion commander. On field telephones at separate communication posts, the Choctaws easily and accurately transmitted the messages. Solomon Louis is credited with choosing the other initial seven
Choctaws who would serve as code talkers and was reportedly appointed
as the chief of the detail (Kahn 1967:550).[11] Within a matter of hours the
location of the eight Choctaws had been shifted until there was at least
one in each field company headquarters (*Bishinik* 1986b, 1994b). In addition the 142d Infantry Regiment was fortunate enough to have two
Indian officers who spoke several of the twenty-six native languages of
the various Native American soldiers, one of whom was most likely
Captain Columbus E. (Walter) Veach, a Choctaw in Company E. Captain
Veach had been in the military service of his state and nation since August of 1908. At that time he enlisted in Company H of the old First
Oklahoma Infantry stationed at Durant, Oklahoma. After about a year
of service he became a first lieutenant in his company and by steady efforts gained the rank of captain. Eventually fifteen Choctaws, aged nineteen to thirty-three, would serve as code talkers in the First World War.[12]

A letter from this period obtained from the National Archives provides the best source of information concerning the development of this
communications strategy and the role played by the Choctaws.[13] In a report to the commanding general of the Thirty-sixth Division, General

Smith, dated January 23, 1919, and entitled "Transmitting messages in Choctaw," this strategy was discussed in detail by Colonel Alfred W. Bloor of Austin, CO, 142d Infantry, and was marked to the attention of Captain Alexander White Spence of Dallas, the official division historian (White 1978:9, 1979:17–18).

Headquarters 142d Infantry, A.E.F.
January 23, 1919. A.P.O. No. 796

From: C.O. 142d Infantry
To: The Commanding General 36th Division (Attention Capt. Spence)
Subject: Transmitting messages in Choctaw

1. In compliance with Memorandum, Headquarters 36th Division, January 21, 1919, to C.O. 142d Infantry, the following account is submitted:

In the first action of the 142d Infantry at St. Etienne, it was recognized that of all the various methods of liaison the telephone presented the greatest possibilities. The field of rocket signals is restricted to a small number of agreed signals. The runner system is slow and hazardous. T.P.S. is always an uncertain quantity. It may work beautifully and again, it may be entirely worthless. The available means, therefore, for the rapid and full transmission of information are the radio, buzzer, and telephone, and of these the telephone was by far the superior,—provided it could be used without let or hindrance,—provided straight to the point information could be given.

It was well understood however that the German was a past master in the art of "listening in." Moreover, from St. Etienne to the Aisne we had traveled through a country netted with German wire and cables. We established P.C.'s in dugouts and houses, but recently occupied by him. There was every reason to believe every decipherable message or word going over our wires also went to the enemy. A rumor was out that our Division had given false co-ordinates of our supply dump, and that in thirty minutes the enemy shells were falling on the point. We felt sure the enemy knew too much. It was therefore necessary to code every message of importance and coding and decoding took valuable time.

19

While comparatively inactive at Vaux-Champagne, it was remembered that the regiment possessed a company of Indians. They spoke twenty-six different languages or dialects, only four or five of which were ever written. There was hardly one chance in a million that Fritz would be able to translate these dialects, and the plan to have these Indians transmit telephone messages was adopted. The regiment was fortunate in having two Indian officers who spoke several of the dialects.[14] Indians from the Choctaw tribe were chosen and one placed in each P.C.[15]

The first use of the Indians was made in ordering a delicate withdrawal of two companies of the 2nd Bn. [Battalion] from Chufilly to Chardeny on the night of October 26th. This movement was completed without mishap, although it left the Third Battalion, greatly depleted in previous fighting, without support. The Indians were used repeatedly on the 27th in preparation for the assault on Forest Farm [Ferme]. The enemy's complete surprise is evidence that he could not decipher the messages.

After the withdrawal of the regiment to Louppy-le-Petit, a number of Indians were detailed for training in transmitting messages over the telephone. The instruction was carried on by the Liaison Officer, Lieutenant [Temple] Black [of Weatherford, Texas]. It had been found that the Indian's vocabulary of military terms was insufficient. The Indian [term] for "Big Gun" was used to indicate artillery. "Little gun shoot fast," was substituted for machine gun, and the battalions were indicated by "one, two, and three grains of corn." It was found that the Indian tongues do not permit verbatim translation, but at the end of the short training period at Louppy-le-Petit, the results were very gratifying, and it is believed, had the regiment gone back into the line, fine results would have been obtained. We were confident that the possibilities of the telephone had been obtained without its hazards.

A.W. Bloor
Colonel 142d Infantry
Commanding[16]

This document later appeared in an Army Security Agency study entitled *Utilization of American Indians as Communication Linguists*

(SHR-120) and is of great historical significance because it is the only known official government document recording the use of Native American code talkers in the World War I AEF files.[17] Bloor's memorandum clearly confirms that Choctaw Indians performed successfully as code talkers during World War I in the Battles of St. Etienne and Forest Ferme, in France. The operation proved successful, as the German forces were unable to break the Choctaw language and code words. Following the capture of Forest Ferme and the withdrawal of the 142d Infantry Regiment from the front line, the eight Choctaws were detailed for training in transmitting messages, even though initial experience found that the Choctaw vocabulary of Anglo military terms was limited. During a brief period of training held at Louppy-le-Petit, a series of formally coded words was devised and used to convey coded telephone messages in Choctaw. While some Choctaw terms were equivalent to Anglo counterparts, others did not exist and, as Bloor's report demonstrates, were quickly developed in a coded form of the Choctaw language to convey equivalents for Anglo military arms and organizational levels. Thus patrol became "many scouts," a grenade became known as a "stone," regiment became "tribe," casualties became "scalps," and Second Battalion became "two grains of corn." The Choctaw vocabulary that was used for transmitting telephone messages combined both regular Choctaw vocabulary and other specialized or "coded" vocabulary invented to convey specific military items.

It was at this point that the Choctaws ceased being simply communications operators with an unknown language and became code talkers. Not only did the Choctaws handle military communications by field telephone, they also translated radio messages into the Choctaw language and wrote field orders to be carried by runners between the various companies. Thus, with the addition of coded Choctaw communications in written form, another means of security was provided to counter the Germans' proficiency in deciphering messages obtained through capturing runners (*Bishinik* 1986b, 1994a; Twin Territories 1991).[18] During the remainder of the war, several other Choctaws in Companies D and E of the 142d Infantry Regiment and in the 141st and 143d Infantry Regiments of the Thirty-sixth Division were instructed to transmit orders by field telephone. The majority of the Choctaws were in Company E of the 142d (White 1979:17; Paul 1973:7).[19]

As the Americans progressively gained control of the surrounding area, they discovered many abandoned German communications lines intact. Already adept at tapping into American telephone lines and breaking radio codes, the retreating Germans had set yet another trap for the Americans by deliberately abandoning their communications lines for the Americans to find and use, thereby allowing the Germans

22   to further monitor American communications. In occupying dugouts and houses recently deserted by the Germans, the advancing Americans faced the almost certain likelihood that the Germans were still monitoring the communications lines in these abandoned structures. Suspicious as to why the enemy would leave intact lines in such exposed areas, Colonel A. W. Bloor, commander of the 142d Infantry Regiment, reasoned that they had been left behind deliberately. He suspected that the Germans hoped that the Americans would tap into the abandoned German lines for their own communications uses, thereby allowing the Germans to monitor the Americans' conversations. One step ahead of the Germans, Colonel A. W. Bloor willingly played into their trap—only he let the Choctaws of Company E, 142d Infantry Regiment transmit messages in their own language to prevent any leak of information and thus used the captured German telephone lines for the Americans' own communications advantages. Captain Ben H. Chastaine of the 142d Infantry described the Choctaws' role in the late stages of the war.

> In the preparations of the 142d Infantry for the attack a novel scheme of keeping the movements of the troops secret was worked out. The entire country was covered by a network of abandoned German wires which were suspected of having been left purposely in such a condition that the enemy across the river could connect up with them and "listen in" to the messages being transmitted to various parts of the American lines. More than once there had been evidence to indicate that such things were being accomplished. To overcome this condition Colonel Bloor selected some of the most intelligent Indians from Company E, composed almost entirely of redmen from Oklahoma, and stationed them at the telephones. These Indians were members of the Choctaw tribe and when the written messages were handed to them in English they transmitted them in their own tongue and it is reasonably assured that no word of this was picked up by the Huns. (Chastaine 1920:231–232)

As a result, the Choctaw Code Talkers were instrumental in helping the American Expeditionary Force win several key battles in the Meuse-Argonne campaign in France. By successfully using their native language to withdraw two companies of troops on October 26, 1918, the eight Choctaw Code Talkers proved the ability of their communications skills. The Choctaws then helped prepare for the following day a surprise attack that led to the capture of the German stronghold at Forest Ferme on October 27, 1918.[20]

Soon a unit of Indian radio talkers was assembled within the 142d Infantry Regiment. With at least one Choctaw man placed in each field company headquarters, the results were so promising that other Indians within the regiment were similarly used for communication purposes, resulting in the use of several of the different Indian languages and dialects contained within the Thirty-sixth Division. Unfortunately, the full extent to which other Native American groups were used for communications service is unknown. Although Bloor mentioned only Choctaws, General Smith and Major George A. Robinson of Dallas, CO, 111th Field Signal Battalion, stated that members of other tribes were similarly used for telephone communications. Likewise, another source from 1945 indicates that "a variety of Indian tongues . . . [were] used by the AEF in the last war."[21] Britten (1997:106) also reports that "several Indian soldiers received instructions in how to transmit messages over the telephone" under supervision of Lieutenant Black, a liaison officer, and Lieutenant Ben Cloud, a Northern Cheyenne attached to the Forty-first Division. It is likely that once word of the Choctaws' success and practicality in using their native language spread through the ranks, other officers were enticed to begin using Native Americans as communications operators. However, due to limited documentation, only Choctaws are presently known to have transmitted messages in intentionally coded vocabulary in World War I. That the tactic of using Choctaw Code Talkers was completely successful was later indicated by a captured German officer who admitted that the attempts by his intelligence personnel to understand the messages through their wiretaps were futile (Twin Territories 1991; Wigginton 1992). Although other regiments similarly utilized Native Americans on a less formal basis, there is no indication that a single message sent in any of the various Indian languages was ever deciphered by the German forces (White 1979:17–18; Tate 1986:432).

Shortly after the war ended, news of the Choctaws' service became public. A November 13, 1921, article by Captain Lincoln A. Levine (Levine 1921) described how the Choctaw language was used:[22]

Messages in Choctaw

The Germans boasted that nothing could happen on the Allied side of the line that they didn't have perfect "dope" on in short order. They had a system of "listening in" on Allied telephone lines that they claimed was infallible. There was a story current in Signal Corps circles during the war concerning a telephone message to the effect that "Petee Dink" wishes to talk with "Grizzly Bear." A listening German broke in with, "Why don't you say Traub and Bullard instead of 'Grizzly Bear' and 'Petee Dink'? Anyway, Bullard is down the line at a conference."

23

24   The German code and language experts boasted that no code or language known to man could "get by" them.

And so one day an American officer treated them to a surprise. What one of these specialists from the land of Kultur heard, with his "listening-in" ear glued to the receiver, was this: "ug blupp. Gwnee blkrup pft kowie! Gmrr-klmpp! Hwee-pstoeck!"

"Donnerwetter! Was ist das fur ein verdammten**!!???" The bespectacled Hun was baffled. He puzzled, scratched his head and nearly choked with amazement.

"What kind of language was this anyway?—this strange and incomprehensible gibberish that came dripping, gurgling and bubbling into his ears in a stream of outlandish vowels and consonants."

Perfectly simple if you knew.

In Company E, 142nd Infantry, there were 150 Indian soldiers commanded by Captain E. W. Horner of Mena, Arkansas. Captain Horner simply detailed eight Indians in command of Chief George Baconrind, to transmit his orders in original Choctaw, pure and undefiled.

Himmel!

Military records of individual servicemen indicate that the Choctaws distinguished themselves in service. All of the members were honorably discharged, and copies of several of their discharge papers contain laudatory comments in several categories, such as "Character: Excellent" and "Remarks: No AWOL and no absence."[23] Tobias Frazier was wounded and awarded the Purple Heart.[24] Victor Brown was awarded the Purple Heart after suffering mustard gas poisoning, a broken nose, and head injuries in combat.[25] Joseph Oklahombi distinguished himself to such a degree in combat that he was declared "Oklahoma's Greatest War Hero" by the *Daily Oklahoman* newspaper. Reportedly underage at the time war was declared, Oklahombi, like many veterans of the time, lied about his age in order to enlist. Because he was an orphan, no one questioned the validity of his age and he was enlisted. A member of Company D, 141st Infantry Regiment, Thirty-sixth Division, Oklahombi was out on patrol during the Meuse-Argonne campaign in southern France. Alone at the time, "Oklahombi discovered a group of 250 German soldiers having lunch in a cemetery. Blocking the only gate to the high-walled cemetery, Oklahombi methodically killed every German who tried to offer resistance or escape. One hundred and seventy-one completely subdued Germans, all that remained alive, surrendered to him. He had killed a total of 79." Oklahombi was later awarded the Croix de Guerre for this action. The U.S. government reported Oklahombi's deeds in an official citation for bravery:

> Private Joseph Oklahombi, Company D, 141st Infantry, under a violent barrage, dashed to the attack of an enemy position, covering about 200 yards through barbed wire entanglements. He rushed on machine gun nests, capturing 171 prisoners. He stormed a strongly-held position containing more than fifty machine guns and a number of trench mortars, turned the captured enemy gun on the enemy, and held the said position for four days in spite of a constant barrage of large projectiles and gas shells, crossed "No Man's Land" many times to get information concerning the enemy, and to assist his wounded comrades.[26]

Oklahombi distinguished himself in another situation by escorting prisoners back to the reserve lines, where he turned them in at a French detention camp. Fellow Choctaw Code Talker Ben Carterby reported the incident, which was written in a firsthand, albeit stereotypical, form:

> An officer saw Oklahombi at a distance coming in with two prisoners. But when he arrived, he had only one man in custody. "Where's the other prisoner, Oklahombi?" he asked. The stoic Choctaw replied simply, "I kill[ed] him." Then before the officer could catch his breath Oklahombi asked, "Want me to go back and kill him some more?"[27]

In 1918 Oklahombi was awarded the Silver Star from General Pershing and the Croix de Guerre from French Marshall Pétain.[28] The medals he won are exhibited in the State Historical Society Building in Oklahoma City. Before departing for France, Oklahombi, having no beneficiary of his insurance, called for the girl of his dreams, whom he had met at a football game while attending Armstrong Academy, to meet him. They were married only a few days before Oklahombi and the other members of the Thirty-sixth sailed for France. While on duty in the St. Etienne region, he was treated by the press as the Indian equivalent of Sergeant Alvin York. After returning home, Oklahombi was approached by representatives from Hollywood interested in making a movie documenting his life and service in the war, similar to that featuring Sergeant Alvin York. Oklahombi declined the offer, however, be-

26   cause it would have required him to relocate to California for the duration of the project.[29]

The Effectiveness of the Choctaw Code Talkers

How effective were the Choctaw Code Talkers? Within twenty-four hours after the Choctaw language was essentially pressed into service and the Choctaws began their communications operations, the Germans' advances were stopped. In seventy-two hours, the Germans had been forced into a full retreat with the Americans on full attack, and less than one month later, World War I ended with the signing of the Armistice on November 11, 1918 (*Bishinik* 1986b; Moseley 1988). After the signing of the Armistice, the Thirty-sixth Division was stationed north of Bar-le-Duc and adopted a new divisional insignia containing a blue arrowhead with a khaki-colored T across it—representing Oklahoma and Texas, respectively—imposed on a khaki background. "Arrowhead" was also selected as the name of a new division newspaper in the Tonnerre area. The "Panther Division" also became known as the Arrow Head Division, and both "Arrow Heads" and "Panthers" became nicknames for individual members (Chastaine 1920:271–272; White 1978:19).

The Choctaw Code Talkers were praised by their company commanders and by the battalion commander, who told the eight Choctaws that he was "putting them in for medals." Although medals were promised to the Choctaw Code Talkers for their communications contributions in World War I, they were never given (*Bishinik* 1986b). During a 1986 honors presentation held for all Choctaw service veterans at the annual Choctaw Nation Labor Day Festival in Tuskahoma, Oklahoma, the families of the original eight Choctaw Code Talkers were posthumously presented with Choctaw Nation Medals of Valor by Tribal Chief Hollis E. Roberts and the Choctaw Nation Council (*Bishinik* 1986a; Moseley 1988; Twin Territories 1991). A marble marker containing the names of the original eight Choctaw Code Talkers was erected at the Choctaw Nation tribal grounds at Tuskahoma. On November 3, 1989—some seventy-one years after the world war—the original fifteen Choctaw Code Talkers were posthumously honored by the French government at the Oklahoma State Capitol Building in Oklahoma City.[30]

The Original Choctaw Code Talkers of World War I

The following is a list of the eight Choctaw men who served as the original code talkers in World War I, their rank, assignment, and residence in Oklahoma:[31]

1. Cpl. Solomon Bond Louis, Hoochatown and Bennington, Oklahoma, 142d Infantry, Co. E.
2. Pfc. Mitchell Bobb, Smithville, Oklahoma, 142d Infantry, Co. E.
3. Ben Carterby (Bismark), Wright City, Oklahoma, 142d Infantry, Co. E.
4. Robert Taylor, Bokchito or Boswell, Oklahoma, 142d Infantry, Co. E.
5. Jeff Nelson, Kullitukle, Oklahoma, 142d Infantry, Co. E.
6. Pete Maytubby, Broken Bow, Oklahoma, 142d Infantry, Co. E.
7. Cpl. James (Jimpson) M. Edwards, Oak Hill, Oklahoma, 142d Infantry, Co. E.
8. Calvin Wilson, Eagletown, Oklahoma, 142d Infantry, Co. E.

To this list may be added the names of at least seven other Choctaws in the Thirty-sixth Division who also served as code talkers in World War I:[32]

9. Albert Billy, Howe, Oklahoma, 142d Infantry.
10. Cpl. Victor Brown, Good Water, Oklahoma, 143d Infantry, HQ Co.
11. Sgt. Tobias W. Frazier, Spencerville, Oklahoma, 142d Infantry, Co. E and HQ.
12. Benjamin W. Hampton, Bennington, Oklahoma (unit unknown).
13. Pfc. Joseph Oklahombi, Bokchito, Oklahoma, 141st Infantry, Co. D.
14. Capt. Walter Veach, 142d Infantry, Co. E.
15. Benjamin Colbert (unit unknown).

OTHER NATIVE AMERICAN COMMUNICATIONS
OPERATORS IN WORLD WAR I

With twenty-six Indian languages and dialects found within the Thirty-sixth Division, we will probably never know how many of these were used for American Expeditionary Force communications due to the spontaneity and minimal documentation of their use. Although the use of Native Americans as telephone operators or code talkers was not widespread in the AEF, several units employed them during the last two months of the war, including Cherokees, Cheyennes, Comanches, Osages, and Yankton Sioux (Hale 1982:4; Britten 1997:107). Hale (1982: 41) reports, "There was also a group of Cherokee soldiers in the telephone service who disconcerted Germans by transmitting orders in their native language." These may have been part of the sixty-eight Cherokees in Company E, 142d Infantry Regiment. As Britten (1997:107) re-

28   lates, "In their discussion of Osage telephone operators, Wendell Martin and Alphonzo Bulz, veterans of the Thirty-sixth Division, remarked that the Osages 'used to love to talk on our telephones and they'd talk in Osage. We used to wonder if Germans could ever interpret those calls.' If the Germans could, they mused, 'it would have confused the hell out of them.'" Documentation shows that at least two other languages were used in a similar fashion, Comanche and Sioux (probably Yankton).

Comanche Communications Operators in World War I

At least thirty-one Comanches served in the First World War.[33] Recent information indicates that Comanche troops in World War I also served as communications operators. Based on recruiting dates of the Comanche Code Talkers for World War II (December 1940 to January 1941), a microfilmed article entitled "The Indian Sign" was printed around 1940:

> An Item from Oklahoma City informs us that A. C. Monahan, director of the Indian Service, has received a War Department request to recommend thirty Comanche Indians for work in the Signal Corps. They would be sent to Atlanta, Ga., for training as Army telephone operators.

> Our Comanches serving with the A.E.F. in France during the World War caused the Germans quite a bit of confusion. . . . Headquarters discovered that the Germans had tapped our telephone wires from advanced outposts at the front. Instead of laying new lines, the Signal Corps merely sent Comanches to man the instruments. The Comanches have no written language and there are not more than thirty white men who can understand their spoken language. None of these is German. When the Germans heard the Indians talking on the Western Front they naturally assumed, after exhausting all their foreign language experts, that code was being used. Their code experts were called in and worked hard on the problem, but these too gave up in despair. They never did discover what the Comanches were chatting about. Evidently the War Department thinks Comanche would prove a nice line of talk for the next war.[34]

A second source, originally issued by the Associated Press in Oklahoma City, was printed in the *New York Times* on December 13, 1940. Entitled "Comanches Again Called for Army Service," this source provides additional evidence of the use of Comanche communications operators in the First World War:

> Oklahoma's Comanche Indians, whose strange tongue not more than 30 white men in the world can fathom, will be ready again to defy decoders as they did in the World War.

> A. C. Monahan, director of the Indian Service, had a War Department request to recommend 30 Indians, fluent in their language and able to understand each other, for enlistment to train in Signal Corps work. He chose Comanches, who have no written language.

> Professor W. G. Becker of the English Department at Cameron Agricultural College, Lawton, and an authority on the tribe, recalled that several Comanches from Southwestern Oklahoma were used for relaying secret messages in the last war, and added:

> "One would be at a telephone at the front in communication with another back at headquarters. They would relay orders in their native language. The Germans had tapped the wires, and it must have driven them crazy."

> The Army plans to send the Indians to Atlanta for training in Signal Corps work, including telephone and radio transmission.[35]

The late Haddon Codynah, a Comanche Code Talker in World War II, stated that he had heard elder Comanche veterans of World War I talk about the use of Comanches and other Native Americans as code talkers in the First World War.[36] Likewise, Albert Nahquaddy Jr. was told by his father, Albert Nahquaddy Sr., that he and other Comanches used their native language during World War I.[37] Although these testimonies demonstrate the use of the Comanche language in the First World War, there is presently no indication of whether any organized code was formed or used due to the absence of available documentation.

The Sioux

In addition to the Choctaws and Comanches, members of an unspecified Sioux (possibly Yankton) tribe also used their native language to provide communications against the Germans in World War I. A brief article from a 1919 edition of *The American Indian Magazine* describes the army's use of their skills:

29

Played Joke on the Huns

Sioux Indians Had Fun for Three Days Talking over a Tapped Telephone Wire

Because of the nature of the country over which American troops fought in the Meuse-Argonne offensive, the Germans found it easy at times to cut in on our field telephone wires.

The commander of one brigade of artillery attached to an American division was particularly annoyed by enemy wire tappers in a heavily wooded section of the Argonne. Code messages from artillery observers were being intercepted by Boche listeners-in and the commander knew, as all armies know, that no code is impregnable when experts get working on it.

The artillery commander took up with the colonel of one of the line regiments the question of the Huns' wire-tapping activities. And the colonel hit upon an idea.

Two Indians, both of proud Sioux lineage, members of one of his company [sic], were assigned as telephone operators. One was to go forward with the artillery observer, the other to remain at the brigade receiving end of the wire which the artillery captain was certain the Germans had that day tapped somewhere along the line.

Now, when two Sioux Indians get talking together in their own tongue, what they say sounds very much like code, but isn't. Anyway, it raised hob with the code experts of certain Prussian guard units.

The Sioux stuck on their jobs for three days and nights. They and the artillery commander and their own colonel enjoyed the situation immensely. If the Germans got any fun out of it they kept it to themselves.

STEUBENVILLE (OHIO) GAZETTE [38]

Britten (1997:107) also provides data on Yankton Sioux telephone communications operators:

Paul Picotte, a Yankton Sioux, expressed great pride about Indian contributions during the war. In fact, he went so far as to make the dubious assertion that Indian telephone operators won the war—

single handedly! "That World War was ended by the Indian boys who were in the service," he boasted. "They were eventually put up to the front . . . in the communication system, and they talked in Indian . . . and the war came to an end."

Another source reports the use of an "All-American Team" in World War I composed of Sioux, Apache, and Comanche Indians from Ft. Riley, Kansas. These individuals laid communications wire from horse-drawn reel-carts and were reportedly chosen by an officer from tribes known for their horsemanship (Time-Life 1993:117). No information concerning the use of their native languages is known.

Although code talkers definitely contributed to the achievements of their respective companies, regiments, and divisions, there is no indication that the war was won solely due to their efforts. There is, however, evidence that German troops were apprehensive concerning the presence of large numbers of Native American AEF troops, who, "through their service as scouts, messengers, and telephone operators, aided the Allied victory and perhaps helped indirectly by demoralizing the enemy" (Britten 1997:108–109).

Three sources (Paul 1973:9; Wright 1986; Aaseng 1992:20) report that Canadian forces in World War I tried unsuccessfully to use Indian languages when their telephone lines were tapped by the Germans. According to Lieutenant Colonel James E. Jones, the Indians "had no words in their vocabulary that were exact equivalents for military terms. For example, they could find no way of transmitting 'machine gun' or 'barrage'" (Wright 1986). The plan reportedly failed because Indian languages did not match up well with Western military terminology. In other words, the military had too many terms for which no Indian equivalent then existed. Dempsey (1983:4) states that among Canadian Indian recruits for World War I, "Language was a common problem . . . since many Indians were unfamiliar with English at first and communication was difficult." The problems of the Canadians in using Native Americans in military communications may reflect a general lack of extensive English fluency among Canadian Indians or the Canadian military forces' failure to devise and implement a code instead of looking for direct cognates or vocabulary equivalents in the existing native languages.

TYPES OF NATIVE AMERICAN CODE TALKING

Prior scholars have failed to distinguish the similarities and differences in defining the two basic forms of Native American military code talking. Data from World War I demonstrate a significant distinction con-

32 cerning the types of Native American military communications operators. A common contention of many writers is that Native American
military communications operators are only "code talkers" if they use
a set of prearranged and formally organized, encoded terms. But how
should those who spoke in their native languages for similar purposes,
but without encoded terms or with only limited numbers of encoded
terms, be viewed? Are they code talkers? While the generic definition of
a code (a formula for secret messages) most commonly conjures up im-
ages of creating new forms of encoded writing based upon an already existing language, what of the intentional use of another language to serve
the exact interests of another group? I suggest that this too qualifies as
a code in that the basic United States armed forces definition of a code
(a system of secret message transmission) is neither specifically limited
to writing nor to the use of an individual group's own language to ac-
complish its communications goals in secret. The difference is that two
different, but related, forms were used to achieve essentially the same
goal. The use of Native American languages with specially designed encoded terms can be classified as Type 1 (Native American languages as
a code with additional encoded terms), while the use of Native American languages without specially designed encoded terms can be classified as Type 2 (Native American languages as unknown languages or as
a code without encoding). The determining factor is largely the presence
or absence of a body of encoded terms that were developed and used.
Aside from the Choctaw data, there is no mention of other groups devising specially encoded terminology. Thus, although some may have
likewise developed a small body of specially encoded military terms as
circumstances necessitated, there are presently no data to formally char-
acterize the other groups, who appear to have served as Type 2 code talkers. In the end, both types functioned for the same military reasons desired by the American Expeditionary Force, secret and secure tactical
and strategic communications. Thus it is important to recognize that at
least two distinct forms of Native American code talkers have existed
since the First World War.

The United States' entrance into World War I in 1917 provided the
first opportunity for Native Americans as a whole to regain full veteran
status since the beginning of the reservation system. Overall, native responses to the First World War came in the form of a tremendous out-
burst of enlistment, patriotism, and tribal and national devotion. This
was a significant turnout at a time when some Native Americans were
still denied United States citizenship and the ability to share in the
constitutional rights for which they were willing to fight and die. Representing a return to acquiring veteran status, servicemen in World War I
were frequently given heroes' farewell celebrations to the accompani-

ment of tribal military society and War Journey songs and dances. Their return during the winter of 1918–1919 provided even greater occasions for celebration as large contingents met incoming servicemen at local train stations. Throughout the summer of 1919, numerous Plains Indian families in Oklahoma sponsored traditional homecomings in the form of large community or tribal encampments, at which scalp and victory dances, and powwows of a social nature, were held. New songs were composed to honor returning veterans, some of which became tribal flag songs among several Plains tribes, such as the Comanche, Kiowa, Naishan Apache, Cheyenne, and Ponca.[39] In most cases the family of each returning veteran sponsored such a celebration.

Comanche, Kiowa, and Naishan Apache elders indicate that during this period the reinvigoration of tribal martial ideology was elevated to that of ethos in support of their young veterans, as the community's attention and daily news focused upon the war (Meadows 1995). Because veterans' celebrations contained dancing, singing, and giving-away, many were still technically illegal and were held in disdain by Indian agents attempting to eradicate them. However, the outpouring of celebration associated with World War I was so great that government Indian agents could not counter it. In 1919, Commissioner of Indian Affairs Cato Sells complained that many Indian veterans had returned from the war in France, where they had "counted coup" in modern form, only to take part in victory dances, watch as their sisters and mothers performed scalp dances, and be ritually cleansed from the taint of combat by tribal medicine people.[40] Celebrations containing scalp and victory dances, naming ceremonies, and inductions into warrior societies occurred in neighboring Cheyenne and Arapaho communities in western Oklahoma. The increased ceremonialism among numerous Plains tribes following World War I demonstrates that the war rekindled past traditions on a widespread basis (Parman 1994:62–63; Britten 1997:84, 149–151). Sparked by the veterans' distinguished service records and their return to active martial combat, the traditional forms surrounding the role of warriors and the culturally appropriate means of honoring them had been revived and experienced by younger generations. While these celebrations were brief in tenure, they were significant because they revived the symbols, ideology, ethos, and community gatherings associated with traditional forms of honoring veterans. Military service in World War I facilitated native reacquisition of martial status, symbols, and meaning in a syncretic form acceptable to both native communities and the larger Anglo society (Meadows 1999). Anglos now came to see Native American servicemen as an asset instead of a threat. The additional use of Native American languages as a military strategy lent further respect. As a result of Native American service in World War I all Indian veterans

33

were officially made citizens in 1919, and citizenship was later given to all Native Americans with the Indian Citizenship Act in June of 1924. As Holm (1996:100) states, "The conferring of American citizenship on American . . . Indians . . . was not necessarily a reward for Indian loyalty. Rather it simply was acknowledgement that Indians were no longer threats to American policy." Scholars continue to debate whether this act was a "reward" to Indians for their service in World War I or a larger politically motivated action (cf. Franco 1999:190–191).

Although its efforts were somewhat hastily and belatedly organized, the American armed forces had discovered and utilized an existing and effective, but previously unrecognized, communications tool—Native American languages combined with coding. The basic premise of using Native Americans as communications operators was that, while codes could be broken, unknown languages, or unknown languages further disguised with encoding, could not. Coded Native American languages (and not writing), as a basis for a crypto-lingual system, offered an extremely valuable, and less decipherable, form of secure communication. The use of Indian troops as telephone operators during the First World War came toward the end of the war, yet received considerable, albeit brief, official and public recognition. The United States had made use of a resource that virtually no other country had yet thought to employ, native languages so obscure that virtually no one else in the world knew them, some of which were then further disguised with systematic coding. Due to sparse military records it is difficult to estimate the exact contributions of Native American code talkers in the First World War. Nevertheless, the success of the Choctaws, Comanches, and others in World War I laid the groundwork for future Native American code talking. It was a tactic that the United States armed forces would not forget.

c·h·a·p·t·e·r · t·w·o

NATIVE AMERICAN SERVICEMEN AND
CODE TALKERS IN WORLD WAR II

WORLD WAR II

Following both the Indian Citizenship (Snyder) Act of June 1924 and the
Selective Service Act of 1940, all Native American men between the
ages of twenty-one and forty-four were subject to the draft. However,
much confusion still existed among both Anglos (including Selective
Service personnel, military officials, and Indian agency superintendents)
and Indians themselves regarding the unique legal, governmental, and
cultural status of Indians. Distinctions between and applicability of the
concepts of wardship, U.S. citizenship, simultaneous statuses of U.S.
and individual tribal citizenship, Indian treaty obligations to the United
States, and the existing status and future retention of tribal sovereignty
created a mass of legal confusion for all involved in Indian administration and the Selective Service (Franco 1999:44–56; Townsend 2000:61–
124). To settle these matters, Congress passed the Nationality Act on
October 14, 1940, granting citizenship to all Native Americans without
impairing tribal property. In reality, this act raised serious questions
concerning issues of tribal sovereignty and the government's jurisdiction in drafting Indians (Franco 1999:46). Eventually the issue of tribal
sovereignty and the draft was settled in court in the case of *Totus et al.
v. United States*, which held that "Congress reserved the right to repeal
or to suspend any treaty during an emergency," and that the Selective
Service Act superseded all previous treaties and laws. A similar finding
was arrived at in the case of Warren Eldreth Green, an Onondaga from
New York (Franco 1999:49).

Because the question of Indian participation in the military had not
arisen in the congressional debates concerning the implementation of

36   the draft, Indian Commissioner John Collier attempted to lobby within the Interior Department for special treatment for Native American soldiers and to expand the role of the Bureau of Indian Affairs (BIA). Collier proposed the formation of an "All-Indian" division administered by the BIA, noting that there were some 42,000 Indians eligible for military service. Anthropologist Oliver LaFarge and Navajo Tribal Council Chairman J. C. Morgan made similar proposals for all-Indian units based on concerns for linguistic and cultural differences, high English illiteracy rates, and the assumption that Native Americans desired to advance their identity as respected and contributing members of American society (Franco 1999:44; Townsend 2000:69). Between 1941 and 1945, the total Native American population was just under 350,000. As part of Collier's overarching attempts to promote cultural pluralism and tribal cultural retention, he maintained that Indians wanted to be separated from whites and have their ethnic identity retained and their specific contributions specially recognized. Although nothing came of his recommendations, Collier did not give up easily on the idea of an all-Indian division (Bernstein 1991:22–23). Increased contact between Native Americans and Anglos came as a direct result of official War Department policies which encouraged Native American integration into all military branches. Despite the efforts of John Collier, the BIA, and Native Americans themselves, Secretary of War Henry Stimson publicly opposed the formation of any all-Indian units, and supported a pro-assimilationist stand on Indian military service embracing "eventual absorption of Indians into the mainstream of American life" (Bernstein 1991:41). Many Kiowa, Comanche, and Apache veterans stated that they were the only Indians in their immediate units and saw few Indians throughout the entire war (Meadows 1995). With a governmental integrationist approach to military unit formation, and no officially segregated all-Indian units, the contributions of 25,000 Indians amongst 15 million other American veterans are often quite difficult to trace (Bernstein 1991:40–41; Bucholz et al. 1996:2; Franco 1999:139).

The exact number of Native Americans serving in World War II will probably never be determined due to several factors. Some individuals did not claim Indian descent and were thus listed as white, which correlated with the antisegregationist and pro-assimilationist policies of the armed forces, which emphasized placing Indians throughout Anglo units. Conversely, the State of Virginia maintained a strongly segregated racist policy whereby all Indians were declared to be of mixed Afro-American descent and could only be listed as Negroes. Not until March 3, 1941, did the War Department order all local boards to determine the ethnic origin of all registrants. However, these designations were often biased by assumptions based on physical appearance and personal association with Afro-Americans (Townsend 2000:87–102). Consequently, there are Native American servicemen whose correct ethnic identity was not recorded.

The Draft in World War II

Some authors have suggested that because Indians became subject to the draft in 1940, this played a major role in the increase of their military service (Bernstein 1991:22–42; Parman 1994:111; Rawles 1996:5). As with World War I, data concerning Native American enlistment prior to the United States' declaration of war against Japan in World War II contest this assertion. Some 4,500 Native Americans were already in the United States armed forces prior to the attack on Pearl Harbor on December 7, 1941, more than 60 percent by voluntary enlistment (Townsend 2000:61). Indian enlistments only accelerated following Japan's attack on Pearl Harbor. "Shortly after Congress declared war on December 8, 1941, Indians flocked to enlist" (Bernstein 1991:42). The number of Indian volunteers more than doubled in the first six months of the war (Collier 1942:29). By November 1942 approximately 8,800 were serving in the armed forces and by the winter of 1942, over 10,000 had registered for the draft. Estimates of Native Americans serving in the United States armed forces during World War II range from over 25,000, along with several hundred women in the Wacs and Waves, to over 44,000.

More than 40,000 other Native Americans aged eighteen to fifty left their reservations and home communities to work in ordnance depots, factories, and other war-related industries across the nation. Approximately one-third of the entire native population left reservation and allotment communities for service in the armed forces or employment in urban settings and represented the first major mass exodus from Indian lands into non-Indian society (Townsend 2000:181). In addition, by early 1945 Native Americans had invested over $50 million in war bonds. Native peoples also made generous contributions to the Red Cross and the army and navy relief societies, as well as large contributions of natural resources: minerals, timber, agriculture, and land for armed forces training facilities and Japanese relocation camps. They also contributed as media figures designed to promote the war effort (Hale 1992; Bucholz et al. 1996:2; Franco 1999:80, 120–148; Townsend 2000:188).

As with enlistments in World War I, Native Americans enlisted at a rate of one and a half times the number that were drafted, and Plains volunteers exceeded inductees by a ratio of two to one (Haynie 1984:7; Bernstein 1991:35, 39–41). Most World War II servicemen were volunteers, not conscriptees (Parman 1994:113). Franco (1999:60) reports an **37**

38 85 percent voluntary enlistment ratio, while Townsend (2000:72) reports that by April of 1941, enlistment among all Indians was fifteen times higher than the number of draftees. By November of 1941, nearly 42,000 Indian men aged twenty-one to thirty-five, almost two-thirds of all eligible Indian males, had fulfilled their requirements for registration (Townsend 2000:61). In 1942, Selective Service reported that "at least ninety-nine percent of all eligible American Indians, healthy males aged twenty-one to forty-four, had registered for the draft" (Franco 1999:62). By the end of the war BIA officials estimated that 24,521 American Indians, excluding officers, had served in the United States armed forces and another 20,000 off-reservation Indians had also enlisted. Although estimates of the total Native American population vary (345,252, Thornton 1987:160; 400,000, Franco 1999:62), this total of 44,500 individuals comprised well over 10 percent of the estimated Native American population of 361,816 in 1942 (Paul 1973:153).

While Native Americans were voluntarily enlisting in significant numbers, some groups, such as the Florida Seminole and the Navajo, experienced deferrals and dismissals due to educational (high levels of illiteracy and lack of English speaking skills) and health reasons. These factors varied greatly from reservation to reservation as high numbers of deferments occurred in some locales, while nearly none occurred in others. These problems were closely linked, in each community, to the existing status of poverty, infectious disease, malnutrition, poor housing and sanitation, and access to adequate school and health facilities. These indices and others had been reported as being substandard throughout the United States in the 1928 Meriam Report and continued to be substandard in the vast majority of Indian communities into the Second World War. Consequently, Native Americans experienced a much higher rate of rejection for military service than their Anglo counterparts. Access to quality housing, clothing, food, and adequate medical facilities was lacking in most locales. Rejection rates varied from state to state, depending greatly upon the population of Indians. While some states with small native populations reported low rejection rates, states such as Arizona with large native populations produced a rejection rate of 27 percent for Anglos, 45 percent for Indians, and 46 percent for Afro-Americans (Townsend 2000:64). On a national level, the majority of Indian rejections (37.5 percent, compared to a 32 percent ratio among Anglos) were caused by failure to pass the military physical exam due to cases of trachoma (nearly 8 percent) and tuberculosis (5 percent), diseases which had become virtually absent among the white population, with ratios of 4 percent and 1 percent, respectively. Age, weight, and gender were other factors (Franco 1999:56–59).

While health conditions from high levels of infectious diseases and malnutrition accounted for many enlistment rejections, low scores on tests designed to determine educational and mental competency were another major factor. Given at induction centers, these standardized tests were modeled on middle-class Anglo culture and were too biased for cross-cultural assessment. In Arizona 12 percent of all Anglos fell below the armed forces' minimum standards, compared to 23 percent of all Afro-Americans and 49 percent of all Native Americans. Inaccurate cross-cultural assumptions by Anglo physicians about Native American demeanor, culture shock in large urban environments, and time orientation also accounted for enlistment rejections (Townsend 2000: 64–66).

Despite greater health problems and more limited educational opportunities, Native Americans were clearly enlisting in great numbers for reasons other than the possibility of being drafted. As Indian Commissioner John Collier stated, "It represents a larger proportion than any other element of our population" (Collier 1942:29). The percentage of Native American participation in relation to their total population was higher than any other American ethnic group represented in World War II, including Anglo-Americans, and this ratio was also higher for some categories involving the number of wounded and killed (Bernstein 1991:55, 61; Haynie 1984:7; Hale 1992; Wigginton 1992). Over one-third of all eligible men aged eighteen to fifty served, but enlistments were as high as 70 percent in some tribes. The Forty-fifth Infantry Division, a National Guard unit from Oklahoma and New Mexico that contained about 1,500 Indians from some twenty-eight tribes, logged 511 days of combat in North Africa, Italy, and southern France, and contained the greatest percentage of Native Americans of any army division, nearly one-fifth (Haynie 1984; Bernstein 1991; Franco 1999:131). Formed from the Arizona National Guard, Company F of the 158th Infantry Regiment, Fortieth Division, was an all-Indian unit made up of members of some twenty tribes that drew its members entirely from the Phoenix Indian School membership and alumni. Later a part of the 158th Infantry Regimental Combat Team, this elite fighting unit trained in hand-to-hand combat, knives, and assault weapons in Panama. It later gained distinction in the Pacific theater, earning the name "The Bushmasters" (Franco 1999:66–67, 164–165).

That Native American patriotism was unsurpassed was reflected in the *Saturday Evening Post* (1942:9), which stated, "We would not need the Selective Service if all volunteered like Indians," and by President Dwight D. Eisenhower (*Senior Scholastic* 1953:6), who stated, "Never did I hear a complaint about the battle conduct of the Native American Indian." Native American performance in the Second World War was rewarded with the highest praise and admiration. The service records **39**

40   of Native Americans during World War II were significant, including over two hundred citations and medals, excluding Purple Hearts. These awards for heroism included: seventy-one Air Medals, fifty-one Silver Crosses, forty-seven Bronze Stars, thirty-four Distinguished Flying Crosses, and two Congressional Medals of Honor, both by Oklahoma Native Americans in the Forty-fifth Infantry Division (Hale 1992: 421). Similarly, Native Americans received thirty Distinguished Flying Crosses and seventy Air Medals in the Army Air Corps, and one Distinguished Flying Cross in the Royal Canadian Air Force. During World War II, 550 Native Americans were killed and 700, or nearly one thirty-fifth, were wounded in action (Haynie 1984:7; Bernstein 1991:53, 55, 61).

For Native Americans collectively, the Second World War marked a defining turning point in the twentieth century. Native participation in World War II, the seminal watershed event of the twentieth century, and later in the Korean War, combined with improved legal and economic conditions, veteran status, concern for the Relocation and Termination Acts, and a developing Indian ethnic awareness movement, did much to revive Native American political and cultural forms. Such was the case with the revival of much Southern Plains Indian culture, including military societies (Meadows 1995). The Comanche Code Talkers were one small element in the larger developing processes of a growing Native American ethnic awareness derived from Native American service in World War II.

THE U.S. ARMY'S DEBATE ON USING NATIVE AMERICANS IN ARMED FORCES COMMUNICATIONS

Despite considerable literature on the Navajo Code Talkers' contributions in World War II, more recent recognition of the Choctaws' and Comanches' service in World Wars I and II, and the fact that there is no evidence that any Native American military communications were ever broken, some critics have expressed views that Native American code talkers' contributions were minimal and relatively unimportant, and could not feasibly have been expanded or used in other ways. In response to these views, this section discusses: (1) the armed forces' debates concerning the use of Native American code talkers, (2) the army's skepticism versus the marines' optimism in using Indian code talkers, (3) the availability of adequate numbers of service-age Indian men who were fluent speakers of their native languages and English, and, most importantly, (4) the possibility that Native American code talking units could have been explored and expanded for a larger military contribution in terms of numbers, methods, distribution, and effectiveness.

During World War II the United States armed forces again decided to use Native Americans for special communications assignments in some branches. However, the main difference in how tribal members were employed was in the army's skepticism versus the marines' optimism concerning the use of Native American communications operators and their native languages for military communications purposes. Despite the documented successes of the Choctaw, Comanche, and other Native American groups in the American Expeditionary Force (AEF) in the First World War, the U.S. Army was reluctant to adopt any large-scale service-wide program using Indian "talkers," considering them too great a liability for secure communications. While the Army Signal Corps appears to have been the first branch to recruit and train Indian communicators (Comanches) for World War II, the army did not develop or expand any other similar units, despite exemplary and effective service throughout the war. One study prejudicially cautioned, "Captured Indian personnel might be forced to introduce false messages into a net employing linguists" (Armstrong 1989:54). Why couldn't any captured non-Indian communications personnel, who were of vastly greater quantity than Indians and thus more likely to be captured, be forced to do likewise?

Correspondence in the now declassified Records of the National Security Agency (RNSA) contains accounts of several meetings among the army, Army Air Corps, and the marines to discuss the adoption of such programs. Despite legitimate concerns for military security, the following letter demonstrates a number of potential and questionable stereotypes, inaccurate assumptions, and prejudices about Native Americans, their languages, abilities, intelligence, judgment, and potential linguistic contributions. Furthermore, it reflects a significant misunderstanding of the relationship between culture and the flexibility and evolution of languages.

8 September, 1943
Memo for Colonel McCormack:

1. It is possible that this idea was "tried with little success in World War I" but it is thought that official records would disclose that the idea was merely suggested and discarded as impractical and dangerous, not only from the standpoint of security but also from the standpoint of accuracy.

2. It is difficult at times for two intelligent and quite fluent speakers to understand each other on good commercial telephone circuits; when the circuits are only fair or bad, as they often are under adverse field conditions, then the quality of the signals becomes so poor that serious misunderstandings are very likely to arise.

41

3. The use of Indians for the purpose indicated will really mean that they would be employed in the capacity of interpreters serving as intermediaries between the unit commanders concerned. The danger of misunderstandings arising from this source, even in ordinary, every day life, is recognized; in military operations, where accuracy in, and proper understanding of technical terminology is important, they may have very serious consequences.

4. Add to the foregoing factors the fact that the vocabulary to any Indian dialect which might be selected will certainly be deficient in military and technical terms, forcing the use of the plain English term, it is clear that security would be lessened. Or, if arbitrary designations were adopted for them, there would soon grow up a code—putting the matter back exactly where it was before, with a considerable loss in efficiency of communication.

5. So long as radiophone and telephone communications are in English unit commanders and security personnel designated to monitor circuits can easily ascertain when and whether or not dangerous violations of security are occurring. If Indians were used, this would no longer be the case and unit commanders would be entirely dependent upon the good judgment of the personnel involved and their individual, personal appraisals or estimates of what may or may not be dangerous to say at a specific time over these circuits.

6. It would be better to employ present methods and personnel with a good code specifically adapted for the purpose. Recent development of a device called "Slidex" gives promise of yielding a good answer to the problem of safe and speedy radiophone communication for forward echelons. Samples of this device will be sent [to] the New Caledonia and other commands as promptly as possible.

W. Preston Corderman
Colonel, Signal Corps [1]

Aside from popular misconceptions about Native Americans in the 1940s (Bernstein 1991; Holm 1996), part of the skepticism toward using Native American communications operators stems from the lack of documentation of their World War I service record. A brief letter dated

September 29, 1943, from J. W. Wright, Colonel, Infantry, of the Army War College in Washington, D.C., to Colonel S. P. Collins, Acting Chief, Signal Security Branch, A.S.F., indicates that the only known documentation of Native American code talkers in the First World War was Colonel A. W. Bloor's January 23, 1919, memo already presented in Chapter 1:

> With reference to paragraph 3, your 1st endorsement, dated September 23, 1943, as addressed to this office, I enclose a copy of an official document (236-32.5) bearing on the use of Indian dialects for code purposes. This is the only document we have ever been able to locate in the official A.E.F. files on this subject.
>
> Very Truly Yours,
> J.W. Wright
> Colonel, Infantry[2]

This lack of documentation points to the fact that the use of Native American code talkers in World War I was an experiment that was extremely limited in numbers, duration, organization, and methods. However, the lack of documentation and the use of several such groups on a "use them if you have them" basis do not indicate that they were in any way ineffective. Colonel Bloor's positive report and the British and French governments' (Hale 1982:41) public recognition of all Native Americans' service in World War I suggest that the code talkers were indeed effective, despite their rudimentary form of organization. More importantly, the fullest military potential of Indian code talkers was neither realized nor explored.

The army's response to the possibility of using Native American code talkers came in a letter dated February 21, 1944, from Colonel Carter W. Clarke, General Staff, Assistant Officer, G-2:

> a. The use of Indian dialects as a substitute for authorized military codes and ciphers violates rules of security. There is information in the ar [Army] Department indicating that, prior to the outbreak of present hostilities, Axis nationals were studying American Indian dialects in both the Eastern and Western sections of the United States. Furthermore, it is known that prior to the outbreak of the present war, Japanese were employed by the Indian Affairs Bureau. A further source of insecurity in the use of Indian dialects lies in the fact that code words must be improvised to fill in deficiencies of the Indian dialects with respect to modern military and technical

43

terms. It must be acknowledged that the use of Indian dialects cannot be assumed to provide security for even a few hours in communications where transmissions can be picked up by enemy intercept facilities.

b. It is conceivable, however, that were [sic] Indian dialects are used as substitute for clear language transmission in rapidly moving front line operations, some advantage may be gained. Under these conditions, if it is considered desirable to utilize Indian dialects an attempt will be made to furnish your headquarters with the required number of Indians.[3]

A letter from Wheat and May, attorneys for Philip Johnston, eventually proceeded to the desk of Major J. M. Marzloff, Air Corps Chief of the Cryptographic Branch. His reply was almost identical to Colonel Clarke's, with paragraphs 4 and 5 more strongly reinforcing the army's opinion that the use of any Indian languages for coded armed forces communications was without merit:

4. . . . it is not evident to this Headquarters how such use of a known native tongue transmitted by radio can afford security over any appreciable length of time.

5. Although the plan has a certain amount of merit as a "stopgap" or as an emergency system of communication, this Headquarters feels that the low-grade security afforded by such a plan would be dangerous to the operations of the AAF, whereas authorized War Department cryptographic systems offer better security than the recommended procedure. It is felt that there are too many "loop holes" in the plan to justify its usage by the AAF. (McClain 1994:124)

However, these conclusions did not inhibit further inquiry into the use of Native American languages. A number of correspondences between March and July 1944 indicate that (1) suggestions were made to the army to expand its use of Native American code talkers and (2) the marines were willing to assist the army by providing logistical assistance and personnel familiar with training Navajo Code Talkers.[4]

A March 10, 1944, letter from Carl Wheat, attorney for Philip Johnston, to Colonel William F. Friedman reveals the acceptance and ongoing use of Navajo Code Talkers by the Marine Corps, as well as news from the Anzio Beachhead in Italy:

Right on the heels of the foregoing news comes a dispatch from the Italian front, proving beyond all doubt that the Navajo system would be of inestimable value to the army. It has been revealed that a critical situation on the Anzio Beachhead was further complicated by the fact that the commander of our forces was unable to transmit information regarding his plight without, at the same time, revealing his weakness to the enemy. Mountain passes were closed by blizzards, barring the passage of couriers, and any attempt to make use of radio communication would have apprised the enemy of his predicament. Here, then, is a classical example of how a method of radio communication which is absolutely secure against enemy interception would be of priceless value. Moreover, it is reasonable to believe that the Secretary of War might now be in a highly receptive frame of mind to give the most serious consideration to a proposal that the Army start a program to train Navajo personnel in the station of communication which the Marine Corps is already using.[5]

The letter went on to offer the services of T/Sgt. Philip Johnston, the man who originated the idea for using and training the Navajo Code Talkers, as well as estimates of some two thousand available Navajos currently enlisted in the armed forces who could be trained as code talkers, while suggesting potential training strategies and possible options for loaning several marines to the army as trainers.[6] Although well intentioned, Johnston's offer directly disregarded marine orders concerning the absolute secrecy of the Navajo project, and it is extremely unlikely that the marines would have allowed any other armed forces branch access to marine programs or marine personnel (McClain 1994:123).

As the army learned of rumors of the marines' program, it began an inquiry into the program's content. At a confidential April 1, 1944, conference held between Marine Lieutenant Colonel Smith and an unidentified army lieutenant, the Marine Corps cautiously discussed its Navajo program. As McClain describes, "the surprising content of the meeting appears to be a carefully constructed smoke screen to deflect the Army's curiosity concerning the Marine Corps code talker program. Paragraphs 1, 4, 7, 11 and 12 give the impression that the men trying to explain the use of the Navajos were careful not to expose their true mission" (McClain 1994:124).[7]

If the Marine Corps intention was to deflect army interest, its strategy apparently worked, as a letter dated June 17, 1944, from 1st Lieutenant Charles E. Henshall, Director of Communications Research, reaffirmed the army's mistrust of using Indian languages in armed forces communications (McClain 1994:125–126):

45

1. In reply to your informal request of 7 June 1944 regarding the attitudes expressed by the Army Ground Forces and Army Air Forces on the use of Navajo Indians for use in radio telephone transmissions, the following information has been obtained:

Army Ground Forces: Lieutenant Colonel James M. Kimbrough, Jr., of the Signal Section of Army Ground Forces informed the writer that Colonel G. B. Rodgers and Colonel O. K. Sadtler took this matter up with G-2 and obtained their feelings and opinions on it. Apparently, G-2 was dead set against the adoption of the plan to use Indians, since it was felt that the security features inherent in the Navajo tongue were not sufficient enough to warrant development for general radio telephony transmissions. It was further objected to that the enemy could obtain translators and after the recordations of sufficient plain text had been obtained, the entire language be subject to successful analysis and compromise.

Therefore, the Army Ground Forces did not feel justified in screening the entire army in search of Navajo linguists.

Army Air Forces: As yet no answer has been received to our request of 13 June 1944 directed to the Army Air Forces on the same subject and we are therefore unable to express to you their feelings on this matter. Upon receipt of this information, it will be immediately forwarded to your attention.[8]

Yet, while the first branch to again employ and train Indian communicators was the Army Signal Corps, the army's Indian code talkers were not the first to see combat action. Eventually, with the U.S. entrance into the Second World War occurring first in the Pacific theater, the U.S. naval air commanders needed fast, secure communications between various airfields to coordinate fighter aircraft escort, bomber strikes, and fighter defense. Following the informal testing of two Creek Indians, the navy's South Pacific Command requested twenty-four well-educated American Indians who spoke the same language. Two separate requests for the recruitment of twenty-four Native Americans for code training followed and included members of Western and Eastern tribes. Problems concerning the location of adequate numbers of well-educated recruits of the same tribe and language are frequently mentioned and are alleged to have proved difficult, as some tribes reportedly did not have a large enough population of service age with the requisite bilingual language skills. Eventually limited use of Native American code talkers was made by the U.S. Navy in World War II (Armstrong 1989:54–55).[9] A number of

Navajos were used by Aircraft South Pacific in the Air Operational Voice Circuit in World War II to order out planes and provide information concerning plane types, numbers, bomb loading, scheduling, rendezvous points, courses, and bearings.[10] A memo from the Armed Forces Security Agency indicates that the Aleuts were recommended for use to the navy in World War II but were not used, probably due to navy concerns for adequate numbers of fluent English-speaking male recruits.[11]

A letter dated January 15, 1944, from Navy Admiral Aubrey Fitch, Commander Aircraft, South Pacific Force, to Commander General, South Pacific, reports:

1. Of the original ten Indians to report only two were selected to receive training for communications work here. It was decided to use these two only after four additional selected Indians were received in order to train sufficient men to man the stations on the voice circuit.

2. . . . Employment of these men has resulted in rapid and accurate transmission of messages which previously required hours to transmit. This method by-passes many of the relays required in sending encrypted dispatches. From the start the service rendered by these men has received favorable comment from all stations on the circuit.

3. It is felt that there should be at least two at each station so that more practice can be obtained by talking together when not transmitting messages. It is also felt that this method of transmission will not remain secure for more than a month or two. Accordingly it is requested that twenty-four Indians of an eastern tribe be made available to this command for training as replacements for the Navajos now being used. Men with a high school education, or preferably with college training, are desired. Due to the urgency with which these men are needed on the circuit it is felt that the luxury of a long training period, necessarily required in the case of the Indians now being used cannot be enjoyed.[12]

However, a later report from the Signal Officer, South Pacific Area, and dated March 31, 1944, relates dissatisfaction with the recruits:

We have just gotten a decision from COMSOPAC that they no longer want the Indians and we have so informed the War Department. That means we will keep the 24 we now have along with allotment of grades and ratings, but will not exchange them for a

47

new batch of eastern Indians speaking a new language as was originally desired. This decision is a relief to me because the whole matter has been pretty much of a nuisance to everybody concerned, as well as having doubtful value in accomplishing any good. Actually only five of the original 24 proved usable but they have been used steadily for several months, using voice codes which change frequently in order to aid in the security.[13]

Despite continuing doubts, some officers, such as Colonel William Friedman, saw the obvious communications potential and campaigned in this direction:

I took up the subject with our Training Branch and . . . they took up the subject with the Marine Corps first and I am glad to say that a very favorable report has been made by certain officers as to the advantages of using trained Navahos for communications purposes. Unfortunately, about the same time we received word from some of our own people who had employed Indians and their reports are far from satisfactory. Of course, I think that the Indians who were tried out in Army units were probably basically unqualified by lack of the necessary education upon which to superimpose the additional qualifications necessary to make good signal personnel out of them. In brief, it is quite possible that our people have reached erroneous conclusions because the experiment they made was faulty.

. . . Informally also I have been told that the Marine Corps would be glad to cooperate with us in any way that they can in connection with rendering us assistance derived from their own training experience and possibly even offering to make Sergeant Johnston available to us. I therefore am going to take the matter up again with the proper people in the higher echelons of the Army and see if they do not want to go into the matter again and take advantage of the more fortunate experience of the Marine Corps. . . . I see no reason why Johnston's experience cannot be used to advantage in the training of men from some other tribe and this is what I am going to suggest.[14]

By the end of June 1944, the Army Ground Forces had officially declined to adopt the Navajo Indian training, despite the proposal to develop code talking among other tribal populations.[15] In July 1944, the Army Air Forces Headquarters announced its decision to decline the adoption of Navajo or other Native American communications operators. Although acknowledging the use of American Indians by the AEF in World War I and the use of Latin by the British in the Boer War, the Army Air Forces defended its position by citing alleged problems with several criteria:

> The need for this type of communication is not evident within the Army Air Forces, . . . it is not evident to this Headquarters how such use of a known native tongue transmitted by radio can afford security over any appreciable length of time. . . . It is recognized that such usage would afford a certain amount of security as well as surprise with the initial usage, but it is felt that the Axis Powers would regard a foreign or strange tongue on the radio as a challenge in glossology or philology rather than a problem of cryptography. It is known that studies of native Indian tongues . . . are available at many of the large reference libraries. . . . Although the plan has a certain amount of merit as a "stop gap" or emergency system of communication, this Headquarters feels that the low-grade security afforded by such a plan would be dangerous to the operations of the AAF, whereas authorized War Department cryptographic systems offer better security than the recommended procedure. It is felt that there are too many "loop holes" in the plan to justify its usage by the AAF.[16]

On July 26, 1944, Colonel Friedman reported the decision of the Army Air Forces not to adopt the use of

> . . . American Indians for communications purposes. . . . I think that the matter can be covered by saying that they do not believe the plan has sufficient merit and freedom from "loop holes" to warrant its further consideration for usage by the AAF. . . . I think this about winds up our correspondence on the subject. I am sure that the matter has been given full and careful consideration by all concerned in the Army and regret that more favorable reaction was not forthcoming.[17]

As we shall see, these largely unfounded misgivings about Native Americans' potential in armed forces communications proved to be a golden opportunity missed, as already demonstrated (prior to July 1944) by various marine Navajo units in the South Pacific theater and by small Native American Army Ground Forces units in the European theater.

There are always a host of grave and legitimate security concerns that arise with almost anything related to military intelligence. Military intelligence requires a tremendous degree of large-scale organization and security. As described by one military historian, there is a "cautious, almost paranoid, nature [to] intelligence personnel."[18] As Maslowski (1995:52–53) points out, intelligence itself makes no decisions and can only assist commanders in making decisions. Intelligence cannot guarantee that commanders make wise decisions and use intelligence reports to their fullest. "Even exquisite intelligence could not *ensure* battle victory; it could only make it easier to achieve" (Maslowski 1995:53). Shy (1986:329) demonstrates this principle in summarizing the results of the first American campaigns in ten individual wars: "Of the ten first battles, the U.S. Army suffered five defeats (Long Island, Queenstown, Bull Run, Kasserine [Pass], and Osan/Naktong) and won five victories. Four of those victories were very costly (San Juan, Cantigny, Buna, Ia Drang)—some might say too costly for the gains achieved."

The military employs communications systems, and the question of obtaining and training adequate numbers of personnel while ensuring security in a war the size of World War II poses legitimate concerns and warrants systematic treatment. To have sufficient personnel for the communications systems of an enormous army system that might be simultaneously employed on several fronts was indeed beyond the ability of all Native American World War II servicemen (25,000) to facilitate. The Navajo Code Talkers were able to be used in a comparatively small organization like the marines, which usually fought on only one island at a time. Although the Navajos were one of the largest Native American populations in 1942, I contend that many other tribal populations contained adequate numbers of available men and enlisted personnel who were fluent bilingual speakers to have furnished personnel to comparable code talker programs. In addition, members of many other tribes were better educated in formal Anglo-structured school systems and had had more lengthy face-to-face interactions with Anglo populations than the Navajo. Considering retrospectively the Navajo and Comanche contributions in World War II, the expansion of these and other Native American communications units would have unquestionably saved numerous lives and possibly even shortened the war in both theaters.

The remainder of this chapter examines the question of whether there were sufficient Native Americans to provide secure coded communications systems for other significant elements of the U.S. armed forces in World War II. To answer this, four criteria must be examined: the feasibility of expanding code talking units, the availability of adequate numbers of Native American men of service age, adequate numbers of service-age Native American men who were fluently bilingual, and factors of security.

Based on the previous information, two important questions arise. First, were there sufficient numbers of eligible, bilingual male recruits in other utilized tribes to have provided the quantity of men needed for code talking units? Second, how can it be assumed that their increased presence would have benefited the U.S. armed forces? I assert that many tribal populations contained sufficient numbers of enlistment-age males who were fluent bilingual speakers to have at least provided the opportunity to develop numerous, but relatively small, code talking units, most of which would have been best suited to division-level organizations.

In 1942 the Navajo tribal population numbered over 25,000, with over 11,600 men. That some 420 code talkers were recruited from their midst is frequently pointed out as evidence of their extensive use in the Marine Corps. The point to consider here is that several tribes smaller than the Navajo contributed to United States armed forces communications, and many others existed. Various moderate-sized populations provided the opportunity to develop numerous code units, with several possible results: (1) distinct individual tribal code talking units, dispersed throughout various military levels, at least as large as an army division (as the Comanches were in the Fourth Infantry Division), (2) periodically interchanging various linguistically distinct Native American code talking units on an irregular basis, thereby constantly making it more difficult for enemy interceptors to become familiar with one of many code talking units, or (3) individual communications units containing a mix of various tribal members trained in their respective ethnic groupings as code talkers and formed in such a way that both the divisional headquarters and respective infantry regiments could have had the option to send a message in one of several coded languages. For example, one message could have been sent in Comanche, while the next were sent, successively, in Lakota, Choctaw, Chippewa, Pawnee, and so on. Thus, for example, as wire teams often contained eight men, an eight-man code talking team of different tribal members would have provided endless possibilities for rotation and exchange with a divisional headquarters, and replacements for casualties would have been simplified with such multiple possibilities. This would also have been advantageous in the event that one or more men were killed or wounded, because communications would not have been dependent upon any one language.

By the fall of 1942, the marines increased Navajo recruitment to meet the demand for code talkers. McClain (1994:99, 201) reports marine requests of one hundred code talkers per division, and a recommended **51**

TABLE 2.1. *States with Indian Populations Exceeding 5,000 in 1940*

Alaska	11,283
Arizona	55,076
California	18,675
Michigan	6,282
Minnesota	12,528
Montana	16,841
New Mexico	34,510
New York	8,651
North Carolina	22,546
North Dakota	10,114
Oklahoma	63,125
South Dakota	23,347
Washington	11,394
Wisconsin	12,265

SOURCE: Thornton 1987:162–163.

minimum of seventy-eight per division continued following the Okinawa campaign in April 1945. However, SRH 120 Document from April 15, 1944, reports: "The normal Marine set-up is 38 Indians per Marine Division. . . . The breakdown of the 38 is 2 per Bn., 2 per Reg't., and 8 per Div. Sig. Co."[19] Despite the numbers involved, cost was never really an issue, as the Comanche and Navajo code formation was performed by tribal members themselves under the supervision, usually, of a single officer.

NATIVE AMERICAN TRIBAL POPULATIONS IN 1940 Thornton (1987:160) estimated the entire American Indian population in 1940 at 345,252, out of a total of 131,669,275 Americans. The Commissioner of Indian Affairs (United States Department of the Interior 1939:Table II) enumerated the Indian population in the continental United States and Alaska under the jurisdiction of the Office of Indian Affairs at 381,861. Individual state enumerations for American Indians in 1940 demonstrated significant population concentrations in specific states. Table 2.1 includes a list of those states with American Indian populations over 5,000 in 1940 (Thornton 1987:162–163).

Collier (Bernstein 1991:22) reported that there were 42,000 Native American men available for military service in June of 1940. As only 25,000 Native Americans served in the military in World War II, including only approximately one-third of all available men aged eighteen to

TABLE 2.2. *Largest Native American Tribes in 1942*

Tribe	Population
Navajo	49,338
Sioux (S. Dakota)	20,670
Chippewa	17,443
Pima-Papago	11,915

fifty between 1941 and 1945, two-thirds remained as potential replacements (Bernstein 1991:22–23; Haynie 1984). It becomes clear that there were significant concentrations of Native American populations in several states in 1940, the year when Native American enlistment in the U.S. armed forces began to increase significantly.

NATIVE AMERICAN TRIBAL POPULATIONS IN WORLD WAR II   In promoting the adoption of the Navajo for code talking, Philip Johnston pointed out the existence of other sufficiently large Native American tribal populations in his initial proposal to the marines in February 1942. Figures provided by Johnston to the marines put the then-current United States Native American population at 361,816 in 180 tribes and showed 230 tribes comprising 56 linguistic stocks in the United States, Canada, and British Columbia. Johnston also reported on their education and bilingual abilities and suggested groups most likely for code talking (Paul 1973:153–156). Table 2.2 lists the largest Native American tribes in 1942.

The most accurate Native American population figures for the World War II period (1941–1945) come from two reports entitled *Statistical Supplement to the Annual Report of the Commissioner of Indian Affairs* for the fiscal years ending June 30, 1939, and June 30, 1945, respectively (United States Department of the Interior 1939, 1945). These data enumerate individual tribes by total population, sex, and residence. For the Indian population in the continental United States and Alaska under the jurisdiction of the Office of Indian Affairs, Table 2.3 lists a selection of the larger existing tribal populations, male populations, and residence as of June 30, 1939 (United States Department of the Interior 1939:Table III). Known code talking groups are in italics.

From these data it is clear that several sizable Native American tribal groups with available male populations sufficient to support code talking units existed. However, as these data demonstrate, size was not the sole factor in the ability to form such units, as tribal populations with

53

TABLE 2.3. *Larger Tribal and Male Indian Populations, June 1939*

Tribe	Total Pop.	Male Pop.	Location
Apache, Jicarilla	733	373	New Mexico
Apache, Mescalero	771	377	New Mexico
Apache, San Carlos	3,082	1,566	San Carlos Res., Ariz.
Apache, Western	2,848	1,508	Ft. Apache, Ariz.
Arapaho	1,198	624	Wind River, Wyo.
Assiniboine	1,597	802	Montana
Blackfoot	4,426	2,272	Montana
Caddo	1,019	503	Oklahoma
E. Cherokee	4,427	1,796	North Carolina
W. Cherokee	40,904	——	Oklahoma
Cheyenne & Arapaho	2,911	1,516	Oklahoma
Chickasaw	4,685	——	Oklahoma
Chippewa (Ojibwa)	6,747	3,472	Turtle Mt., N.D.
Chippewa	6,060	2,376	Great Lakes Agency, Wis.
Chippewa	13,384	6,702	Consolidated Chippewa Agency, Minn.
Chippewa	434	224	Isabella Res., Mich.
Chippewa	100	——	Bay Mills, Mich.
Chippewa	487	244	Rocky Boy's, Mont.
Choctaw	16,641	——	Oklahoma
Comanche	2,332	1,136	Oklahoma
Creek	8,607	——	Oklahoma
Crow	2,237	1,135	Montana
Hopi	3,339	1,738	Arizona
Iroquoian			
Cayuga	206	——	New York
Mohawk	1,600	——	St. Regis, N.Y.
Oneida	3,311	1,662	Wisconsin
Oneida	286	——	New York
Onondaga	663	——	New York
Seneca	2,717	——	New York
Seneca	611	——	Tonawanda, N.Y.
Seneca	763	376	Oklahoma
Kiowa	2,344	1,126	Oklahoma
Menominee	2,314	1,174	Menominee Res., Wis.
Mohave	516	294	Colorado Riv. Res., Ariz.
Mohave	352	197	Ft. Mohave, Ariz.
Navajo	25,623	11,658	New Mexico, Arizona, Utah
Omaha	1,730	910	Nebraska
Osage	3,672	1,857	Oklahoma
Ottawa	433	224	Oklahoma

TABLE 2.3. *(continued)*

Tribe	Total Pop.	Male Pop.	Location
Papago	5,518	2,777	Papago Res., Ariz.
Papago	513	262	San Xavier Res., Ariz.
Papago	112	66	Gila Bend Res., Ariz.
Papago	178	94	Ak-Chin Res., Ariz.
Pawnee	996	507	Oklahoma
Pima	4,301	2,221	Pima Agency, Ariz.
Pima	1,030	524	Salt River Res., Ariz.
Ponca	842	423	Oklahoma
Ponca	395	193	Nebraska
Potawatomi	2,911	1,469	Citizen Band, Okla.
Potawatomi	1,077	557	Kansas
Potawatomi	145	72	Hannahville, Mich.
Puebloan			
Acoma	1,210	612	New Mexico
Isleta	1,189	641	New Mexico
Jemez	703	362	New Mexico
Laguna	2,493	1,290	New Mexico
San Felipe	654	352	New Mexico
San Juan	589	292	New Mexico
Santa Clara	444	227	New Mexico
Santo Domingo	920	535	New Mexico
Taos	799	403	New Mexico
Zuni	2,220	1,234	New Mexico
Sauk and Fox	471	234	Iowa
Sauk and Fox	889	449	Oklahoma
Sauk and Fox	130	60	Kansas
Seminole	1,789	——	Oklahoma
Seminole	581	278	Florida
Santee Dakota	1,294	678	Nebraska
Shoshone	1,513	780	Ft. Hall, Idaho
Shoshone	1,184	584	Wind River, Wyo.
Shoshone	132	60	Washakie Sub-agency, Utah
Teton Lakota	28,578	14,631	South Dakota
Teton Lakota	1,808	889	North Dakota
Ute	1,317	676	Uintah and Ouray, Utah
Winnebago	1,268	660	Nebraska
Yakima	2,972	1,404	Washington
Yankton Nakota	1,030	523	Ft. Totten–Devils Lake, N.D.

SOURCE: United States Department of the Interior 1939:Table III.

56   known code talking units varied from groups as large as the Teton Lakota, with a total population of 28,578 (14,631 males), and Navajo, with
a total population of 25,623 (11,658 males), to the Comanche, with a total population of 2,332 (1,136 males), the Pawnee, with a total population of 996 (507 males), the Sauk and Fox of Iowa, with a total population of only 471 (234 males), and the Hopi, with a total population of
3,339 (1,738 males). Because all of these groups could have supported
larger numbers of code talkers in their respective units than are recorded
(420 Navajos, 19 Sac and Fox, 17 Comanches, 11 Hopi, etc.), the numbers of available speakers and fluency in native languages become significant criteria in comprehending the underutilization of Native Americans as code talkers during World War II.

NUMBERS OF NATIVE SPEAKERS   Chafe (1962) provides the first comprehensive estimates of speakers of Native American languages in the
twentieth century. His report combines results from approximately 250
questionnaires to anthropologists, teachers, government administra-
tors, and native speakers themselves; his own fieldwork; and the reports
of linguists with firsthand experience. Despite the likelihood of varia-
tion in attempting to accumulate such estimates, the results are believed to be generally accurate; and revisions in only eleven groups, most
of which he had underestimated, were made in a subsequent update
(Chafe 1965). Chafe (1962) provided estimates for contemporary Native
American populations (including all ages and sexes) in relation to: (1) the
approximate number of existing speakers, (2) their minimum age group-
ing, and (3) their geographical location. He also divided existing Native
American languages into five categories: (A) languages with fewer than
10 speakers, (B) languages with between 10 and 100 speakers, (C) languages with between 100 and 1,000 speakers, (D) languages with between 1,000 and 10,000 speakers, and (E) languages with more than
10,000 speakers (1962:170). These data allow an examination of the feasibility of expanded and/or additional Native American code talking
units. For most tribes the numbers of bilingual speakers only increase
the further one examines back in time. Only categories D and E concern
populations of militarily relevant scope. Populations with known code
talkers are italicized.

In category D, Chafe (1962:170, 1965:346) identified forty-seven native populations in America and Canada containing between 1,000 and
10,000 current bilingual speakers (code talking populations are in italics): Western Apache, Arapaho, *Assiniboine*, Blackfoot, Carrier, Cherokee, Cheyenne, Chickasaw, Chipewyan, *Choctaw*, *Comanche*, *Creek*,
Crow, Halkomelem, *Hopi*, Isleta, Jemez, Keresan, *Kiowa*, Kutchin, Lil-

looet, Micmac, Mohawk, Montagnias-Naskapi, Nootka, Okanagan, Omaha, *Oneida*, Ottawa, Northern Paiute, Southern Paiute, Papago, Pima, Santee, Seneca, Shoshone, Shuswap, Slave, Tewa, Thompson, Tlingit, Tsimshian, Ute, Winnebago, Yakima, Yankton, and Zuni.

In category E, Chafe (1962:170) identified six additional native populations in America and Canada with more than 10,000 bilingual speakers (code talking populations are in italics): Cree, Inupik Eskimo [Inuit], Yupik Eskimo [Inuit], *Navajo, Ojibwa [Chippewa]*, and *Teton [Lakota]*.

While several groups in category D had sufficient numbers during World War II for small code talking units, of which some did (Choctaw, Comanche, Creek, Hopi, Kiowa, Oneida), all of those in category E were sufficiently large to have large code talking units composed from their numbers. Of those groups in category E, only the Navajo were used in a large unit (420 code talkers), while only small contingents of Ojibwa (Chippewa) and Teton Lakota were used. Even more ironic is the fact that some members of tribes listed in category C, or languages with between 100 and 1,000 speakers (Fox or Mesquakie, and including the Sac or Sauk [Sauk and Fox], and the Menominee, Pawnee, Seminole), served as native communicators in World War II. Therefore total tribal population size was again not the sole determining factor in the utilization of Native Americans for military communications based on their native languages.

Although these statistics are based on 1962 data, we can examine a number of groups which held potential for code talking service in World War II. What is important to recognize in these data is that (1) while the numbers are based on figures current in 1962—some seventeen years after the end of World War II, and (2) while the total population had increased from 1941–1945 to 1962, the total number of bilingual speakers in many tribes had generally decreased. Thus most populations contained a higher percentage of bilingual speakers in 1941–1945 than in 1962. As with the problems in obtaining an accurate census of any large population, determining the exact numbers of bilingual speakers in 1941–1945 is virtually impossible and is not as important as recognizing that adequate numbers of them existed in several Native American groups in the period between 1941 and 1945. Although members of some tribes with as small a total population as around 1,200 to 2,600 individuals (and presumably fewer native speakers) performed military communications in World War II in their native languages, which demonstrates linguistic contributions and abilities from relatively small populations, only those populations with 1,000 bilingual speakers or more in 1962–1965 are included in Table 2.4 (Chafe 1962, 1965). Populations with known World War II code talkers are again in italics. **57**

58 TABLE 2.4. *Tribal Populations and Estimated Bilingual Speakers in 1962*

Tribal Population	No. of Speakers	Location
Apache, Jicarilla	1,000	U.S.
Apache, Mescalero	1,000	U.S.
Apache, Western	8,000–10,000	U.S.
Arapaho	1,000–3,000	U.S.
Assiniboine (Stoney)	1,000–2,000	U.S. and Canada
Blackfoot	5,000–6,000	U.S. and Canada
Carrier	1,000–3,000	Canada
Cayuga	500–1,000	U.S. and Canada
Cherokee	10,000	U.S.
Cheyenne	3,000–4,000	U.S.
Chickasaw	2,000–3,000	U.S.
Chipewyan	3,000–4,000	Canada
Choctaw	10,000	U.S.
Comanche	1,500	U.S.
Cree	30,000–40,000	U.S. and Canada
Creek	10,000	U.S.
Crow	3,000	U.S.
Inupik Eskimo	40,000–50,000	U.S. and Canada
Yupik Eskimo	13,000–14,000	U.S. and Canada
Halkomelem	1,000–2,000	Canada
Hopi	3,000–5,000	U.S.
Isleta	1,000–2,000	U.S.
Jemez	1,200	U.S.
Keresan	7,000	U.S.
Kiowa	2,000	U.S.
Kutchin	1,200	U.S. and Canada
Kwakiutl	1,000	Canada
Lillooet	1,000–2,000	Canada
Micmac	3,000–5,000	Canada
Mohave	1,000	U.S.
Mohawk	1,000–2,000	U.S. and Canada
Montagnais-Naskapi	5,000	Canada
Navajo	80,000–90,000	U.S.
Nootka	1,000–2,000	Canada
Ojibwa	40,000–50,000	U.S. and Canada

NATIVE AND ENGLISH LINGUISTIC FLUENCY   Determining exact enumerations of fluent speakers on a tribal basis after significant and permanent external Anglo contact at any point in time is virtually impossible (Chafe 1962, 1965; Hollow and Parks 1980:73–75). Potential factors affecting the native language fluency of Native American ser-

TABLE 2.4. *(continued)*

Tribal Population	No. of Speakers	Location
Okanagan	1,000–2,000	U.S. and Canada
Omaha	1,000–3,000	U.S.
Oneida	1,000–2,000	U.S. and Canada
Ottawa	1,000–2,000	U.S.
N. Paiute	2,000	U.S.
S. Paiute	1,000–3,000	U.S.
Papago	8,000–10,000	U.S. and Mexico
Pima	5,000	U.S. and Mexico
Santee Dakota	3,000–5,000	U.S. and Canada
Seneca	2,000–3,000	U.S. and Canada
Shoshoni (including Gosiute)	5,000	U.S.
Shuswap	1,000–2,000	Canada
Slave	1,000–2,000	Canada
Taos	1,000	U.S.
Teton Lakota	10,000–15,000	U.S.
Tewa	2,000	U.S.
Thompson	1,000–2,000	Canada
Tlingit	1,000–2,000	U.S. and Canada
Ute	2,000–4,000	U.S.
Winnebago	1,000–2,000	U.S.
Yakima	1,000–2,000	U.S.
Yankton Nakota (excluding Assiniboine)	1,000–2,000	U.S.
Zuni	3,000–4,000	U.S.

Other Groups That Used Native American Language–Based Military Communications in WWII

Menominee	300–500	U.S.
Pawnee	400–600	U.S.
Fox and Sauk	1,000	U.S.
Seminole	300	U.S.

SOURCE: Chafe 1962, 1965.

vicemen in World War II include varied levels of isolation or proximity of individual native communities to Anglos; formal Anglo education; age of entry into, duration of enrollment in, and experiences in boarding schools; intertribal and non-Indian intermarriage; assimilation; and changes in residence. All of these factors produce numerous situations

60   that may have led to a loss of native language fluency. Because quanti-
fying linguistic fluency in Native American populations would require
more in-depth attention than the standard procedures involved in taking a regular census (which contain several subjective flaws in processes
of determining ethnicity), determinations of linguistic fluency can be
highly subjective (Hollow and Parks 1980:74).

Chafe (1962:170) correlated native languages with three population
groups in which most or all speakers were: (1) of all ages, (2) over twenty
years of age, or (3) over fifty years of age. Although Chafe (1962:163) ad-
mits that the age distributions are less reliable than the estimates of total speakers, they clearly indicate an expected increase in the number of
native language speakers with increasingly older ages. The total distribution of native-speaking cohorts is not of significance here, only those
cohorts eligible for military service in World War II. Chafe's (1962, 1965)
data indicate a high correlation of native language fluency with individuals fifty years and older in 1962. Using 1962 as the base year, fifty years
would extend back to 1912. The birth dates of the vast majority of World
War II veterans fall into the period ranging from 1900 to 1926. Thus a
high degree of fluency correlates with Native Americans of the appropriate age for service in World War II.

While many Eastern Algonquian languages were spoken by only a
limited number or were already extinct by 1940 (Goddard 1978:71),
many other areas contained significant numbers of bilingual speakers.
In most Plains, Great Lakes, and Great Basin, and in some Southeast
and Northwest Coast tribal populations, individuals born around 1920
are fluent in their native language as well as in English. In my own fieldwork, rarely have I encountered a Comanche, Kiowa, Kiowa-Apache,
Cheyenne, Lakota, Crow, Creek, or Cherokee born before 1930 (and
thus generally within the pre-1926 World War II veteran age range) who
was not fluent in his language to the degree of being able to communicate in everyday conversation. Those who were not fluent usually described combinations of the factors listed previously as the reason(s)
why. Most individuals of this age group can and still do "use the language fluently in normal, day-to-day conversation," the definition which
Hollow and Parks (1980:74) use in determining a speaker among Plains
tribes. The prevalence of linguistic fluency among most contemporary
Native American World War II veterans, and the fact that many learned
English as a second language upon entering formal boarding and public school programs, also support assuming the fluency of veteran-age
natives.

Although the navy reported problems in obtaining adequate numbers
of Indians who all spoke the same native language and who all had an

TABLE 2.5. *Percentage of Native American Illiteracy,*
1900–1930

1900	1910	1920	1930
56.2	45.3	34.9	25.7

SOURCE: United States Department of Commerce 1937.

adequate command of English, government census data indicate that by
1930 most Native Americans over the age of ten were literate in speaking, reading, and writing English. Data from the 1930 census for *The In-*
dian Populations of the United States and Alaska (United States Department of Commerce 1937:143–154) indicate that despite the lack
of a specific testing method to determine the ability to read and write,
illiteracy (defined as the inability in any person over the age of ten to
read or write either in English or another language) was rapidly declining among Native American populations. Table 2.5 demonstrates the declining percentage of illiteracy in Native American populations between
1900 and 1930.

Likewise, the percentage of Native Americans unable to speak English was relatively small by 1930 (United States Department of Commerce 1937:155–163). By 1930, nearly all Native Americans over the
age of ten were able to speak English, with the exception of tribal populations in Arizona, New Mexico, and Utah. In addition, tribal populations in these three states contained nearly no members born after 1910
who were unable to speak English. Even in conservative tribes such as
the Zuni, nearly everyone aged ten to nineteen in 1930 is reported as
having been able to speak English. In states such as Kansas, Michigan,
and North Carolina, less than 3 percent of all Native Americans over the
age of ten were unable to speak English in 1930, and these were primarily elder men and women, the majority of non-English speakers in nearly
every Native American population at this time (United States Department of Commerce 1937:155–163). Table 2.6 illustrates these data.

In addition, data in Table 2.7 on the percentage of non-English-speaking Native Americans by tribe and sex (United States Department of
Commerce 1937:158) reinforce the previous data, demonstrate that a
greater percentage of male than female Native Americans were fluent
in English, and show that code talking was performed by groups with
both extremely high and low levels of non-English-speaking tribal populations. Tribal populations with known code talking service in World
War II are italicized.

61

TABLE 2.6. *Percentage of Non-English-Speaking Native Americans Aged Ten and Over, 1900–1930*

Year	Total Pop.	Number	Percent
1930	238,981	40,651	17.0
1920	176,925	36,752	20.8
1910	188,758	59,055	31.2
1900	171,552	72,583	42.3

Male

Year	Total Pop.	Number	Percent
1930	123,469	18,233	14.8
1920	91,546	17,469	19.1
1910	96,582	26,705	27.7
1900	86,504	32,309	37.3

Female

Year	Total Pop.	Number	Percent
1930	115,512	22,418	19.4
1920	85,379	19,283	22.6
1910	92,176	32,350	35.1
1900	85,048	40,274	47.4

SOURCE: United States Department of Commerce 1937.

From these data the following become apparent:

1. Limited code talking was performed by groups which fit Chafe's (1962) category C, or languages with between 100 and 1,000 speakers, as well as larger categories D and E. Therefore, adequate numbers of available young men who were fluent speakers was not a problem in most Indian communities of nearly 1,000 total population or greater.

2. Many Native American populations contained adequate numbers to devise code talking programs for at least an army divisional level of military organization.

3. Only three groups, the Navajo, Comanche, and Hopi, are known to have had formally developed Type 1 code systems in World War II.

4. Probably fewer than 650 of the 25,000 Native American servicemen (including 420 Navajos, 17 Comanches, 19 Fox, and 11 Hopi) in World War II were used for military communications based on their native languages.

TABLE 2.7. *Percentage of Non-English-Speaking Populations by Tribe, Aged Ten and Over, in 1930*

Tribe	Tribal Total	Male	Female
Navajo	71.0	66.6	75.6
Papago	49.8	46.2	53.5
Zuni	44.5	42.4	47.4
Ute	34.3	30.8	38.6
Tanoans	30.2	31.2	29.1
Seminole	27.5	23.6	31.7
Cheyenne	26.8	23.9	29.7
Apache	24.8	19.3	31.1
Hopi	22.4	23.0	21.7
Yuma	17.7	14.7	21.1
Assiniboine	17.5	15.3	19.8
Shoshoni	17.2	14.1	20.5
Comanche	14.3	11.4	16.9
Crow	13.8	12.1	15.7
Dakota	13.2	10.5	16.1
Pima	11.6	11.0	12.2
Creek	11.0	7.9	13.9
Winnebago	7.7	2.6	12.9
Chippewa	7.4	4.4	10.7
Iroquois	4.6	2.6	6.7
Menominee	4.5	2.9	6.6
Cherokee	4.2	3.5	5.0
Potawatomi	4.0	2.0	6.3
Choctaw	3.6	1.9	5.3
Ottawa	2.7	1.0	4.7
Osage	2.2	1.6	2.8
Chickasaw	1.6	0.6	2.6
Delaware	1.0	0.3	1.6

SOURCE: United States Department of Commerce 1937:158.

5. The Southwest, Southeast, Plains, and Great Lakes area tribal populations represent the most likely populations for the development of code talkers in 1940 due to the size of their tribal populations and estimates of fluent speakers.

6. Lists of World War II veterans from several tribes and veterans' memorial statues (Comanche, Kiowa, Cheyenne, Choctaw, Cherokee, Lakota) indicate that several groups had adequate numbers of bilingual male servicemen for developing and/or increasing code talking units, and as replacements for casualties. While exact numbers are unavail-

64 able, the prevalence of fluent speakers in the age range which served in World War II was very high in proportion to those who were not.

7. Most Native Americans born after 1910 were able to speak English, the majority of nonspeakers were elderly tribal members, and a greater percentage of male (potential servicemen) than female Native Americans were fluent in English.

8. Sufficient service-age men who were fluent native and English speakers existed in both enlisted and potential civilian reserve populations. Population statistics demonstrate that nearly two-thirds of all available Native American men aged eighteen to fifty remained as potential reserves and never saw military service.

9. Only sixteen of the sixty-three tribes listed above are known to have been used in Native-American-language-based U.S. military communications in World War II (see Appendix G), which suggests larger external (governmental and military policy) reasons and not a shortage of available Native American civilian men, enlisted men, and fluent bilingual speakers.

Questions of Security

Finally we must ask, would Native American code talking have been secure? The critical factor in determining the size, extent, and use of Native American code talkers is found in United States military and organizational policy preferences. The most commonly cited vulnerability in using Native American languages for military communication is whether or not an ethnologist, anthropologist, linguist, or some other American or foreign scholar had studied and, more importantly, recorded the native language. The Navajo language was embraced by the marines in May of 1942 because of its linguistic difficulty, because it had allegedly not been formally recorded, and because reportedly fewer than thirty non-Navajos understood the language. However, by 1940 a Navajo-to-English reader and a phrase book in Navajo and English had already been written by the Indian Medical Service and a study for a Navajo dictionary was already under way (United States Department of the Interior 1940: 386–387). In addition, various Apaches, Hopi, Zuni, other neighboring tribes, and a limited number of Anglos including Philip Johnston, understood "Trading-post Navajo" (McClain 1994: 25). In his proposal to Major General Clayton B. Vogel to consider adopting the use of Navajos as code talkers, Philip Johnston pointed out the fact that several texts in Navajo had already been written:

> All Indian languages are classified as "unwritten" because no alphabets or other symbols of purely native origin are in existence. In a

few cases, these aboriginal tongues have been reduced to writing by American scholars, who have developed alphabets adapted to the expression of the difficult consonants involved. A notable instance in point is the Navajo Dictionary compiled by the Franciscan Fathers of Saint Michaels, Arizona, who have also translated portions of the Bible, and written other texts in the Navajo tongue for the use of their students. Recently the United States Bureau of Indian Affairs has inaugurated a program of writing Navajo texts for study in reservation schools. However, a fluency in reading Navajo can be acquired only by individuals who are first highly educated in English, and who, in turn, have made a profound study of Navajo, both in its spoken and written form. (McClain 1994:241–242)

Although it was often difficult to distinguish foreign linguists and ethnographers from government agents, several foreign individuals conducted linguistic field research on Native American languages in the early 1900s. Marine Corps combat correspondent Mt. Sgt. Murray Marder (1945:6) cites a marine report indicating that Germans disguised as art students and anthropologists had been studying Native American tribal dialects for some twenty years prior to the beginning of World War II in 1941. Around 1980, the U.S. government declassified documents which indicate that German and Japanese language experts attempted to gain fluency in Native American languages prior to World War II. Mindful of the successful use of Native American languages in World War I, German and Japanese agents attempted to learn Native American languages to enable the interception and translation of any possible future messages transmitted in these languages (Marder 1945; McCoy 1981:75). Gunter Wagner, a linguistic anthropologist from Germany, conducted fieldwork on the Comanche language in 1932.[20] As World War II Comanche Code Talker Forrest Kassanavoid recalled:

Back in about 1939, some Germans came to the United States to study anthropology at Columbia University. They came out here to a German missionary Church near Indiahoma to study native languages. They didn't look like students to us—they were in their 30's. We were told later that just at the end of the summer, they were all arrested. We heard the FBI came in and arrested them.[21]

Furthermore, foreign diplomats were found to have been among the chief customers of the Bureau of Indian Affairs for the purchase of publications, and publications of the Bureau of American Ethnology, many of which dealt with Native American languages, were available to foreign readers. Fieldwork and attempts by German and Japanese scholars

66 to learn Navajo and other Native American languages prior to World War II are recorded, and some Japanese personnel had even been employed by the Interior Department's Bureau of Indian Affairs (Armstrong 1989:55; Bixler 1992:43; *New York Times* 1945). Bixler (1981:58–59) records one instance of a post–World War II attempt of a Japanese to infiltrate and gain further knowledge of the Navajo language. The marines were encouraged to use the Navajo because of the difficulty of their language, the knowledge of it by fewer than thirty non–Native Americans, and the apparent lack of foreign inquiry, characteristics that classified the Navajo language as a "hidden" language. Foreign attempts to learn these Native American languages proved unsuccessful, and the use of Native American code talkers in World War II proved invaluable for the American forces.

By late 1944, the Japanese had identified the marines' code talkers as Navajo and attempted unsuccessfully to interrogate Joe Kieyoomia, a Navajo prisoner of war who was not a code talker (McClain 1994:118–121). Although Kieyoomia was a fluent Navajo speaker and was subjected to several forms of interrogative torture, he was unable to provide any clues to the code. Although a very difficult language, Navajo had been recorded in several sources, and had the top Japanese cryptologists acquired these written sources, events might have transpired differently. In reality, by 1940 more Native American groups had had some linguistic and ethnological work performed concerning their language than had not.

However, what is often not realized is that regardless of the Native American language in use, English had unquestionably been studied at greater length and better documented than any other foreign language known to the Axis powers, and because English served as the basis for most American encoding systems, the Axis powers had a more solid base from which to attempt deciphering it than with a less-well-known native language. Native American languages vary greatly in their complexity; some are relatively easy for non-Indians to learn, while others are extremely difficult. The difficulty of some Native American languages and their potential for military communications are further illustrated by an examination of some of the structural qualities of Kiowa. While only a few Kiowas made wartime use of their language, on an irregular noncoded basis, over three hundred Kiowas served in World War II. The Smithsonian Institution's Bureau of American Ethnology published John P. Harrington's (1928) *Vocabulary of the Kiowa Language*. Yet Harrington's vocabulary only scratched the surface of the complexity of the language. Kiowa is an extremely difficult language for a non-Kiowa to learn for several reasons. First, Kiowa is a tonal language, having ten possible pronunciation pitches for every single syllable and one hundred possible pronunciation pitches for every two-syllable word (only a few of which have any assigned meaning). Kiowa contains a hearsay tense not found in English, lacks the equivalent of English articles, and has 550 syllables. Grammatically, Kiowa has nouns, verbs, adjectives, and verbal-adjectives. Furthermore, Kiowa contains a complex system of seventy pronoun forms which differ greatly from English pronouns, and contains a system of multiple and irregular use of dual embodiment in pronoun forms (two subjects conveyed in a single pronoun form). Kiowa is also characterized by frequent contractions or "clipped forms," agglutination of numerous words and clauses into lengthy expression, and contains an irregular pattern of expressing single, dual, and triplural forms for any object—the rules for which have still not been completely and grammatically understood or recorded to this day by Kiowa or Anglo scholars.[22]

Most codes are based on the coder's native language, and if the language is a widely used one, it will also be familiar to one's enemy, and, regardless of how good the code may be, the enemy will eventually master it (Kahn 1967). However, the use of "hidden" languages, or those that (1) are little known by non-native members of the group and (2) have no written form, can be very effective for the communication transmissions of a second group. During World Wars I and II, many Native American languages existed that are classifiable as hidden languages. It is precisely because of these factors that Native Americans and their languages were able to make such a unique contribution in American military communications during World Wars I and II.

World War II Native American Code Talker and Communications Operator Distribution

During World War II members of at least sixteen tribes served as code talkers in at least three different agencies and sets of code talker programs (see Appendix G). Despite the army's decision not to adopt large units of trained Native Americans as code talkers, small units were used throughout various army divisions. While the Comanches and other groups such as the Oneida, Chippewa, Sac and Fox, and Hopi served in the Army Signal Corps, other groups of Native American communications operators such as the Navajo served in the Marine Corps, while limited numbers of Navajos and Creeks served in the navy. While other Comanches had already joined or were later recruited into various branches of the U.S. armed forces, those who served as code talkers were of the only known Oklahoma tribe recruited exclusively for formal military code training during World War II.

While the Navajo have received considerable recognition for their ser- **67**

68   vice in the Pacific theater, several other Native American groups also participated in various communications operations. Members of several tribes, including the Comanche, Chippewa, Choctaw, Creek, Hopi, Kiowa, Menominee, Navajo, Oneida, Pawnee, Sac and Fox, Seminole-Muscogee, Sioux (Lakota and Dakota), and Assiniboine, were used in operations involving both Type 1 (encoded) and Type 2 (noncoded) code talking (Paul 1973:7; Bernstein 1991:46; Rodgers n.d.).[23]

Recent data indicate that a group of eleven Hopi in the army's 223d Battalion used some degree of Type 1 coded communications. Franklin Shupla, Travis Yaiva, Floyd Dann, and others were shipped to Hawaii for jungle training, then shipped to participate in the latter stages of the battle for Guadalcanal. According to Shupla, group members "went to extraordinary lengths to use Hopi words and concepts to come up with terms for battle" during several months of training near Dateland, in southern Arizona in 1943. Terms such as eggs (*nu-hu*) for bombs, a house on water (*bah-ki*) for ships, and different types of birds to designate planes, such as ducks (*pa'h-we-waka*) for seaplanes and chicken hawks for dive bombers, were used. Although the full extent of their training and code formation is unknown, the code's preparation prior to combat suggests it is of a Type 1 form. The Hopi first used their language in combat in the Marshall Islands and later at New Caledonia, before being reassigned to Leyte as part of Douglas MacArthur's return campaign to retake the Philippines. The Hopi also had fun with their secret language, which allowed them to make jokes about their commanding officers to one another. The full content of the Hopi code and the extent of its use have yet to be recorded.[24]

While the Comanche, Navajo, and Hopi served as Type 1 code talkers, or those with formally organized training and encoded terms, members of many other Native American nations appear to have served mainly as Type 2 code talkers, or those who did not undertake precombat code formation and who subsequently communicated only in their everyday noncoded language, but with the same purpose of transmitting secret military communications. Although additional research is needed for several groups, characterization as Type 1 or 2 code talkers is suggested (Appendix H) for each known tribal unit based on existing data. Extensive future research and travel will be necessary to elicit the particular structure and characteristics of each code talking group, and may result in some revision of the classifications offered here.

The *United States Marine Corps Manual of Military Operations Specialties* defines "Code Talker," in entry 642, as one who:

Transmits and receives messages in a restricted language by radio and wire. Sends and receives messages by means of semaphores and other visual signal devices. May perform field lineman, switchboard operator, or other communications duties. (McClain 1994:226)

Examination of this definition demonstrates that it applies to both classifications of Native American code talkers (coded and noncoded) as defined in this work.

The initial optimism about recruiting members of various Native American tribes for signals communications was in the Army Signal Corps. In the autumn of 1940 seventeen Oneida and Chippewa from Michigan and Wisconsin joined the Thirty-second Infantry Division for the specific purpose of receiving training in adapting their native languages for radio communication. Under Lieutenant Colonel Glenn B. Arnold, signal officer for the Thirty-second Division, and trained by Lieutenant Newton L. Chamberlain, the seventeen men were assigned as radio operators in three communication nets. Nine men from western Wisconsin were with the provisional antitank battalion net, four from northern Wisconsin were with the Fifty-seventh Field Artillery Brigade, and four from northern Michigan were assigned to the division command. Shortly after the induction of the Oneida and Chippewa, a group of Iowa Sac and Fox were recruited for training as native communications operators in World War II. A February 15, 1941, news release from Omaha, Nebraska, to the *New York Times* reports the group's formation. "Eight Indians from the Sac and Fox reservation near Tama, Iowa, attached to the 18th Iowa Infantry, will be trained to operate walkie-talkie and field telephones for vital communication between front lines and battalion and regimental headquarters. They will speak their own dialect, so that an enemy would be unable to understand their reports even if their messages were intercepted." Heading the group was Dewey Youngbear, the grandson of tribal chief Youngbear, and the son of Robert Youngbear, who had served in World War I with the 168th of the Rainbow Division as a cannoneer. Other members included Frank and Willard Sanache, Judy and Mike Wayne, Dewey Roberts, Edward Benson, and Melvin Twin. Eventually a total of nineteen Sac and Fox Indians are reported to have served as code talkers in this division.[25] Following their initial communications training, these individuals used their native languages in wargames maneuvers while training in Louisiana. With optimism prevailing within the Army Signal Corps, seventeen Comanches from Oklahoma were recruited in December and January of 1940–1941.

While the Oneida, Chippewa, Sac and Fox, Comanche, and Navajo were intentionally recruited to be trained as code talkers, many other Native Americans were used in more informal, noncoded, "use them if you have them" contexts. Choctaws again served during World War II as

69

communications operators in Europe. Company K, 180th Infantry Regiment, Forty-fifth Division contained an all-Choctaw platoon (Wigginton 1992; Moseley 1988; *Bishinik* 1987a). Tribal members such as Staff Sergeant and later Lieutenant Schlicht Billy, Corporal Andrew Perry, Sergeant Davis Pickens, and Pfc. Forrester T. Baker, all of Company K, 180th Infantry Regiment, Forty-fifth Division, conversed in Choctaw on Model 536 radios for short-range communication. Transmission of exact locations and details of opposing forces without fear of German interception resulted in deadly consequences for the enemy. While there is no indication of any formal code training or that they used a formally developed code at this time, their service was just as effective as in the First World War, as there are again no indications that any Choctaw messages were ever deciphered.[26]

A number of Sioux were assigned to reel-cart teams with the Third Battalion and were known as the "All-American Team" because the drivers were all reportedly full-blooded Sioux Indians except one who was of mixed descent. Suspecting that the Germans had deciphered the U.S. communications codes, members such as Private Simon Broken Leg and Private Jeffrey Dull Knife spoke in their native language across their Signal Corps links while fighting in the Ardennes.[27] Other Sioux Indians performed code talking in the Thirty-second Field Artillery, which supported the Nineteenth Regimental Combat Team in North Africa, Sicily, and Normandy. Garfield T. Brown of Allen, South Dakota; Anthony Omaha Boy of St. Francis, South Dakota; and John C. Smith of White Earth, Minnesota, are reported to have used Type 2 code talking. Serving in the headquarters battery, one of the men had the idea that he could talk to his friend in the forward observer post in their tribal language, a faster method than the standard encoding and decoding used to send messages (Marshall 1994).

In the Pacific other Lakota and Dakota speakers served as radio communications operators in the 302 Reconnaissance Team in the First Cavalry Division from 1942 to 1945. The group was formed from Sioux soldiers assigned in Australia and included Philip LaBlanc (Lakota), Edmund St. John (Lower Brule'), Baptiste Pumpkinseed (Lakota or Rosebud Sioux), Eddie Eagle Boy (Cheyenne River Sioux), Guy Rondell (Sisseton Wahpeton Dakota), and John Bear King (Standing Rock Sioux). All worked in two-man reconnaissance teams, using their Lakota and Dakota language dialects to relay U.S. communications and to report enemy troop strengths, locations, and armaments. Known as "MacArthur's Boys," members addressed each other over the radio as "tahansi" (cousin). There is also a report of a group of five Assiniboine Code Talkers in Company B of the 163d Infantry Division, which included James Turningbear and others.[28]

Similarly, a few Kiowas, including John Tsatoke, James Paddlety, and Leonard Cozad Sr., in the 689th Field Artillery Battalion, XX Corps, under Generals Walker and Patton in the Third Army, used their language for communication transmissions. Although no formal training or encoding was used, the periodic use of such battlefield communications undoubtedly helped to minimize the danger of successful enemy interception (Wigginton 1992).[29]

Ambrose (1994:144) reports the use of Cherokee Code Talkers in World War II. Edmund Harjo, a Seminole Indian and a member of the 195th Field Artillery Battalion, was walking through an apple orchard in southern France on a Sunday afternoon a few days following D-Day, when he heard an Indian singing under a tree. Harjo immediately recognized the language as Creek, a dialect of the Muscogean language. When a captain heard them conversing later, he put them to work on opposite ends of a radio (Moseley 1988). Walker (1980:145) reports interviewing, near Checotah, Oklahoma, Leslie Richards, a Muskogee Creek who stated that he and a fellow Muskogee-speaking Seminole from Florida had used their native language in the army during the Aleutian campaign of World War II. In playing a practical joke on the men, an officer discovered their shared language, as a consequence of which they were assigned to special duty as "dispatchers," communicating with one another over shortwave radio during the remainder of the campaign. While some tribes received impromptu code training, most appear to have been used to communicate in their everyday noncoded languages.

Several incorrect statements have been made, concerning the role and extent of Native American code talkers, which this work hopes to clarify. Kahn (1967:550) misleadingly asserts that "During preparations for World War II, the Signal Corps tested Comanches and Indians from Michigan and Wisconsin in war games, but most of the code talkers in the combat itself were Navajo." While this is statistically true, he significantly downplays the role of these other units across the European and Pacific theaters of World War II. Likewise, Paul (1973:7) mistakenly states that "Actually, during World War II, Indians of many tribes spoke across enemy lines in Africa, Sicily, and the South Pacific—Comanche, Creek, Choctaw, Menominee, Chippewa, and Hopi. But in each case the Indians were speaking in their own tongue—not in code." Bixler states of the Navajo code in World War II, "It is the only code (language or otherwise) that has never been broken by the enemy" (1992: 43), and "so was born the only code the enemy was never able to decipher" (1992:48). McClain (1994:23) states that the "Army Signal Corps field tested Comanche personnel from Michigan and Wisconsin" (probably the Oneida and Chippewa from Michigan and Wisconsin who trained in native language code work with the Thirty-second Infantry **71**

Division), that "fifteen Oklahoma Comanches" were recruited for duty in language communications (there were seventeen Comanche recruits), and that they "occasionally substituted Comanche words for military terms during combat in the European Theater of Operations. But these substitutions never developed into a full-scale Comanche-based, specifically-designed combat code." Durrett (1998:v) adds, ". . . and the Navajo Code is the only oral combat code that was never broken."

As we shall see in Chapter 3, a formally based Comanche combat code was indeed developed, before the Navajo code, and used in Europe. Contrary to assertions that only the Navajos used a code in transmitting and receiving messages, the Comanche code was developed at least a year and a half prior to the formation of the Navajo Code Talker training program, and differed qualitatively little from that of the Navajos. While these special Army Signal Corps and regular infantry units never involved more than fifty Indian men, the Marine Corps expanded the concept to a broader scale (Bernstein 1991:46). The Comanches, Choctaws, and other groups have long been overshadowed, largely because of the sheer size of the Navajo unit, a reflection of army policy and not Native American potential.

Having the largest existing Native American population of nearly fifty thousand, a language that was known by only twenty-eight non-Navajos, none of whom were German or Japanese, and given the extreme difficulty involved in learning their language, the Navajo were a logical and favorable choice for military purposes (Kahn 1967:550; Paul 1973). As Sergeant Murray Marder described, "One of the reasons that prompted the Marine Corps to adopt Navajo—in preference to a variety of Indian tongues as used by the AEF in the last war—was a report that Navajos were the only Indian group in the United States not infested with German students during the twenty years prior to 1941."[30] However, as we shall see, other groups such as the Comanches, despite their small size, made similar and considerable contributions as code talkers in World War II.

"GET HIM BACK ON THAT SCALE AND WEIGH HIM AGAIN!"

THE RECRUITMENT OF THE COMANCHES

In 1940 the United States Army consisted of only 400,000 men and two infantry divisions. Infantry divisions at this time contained between eighteen and twenty thousand men each. Two new infantry divisions, the Third and Fourth, were later added. Still later, armored divisions were activated due to the success of the German panzer divisions in Europe. Most Indians from the Plains region served in the Nineteenth Iowa Infantry Regiment, the 147th Field Artillery Regiment from South Dakota, the Fourth Army Infantry Division, and the Forty-fifth Infantry Division. The Comanches served in the Fourth Infantry Division, Fourth Signal Company. The Fourth Infantry Division was activated on June 1, 1940, at Ft. Benning, Georgia, and the Fourth Signal Company served as the communications unit for that division. The Fourth Infantry Division was reorganized as the Fourth Division (Motorized) on August 1, 1940, then as the Fourth Infantry Division (Motorized) on July 11, 1941, and later as the Fourth Motorized Division.

The Fourth Infantry Division was a modified infantry division designed to test a new mobile form of organization. The army was addressing the problem of keeping infantry troops up with the faster advances of the developing tank formations. Although the Fourth Division structure was largely unchanged, the number of vehicles in the division was increased dramatically. In 1940 a normal infantry division had relatively few motor vehicles, and when it became necessary to move an entire division some distance, truck companies and other transportation units were brought in from outside sources for the duration of the move. The Fourth Division (Motorized) was organized to have enough organic trans-

74   portation to move the entire division on its own. Accordingly, nearly every truck in the division pulled a cargo trailer, and many individuals, such as communications operators within the signal company, were often given a second duty as a truck driver. Job description entries in the tables of organization were frequently marked "Also drives truck."

In preparation for World War II, a number of Native American tribes were examined by the army as potential candidates for code talking. An elimination process was undertaken until only the Hopi, an unnamed Apache group, and the Comanches remained. Of these, the Comanche and Hopi were finally chosen from which to recruit code talking units.[1] Largely due to limited prior ethnographic and anthropological inquiry, the Comanche language had not yet been adapted to any standard written form and thus, as an unwritten language, held great promise for army communications, as it would be more difficult for an enemy to decipher. By October 1940 plans to use Comanche recruits for verbal communications were under way.[2] Although other Comanches were already in the army by late 1940, those who would serve as code talkers were specially recruited between December 1940 and January 1941 for communications training. Their recruitment preceded that of the Navajo by some sixteen months, as the idea to use Navajo as code talkers did not develop until well after the attack on Pearl Harbor (Paul 1973:8).

Credit for conceiving the idea of using Indian languages for coded military communications has long been given to Philip Johnston, a civil engineer living in Los Angeles who had grown up on the Navajo Reservation and spoke the language with some degree of fluency (Paul 1973). Following the attack on Pearl Harbor on December 7, 1941, Johnston conceived of the idea in late December 1941 or early January 1942. According to Paul, who interviewed Philip Johnston:

> It all started when he saw a newspaper story one day concerning an armored division on practice maneuvers in Louisiana where they were trying out a unique idea for secret communication—attempting to establish some sort of system using several of their Indian personnel. The news item sparked the concept of a code based on the complex Navajo tongue. (Paul 1973:8)

Similarly, Escue states, "Before entering the Second World War, communication using Indian languages was tried with indifferent success by a tank corps in Louisiana, but Johnston's idea of developing a code based on an Indian language was unique" (1991:15). As we shall see, Johnston's idea was not totally unique, as Indians from Michigan and Wisconsin were participating in Louisiana War Games in the first week of September 1941. The Comanches who participated in the IV Corps Louisiana Maneuvers in August of 1941 in Dry Prong, Louisiana, returned to Ft. Benning on August 27, 1941, where they began forming their code.[3] Based on Paul's interview with Johnston himself, Johnston read of the Louisiana project and developed the idea that the Navajo could be similarly used (Johnston 1964; Paul 1973:8; Parman 1994:113; McClain 1994:24).

The article that Johnston read may very well have been that printed in the November 1941 issue of *The Masterkey*, which summarized the use of Michigan and Wisconsin Indians of the Thirty-second Division in the Louisiana War Games:

> The classic World War I trick of using Indians speaking their own languages as "code" transmitters, is again being used in the Army, this time during the great maneuvers in the South, says *Science Service*. Three units of the 32nd Division have small groups of Indians from Wisconsin and Michigan tribes, who receive instructions in English, put them on the air in a tongue intelligible only to their listening fellow-tribesmen, who in turn retranslate the message into English at the receiving end.
>
> The Indians themselves have had to overcome certain language difficulties, for there are no words in their primitive languages for many of the necessary military terms. In one of the groups, ingenious use was made of the fact that infantry, cavalry, and artillery wear hat cords and other insignia of blue, yellow, and red, respectively. The Indian word for "blue" thus comes to mean infantry, "yellow" means cavalry, and "red" means artillery. The Indian term for "turtle" signifies a tank.
>
> The Indians had to be carefully selected, for many of the men entering the service had forgotten the language of their forefathers, and others could not translate it into English very readily. However, thanks to the efforts of Lt. Newton L. Chamberlain of Grand Rapids, Mich., a total of 17 properly qualified Indians were picked out and trained for the job.
>
> The Indian "coders" work in pairs. It is of course necessary for both members of a pair to be of the same tribe, for the language of one tribe is as unintelligible to that of another as it is to white men. (1941:240)

Johnston later presented his idea to Lieutenant Colonel James E. Jones, the area signal officer at Camp Elliot, north of San Diego, in late

76   December of 1941 or early January of 1942. That Johnston presented his
idea after the attack on Pearl Harbor also suggests that he had knowledge of the Louisiana War Games. Two weeks later Johnston arranged
for several Navajo men to demonstrate their ability to transmit messages in Navajo over field telephones. With Jones's support, Johnston
proceeded to present the idea in a formal document which Major General Clayton B. Vogel, at Camp Elliott, forwarded to the Commandant of
the United States Marine Corps in February 1942. In March, Major General Vogel wrote to the Commandant of the United States Marine Corps
praising the Navajo demonstration and recommending the recruitment
of a force of Navajo for communications purposes. Finally, the first recruitment of Navajo did not occur until April of 1942 (Paul 1973:11;
Hale 1992:412), and the graduation of the first Navajo platoon from boot
camp did not occur until June 27, 1942. Code formation came later that
year (McClain 1994:61).

   A great emphasis was laid on maintaining the secrecy of the Navajo
project (McClain 1994:77, 91–98). In several separate instances, the secrecy of the Navajo training program was placed in potential danger. After effective service by the Navajo at Guadalcanal, and despite directions
that no publicity be given, the January 23, 1943, issue of the Marine
Corps camp paper *Chevron*, and the January 27 edition of the *San Diego
Union* newspaper both ran articles alluding to the use of the Navajo
and their language (McClain 1994:91). Later that summer, James M.
Stewart, then General Superintendent of the Navajo Indian Service,
published a five-page article on the Navajo, entitled "The Navajo Indian
at War," in the June edition of *Arizona Highways* magazine. The uniqueness and basic composition of the training and use of Navajo were
specifically described:

> The U.S. Marine Corps has organized a special signal unit for
> combat communication service. A platoon of thirty Navajo was
> recruited in the Spring of 1942. Its members were trained in signal
> work using the Navajo language as a code, adapting a scheme tried
> with considerable success during World War I, when the enemy was
> completely baffled by the employment of an Indian language in
> front line communication. The thirty Navajo Marines performed
> their duties so successfully that the plan was expanded, a recruiting
> detail was sent back to the Navajo Reservation in the early autumn,
> and by early December, 67 new boys were enlisted. Two members of
> the original detachment went back as corporals to assist in explain-
> ing the work to eligible Indians. (Stewart 1943:22–23)

   Thus, as demonstrated by the army's recruitment of Comanches and
other Eastern Indians, the idea to use Native American code talkers in

World War II preceded the code talker program of the Marine Corps. Military records demonstrate that formal code training and field practices had already been undertaken by the Comanche unit in the Fourth Signal Company, Fourth Infantry Division, prior to Philip Johnston's idea to form a Navajo unit. The Comanches had already completed their general communications training and finished their specialized code development in late September and early October of 1941 at Ft. Benning, Georgia, whereas the first platoon of Navajo was not recruited until April 1942 and did not complete training until late in the summer of 1942 (Paul 1973; Tully 1995). The Comanche unit had already used its code talking abilities in the First Army Carolina Maneuvers in November and December of 1941 at Ft. Jackson, South Carolina, and in the Carolina Maneuvers (Area 7) in July 1942 (Stanton 1984:81).[4]

McClain (1994:94–98, 122–127) discusses how Johnston leaked extensive information about the Navajo program, which led to a heated investigation. By June 1942, the army was attempting to ascertain if marine Indian code talkers actually existed and whether using Indian code talkers in the Alaskan theater was feasible (McClain 1994:96). As McClain explains:

> Whether Marine Corps Headquarters was aware of the Army's interest in the Navajo is not known as there are no documents to indicate any damage control concerning the Army's interest. The reply that Colonel Townsend received from Major Hiser, however, is amusing to say the least: "No information is available to this office except in rumor form. However, investigation is continuing and results will be forwarded if they seem worthy of consideration." It is rather clear that neither Colonel Townsend nor Major Hiser were aware that the Army had a unit of talkers comprised of Comanches who were serving in the European Theater of Operation. (1994:97)

In light of the earlier correspondence among the navy, army, and marines, it is not clear why they would not be aware of the army's Comanche unit. Although the Comanche were trained earlier than the Navajo, they would not become combat-active until June 6, 1944.

THE FORMATION OF THE COMANCHE CODE TALKERS

The initial stimulus leading to the use of Native American code talkers and communications operators in World War II appears to have resulted from formal requests from the United States War Department for recommendations of various Native American groups for potential recruitment and communications training in late 1940.[5] According to an As-

78 sociated Press release, the decision to choose the Comanches was made by the Director of the Indian Service, A. C. Monahan. After receiving a request from the War Department for thirty fluent Indians for training in the Signal Corps, he chose the Comanche because their language was unwritten. Within the Comanche community, however, exactly who developed the idea and who decided to use the Comanches as code talkers remains a hotly disputed topic to this day. The basic dispute centers around assertions by Bill Karty (a fellow Comanche who was responsible for helping to recruit some of the code talkers) that he originated the idea of the military using the Comanches as code talkers, and those of others (including some of the actual code talkers), who insist the idea came from the army.[6]

According to Haddon Codynah, who was then working in the CCC-ID (Civilian Conservation Corps—Indian Division), an army colonel came to the Anadarko Indian Agency to talk to Superintendent W. B. Mc-Cowen about the possibility of recruiting a group of Comanches to serve as code talkers. The colonel thought that some of the Comanches might want to enlist as a group before the draft started. Supporting the idea, Superintendent McCowen called Bill Karty, a fellow Comanche then working for the Anadarko Indian Agency as a civilian director of the CCC-ID camp at Ft. Cobb, Oklahoma.[7] McCowen gave Karty the task of contacting and recruiting potential members. Karty then proceeded to travel to various rural Comanche communities (mainly around Walters, Oklahoma), during December 1940, to contact various young, unmarried Comanche men who were fluent speakers of the Comanche language about potential special duty service in the Army Signal Corps.

As the late Haddon Codynah explained in 1987:

> Well he [Karty] didn't get the idea. Like I say it came through the Superintendent up here. . . . He was working for the people [CCC-ID]. . . . Like I say, this colonel, an Army officer, came to our Superintendent there at Anadarko, at the agency. He came and talked to him, talked to him about what he thought. . . . All right, back in 1938–39, somewhere along in there, that's when this colonel came to the Superintendent over here and talked to him, what he thought about the younger Comanche people, some of them was going to get drafted anyway you see. And finally they brought that up about those code talkers then. He [McCowen] said well that would be a good idea if we could, it would be all right with me. Some of them might want to volunteer before they get drafted. He said we could start that. Its all right. So there, what they talk over and wanted to do was a pretty good idea and then they called this guy Bill Karty, but he was working for the agency you know. And they called him

in, and talked to him, to see what he thought about it, and about him recruiting. He said well its all right if you all say so. . . . So all right they turn it over to him as a recruiter, that's where it went from there.[8]

Although Karty explained that they would use their language for communications purposes, the exact extent of their future duty was apparently not fully known to some recruits at this time.[9] Remaining code talkers indicated that whether the concept of code talking was directly explained to them or not, it quickly became apparent in the recruitment process, long before the actual code training began.

Many of the code talkers dropped out of high school to enlist. Roderick Red Elk recalled that he was home from high school on Christmas break when Karty came to visit and recruit him. Seven or eight of the Comanche Code Talkers were recruited by Bill Karty, whose primary role was in soliciting potential recruits for army code talkers. Albert Nahquaddy Jr. was recruited by World War I Comanche veteran John Wahkahquah and a U.S. Army officer while home on a weekend visit from Wichita, Kansas.[10] Another code talker described how he decided to enlist to become a code talker:

Well when I was a senior in high school at Haskell Indian School at Lawrence, Kansas, I came home for Christmas vacation of 1940. And when I got there I was around visiting my friend and that's when my cousin across the road told me that he was going, Larry Saupitty, my aunt's boy. And later I heard the other boys was going that I go to school with at Ft. Sill Indian School. So I went home and told Mama what they were going to do. They were going to make a special unit of Comanches that could speak their tribe [tribal language] fluently. So since my kin folks was going I said, "I might as well go with them." So we signed up because Hitler was already raising Cain over there in Czechoslovakia, and Poland, and all that. We talked about it at Lawrence, Kansas, in one of our classes, in science or something like that, you know. Mama said, "Go ahead if you want to." So that's when I went with the guys to Oklahoma City and we all joined up.[11]

As Charles Chibitty (Hidden Path 2000) explained, "I finally talked Momma into letting me drop out of school and go with the other boys because my little cousin was going. . . . So he was going, so Momma consented and I promised up and down that I would finish high school when I got back. But it took me four and a half years to get back." Other recruits responded as a result of other means such as hearing from relatives, or from local newspaper ads. Not being able to afford to go to college, Forrest Kassanavoid was prompted to join after seeing an army advertisement in the Lawton newspaper that specifically asked for young Comanche men who could speak the Comanche language fluently. Although the article did not state the reason for the fluency prerequisite, Kassanavoid stated, "Everyone realized that's what the language was going to be used for, so everyone basically suspected why and already knew."[12] While the army had planned to recruit thirty Comanches for the program, a total of twenty-one were initially recruited. Seventeen eventually enlisted and trained as code talkers, of whom fourteen eventually served overseas in Europe. Eight of the final seventeen recruits were from the Walters community in Cotton County, Oklahoma.[13]

Background

As described in the 1928 Meriam Report, major differences in culture, language, housing, wealth, formal education, and other areas existed between most Native American and Anglo recruits (Meriam et al. 1928; Parman 1994:83–88). The greatest differences between the Comanche recruits and Anglo recruits at this time were that the Comanches were all bilingual and to some degree bicultural, and all but one of the Comanche recruits had completed several years of military-style regimented training at the government-run Bureau of Indian Affairs' Fort Sill Indian School near Lawton, Oklahoma. Although all three criteria provided the Comanches with a distinct advantage in comparison with many of their Anglo fellow servicemen, the Indian school training would provide a distinct advantage in terms of adjusting to military training and lifestyle. At Fort Sill Indian School, these recruits had completed educational levels equivalent to a high school diploma. In 1940, the Comanches were a tribal population guaranteed certain select services through formally signed treaties with the United States government. However, these services have always been underfunded and poorly administered, and many Comanche at this time were economically worse off than many Anglo recruits. The ability to obtain a full-time job through military service was mentioned as a reason for enlistment by veterans of many tribes I have interviewed, including some of the code talkers. As Forrest Kassanavoid described:

> I was going to school and that was right at the end of the Depression. It was hard to find a job, so I decided to join the Army. Recruiting was intensive at that time, because they were trying to get the

Army up to about 400,000 men. . . . Several of my Comanche friends joined the infantry, and they went to Fort Sam Houston, Texas. I was hoping to go with them, but when I heard they were recruiting Comanches for the Signal Corps, I thought I'd try that instead—we went to Fort Benning, Georgia.[14]

The seventeen members came from various Comanche tribal communities and represented a cross-section in terms of education, income, and cultural background. However, the Comanches had the advantage of being able to communicate and function in two diverse cultural systems, Comanche and American. What was different was their bilingual ability in Comanche and English, their traditional cultural upbringing, and their tribal heritage of having descended from a culture which emphasized a strong martial ideology and ethos. Because the Comanches entered the reservation in 1874–1875, further military service was extremely limited, as all intertribal warfare was stopped and as the only opportunity for military service was as scouts for the United States Army. A few Comanches served as Army Scouts between 1892 and 1897 in Troop L of the Seventh Cavalry at nearby Ft. Sill. At least thirty-one Comanches served in World War I. While these servicemen were honored with traditional farewell gatherings and the singing of military society songs upon their departure, and later homecoming celebrations including social and military society songs and dances, their small numbers precluded the large-scale revival of the earlier Comanche men's societies and ceremonies. This prewar militarization context is essential to understanding the Comanches' position in 1940. While most traditional Comanche military society dances and ceremonies were dormant by this time, they were still well known. In addition, Comanche, and not Anglo-American, culture remained the primary context in which this generation of individuals was raised, with Comanche language, kinship, singing, dancing, and community social and economic activities comprising the basis of daily interaction. This remaining traditional cultural context had far-reaching postwar effects on the Comanches' service in World War II and subsequent large postwar cultural and veteran ceremonial revivals (Meadows 1995:302–390).

In terms of formal education and face-to-face interactions with Anglos, the Comanches were far more experienced than most Navajo at the start of the Second World War. Many Navajo were from remote portions of their reservation lands, and only 102 of 420 had attended federal high schools (Paul 1973:105–113). The Navajos' fewer off-reservation experiences, lack of knowledge of English, and general reluctance to send children to boarding schools produced initial difficulties in adjusting to

81

TABLE 3.1. *The Comanche Code Talkers*

---

(1) Cpl. Forrest Kassanavoid [Marked or Painted Wing (Feathers)], Indiahoma
(2) Pfc. Roderick Red Elk, Walters
(3) T/5 Charles Chibitty [Holding On], Mt. Scott–Porter Hill
(4) T/5 Wellington Mihecoby [War Face], Geronimo
(5) T/5 Simmons Parker, Cache-Indiahoma
(6) Pfc. Larry Saupitty [Many (Cheyennes) Came], Mt. Scott–Porter Hill
(7) Sgt. Melvin Permansu [Fur Taboo], Walters
(8) T/5 Willie Yackeschi [Crying and Holding On], Walters
(9) T/4 Morris Tabbyetchy [Sunrise], Cache-Indiahoma
(10) Pvt. Perry Noyabad, Cyril
(11) Pvt. Elgin Red Elk, Walters
(12) T/4 Haddon Codynah [Sitter], Walters
(13) Pfc. Robert Holder, Walters
(14) T/5 Clifford Otitivo [Brown or Tan Non-Indian], Cement-Walters
(15) Albert (Edward) Nahquaddy Jr. [Peeling (tree bark)], Walters
(16) Anthony (Tony) Tabbytite [Hole in the Sun], Cement-Walters
(17) Ralph Wahnee [Fox or Little Fox], Cyril-Fletcher

---

regimented military-style training schedules (Paul 1973; Escue 1991). In contrast, all but one of the Comanches had attended various Indian boarding schools, and all were in greater geographic proximity to Anglos.

The Comanches were recruited in a total of four separate groups which left Oklahoma City, Oklahoma, during December 1940 and January 1941. Bill Karty led to the recruiting station in Oklahoma City the first group of ten men, which included Wellington Mihecoby, Simmons Parker, Willie Yackeschi, Morris Tabbyetchy (also known as Morris Sunrise), Elgin Red Elk, Robert Holder, Clifford Otitivo, Albert (Edward) Nahquaddy Jr., Tony Tabbytite, and Ralph Wahnee. The second group of three Comanche recruits included Roderick Red Elk, Charles Chibitty, and Haddon Codynah. The third group included Forrest Kassanavoid, Melvin Permansu, and Larry Saupitty. Perry Noyabad was the only Comanche member in the fourth group. At least four other Comanche men passed their physicals but chose not to join for personal reasons: George Woogie Watchetaker (Chibitty's half brother), Lester Poahway, John Woosypitty, and Clifford Treetop. Watchetaker and Poahway were with the third recruit group.[15] Table 3.1 lists the seventeen members who were trained as code talkers, their military rank, translations of their family surnames, and their home community.[16]

Of the seventeen men trained for code talking, Nahquaddy, Tabbytite, and Wahnee were later discharged from the army after their training and did not serve overseas. Other Comanches later tried to join the code talkers (including Bill Karty, who was turned down because he was married and had dependents); however, the army did not enlist any more for code training.

Why did Native Americans enlist in the United States armed forces in such great numbers during World War II? Clearly, individuals held a wide variety of personal motives for such decisions based on factors of tribal and family warrior or military service traditions, employment, boarding school experiences, religion, degree of assimilation, a desire to travel, and issues of citizenship and ethnic identity. But what are the larger factors and patterns behind the widespread enlistment of Native Americans in World War II?

Dating back to World War I, most studies of Native American military service in the United States armed forces have essentially explained Indian entrance into the military as a form of continuing dependency, largely as an attempt to legitimize themselves as American citizens through military service (cf. Holm 1996:20). Emerging from Third World Latin American and African scholars, dependency theory grew in popularity after 1970, especially among political scientists and scholars emphasizing international relations. The increased use of history in dependency literature led to an increased awareness and examination by Western scholars. Dependency theory focuses on the process by which peripheral regions are incorporated into the global capitalist system, and the resultant political, economic, and social changes, or "structural distortions," that occur. Dependency theory generally examines the development and effects of differentially or asymmetrically structured economic relationships between peripheral groups and capitalist entities that arise through the development and expansion of an economy to which the former is subjugated, and the subsequent social transformations (White 1982:xiii–xix).

Dependency is seen as a multifaceted process, resulting not from any one material or economic process that alters or subordinates all else, but from a complex interaction of environmental, economic, political, and cultural influences that develop to the point where they deny some groups the ability to expand or remain self-sufficient. Theorists then examine the impact of conditioning of one economy on the other. Reflecting some earlier tenets of historical particularism, the specific combination of factors and their results is then understandable within specific histories (White 1982:xii–xix).

Theoretically, the Comanche Code Talkers serve as a case study

84   which demonstrates that Native American motivations for enlisting in
World War II and many other conflicts continue along complex, yet
largely culturally based, forms rather than following the solely assimilationist models proposed in prior historical works relying on dependency theory. Several authors have already documented the various factors behind Native American military service (Holm 1996; Britten 1997;
Franco 1999; Townsend 2000). Native Americans did not join the armed
forces in World Wars I and II solely to prove or to legitimize themselves
as American citizens; many already knew that they held dual citizenship, first, as members of their respective tribes and then, as Americans,
via the allotment process, the 1924 Indian Citizenship Act, and the 1936
Oklahoma Indian Welfare Act. Most joined for a complex combination
of: (1) traditional sociocultural influences (warrior-based themes), (2) acculturative influences (boarding school), (3) contemporary economic
factors (employment), and (4) patriotism for the defense of their own
lands and peoples and the United States. The opportunity to (5) use their
unique linguistic skills and to (6) remain in a select Native American
unit with fellow Comanche kinsmen provided two additional incentives
for these men during World War II.

   That the opportunities for military service and the overwhelming
majority of economic opportunities were Anglo-dominated during Word
War II is true and reflects some elements of dependency; however, other
cultural and ideological factors suggest otherwise. The motivations for
participating in these activities, primarily as volunteers, and the manner in which Native Americans chose to do so based on the continuation
of traditional values, ideologies, and, as with code talkers, the unique
circumstances in which they could use their native language, reflect
other factors of cultural continuity, adaptation, and syncretism of related
yet culturally different martial systems, consciously derived by Native
Americans and acceptable to them on their terms. As with other Native
Americans in United States military service, the Comanche Code Talkers demonstrate how a group of individuals syncretized military service
in a basically foreign institution with a strong sense of their own ethnic and martial identity—a uniquely Comanche sense of identity. In
doing so, they gave service in the United States military a meaning far
beyond that of dependency and simply legitimizing themselves as American citizens.

   To understand Native American motivations for enlisting in World
War II, one must acknowledge that the syncretization of Native American and American military systems was by now well established and
continued as a unique Native American cultural form with syncretic
tribal customs and traditions including honoring and naming ceremonies, the incorporation of the American flag, tribal flag songs, various

forms of scalp and victory or celebration dances, and participation in Anglo and/or establishment of Native American Veterans of Foreign Wars (VFW) and American Legion posts. The motivations for Native American enlistment in World War II closely parallel those in the First World War. The primary difference is that the scale of involvement was now larger and the processes of syncretization and service in the United States armed forces were more firmly established. By World War II the only way for Native Americans to obtain traditional martial roles was through United States military service, which by 1940 had combined past and present traditions in a syncretic adaptation to the current cultural situation. As only one example, Comanches had syncretized the cultural values and knowledge handed down from the prereservation and reservation periods with the experiences of their elders who were World War I veterans. Consequently, the Comanches again enlisted, largely because of factors related to their own social and cultural backgrounds and not from the preconceptions and stereotypes of the larger American society (Meadows 1995; Holm 1996).

Throughout the 1930s, significant socioeconomic improvements were made during the administration of Commissioner of Indian Affairs John Collier. Programs in vocational training and practical education, and work experience gained through participation in the CCC-ID, had increased on- and off-reservation job opportunities. Visible increases in health care, landholdings, and profits from livestock values and agricultural productivity were all evident. In addition, individual and tribal income levels had reached an all-time high (Townsend 2000:74). The Indian Reorganization Act of 1934 and the Oklahoma Indian Welfare Act of 1936 had resulted in significant changes in Indian cultural, religious, and linguistic freedom, while permitting some movement toward sovereignty with the reformation of tribal governments, business committees, and tribal constitutions. While many problems still existed, improvements were clearly evident.

In light of the Collier-era reforms during the 1930s, social and ethnic acceptance within the greater non-Indian populace was increasingly an issue for many Native Americans who were struggling to improve their condition throughout the Depression years. Although Native Americans did seek to establish greater equality as individuals and Indians, and an identity as contributing members of American society, the vast majority were not willing to do so to the exclusion of their respective tribal identities. That Native Americans were restrengthening their tribal cultures while simultaneously pursuing political and economic improvement to more firmly establish their political and economic position within the United States counters the contentions of dependency theory that Native Americans joined in vast numbers primarily to demonstrate assimilation, legitimize themselves as American citizens, and gain social acceptance in the non-Indian world. Native Americans did not join the armed forces in World War II to legitimize themselves as American citizens, as the majority already knew they were both members of their respective tribes and American citizens through the allotment process, Native American service in World War I, and the Indian Citizenship Act of 1924. Townsend (2000:77) provides several examples that demonstrate a widespread Indian awareness of their dual citizenship in the early 1940s. During World War II most Native Americans again joined the armed forces because of a complex combination of (1) traditional culture (warrior-based themes), (2) acculturation (boarding school), (3) contemporary economic factors (employment), and (4) tribal and national patriotism.

Several Comanche veterans I interviewed believed that it was only a matter of time until the United States became involved in World War II, and thus many Comanche men preferred enlistment to being drafted. Interviews with Comanche World War II veterans indicate that they were well aware of the cultural traditions associated with the military service and return of prereservation warriors and World War I Comanche veterans. As with the First World War, military service brought World War II veterans a tremendous level of respect in their tribal communities and from other Native Americans. By enabling them to protect their land and people, military service in the United States armed forces, now in syncretic form, once again linked native peoples to traditional tribal and family male cultural roles and heritage as warriors. Because military service provided a means for Indian men to achieve these roles in a manner that was essentially viewed as a continuation of, and thus being in accordance with, their traditional value systems, it was seminal in the widespread reinvigoration of martial ideology and ethos. Because traditional warriors' activities often involved cultural rituals such as parades, songs, and dances, these activities further consolidated support for veterans in their home communities.

The protection of the tribal people and their remaining lands and the deeply ingrained association of ethnic identity and geographical community were additional motivations. Many Native American World War II veterans I visited with emphasized their desire to join in the common defense of tribal lands and America, indicated that they were clearly fighting for "their" country, and saw any enemy attack on the United States as an assault on them as well. Although tribal ownership of lands had been greatly reduced by 1940, the ideology associated with the protection of one's homeland was prevalent, as was concern with the possibility of being conquered by another foreign power. Despite considerable Nazi propaganda aimed at swaying Native American support for Germany, Native Americans were well aware of Germany's exterminationist policies toward minorities, a potential threat should the United States fall.

By reaffirming a widespread sense of individual, tribal, and ethnic self-worth, and establishing a cornerstone for Indian pride, military service again provided not only a contemporary link to past warrior roles and prominent social status, but resulted in an even larger revival or reinvigoration of many tribal cultural forms than after World War I, including song, dance, ceremony, economic redistribution, religion, and naming customs (Meadows 1995; Holm 1996). Thus while significant Indian military service gained widespread non-Indian support, it simultaneously served to restrengthen traditional culture and ethnic identity within the tribal communities. Thus a syncretization of two previously distinct military traditions allowed for the continuation of Comanche martial values and culture through what was then the only available means, United States military service. In turn, the militarization context as it affected the Comanche Code Talkers in World War II serves as a reflection of the larger regional (Kiowa, Comanche, and Apache) and national (pan-Indian) processes tying the service of most Native American veterans in World War II to their traditional military cultural structures (Meadows 1995).

The United States government and various newspapers and periodicals highlighted a widespread and highly romanticized media campaign promoting a stereotyped pan-Indian image based on an alleged correlation between the renewal of warrior spirit and tradition and the prevalence of Indian enlistment. Much attention was given to data concerning Indian enlistment and accounts of native combat heroism. Although these representations held some truth for many tribes, many other crucial factors were involved in the widespread enlistment of Native Americans, and the use of such imagery was largely political and misleading. Such accounts were well received by the non-Indian public, who eagerly consumed the undeniably enticing human interest stories. However, these accounts were used largely by an assimilationist-minded government wanting to demonstrate the compatibility of Indians and whites in service while advancing the popular belief that most Indians favored assimilation (Townsend 2000:78–79).

Government-run Indian boarding schools constituted another important factor in native enlistments. The experiences gained from years of schooling in an atmosphere of military-style discipline and schedules further preconditioned many Native Americans to regimented daily activities. This educational foundation in turn facilitated the prompt adjustment of Native American men to basic training and military service. By familiarizing Native American men with many of the initial activities associated with induction into military service, the boarding school experience unintentionally aided in preparing Native American soldiers to renew and regain their position as veterans by combining traditional values with service in a modern military structure.

Financial considerations were an additional significant factor. The Second World War provided military and economic opportunities on a much larger scale than World War I. In contrast to Holm's (1996:101) findings in studying Vietnam-era veterans, economic motivations played a significant role in enlistment decisions of the World War II veterans I have spoken with from several tribes. With the effects of the Depression still lingering, unemployment was high. The remaining code talkers and tribal elders indicate that most young Comanche men at this time were just out of high school and were unemployed. While limited federal aid and bureau-funded work projects provided limited and irregular sources of income, the prospect of gaining some form of specialized training applicable to later civilian life offered the possibility of more stable employment and prompted many to consider military service. With continuing economic instability, life in the army appealed to many Native Americans by providing both military service and a stable source of income for enlisted servicemen. Economically, this also benefited many in the home communities, as many servicemen sent much of their earnings to their families.

As with most Native American men of service age in 1940, all of these factors affected the Comanche recruits' considerations of enlistment. However, the situation concerning Native American code talkers created two additional motivations for enlisting that significantly differed in comparison with other native servicemen. The primary reasons given by the Comanche Code Talkers I interviewed for joining to serve as a code talker involved (1) the realization that they would probably be drafted soon, (2) the desire to serve in a unit with fellow Comanches, (3) the acknowledgment that their language could provide a unique service, and (4) reliable employment. Of these factors, the two most commonly mentioned by the code talkers were the desire to (1) "stick together" as a specialized all-Comanche unit and (2) provide a specialized communications skill through the use of their language. Group cohesiveness again reflected earlier kinship, war party, and warrior society practices. These opportunities provided additional incentives for enlisting as code talkers.

Five of the Comanche Code Talkers gave very similar reasons for their enlistments. Haddon Codynah, then working under Karty in the

CCC-ID, stated that he joined to serve with fellow Comanches and to obtain work.[17] Roderick Red Elk commented:

> What interested me about it was I knew all the people that they were recruiting. It would be just like home, just like all those seven or eight or nine people that lived in that Cotton County area. See I knew all of them so that would probably be an enticement to go into a branch of service where you know a bunch of them.[18]

> I knew all the guys who would be in the unit, and that enticed me. I knew about the war and knew we would get into it sooner or later.[19]

Another code talker reflected:

> We was probably going to get drafted anyway in a year or two later you know, so in order to stick together, we just went.[20]

Forrest Kassanavoid similarly explained his reasons for joining:

> Well my reason for joining was I had finished high school in the middle of the year and I didn't have no money to go to school on, and I was going to join the Army anyway. So when this came along I just thought, well that's an opportunity to join a unit where you'll know somebody instead of going to a unit where you didn't know anyone. So I was going to join the Army anyway, so if I didn't I'd probably be drafted within a year or two, so that's the reason why I joined up.[21]

> We knew we would get into it sooner or later, so when I found out I would be in a unit with good friends, it made the decision easier.[22]

Likewise, Albert Nahquaddy Jr., who was related to eleven of the other sixteen recruits, stated that when the others told him of their decision to enlist and that he would be "left behind," he decided to join as well:

> They were getting them [the recruits] all together and when I came home from Wichita, Kansas on the weekend, they was all getting ready to swear them in, in Lawton, and of course I was kin to all of them but five guys, and they asked me, they said, "Why don't you just come and go with us," they said. "You're going to be left here alone. . . ."[23]

"GET HIM BACK ON THAT SCALE AND WEIGH HIM AGAIN!"

The second group of Comanche recruits, which included Roderick Red Elk, Charles Chibitty, and Haddon Codynah, were almost not recruited due to circumstances encountered during their physical examinations. These men were preparing to enlist on New Year's Eve, December 31, 1940, at the recruiting station in Oklahoma City. Being the youngest of the seventeen, Roderick Red Elk had to have his parents sign a permission slip to join. During the physicals, it was discovered that Red Elk was under the required enlistment weight of 122 pounds. The other recruits all passed the required weight for their height and age. The recruiting sergeant told them that he could only take those who passed their weight exams. Codynah and Chibitty told the recruiting sergeant that if he wanted them, he would have to take Red Elk as well. The sergeant gave them twenty-four hours to get Red Elk from 112 up to 118 or 119 pounds. That evening Red Elk ate bananas and he drank large amounts of water throughout the night in an attempt to attain sufficient weight by the following day. When Red Elk was weighed again the next day, he had gained to 115 pounds, but was still underweight. After deferring his enlistment, the recruiting sergeant stated, "Boys, I guess we're going to have to lose you all." Desiring that they all remain together, the other Comanches reaffirmed that if he didn't enlist Red Elk, they would not enlist either. About this time, a lieutenant came in and overheard the situation. Faced with this, the lieutenant decided that the sergeant "might have made a mistake" and ordered him to weigh Red Elk again. In reweighing Red Elk, the lieutenant found his weight to be adequate.

As Red Elk recalled, the lieutenant sternly ordered the sergeant, "Get him back on that scale and weigh him again." "They put me back on and I looked down and the Lieutenant had his foot on the scale." When the sergeant saw what was happening, the lieutenant again firmly ordered him, "Sergeant, you just watch the weight." "They got me up to 118 pounds, so they signed me up" (Red Elk 1991:113). Whether the lieutenant knew of the Comanches' destination and their future communications role in the Fourth Infantry Division is unclear. Nevertheless, he decided the participation of the three members by providing Roderick Red Elk with a third foot to ensure he made the required enlistment weight.[24]

As Red Elk concluded:

They had our tickets all ready and the Sergeant said, "Well those other guys think so much of you that I'm going to put you in charge." I was the youngest one of the whole group. He gave me the jacket with all of our orders and they took us to the train where we headed for Georgia. We had a good laugh about that—me passing the physical. (1991:114)

The purpose of forming the Indian code talkers was to speed up communications by eliminating the slow process of encoding, sending, receiving, decoding, translating, and relaying military communications. All recruits were required to be fluent in the Comanche language, a primary reason for their selection, as well as to be unmarried. Those chosen were all individuals who had been raised with the language in their families and communities. In 1940, the Comanche language remained the primary language in most Comanche families, and the code talkers' generation grew up speaking Comanche as their first language. Although several band-related dialects of the Comanche language existed, they were mutually intelligible and presented no problems to the Comanches.[25] That many Indians found themselves in the position to help in wartime communications is a striking irony, since genocide and later assimilation of language and culture had been the larger American governmental policy which continues to affect the Comanches to the present. Perhaps the most ironic facet of the history of the Comanche Code Talkers is that the United States military forces were actively seeking Native Americans to practice what they had been instructed not to do and punished for, for many years—speaking their native languages. Beginning in the late 1870s and continuing throughout the 1930s, the Comanches, like other tribes, were instructed in Indian boarding schools not to speak their native language because it was thought that such languages were detrimental to the academic and economic advancement of individuals and would have no place in the future. Like other Indians sent to government-run Indian boarding schools, the Comanches were forced to adopt and function in a paramilitary style of life. Students were well versed in regimented dormitory life, including regulated schedules for arising and going to sleep, bunk making, shoe shining, dormitory cleaning, academic classes, and marching to all activities and meals. In addition, physical training, including boxing, served to physically strengthen students. Tom Holm reports that Indian boarding schools were in many aspects similar to Prussian regimental schools.[26]

The significance of the militarization of the Indian boarding school experience was that while it (1) familiarized Native American children with English language and educational structures, it (2) did so in a form which was militarily oriented. By having years of regimented military-style training since early childhood, these individuals were well trained in many aspects normally associated with basic training, making military service more familiar, appealing, and easier to adapt to. This training, combined with traditional Comanche cultural values emphasizing and recognizing military service as the primary means to male social status, preconditioned many students for military service in World War II. Essentially, most Comanche soldiers were thoroughly grounded in dual military protocol and procedures before their entrance into military service. This aspect made Native Americans qualitatively unique in comparison to many of their Anglo counterparts.

By 1940, however, with the approaching war, the army was seeking fluent Native American speakers for their valuable linguistic contribution in the Allied war preparations. Forrest Kassanavoid described his experiences at the Fort Sill Indian Boarding School near Lawton, Oklahoma:

> They discouraged you, . . . they didn't want you to speak Comanche because . . . they were going to do everything they could to break you away from that lifestyle you had lived as an Indian, you know. . . . Of course when you went home from the boarding school you spoke Comanche most of the time. . . . We all spoke Comanche in our families. Before the war very few Comanches didn't know the language of their ancestors.[27]

> Prior to World War II, very few Comanches did not speak Comanche. The only ones who didn't, lived away [from the area]. Everyone spoke it fluently.[28]

Another code talker reflected on the attitudes of Indian boarding schools toward the retention of native languages and the military's later requests for natives' help:

> And we were forbidden at that time to talk Comanche. That was strictly a no-no, and if we did talk Comanche, we got strictly punished . . . paddled or forced to wax floors. . . . You got punished for talking Indian. So when we see them coming, when we're talking Indian, we hush-up real quick. Like I say, they was always trying to make little white boys out of us. But still, when Hitler started kicking around, they was looking for Indians, and they come back to us and asked us to use our language for that special unit, to use to send messages.[29]

Charles Chibitty described the prohibition on native languages during his years as a student:

> I went to Fort Sill Indian School when I was little. And while I was going to school there, way back in '26, '27, on up to 1930, we were forbidden to talk our tribal language. Not only at Fort Sill, but

Riverside, Concho, and all the other Indian schools. But it never really worked because when we got home that's all we talked, was Indian, and when we got caught talking Indian at Fort Sill Indian School we got punished for it. And me and my cousin Larry Saupitty . . . when we was talking Indian and we see a teacher or somebody, a faculty or some kind coming down, we always hush up. We laugh and everytime we say, "I think they're trying to make little white boys out of us." That was so, not only at Fort Sill, but at Riverside, Concho, and the other Indian schools. They wash my mouth out with that old yellow soap and they tell me to stop talking that dirty language. (Hidden Path 2000)

Although officially prohibited in schools, Comanche continued to be spoken away from the school faculty and in the Comanche communities, where it remained the dominant language for most Comanches of this generation. Once forcibly discouraged, native languages and Native Americans' bilingual advantage were now valued by the American military in wartime. What the American government had tried to eradicate, it now came asking to be reinvigorated. Yet despite the United States' attempts at forcing assimilation on Native American cultures and languages, many individuals of this generation retained their cultures, and thankfully, for the United States' benefit, their native languages.

BASIC TRAINING: "THERE'S SOMETHING WRONG HERE.
YOU GUYS AREN'T SUPPOSED TO KNOW ALL THIS."

Assigned to the Fourth Infantry Division, the four groups of Comanche recruits arrived by train at Columbus, Georgia, and then went to Ft. Benning, Georgia, for basic training during late December 1940 and January 1941. The Fourth Infantry Division, also known as "The Fighting Fourth" and, from its distinctive Ivy League patch modeled as a play on the Roman numeral four, the "Ivy Division," was originally formed at Camp Green in North Carolina in December of 1917 under the command of Major General George H. Cameron. Six months later it was sent to active duty in World War I in France. In sixty-nine days of active combat service the Fourth saw action in the front lines and as reserves, and received battle honors for five major campaigns: the Second Battle of the Marne, Chateau Thierry, St. Mihiel, Verdun, and the Argonne Forest. With the beginning of the Aisne-Marne campaign on July 18, 1918, units of the Ivy Division were organized and assigned to several French infantry divisions. In August, the Fourth was reunited for the final days of the campaign. In helping to defeat sixteen German divisions, the Fourth Division took approximately 5 percent of all AEF battle casualties in World War I. Suffering 11,500 casualties, the Fourth was the only division to serve in both the French and British sectors of the Western Front. After brief post-Armistice occupational duty, the division was sent home and deactivated.[30]

On June 1 of 1940, the Fourth Infantry Division was reactivated at Ft. Benning, Georgia. The Fourth Signal Company was organized as the communications unit for the Fourth Division. Enlisted cadre for the company were transferred from the Second Signal Company at Ft. Sam Houston, Texas. Enlisted personnel were recruited largely from Pennsylvania, Maryland, Virginia, and Tennessee. Later, in February 1941, the company received its first selectees. An additional five hundred men were also assigned to a Provisional Signal Training Battalion that was staffed by Fourth Signal Company personnel. This provisional battalion trained the men in wire, message center, and radio procedures for the communication detachments and sections in the regiments, battalions, and companies of the division.[31]

After arriving at Ft. Benning and staying briefly in a staging area for new recruits, the recruits were checked into their assigned companies, where they were issued their barracks assignments and their clothes— excess World War I–issue uniforms consisting of wrapped leggings, wide-hipped breeches, and campaign hats—all wool garments. As Roderick Red Elk recalled, "You've seen those wrap leggings and big old riding breeches, and those big smokey hats? That's what they issued us" (Bryant 1993a:21). The Comanche recruits were all placed in the same barracks as part of a recruit platoon in a training program. The Comanches were under Company First Sergeant Charles Hurst and two drill instructors, Sergeants Clifford Rate and John Boozer.[32]

Most of the Comanches' surnames were poorly attempted English spellings of their Comanche pronunciation, which became standard family surnames on government BIA (Bureau of Indian Affairs) tribal enrollments. As only five of the seventeen Comanche recruits had English surnames (one with an English surname and four with English translations of Comanche names as surnames), the Comanches found that the military personnel initially had great difficulty in pronouncing their surnames. Charles Chibitty (Hidden Path 2000) described the instructors' problems with their Indian surnames, "When we got to Ft. Benning, Georgia, while we was in boot training, Sergeant Boozer and Sergeant Rate, they was in charge of us. For a while they always holler at us, 'All you Indians line up,' because they couldn't say our Indian names." As one member recalled, "The Sergeant used to say, 'OK. All you Indians line up,' before he got to know the names pretty good."[33]

Probably no theme better characterizes the Comanche Code Talkers' experiences in basic training than being underestimated. The Comanches were continually underestimated in many facets of their knowledge, prior experiences, and linguistic and physical abilities. Naturally, the average Anglo recruit in 1941 had not experienced years of regimented military boarding school training, which had already familiarized the Comanches with much of the military procedure covered in basic training. The Comanches continually challenged the expectations and stereotypes many of their non-Indian officers and fellow servicemen held concerning Indians. On the second day of basic training, all seventeen Comanche recruits made roll call. Unaware of the Comanches' experiences in Indian boarding schools, and intending to have his usual fun with a bunch of bewildered new recruits, the drill sergeant began to call out various military commands. Because all but one of the seventeen Comanches had gone through Indian boarding schools, they were familiar with the military-style routine. As Roderick Red Elk recalled:

> The drill sergeant got us out there and was going to have some fun with a bunch of raw recruits. He was going to put us through the paces. He started giving commands. There were sixteen of us that knew exactly what commands he was going to give and we knew how to march because we'd all been in boarding schools. There was only one of the guys that didn't go to boarding schools and instead of going right, he'd go left every time. I'm not going to mention any names, though! But anyway, we surprised the drill sergeant. He'd give us right face, left face or marching and he'd give us about face and we'd just do it like we'd been in the Army all our lives. He was amazed. He halted us and we stopped. He asked us if we were sure we were raw recruits. We told him "yeah, we just got in." So he dismissed us. (1991:114)

Red Elk elaborated on how they continued to baffle their drill sergeant:

> The next morning, he came to the barracks and said he was going to show us how to make the bunks up—the military way. We were already up and had our bunks made, and here he came and looked— and he was surprised again. We really had him going. He just scratched his head, he couldn't figure it out. He reached in his pocket and pulled a quarter out and threw it on the bed and it just jumped right back at him. He said, "There's something wrong here. You guys aren't supposed to know all this." So one of the fellows told him that all of us except one had been in boarding school and we march everywhere we went. We knew all the commands that he had and one of the things they taught us was how to fix a bed:

95

tight—just like the military. We had to shine our shoes too. That was another thing he couldn't get over, that we knew how to shine our shoes. From then on we got along pretty good with the drill sergeant. (1991:114)

We already knew how to make bunks you know, so that a quarter would bounce. We knew how to shine our shoes. We marched every place we went. That's what really got the drill sergeant.[34]

Roderick Red Elk recalled how, when the Comanche recruits were sent to qualify for rifle training at the rifle range, their instructors truly became suspicious. When all qualified as experts on the range, the instructors accused them of having been in the military before because they already knew what they were supposed to be there to learn, but they had not.[35] Charles Chibitty continued:

When we was on the firing range over there, I don't know where that rabbit came out of between the targets and where we was. And pretty soon there was dust flying around that rabbit where he was running. And Sergeant Boozer was a hollering and getting after us, but we didn't pay no attention, we just shot after him until he got out of sight.[36]

Forrest Kassanavoid attended a public school at Indiahoma, Oklahoma, before being sent to Fort Sill Indian School at the age of twelve. Although Kassanavoid stated that he was most surprised by the more regimented and schedule-bound structure of the boarding school, he explained how boarding school life helped in the adjustment to army life:

We knew close order drill, we knew how to make beds, and then we were regimented, we had to march every place we went. And we all dressed, we practically all wore the same kind of clothes when we were there. . . . Of course everything was done by the numbers (. . . marching, daily work and study activity schedules by military time) there at the Indian School, so that gave us a good preparation when we went into the Army. . . . See they cut our drill, our training time in half, because we already knew close order drill and we knew all about barracks life and how to make beds, . . . when to go to bed, and all that kind, so we didn't have to go through that.[37]

As another code talker described, the years of drilling and training in Indian boarding schools made the Comanche recruits already prepared for military life:

They couldn't get over how we was so good in drilling and making our beds. So one of the boys told them that we did that in Indian school. We drilled in Indian school. We had companies back in the late [19]20's, I was in C Company. So we learned the army way of living there at Indian school.[38]

The Comanches' willingness and ability to take a hard assignment and make light work out of it without complaining pleased their training officers at Ft. Benning tremendously. Indians excelled at basic training, as reflected by the acclamations of their commanding officers. As First Sergeant Charles G. Hurst stated, "Those Indians are the best morale tonic on the shelf. They take a hard job and make a game out of it. We could use more like 'em. . . . If we don't keep 'em busy, they're always playing pranks on somebody."[39] The other, non-Indian recruits also couldn't help but like the Comanches, as groups of Comanche and Anglo soldiers frequently went into town together during their off-duty periods on Saturday and Sunday afternoons. One code talker went to a friend's home in New York, where his parents were delighted to meet "a real Indian." Forrest Kassanavoid recalled that because they received no special treatment in basic training and once the Anglo troops realized that they spoke English, the Anglos became friends with the Comanches and liked them very much.[40]

One article published during July of 1942 stated, "Their pale face buddies like them because of their good humor, willingness to work and ability to stand up under the rough work and come out grinning."[41] The prior experience in Indian boarding schools resulted in their basic training at Ft. Benning, which normally lasted six weeks, being cut to two weeks.[42]

Although many of the Comanches knew the basic reason for their recruitment, they had not been officially told that they would be forming and using a code. Only after basic training were they formally assigned to communications and told that they would be an ultraspecial group. The seventeen recruits trained in all aspects of communications between early February and August of 1941. Fellow company member John Eckert reflected that as the signal company contained only around three hundred men, everyone got to know almost everyone else.[43] Their training included instruction in wire, radio, telephone, and telegraph (Morse code) use and repair; semaphore construction; and minor repairs on communications field equipment. Although now assigned to different communications units, they remained in neighboring barracks and were in close contact with one another. After their initial communications training they were reassigned to different areas of communications. Most went to various sections, including radio and wire sections. Forrest

"GET HIM BACK ON THAT SCALE AND WEIGH HIM AGAIN!"

Kassanavoid stated that he was given the opportunity to select an assignment and thus chose the "wire section," which included the construction and use of telephones and telegraphs, and the laying of lines between command levels.[44] In addition to receiving special communications training, all performed regular duties such as guard duty, kitchen duty, and sanitation, and took training in anti-aircraft, amphibious, and routine fighting skills. They also learned how to lay communications lines while under fire. One member of the code talkers remarked that he was a little disappointed initially, as he thought they would start code training sooner.

By August of 1941, plans for specialized code talker training were ready to be implemented. On August 1, 1941, the Fourth Signal Company was moved to Dry Prong, Louisiana, where it participated in the IV Corps Louisiana Maneuvers in the Louisiana swamps. The Comanches operated with the signal outfit near the front lines of the simulated battles. Their performance in the Louisiana Maneuvers at Dry Prong, Louisiana, from August 1st to the 17th, 1941, also pleased their commanders. As one of the code talkers commented, "We were used to hunting, fishing, and living in the outdoors. It was easy for us to work in the maneuvers."[45] This member recalled one of the more humorous incidents. While practicing war games on the maneuvers, he and another of the code talkers were captured by the opposing side. While watching their guard, he spoke to his companion in Comanche, "He's gonna smoke, when he does, I'll kick him in the leg. You grab him and throw him down and we'll run off." As the guard was caught totally "off guard," the plan worked. Standing over their newly captured guard, he jokingly said, "We have to kill you now." "Pow," they said, pointing their finger at the surprised guard, after which the two Comanches ran off into the woods and escaped. Thus, during the maneuvers, none of the Comanches was officially "captured."[46]

The Comanches would soon be assigned under an officer to begin formal code training. Upon graduation from West Point in June 1941, Lieutenant Hugh F. Foster Jr. was assigned to the Fourth Signal Company, Fourth Division. He reported for duty on August 8, 1941, joining the company while it was on maneuvers near Dry Prong, Louisiana. On August 27, 1941, the Fourth Division returned from the Louisiana Maneuvers at Dry Prong, Louisiana, to Ft. Benning, Georgia. Shortly thereafter, the division signal officer, Major Terence J. Tully (USMA 1920) called Lieutenant Foster to his office and told him that the company had seventeen Comanche Indians who had all been recruited from one general area with the intention of using their native language as a simplified verbal code. He then said that from that moment on Foster was responsible for training them, and was directed to work with them to develop a code that would both meet field military requirements and be unintelligible to any other Comanche outside of the group of seventeen.[47] Thus, if any Comanches in another unit were captured and subjected to "forceful interrogation" by the enemy, they could not give the code away. As Foster recalled, "I was told the decision was to recruit a group from one locale, all from one tribe, so they would have lingual commonality which might not be shared by other groups, even of the same major tribe."[48] The methods for accomplishing this assignment were left totally to Lieutenant Foster's discretion. In addition to organizing and supervising the code talkers' training, Lieutenant Foster also served as mess officer, wire construction platoon leader, and member of courts martial, besides holding other duties.

Lieutenant Foster had just recently been commissioned by choice in the Signal Corps. In 1941 West Point graduates were only commissioned in a combat arm (Engineers, Signal Corps, Cavalry [Armor], Infantry, Field Artillery, Coast Artillery) in the Quartermaster Corps. The Corps of Engineers and the Signal Corps were designated as both combat arms and technical services because (1) they operated in the forward areas with other combat elements, and (2) they also had extensive technical responsibilities in the design, procurement, issue, and repair of their own equipment, some of which, like telephones, were used by other elements as well. If a graduate chose the Army Air Corps, he was also assigned to a basic branch, and if he washed out of flight school, he reverted to duty in that basic branch.

Ironically, Foster's assignment to the Fourth was completely a mistake. As Major General Foster recalled:

In 1941 the normal procedure was that upon graduation one was sent to a Branch School for the Branch Basic Officers Course, where you were taught the details of your specific duties as pertained to your branch. . . . It was not until about a few weeks before graduation that each cadet knew what branch he was assigned to, so the curriculum had to be all things to all people. . . . As it happened in my case, through administrative mishap at the Department of the Army I was assigned to duty with the 4th Signal Company, not to the Basic Officers Course at the Signal School. The school was expecting me, but I never got the word. I was so deep in the Louisiana swamps the orders never reached me, and I never received the specialized instruction I should have received, so it was an uphill struggle for me all the way. I had to learn by practical experience.[49]

99

100   Faced with the assignment to devise a coded form of communication in a language in which he did not know a single word, Foster met with the Comanches. As Major General Foster described:

> I met with the 17 Comanches for a general discussion about our objective. It soon became evident that I had a couple of problems: (1) There is no written Comanche language, so it was entirely memory for them. (2) Whatever we came up with was supposed to be unintelligible to any other Comanche Indian. (3) There were no Comanche words for many essential military terms, e.g., "overpass," "underpass," "howitzer." The Comanches had one word for airplane, but no way to differentiate between a bomber, a fighter, a scout plane, a pursuit plane, etc. The Comanches had a word for gun, but no way of differentiating between a mortar (small and portable, small projectile, high trajectory, short range), a "gun" (large projectile, long range, flat trajectory), and a howitzer (large projectile, short range, high trajectory), etc. It was in these military-specific terms that the codewords were to be employed. (4) I was not going to come up with an entire new Comanche language.[50]

In light of the fact that the Comanche language was unwritten, and unknown within the military, and that the Comanche recruits came from several bands with occasionally slight, but significant, dialect (linguistic band and divisional) differences, Foster realized that the formulation of terms would be difficult. Eventually he decided that the formulation of codes for the military terms was best left to the recruits themselves to figure out, something previously unheard of in traditional army intelligence.

CODE FORMATION AND TRAINING

As the tensions in Europe and the Pacific increased, the Fourth Division continued its training. Returning from Louisiana, the Fourth Division was again stationed at Ft. Benning from August 27 to October 30th, 1941. The majority of the actual code formation was undertaken in late September and early October of 1941 at Benning.[51]

The Comanche trainees were also taught to differentiate various types and calibers of weapons, armored vehicles, and airplanes, much of which had no existing counterpart in Comanche. Although they were frequently referred to as "code talkers," the majority of communications performed by the Comanche Code Talkers were in everyday non-coded Comanche language, with specialized military language in coded form. Many military-related items already existed in regular Comanche language, such as geographical forms including mountains, rivers, hills, and roads, and military subjects such as soldiers and guns, and thus did not need coded terms. Code was used for the nearly 250 terms for various American military and modern geographical forms having no common equivalents in the Comanche language, such as machine gun, mortar, bomber, fighter, and tank. These "coded" terms were not intelligible to other non-code-talker-trained Comanche servicemen and were used largely as nouns inserted into regular noncoded Comanche sentences. Coded terms were thus used only in sending messages and not in everyday language. While most of each message sent was spoken in everyday Comanche language, the numerous insertions of specially coded military terms made it impossible for anyone not trained in the code to understand. Most messages were simply translated from English into Comanche (including code words), sent in Comanche over the telephone or radio, and then translated from Comanche back into English by the receiving code talker, who relayed the messages to his unit. Thus speed, accuracy, and security were all ensured.

This strategy accommodated two crucial criteria in military communications: (1) an accelerated form of voice communication avoiding the need to encode, send, receive, decode, and translate messages through writing and machines, prior to relaying messages, and (2) assurance of security in communications transmissions. As Forrest Kassanavoid reiterated:

We spoke Comanche that even other Comanches couldn't understand. . . . A Comanche who was not a code talker would not understand very well because of so many code words and names.[52]

While Lieutenant Foster provided the list of military terms in English for which Comanche terms were needed, the Comanches created the actual code terms themselves. Everyone had to agree on each term to enable standardization before proceeding to the next term. When the men agreed on a word Lieutenant Foster wrote it into a small green notebook. Part of the training involved drilling by counting in Comanche to ensure exact numbers, which would be crucial during the war. As Lieutenant Foster described:

In a small pocket notebook I had written a list of about 200 terms. In some cases words like "hospital" and "railroad" already existed, but there might be multiple ways of expressing the idea. I saw no need to change such words as long as all the Comanches agreed on how they would say the word. . . . I named a term and the Comanches gathered in a group and spoke in Comanche while they suggested and discarded phrases until they finally reached agreement. They told me in Comanche what they had agreed upon and I wrote in my pocket notebook the term in English followed by my brand of phonetics for the way the Comanches decided to say it. I was certainly in no position to argue the point with them.[53]

The Comanche recruits were thus faced with the need to develop extensive terminology for a large number of military items, many of which did not exist in their language. As with the circumstances experienced by the Navajo (Begay 1981:91) in the formation of their code words, many of the code terms were drawn from the Comanches' own perceptions of their natural and cultural environment: their land, tribal culture, and familiar objects, sights, and sounds. While virtually every language occasionally borrows terms or loan words from other languages to name new objects or concepts, many new words are also created from within the existing components of a language. Although the Comanches had integrated various loan words from Spanish, French, English, and even other neighboring tribes, they often created new words themselves for such things as the horse, automobiles, airplanes, sewing machines, and firearms. For the required code terms, the Comanches created a new lexicon based largely on new combinations of existing words.

The Comanche language traditionally had only one generic term for all types of guns (tawo'i'), which included rifles and pistols. The later development of various tank guns and artillery pieces necessitated specific terms to distinguish these different types of firearms. Various prefixes were created and added to the existing Comanche word for gun to differentiate the many types of firearms used by the army. Combinations of the Comanche words for individual numbers, and the words "big," "small," and "gun," were used to differentiate various types and calibers of manual firearms and artillery pieces. Such was the case for devising a term for machine gun. Because the machine gun made a staccato "rat-a-tat-tat" sound, one of the Comanches associated its sound to that made by his grandmother's treadle sewing machine that was pumped by foot. Thus "sewing machine gun" (tutsahkuna' tawo'i') became the Comanche code word for a .30-caliber machine gun, while a .50-caliber machine gun was distinguished as a "big sewing machine gun" (piatut-sahkuna' tawo'i').[54]

Roderick Red Elk recalled how the group decided on a code term for the tank:

Well we kind of set around in groups you know and we kicked it around [the proposed term] and we all agreed on something and we'd go with it. We would sit around just like this, just kind of battin' the breeze. We got to talking about that and somebody come up with an idea to call a tank a turtle. Somebody asked him why. He says, "Well the only reason I came up with a turtle is a turtle is like a tank. It's got a hard shell and that's the only reason I believe we could associate the turtle with a tank." We kicked that around and as we passed one word we would write it down.[55]

The same process had to be repeated for various types of artillery and aircraft. Artillery was distinguished by the caliber size, using standard Comanche numbers, and by the addition of "big" and "small." As a result, various prefixes of names or numbers were added to the basic word for gun to distinguish various forms of firearms. Thus, wahatᵫ mo'ovetᵫ piata'wo'i'—literally, "two-fives or double-five big gun"—was used to specify the .55-caliber Howitzer "Long Tom," and "8, 8 big gun" was used to designate an .88-caliber artillery piece, while "forty turtles" equaled forty tanks. Other terms simply referred to larger-caliber artillery as piata'wo'i' (big guns/cannons), and smaller-caliber artillery as tᵫtaatᵫ piata'wo'i' (small big guns/cannons).[56]

Thus, Comanches associated these modern military inventions with existing familiar elements. Similarly, because only one word existed in the Comanche language for all types of airplanes, new terms also had to be created for different types of planes, and the same principle of a base word with various prefixes was used for distinguishing different types of aircraft. As Roderick Red Elk explained:

That airplane, now that was something else too. There's so many different types. The very first thing they wanted to know was about a bomber. Now how are we going to tell them it's a bomber? We did the same thing, we kicked it around and kicked it around and somebody come up and said, "Hey I got an idea." He said, "We can't get an association real close," but he said, "I got an idea." So we said, "Let's have it." He says, "Let's call it a pregnant airplane." Somebody asked him why. "Well you see all those bombs under the wing, see those two big 500 pounders under there. You look up in the sky and look at it. What does it remind you of?" Somebody said a pregnant woman. So that's how the bomber got its name, no'avakatᵫ hutsuu, pregnant bird.[57]

With bombers as "pregnant birds," the bombs inside became known as "baby birds." Different terms also had to be created for different types of enemy. Each session Foster introduced five or six new words and held reviews of all words previously agreed upon. Everyone contributed in the creation of coded terms. As Forrest Kassanavoid recalled:

103

He'd [Lieutenant Foster] just throw the word out to us and then we'd all get into a little huddle . . . different guys, and then we'd get together and say all right maybe this is what we ought to call it and we'd agree on some particular word, you know.[58]

Eventually Foster developed a list of approximately 250 military words for which there were no existing Comanche counterparts, and thus a code term for each was devised. The remaining code talkers stated that too much time had passed to remember exactly who devised each code term; however, they all indicated that some members devised many terms while others devised fewer terms. Forrest Kassanavoid remembered devising the term for a bayonet—tawo'i' nahuu', or "gun knife."[59] As one code talker explained, "There was three major things we talked about: a tank, a machine gun, and an airplane." The code terms remembered by the surviving members and Major General (Ret.) Hugh Foster are listed in Appendix F.

Because the Comanche recruits spoke both Comanche and English fluently, the extent of coding needed was limited. Training was generally limited to no more than two hours a session or half of a day, three days a week, for four weeks. While the training was conducted over a period of some four months, the majority of the coded terms were devised and perfected within about four weeks. As Haddon Codynah described the initial code formation, "It was not a peaceful time. Everybody had his own pet term for something—and one was about as good as another—but we finally came up with a code that worked. . . . We must have driven them crazy. We almost went crazy ourselves figuring out the original code."[60]

In good weather the group often met outside under a tree for code training sessions. The code talkers spent most of their time in the Harmony Church Area of Ft. Benning, where the Fourth Signal Company barracks, orderly room, supply room, motor pool, and other resources were located. On inclement days, they met in a classroom building. The schedule for training varied according to circumstances and the numerous other duties that individuals held, which sometimes forced classes to be canceled. To test the use of the code, field practices were conducted. One day a week was usually spent in field exercises, where communications equipment was set up two to three hundred yards apart, out of the range of vocal, visual, and physical contact. Connecting lines were then linked to a switchboard, and practice in sending and receiving messages in coded Comanche was held with Lieutenant Foster providing various messages to be sent. During garrison training, messages were taken from segments of newspapers, magazine articles, weather reports, or anything close to hand. Since the operators knew that no one would

TABLE 3.2. *Fourth Infantry Division Code Terms (SHAFE [Supreme Headquarters Allied Forces Expedition])*

1st Army—Master
3rd Army—Lucky
12th Army—Eagle

7th Corps

4th Infantry Division—Cactus
  8th Infantry Regiment—Cabbage
  12th Infantry Regiment—Cargo
  22nd Infantry Regiment—Caisson

4th Signal Company—Canine

Detail of 8th Infantry Regimental (Cabbage) Levels
  Regimental Commander—Cabbage 6
  Chief of Staff/Executive Officer—Cabbage 5
  Supply—Cabbage 4
  Operations—Cabbage 3
  Intelligence—Cabbage 2
  Personnel/Adjutant—Cabbage 1

Detail of Battalion Levels
  Individual Battalions
    1st Battalion—Red
    2nd Battalion—White
    3rd Battalion—Blue

Individual Companies (by standard Phonetic Alphabet)
  1st Rifle Company or A Company—Able
  2nd Rifle Company or B Company—Baker
  3rd Rifle Company or C Company—Charlie
  Weapons Company or D Company—Dog

---

be receiving their messages, even jokes were used for practicing the transmission and reception of messages.

Members also had to memorize, in addition to coded Comanche terms, numerous code names for the various units of command under the Allied forces in the European front. Each division had an associated set of code names, from the divisional level down to individual companies, that were composed of standard English words. Table 3.2 lists the standard code terms for the Fourth Infantry Division.

An operator simply rang up the line he needed and specified in English the list of code terms, which indicated the level he needed to speak with. Thus, "Cactus 6" = the division commanding general, "Cab-

106   bage 6" = the Eighth Infantry regimental commander. "Cactus, Cabbage, Red, Able" designated the Fourth Infantry Division, Eighth Infantry Regiment, First Battalion, First, or "A," Company. "Cabbage Red 6" designated the Eighth Infantry Regiment, First Battalion, regimental commander, and so on. These terms were never changed throughout the war. When assigned out in a regiment, members often sent messages back to the Fourth Signal Company construction team or wire chief (Canine 6, the company commander of the Fourth Signal Company), or to the Fourth Infantry Division operations officer (Cactus 3). In sending a message (1) an operator first rang up the other end in English using English code terms such as "Hello, give me Cabbage 6" (the Eighth Infantry regimental commander); (2) the sending operator would then say in English, "Give me one of the code talkers"; (3) then he would send the actual message in coded Comanche.[61]

As Forrest Kassanavoid explained:

You would say "give me one of the code talkers" and they'd put him on. You'd say it in English and then you'd give him the message [in Comanche]. Hell, the Krauts could probably tell you who you were going to talk to, but once you started talking code in Comanche, they wouldn't know what the Hell you were talking about.[62]

Another code talker similarly reflected:

I often wondered what those Krauts thought when they heard it. They probably said, "What the heck is going on there anyway?"[63]

Impromptu Alphabetic Spelling

In addition to using the list of coded military terms, the impromptu use of informal coded spelling made the Comanche code even harder for the enemy to decipher. The Navajo Code Talkers employed a standardized alphabet by spelling in English using the first letters of translated Navajo words. For example, Saipan could be spelled Disbeh = sheep, wolla-che = ant, tkin = ice, bi-sodih = pig, be-la-sana = apple, nesh-chee = nut, with multiple and interchangeable forms for frequently used letters such as vowels (Paul 1973). As an unwritten language, Comanche had no standardized alphabet in 1941, and none was ever developed during training. Yet despite the absence of a standardized alphabet, the Comanche Code Talkers were able to remedy this communications problem with the same method that was employed by the Navajo Code Talkers, through the use of a form of alphabet-based impromptu spelling.

While the Comanche language contained many words which did

not necessitate coding (such as mountain, river, hill, road), proper place names posed a problem, as they were both necessary and without any existing analogous term in Comanche. Impromptu spelling was used only rarely and informally when a code talker needed to spell out an object or, more commonly, a proper place name, such as Paris or Berlin, for which there was no Comanche equivalent, for which no coded military term had been devised, and that could not be spoken in regular English for security purposes. Thus, Comanche words were informally used to convey and represent the letters of the English alphabet, according to the first letter of the English translation of each Comanche word.

Charles Chibitty (Hidden Path 2000) explained that when reading maps in Comanche over the phone or on radio they would call out numbers from the top and sides of the map to designate an area by their point of intersection. They would then indicate whether they were at or near that location. When asked what town they were closest to, the other code talker would respond with "Meekununa" (Now listen to me) and begin to speak a list of Comanche words. When translated into English, the first letter of each word would spell out the name of the designated town. As one member explained:

> When we can't say something, we say, "Meekununa: Now listen to me." The first thing that comes into mind, we say it and take the letter of the first word [the first letter of the word translated into English] and we could spell anything out. . . . That's the way we spell names.[64]

In other words, an impromptu and noncoded Comanche word was picked for each English alphabet letter according to the first letter of its English equivalent. Thus saddi (dog) represented the letter D, tuhka (eat) the letter E, sonipu (grass) the letter G, and so on. As another member explained, a code talker would simply say, "now listen to me," and pronounce a list of words that the receiving operator wrote down and, realizing that they were neither grammatical sentences nor code terms, immediately recognized as spelling. Thus, by reciting a list of Comanche words for translation into English, the code talkers could spell out proper place names such as towns, identify objects lacking prior Comanche or code terms, report locations, or clarify messages if the receiving code talker was unable to hear or understand what had been said. In addition, spelling could also be used with standard Comanche numbers to specify planes such as the P-47.[65]

One member indicated that a code talker might say that he was going to primarily use words from a specific category to spell with, such as all animals. Thus, for example, Paris could be spelled out as Wasape'atuhkapu (pear) = P, aniku'ra (ant) = A, and so on.[66] In other cases a variety of unrelated words might be used. Thus any Comanche word could potentially be used to represent the first letter of its English counterpart. Haddon Codynah elaborated on the process:

> Like A B C, alphabetic. Well for a B, maybe we call it a bear and then we put . . . how we would say it in Comanche and spell it as close as we can ourselves and put it down. Bear—wasa'pe. Wasa'pe means bear. . . . See we got that all down in groups and when we went to give a signal we just call that this and say it in our own Indian language and write it down and we can make out a message ourselves. We could say different types of guns, trucks, and this and that, describing them in Army [style], nothing but Army [style]. And we write it down, we write it down in Comanche as close as we could spell it. And each one of us we knows what it's all about. See we all learned the same thing. . . . Boy you heard some Comanche talking when we started up.[67]

One of the code talkers recalled a humorous incident during a demonstration of their code talking for a group of officers while training in Georgia:

> One time we were at Augusta, Georgia, at the golf course and we were doing it [an exhibition] for the big brass, generals, colonels, and everything. And one of our code talkers that went to college then was Morris Sunrise Tabbyetchy. When he got through with his message the officer looked at it and said, "This man don't know how to spell. It's misspelled."[68]

Several features made the Comanche code nearly impossible to break. Foremost, it was contained only in the heads of Lieutenant Foster and the seventeen Comanche Code Talkers. Second, while the code terms were standardized among the members, the occasional spelling was randomly chosen by the operator and thus was nonstandardized in selection. Third, there was little in the form of records and paperwork, and no written Comanche language or alphabet. Finally, Lieutenant Foster had the only complete written copy of the code terms and later lost his original code book in the sands of North Africa, while serving in the North African campaign.[69]

Publicity and Recreation

While great efforts were made to keep the training and future use of the Navajo as code talkers secret (Paul 1973; Tully 1995), no such attempt was made with the Comanches. Members indicate that other Comanches at home knew that they had been recruited for the purpose of speaking Comanche, but had no real knowledge that they were using a formally devised code. Although their training was known in the Comanche community, it was difficult for the recruits to fully inform their relatives back home of what they were doing. As Roderick Red Elk explained:

> We couldn't tell them about what we were doing on this code part. Heck, we didn't even know what we were doing to be real truthful with you. We were making up things as we went. We were laying our own ground rules is what we were doing.[70]

Members of the Comanche unit indicate that security was apparently not a concern. Indeed, the surviving code talkers indicate that some of the local officers even utilized their presence in recreational events as a means to gain prestige among the other local officers. More dangerous, however, was the well-publicized media exposure throughout the eastern United States coastal region. Shortly after their basic training at Ft. Benning, publicity throughout the East Coast frequently featured newspaper articles, with close-up pictures of the code talkers, describing their training and the uniqueness of their language as a coded communications device. Several articles specifically stated that the Comanche language was being used in coded form. One member even remembered the Associated Press coming to do an article and take photographs of them. A number of newspaper clippings provided by the surviving code talkers, of articles originally published between the spring of 1941 and March of 1942, demonstrate the lack of concern for security surrounding the code talkers' training at Ft. Benning, Georgia.

As one article from the *Sunday Ledger-Enquirer* of Columbus, Georgia, publicly stated:

> And they're all volunteers. But behind it there's a story. The Comanche language is unwritten. Up in the battle lines it can't be decoded. Tapping into a telephone or intercepting a radio message would do an enemy no good, no matter how alert the enemy was in decoding messages. So with that in mind, an official at——[illegible] sent his request to the War Department. The War Department, sympathetic with the idea, made it known to the Department of the Interior. The Department of the Interior spread the word around over the various tribes in the west that the Great White Father had need for his subjects, but only for a certain number. . . . The competitive spirit ran high. The tribes were maneuvered through an

"GET HIM BACK ON THAT SCALE AND WEIGH HIM AGAIN!"

elimination process until they had dwindled to three, the Comanches, the Hopi, and the Apaches, and in the finals the Comanches came out on top. Their tribe was chosen.[71]

A similar article entitled "4th Signal Grew with Division," also contained a picture of the group, detailed descriptions of the Fourth Signal unit's formation, and the role of the Comanches as code talkers. Surprisingly, this article was published by the Fourth Division (Motorized) itself:

> When the Fourth Division wishes to convey a message which cannot be understood or decoded by the enemy, it merely calls upon the Comanche Indians, who are assigned to the 4th Signal Corps [Company]. An unrecorded language, the Comanche tongue is completely unintelligible to anyone but a Comanche.

and:

> A dozen Comanche Indians from Oklahoma reported as a unit last December and January. Chosen primarily because the Comanche language is an unrecorded one and valuable for secret communication, the Comanches proved to be among the ablest men in the Company. In February 1941, the Company received 345 selectees from signal training for work throughout the Division. After an intensive two month training, 110 selectees remained with the Company and the others were distributed throughout the Division.[72]

Although written in a light spirit and containing much stereotyping of Indians, these newspaper articles, in hindsight, represented a potentially serious threat to military security. Not only had the media publicly stated that the Comanches had been chosen as communications operators, but they had also relayed information pertaining to the elimination of other tribal languages from possible wartime use. Had the Comanche code been used more frequently or widely in the European theater and had this broadcasted information fallen into the wrong hands, the Axis forces might have had time to counter the usefulness of the Comanche language, or, having captured any of the code talkers and identified them through these numerous media pictures, could have subjected them to forceful interrogation. However, the small size of the Comanche unit precluded the usefulness of any such actions by Axis forces. The lack of secrecy was also recognized by all of the code talkers, who indicated that there was not any real effort to keep their activities secret from the heavy publicity of East Coast newspapers. As one code talker described, "There was no need to keep it secret, others simply couldn't understand the Comanche language, and even other Comanches didn't know the code words."[73]

Despite the newspaper and popular press, most fellow soldiers, by their own accounts, had little or no idea what the Comanches were really doing. In addition, measures were taken to ensure the secrecy of the actual code formation and use of the code in field exercises. As fellow Fourth Signal Company member Ernest Stahlberg described, during their time at Ft. Benning "they were isolated from us during [their] sessions with Lt. Foster. We were told to stay away, although at the time I didn't know why. Even in combat very few knew of them. . . . While training as talkers we were ordered to stay away from all the 'sessions' given by Lt. Foster." In reading a draft of this manuscript in 2000, Stahlberg, who was partners with code talker Simmons Parker in combat, remarked, "I am being educated about the 4th Division and the Code Talkers. Most of it is new to me. That's how secret everything was."[74]

Despite their numerous duties as communications operators, the Comanche Code Talkers were actively involved in two forms of well-publicized recreational activities during their training at Forts Benning and Gordon, performances of traditional song and dance, and boxing.

DANCING EXHIBITIONS   One day while the code talkers were out in the woods on a field exercise practicing radio communications, the group took a break, during which their sergeant temporarily left the group. One of the Comanches started singing an Indian song over the radio, to which a couple of the others jumped up and started dancing. Returning unexpectedly, the sergeant caught them in the act, but remained behind a tree watching them. When he stepped out from behind the tree, the embarrassed performers stopped. Curious about the activity, the sergeant began to inquire about the singing and dancing. A couple of days later, the sergeant asked the Comanches if they could perform for a crowd, an invitation they gladly accepted. Two of the members, Charles Chibitty and Simmons Parker, sent home for their war dance costumes, which were sent to them. With these two as dancers, the others went along to sing and provide music for them. Needing a drum to perform, the Comanches were given a two-and-a-half-ton truck and money to go to town and buy some hides. Obtaining two cattle hides from a local slaughterhouse in Columbus, Georgia, and a truck wheel rim, they made their own drum. Some of the members remembered Sergeant Boozer being so enthusiastic about the activity that he brought them beer to drink.[75]

Soon after this performance, the Comanches were taken to Colum- **111**

112   bus, Georgia, where they performed for the Chamber of Commerce. Afterward, the local newspapers lit up with the following headlines: "Wild Comanches Have Hit Columbus, Georgia." The company was immediately flooded with requests for the group to perform, for which their sergeant became their unofficial "agent." Major Terence J. Tully (the division signal officer) and Sergeant John Boozer went along for publicity. While stationed at Ft. Benning and Camp Gordon, Georgia, the Comanches frequently performed songs and dances for different companies on the bases. Wellington Mihecoby and Morris Tabbyetchy served as spokesmen for the dance troupe, explaining the different types of songs and dances to the spectators. The Comanches performed mostly for military personnel and their families, most of whom had never seen any form of Indian dancing. Individual companies would invite them to perform, sponsoring a big feast and cold beer afterwards. While the majority of the Comanches' cultural performances were limited to their assignments at Ft. Benning and Camp Gordon, they also performed at local YMCA gymnasiums for civilians near Ft. Benning. Wherever they went, headlines of "Wild Comanches Hit Town" preceded their performances. As their popularity grew, the Comanches increasingly made friends everywhere and were virtually "on tour," performing throughout Georgia, Mississippi, Alabama, and Florida.[76]

THE FOURTH SIGNAL COMPANY'S COMANCHE BOXING TEAM During peacetime, U.S. Army athletics were very popular and avidly supported. While at Ft. Benning, Lieutenant Keene, a collegiate athlete himself, formed an all-Comanche boxing team during the winter and early spring of 1941–1942 and served as its manager and promoter. However, as with the Comanches' experiences in basic training, the army was in for yet another surprise with its Comanche pugilists. As many of the Comanches had been involved in boxing programs during their boarding school days, several of them were quite adept in using their fists. Most of the members had boxed at Fort Sill Indian School, while Charles Chibitty had boxed at Haskell Indian School in Haskell, Kansas, and Wellington Mihecoby had boxed at Cameron College in Lawton, Oklahoma. Melvin Permansu had won more than one Oklahoma State Golden Gloves title in the 112-pound category while at Fort Sill Indian School in Lawton, Oklahoma. Albert Nahquaddy Jr. recalled that their training sergeant, Sergeant Boozer, once asked the group if any of them wanted to fight him. When they all enthusiastically volunteered, he suddenly changed his mind.[77]

    Because they had no real facilities, training was initially held in their barracks. When the team first started, the Comanches had a member for every category except light-heavyweight (175). The team had its first

TABLE 3.3. *The Fourth Signal Company Comanche Boxing Team*

Simmons Parker—flyweight (112)
Melvin Permansu—bantamweight (118)
Ralph Wahnee—featherweight (126)
Anthony (Tony) Tabbytite—lightweight (135)
Charles Chibitty—welterweight (147)
Elgin Red Elk—middleweight (160)
Anglo substitutes used—light heavyweight (175)
Perry Noyabad—heavyweight (up to 201)
Wellington Mihecoby—Trainer

meet with the Ft. Benning Military Police Company boxing team and won every match except one—the one category which the Comanches had to forfeit—light-heavyweight. The following day the local newspaper headlines read "Wild Comanches, Gone Crazy. They're Whipping the M.P.'s." The next day, the M.P. who had won the forfeited category came to the Comanches and asked if he could join their team. Throughout World War II many non-Indians commonly called Indians by nicknames such as "Chief," regardless of tribe or status. In turn, the Comanches, who had distinctly Indian-sounding surnames, dubbed their new Anglo teammate "Chief Buffalo." As one code talker explained, "We took him and made an Indian out of him." With a complete roster, the Comanches proceeded to make and to take challenges from different company teams. The Comanches sailed through the matches with relative ease. Table 3.3 lists the members of the team and their respective weight categories.[78]

The Fourth Signal Company's Comanche boxing team became so popular among the Fourth Division and the officers that it was given extra time to train, had its own "training" table at the mess hall, and received special meals. One of the code talkers recalled how they got out of a lot of extra duties, such as guard duty and K.P., because their fellow soldiers were so supportive of them as their company boxing team. Several of the Comanche boxing team members distinguished themselves further in the ring. Elgin Red Elk won the 160-pound class Georgia State Golden Gloves championship in Atlanta, Georgia, and Melvin Permansu went to the finals in the bantam weight.[79] Charlie Chibitty won three straight fights by knockout. A newspaper account of one of his fights describes the young fighter's tenacity:

Private Chibitty, a wily Indian slugger from the 4th Signal Company, won an unpopular decision over Pvt. Brock of the 29th Field Artillery Battalion in a lightweight class III bout. Brock landed the more solid blows throughout the fight, shaking his foe with hard right crosses to the jaw in the third, but the Indian won the nod on the basis of a consistent left which he kept in Brock's face during the entire bout.[80]

Originally slated as a citywide amateur tournament, an exhibition boxing tournament was held in Golden Park, and brought together some of the best fighters from Ft. Benning, Columbus, and Phoenix City, Georgia. Several of the Comanche boxers entered, and once again, Ft. Benning's Fourth Signal Company boxers walked off with several of the honors, taking four of the many bouts, and two by KO's. As the report of the fight described:

> Ralph Wahnee stopped Tom Harmon of the 29th Infantry in the third round after a slugfest that raised the fans from their seats. Charlie Chibitty, packing dynamite in both fists, stopped Pennington cold in the first round and won the bout when referee George Ross stopped it after seeing that Pennington was clearly outclassed.

Comedy for the evening included a battle royal between four Afro-American soldiers. The bout was called when the referee was knocked out![81]

In another match, the Comanches were challenged by the Twenty-ninth Field Artillery Battalion, the current post champs. Their newly made friend from the recently defeated military police boxing team again fought for the Comanche team, which still had no light-heavyweight. Charles Chibitty remembers getting floored in the match, and after a heated exchange of words with his opponent, proceeded to knock him out in the second round. The Comanches won the match handily and became the post champs.[82]

Forrest Kassanavoid recalled another humorous incident during the group's boxing days. An Anglo soldier named Chambers was friends with one of the code talkers and, although not particularly adept at boxing, frequently sparred with them. Prior to one upcoming match, Ralph Wahnee was sick, and the company doctor would not let him fight. At the suggestion of the other Comanches, Lieutenant Keene thought it would be all right to let Chambers fight at 126 in place of Wahnee. Because Chambers had a somewhat clownlike personality, everyone thought he would lose, which would not make the other team look so bad if the Comanches lost at least one match. When the match finally started Simmons Parker (112) quickly knocked his man out. Likewise, Melvin Permansu (118) quickly defeated his man. Entering the ring to fight in the 126 category, Chambers began shuffling around and displaying his agility, as boxers often do before starting. However, the other team failed to provide a man, and eventually its coach threw in a towel to forfeit the category. With everyone expecting him to lose, Chambers won, even if it was by forfeit. "The next day Chambers was a big hero," Kassanavoid recalled.[83] As their successes continued to pile up, the Comanches retained their boxing success as divisional champs. As their popularity grew, the entire company became avid fans of the Comanches and regularly turned out to see the Comanches fight.

The widespread and stereotypical media exposure had an effect on the local Georgia residents. Apparently some of the recruits who had been stationed longer at Ft. Benning than the Comanches were a little jealous of the immediate and constant attention and publicity that the newer recruits received. As a result, the Comanches were frequently challenged by GIs who wanted to test them. The media also gave the local Georgians a stereotypical image of the group as "Wild Comanches." As Roderick Red Elk recalled:

The natives there in Georgia were kind of, well write-ups like that in the paper, I guess is what scared them. They were kind of afraid of us. We'd go to town and there was always two or three of us together, they'd see us coming and they'd just move over to the other side of the street like they was, you know, really afraid of us. . . . I guess it was just those write-ups saying there was some "Wild Comanches" in town. Other than that, we never did have any trouble. We had some trouble with other branches of the service, I guess on account of those write-ups that's the only thing I know of. . . .

They were always challenging us, to meet them downtown. They didn't think we were that tough. I guess they was gonna, they just had to try and see. . . . We took care of ourselves pretty good.[84]

As word of their boxing skills spread, the respect the Comanches received increased, while the confrontations prompted by fellow soldiers decreased. Eventually, the Comanches could not get any further challenges from any teams. As Roderick Red Elk described:

One day they called and said they couldn't get any more matches, but there was one guy that would like to have an exhibition bout. He said, "You all look good. Just pick any of your men." We asked him, "What weight?" and he said, "Oh, he's probably about middle weight." So we go down there and put our middle weight in and we told him, "Now just play with him, don't try to hurt him. Just work

115

116   in there, jab him, hit him, and go out." Well, like all good things, everything had to come to an end. This old boy got a little too cocky and he'd run in there and jab him and hit him and run out and dance around. All at once, this old boy put a hay maker on him and knocked him colder than a wedge. It took us about ten minutes to revive him. When our fellow comrade [Elgin Red Elk] got knocked out, that put the quietus to our boxing career. (1992:2)

Later, in 1942, the boxing team was temporarily discontinued when Lieutenant Keene and the Comanches were given different assignments. However, the Comanches continued to box at Ft. Benning, Camp Gordon, in South Carolina, and later at Ft. Dix, New Jersey.

Movements and Final Training

After returning from Dry Prong, Louisiana, on August 27, 1941, the Fourth Division remained at Ft. Benning until it was moved to Ft. Jackson, South Carolina, on October 30, 1941, to participate in the First Army Carolina Maneuvers of 1941. The Fourth Division returned to Ft. Benning, Georgia, on December 3, 1941, just prior to the attack on Pearl Harbor. After several additional weeks of training, the Fourth Division transferred from Ft. Benning, Georgia, to Camp Gordon, near Augusta, Georgia, on December 29, 1941 (Stanton 1984:82). Lieutenant Foster (wire platoon leader) and the code talkers were moved to Camp Gordon in advance to install telephone communications for the division. To prepare for training exercises, the signal company always had to enter the field prior to the rest of the division to install the basic wire network for telephone and teletype communications. Following such exercises, the signal troops remained behind to collect the miles of wire and cable that had been installed over a very large area. As this customarily took four to ten days, and everyone had additional duties, the code talkers were precluded from holding any formal training sessions. Consequently, as the signal company's duties generally made them arrive in advance and depart after the remainder of the division, their movement dates do not correlate with the official dates for the entire division. With the final code training completed, other communications training and practice were undertaken at Camp Gordon.

At Camp Gordon radio training and telephone communications work increased as members laid the communications wire for upcoming war games. Albert Nahquaddy Jr. recalled a humorous incident involving how they talked Lieutenant Foster into climbing up one of the poles they were running lines along: "So we got him up there and sure enough the Division Signal officer came by and said, 'What are you doing up there,

Foster? Get off of that pole. Let them boys do that.'" The members got quite a laugh out of seeing how fast Lieutenant Foster came down the pole as he was reprimanded by a senior officer.[85]

In early February 1942, Foster was promoted to 1st lieutenant and, although requesting to remain with the Fourth Division, was ordered to Harvard University in March of 1942 and later to MIT for graduate studies for secret training on radar electronics. He never saw the Comanches again until long after the war. Foster later served in North Africa and Italy, and went on to have a distinguished military career, retiring on September 1, 1975, as a major general.[86]

The Fourth Infantry Division (Motorized) proceeded to the Carolina Maneuver Area for more training on July 7, 1942, before returning to Camp Gordon, Georgia, on August 31, 1942. On April 12, 1943, the division was transferred to Ft. Dix, New Jersey, where it was redesignated as the Fourth Infantry Division on August 3 (Stanton 1984:81–82). While at Ft. Dix, the division undertook anti-aircraft training in vehicles containing new .50-caliber machine guns in nearby Massachusetts. In July 1942, the Fourth was alerted for overseas duty and pulled from the Carolina Maneuvers, but was instead prepared for additional training in Florida.

After returning to Ft. Dix, the division next went to Camp Gordon Johnston near Pensacola, Florida, on September 19, 1943, for II Corps Carrabelle Maneuvers, which included newly developed methods of amphibious training with landing craft personnel (LCP) boats. Here they practiced invasion training on beaches and learned how to swim with their clothing and full gear on. Roderick Red Elk recalled another of the group's humorous incidents:

We go down there to take training and the first thing they asked was if we knew how to swim. Naturally Indians are not very good swimmers, so we all held up our hands and said, "We don't know how to swim." So we were excused from taking amphibious training, but we started swimming classes. They took us out to a pool and made us jump off the big platform that was out there. When the instructor wasn't watching, we'd get out there and start water fighting. We went to school like that for a week and a half and they finally caught us and kicked us out. They said, "You guys know how to swim, you're just pulling our leg." (1992:3)

Forrest Kassanavoid remembered this same incident when the members of the group produced "some mud crawling and crazy strokes like you never seen," which resulted in their getting some "easy" days around the pool to "practice" their swimming.[87] The Comanches finished their **117**

118 amphibious training, then were moved again. It was at this point that members stated they knew they were making the final preparation before going overseas.

Following this training, members were allowed a brief furlough to return home. Numerous Native American Church prayer meetings, Christian church prayer meetings, and traditional blessings were held for the departing servicemen of many tribes, who knew that they were about to go overseas (Meadows 1995). The practice of holding Native American Church (peyote) meetings to pray for and bless departing servicemen, including giving them a blessed peyote button to carry in a small leather bag on their person in combat, was a common form of religious and community preparation for Plains Indian servicemen in World War II (Holm 1993; Meadows 1995). As Haddon Codynah recalled:

> There was a peyote meeting for me at the church. I was given a piece of peyote that had been blessed to keep me from harm. I think all the others were given one too. It must have worked, for all of us came back home. Yes, I still have it.[88]

Nearly all of the Comanches had small peyote buttons given to them in small leather pouches or bundles to carry on their person while overseas and in the war as a means of personal protection. Forrest Kassanavoid recalled how his father gave him a small bundle containing a peyote button during his furlough about six months before being sent overseas. Some wore them around the neck while others carried them in their pockets. Coming from a strong Christian-oriented family, Morris Sunrise did not carry peyote.[89] Traditional Comanche songs were often dedicated by elders and dance-oriented "Powwow People" to Comanches serving overseas. Radio station WNAD in Norman, Oklahoma, featured an hour-long Saturday morning program called "Indians for Indians Hour," in which members and singing groups of various tribes were invited to perform live. A friend of Forrest Kassanavoid's grandmother dedicated a song to him overseas during one such program.[90]

Preparing to go overseas, the Fourth was again moved to a holding area at Ft. Jackson, South Carolina, on December 1, 1943. The men were next staged at Camp Kilmer, New Jersey, on January 4, 1944, where they received inoculation shots and were processed to go overseas. The Fourth Division was then moved to New York on January 18. The Fourth was again moved to New Jersey, where three members, Albert Nahquaddy Jr., Anthony Tabbytite, and Ralph Wahnee, were discharged at Ft. Dix, leaving only fourteen code talkers.[91] The Fourth Division sailed from Hoboken, New Jersey, in a large convoy of British transport ships, arriving in Liverpool, England, on January 26, 1944 (Stanton 1984:81–

82). The Fourth Signal Company boarded the U.S.A.T. *George Washington* on January 18, 1944, and arrived in Liverpool on January 29, 1944.[92] Haddon Codynah recalled their departure:

> We was in Camp Kilmer, New Jersey, when we processed, the whole division. . . . They loaded us up one night on a train and took us down to the docks. I don't know whether it was New York, Brooklyn, or wherever the ships were, and we couldn't even see outside, they pulled down the curtains and wouldn't let us see until we got down to the docks. Then we started, of course we had our duffel bags, that was all we had, what we could carry. Then we got off that train and they marched us through. We heard a band playing, it was the Salvation Army that was playing. Boy we seen a big ship there and big doors open, big planks, and they marched us on there. We loaded up all that night as far as I know. I guess the whole division was loading up. I don't know, later on that night or that [following] morning, we finally heard that propeller moving, you know, begin to crank up. You could tell it was beginning to move a little bit. . . . They wouldn't let us get out of where our quarters was for about a couple of days until we got out at sea.[93]

Roderick Red Elk recalled that nearly everyone on the ship suffered from seasickness and wouldn't go to the mess hall.[94] Taking an indirect, zigzagging route, the trip took several days. Upon arriving in England, they were sequestered with other American troops at Tiverton, Devon. After receiving their equipment, the soldiers waterproofed all of it in preparation for the damp Northern European environment. Although limited by space, communications and some physical training were held throughout the English countryside. By May 1944, the Fourth had moved to a secluded marshlands area, as preparations for Operation Overlord (the invasion of France at Normandy) neared completion. Here, mock-practice invasions using large landing craft with tanks and vehicles, and including simulated explosions, gun and artillery fire, and casualties, were held two to three times a month. On the night of April 27–28, 1944, VII Corps was undergoing training practice, known as Operation Tiger, for the eventual landing at Utah Beach. Missed schedules, subsequent traffic jams of ships, and the late arrival of naval craft at embarkation points created many logistical problems. Even worse, German E-boats slipped past the screen of British destroyers, sinking two LSTs (landing ship, tank) and damaging six others. More than 749 men were killed and 300 wounded by the explosions or drowning (Ambrose 1994:139). The Comanche Code Talkers were among the lucky.

119

The code talkers and the Allied troops had finished their training. While in England, Comanche Code Talker Morris Sunrise was transferred to the I-Corps for his skill in cryptography. With only thirteen Comanche Code Talkers remaining in the Fourth Signal Company, D-Day was fast approaching.

"ʉTEKWAPA NAKA: I HEAR WHAT YOU SAY."

MILITARY ORGANIZATION AND COMMUNICATIONS SERVICE

To understand the role of the Comanche Code Talkers prior to their initial entry into combat, and their functions during the Second World War, it is necessary to gain an understanding of the organization and workings of a United States Army infantry division in 1941. While this brief chapter is of a detailed and technical nature, it is necessary to fully understand the communications systems the Comanches learned and adapted to, and the manner in which they related their experiences as code talkers—in the military language as used by the United States Army Signal Corps.[1]

Distribution and Organization

In the 1940s, the infantry division was the main instrument of the army. "An infantry division is the smallest unit, composed of all the essential ground arms and services, which can conduct by its own means operations of tactical importance" (Hoegh and Doyle 1946:412). During World War II airborne and infantry divisions were structured as follows: at the base, a squad (usually nine to twelve men), then three squads to a platoon, three or four platoons to a company, three or four companies to a battalion, three or four battalions to a regiment, three or four regiments to a division, plus attached engineers, artillery, and other support personnel. On D-Day, U.S. infantry divisions contained between fifteen and twenty thousand men at full strength (Ambrose 1994:15). Table 4.1 illustrates the Fourth Infantry Division (Motorized) in 1941.

As of 1941, an infantry division had three infantry regiments, each of which had three rifle battalions, a division headquarters company (HQ),

TABLE 4.I. *The Fourth Infantry Division Combat Organization, 1944–1945, Showing Comanche Code Talker Distribution*

Active Units on Front Lines		Reserve Units
Rifle Companies	Rifle Companies	Rifle Companies
Rifle Battalion	Rifle Battalion	Rifle Battalion
*Art. Battalion	Art. Battalion	Art. Battalion
(2 code talkers)	(2 code talkers)	(2 code talkers recalled to division)
	(occasionally)	(occasionally)
*Inf. Regiment	Inf. Regiment	Inf. Regiment
(2 code talkers)	(2 code talkers)	(2 code talkers recalled to division)

Division Artillery
(2 code talkers)

Engineer Battalion

**4th Division Headquarters and Signal or Communications Center
(up to 6 code talkers near the Divisional Signal Center)

(Ordnance Company, Quartermaster Company,
Military Police, Medics, etc.)

I Corps (One to Five Divisions)
(Organic Artillery, Engineers, Signal Corps, and other units)

ARMY

*Code talkers most commonly provided communications between division and regiments, and sometimes between regiments and battalions.

**For a complete listing of organization and location of the Fourth Infantry Division (1941–1945) and its overseas wartime assignments, see Appendix C.

a heavy weapons company, plus assorted support elements. When a division was engaged in combat only two regiments were normally committed, with the remaining regiment as a reserve. Each division also had numerous other organic elements, such as division artillery, an engineer battalion, an ordnance company, a quartermaster company, military police, and medics. Each rifle battalion had a headquarters plus three rifle companies and a heavy weapons company equipped with mortars, heavy machine guns, recoilless rifles, etc.[2]

A corps was a tactical headquarters to which anywhere from one to five divisions were assigned, depending upon present needs. In essence, a corps was a "managerial" headquarters with organic artillery, engineers, signal corps, and other units that supported all elements of all assigned divisions on an "as needed" basis. Each individual corps was designated with Roman numerals, such as II CORPS (Second CORPS). Divisions frequently "floated around" on the battlefield and were reassigned from one corps to another according to current needs. Which divisions were assigned to a corps was often influenced by geographic features such as rivers, valleys, mountains, ridges, etc. A corps is not in the normal chain of logistic support from divisions to the rear echelons of support, but the corps is in the chain of command between an ARMY and a division. The number of corps assigned to an ARMY depended upon factors such as the size of the area to be controlled, the terrain, and mission involved.[3]

The Comanche Code Talkers were assigned to the Fourth Signal Company of the Fourth Infantry Division (Motorized). For the complete organizational structure of the Fourth Division from 1941 to 1945 see Appendix A. As of 1941, the Fourth Division was the only motorized division in the entire U.S. Army, and was established as an experimental structure to see how many vehicles of what types would be required for a divisional level of operations, and to determine what advantages or disadvantages were associated with particular configurations of vehicles. There was no specific relationship between the Fourth Infantry Division and the FOURTH ARMY. According to military usage, the identification of an ARMY in the field was always spelled out in capital letters to preclude confusion in sending and receiving messages.

Although trained as a group in the Fourth Signal Company, the thirteen Comanche Code Talkers who later saw combat action were distributed throughout the three infantry regiments, division artillery, and the division headquarters signal center. Radio and construction teams made up the signal detachment attached to a regimental combat team (an infantry regiment, field artillery battalion, company of engineers, medics, sometimes tanks, etc.). The Fourth Infantry Division consisted of the Eighth, Twelfth, and Twenty-second Infantry Regiments. Normally, each infantry regimental combat team (rct) contained a regiment of infantry, a battalion of artillery, a company of engineers, a company of medics, and several detachments—including a signal detachment with a radio team and a wire construction section of twenty-four men. Most of the code talkers were in either the radio or wire construction team. A pair of code talkers were assigned to each infantry regiment or regimental combat team (rct) and another pair to each attached artillery battalion. Each regimental combat team had a command post containing a signal detachment consisting of a radio team, and a wire team of six to eight men. The code talkers were usually members of the regimental radio or wire team, performed general duties, and were called as needed for communications jobs. At the regimental command post all members of the radio and wire team were usually within talking and

123

124   hearing distance of one another, and thus could be called over and instructed when needed. The two men forming a pair of code talkers were often members of the same platoon or section. Thus, for three infantry regiments (the Eighth, Twelfth, and Twenty-second) and four artillery battalions (the Twentieth, Twenty-ninth, Forty-second, and Forty-fourth) in the Fourth Infantry Division, as many as eight to ten code talkers were normally assigned to active positions simultaneously, as one infantry regiment and one artillery battalion were usually held in reserve.[4]

The Comanche Code Talkers were primarily used by officers at the divisional and regimental headquarters, and in battalion-level infantry and artillery units.[5] Only occasionally did individual companies on the front lines use code talkers. Radio teams were split up widely among the regiments, and members from the message center frequently traveled back and forth between the regiments carrying messages by jeep. Code talkers were sometimes rotated frequently, while at other times they remained with specific regimental units for lengthy periods. Each pair of code talkers remained at their assigned positions until one or both were relieved for rest or due to wounds received in service. Members were also periodically recalled for duty at division headquarters. Whenever an infantry regiment was relieved and placed in reserve, the four code talkers assigned to that regiment and its artillery battalion were generally recalled and sent back to the divisional headquarters. The remaining core of code talkers were located at the divisional headquarters near the signal center, where at least two were always on duty. The surplus of code talkers provided support for those code talkers currently assigned to individual combat units, and in addition to working at the divisional signal center, served as replacements for rotations. The ability to rotate code talkers resulted in a constantly available source of interchangeable replacements. Individual assignments and experiences varied, as some individuals were attached to only infantry regiments throughout the entire war, while others spent most of their time assigned to artillery battalions. Others had more varied assignments, moving between different organizational levels within the division. The periodic replacement of the members also ensured that most were familiar with the functions associated with providing communications for various infantry, artillery, and support elements.[6]

The Comanche Code Talkers were distributed by the regimental commanding officer (RCO). Their distribution changed in accordance with the width of the front and the intensity of the fighting. Members emphasized that because the European theater was a "fluid" war, the front frequently changed, and it was sometimes difficult to know exactly how close the enemy was. At Normandy, all of the code talkers were relatively close together in various regimental and divisional headquarters assignments. However, as the Allies advanced farther into Europe, the front widened and the code talkers were increasingly farther from one another. Individual pairs assigned to their respective infantry regiments and artillery battalions often did not see others for weeks or months at a time. Some code talkers did not see other members of the unit for periods of up to eleven months during the war. As Forrest Kassanavoid recalled, "Once we really started advancing, we didn't see some of the others until the war was almost over."[7] When recalled or recovering from light wounds, code talkers assigned to the divisional headquarters were often in daily contact with those presently assigned to the divisional headquarters. But even then they were sometimes separated and out on regular duties for periods of time. Occasionally, the members had the opportunity to speak to one another on the phone, but only occasionally, briefly, and for messages. When assigned to an infantry regiment, the code talkers were right up near the front lines. Although much of the European campaign was conducted during inclement weather, the code talkers stated that on clear days German troops were often within plain sight. Despite the varied locations of their assignments, all of the code talkers were always within range of enemy fire, as the division was never totally out of the combat zone. Because the rear echelon of the division was generally no more than one mile behind the front lines, it was always easily within the enemy range of fire. Sometimes the division pulled the support units too close to the front lines and they also received fire. Some of the code talkers stated that the bombing, strafing, and artillery fire they experienced were often worse at the divisional level than on the front lines.

Communications

The code talkers served as wire linemen, teletype operators, telephone switchboard operators, and motor messengers. Teletype, radio, wire operations, message center, and cryptographic operations were located in separate platoons. Within the wire platoon, there were separate sections for the linemen and the switchboard operators. Although most of the Comanches were in the wire platoon, they were dispersed throughout all these areas. At the divisional message center, the Comanches encoded and decoded messages as they sent and received them. As Ernest Stahlberg recalled of his and his partner Simmons Parker's service, "We were in the Message Center section. We delivered maps and overlays and secret documents for the various infantry and other units, especially at Bastogne, the Battle of the Bulge, and many other times."[8]

The primary duty of the Code Talkers in World War II centered on establishing and maintaining communications between the division and the regimental command (the individual infantry regiments) by wire. From the infantry regiment forward to its individual battalions and companies, each infantry regiment usually took care of its own communications and lines. Occasionally, however, the code talkers also provided additional communications between the infantry regiments and their battalion levels. Many communications links involved stringing wire with the aid of specially built trucks which held large rolls of field wire in the back. The wire was rolled out along a road or wherever the most direct route between a regiment and the division was. The code talkers then periodically attached the wire to tree stumps, fences, or other items that prevented the wire from getting run over and broken by tanks or any vehicles. Both Allied and Axis wires were frequently laid along the same course and were commonly clustered at trees, fence posts, intersections, or other convenient locations. Identification of individual communications lines was necessary, and all wire lines were periodically marked with colored identification tags containing the code name assigned to a particular unit. This allowed faster identification of one's line for linking in to receive or send messages and for checking for any broken lines to repair. Although lines were normally run along the ground, they were often placed on poles in locations with tank traffic to prevent the breaking of lines.

Near the front lines, the advancement of vehicles was frequently stalled by difficult terrain or intense artillery shelling. In these circumstances a team of two code talkers laid the wire manually, unrolling it by walking it on a smaller reel carried on a pipe handle. In 1944–1945, model W-110B telephone wire was used and consisted of a twisted pair of wires. Each wire had three steel and four copper conductors spiraled together, covered with rubber, overcovered with a woven cloth sleeve, then overcovered again with a tarred substance containing flecks of mica. W-110B wire was issued in one-mile reels for installation via trucks, and one-half-mile reels for laying by hand.[9] While the danger of shelling increased with proximity to the front, communication between the regiment and division depended upon the wire team being able to reach the regiments, to connect the two switchboards together with wire. The majority of wire strung by the Comanches connected either the division and infantry regiment or the division and division artillery. Occasionally other support units (engineers, medics, etc.) were linked through wire by the code talkers. The corps (the next echelon above the division) then brought a large round cable down to the wire team, who linked them to the division. Due to the cumbersome nature of these large cables, the corps was sometimes unable to get a cable to the division, and the wire team linked the corps and division with regular field wire. Shelling was always a danger during such communications work, and installing and recovering tactical wire required a great deal of running and real stamina. Major General Foster recalled that "the Comanches were good runners."[10]

Forrest Kassanavoid recalled being in France after the invasion, when he and others were tying lines together near dark. Coming to a railroad crossing, they were trying to decide whether to run their lines over or under the track. The local French told them that no trains had used the tracks since the Germans had invaded the area, so with no train traffic to cut the wires, the wire crew decided to run the line directly over the track to save time with night approaching. Barely an hour later, however, some American soldiers who had found a manually propelled handcart were seeking some entertainment and went for a ride down the tracks. They quickly severed the line. Kassanavoid and others then had to locate the break and splice it in the dark.[11]

Occasionally, code talkers provided communications between the regimental and battalion levels, which brought them much closer to the front lines. Each battalion had several line or rifle companies ahead of it which formed the actual front line. The battalion was directly behind these companies, and each battalion had one six-line switchboard. When code talkers worked at battalion headquarters they were very close to the front lines and were frequently subject to small-arms and mortar fire. Forrest Kassanavoid remembered being at a battalion headquarters in Germany when the battalion's advance had stalled. Just before dark, the battalion began to receive heavy machine gun fire from across the valley and took shelter in the basement of a farmhouse. Eventually, a number of rifle companies, moving up without protection or entrenchment, advanced to push back the German forces, allowing the battalion to continue its advance.[12]

Although wire and telephone were the major means of communication, radio was often used, since wire and phone lines were frequently knocked out from incoming artillery shelling. According to Forrest Kassanavoid, most regimental commanders preferred wire or telephone communication over radio communication because it allowed one to speak directly with the desired person. Radio required one to go to the location of a radio vehicle to send and receive messages, involved the use of many required terms such as "over and out," and often depended upon the use of a radio operator to send, receive, and then report messages, whereas wire communication provided a more direct and immediate link between two parties. According to Kassanavoid, most commanding officers wanted to be able to pick up a phone, place a call, report or check on a situation, and then hang up right where they were.[13] When the Comanches needed radios, they used both SCR (Signal Corps Radio) Model

"ᵁTEKWAPA NAKA: I HEAR WHAT YOU SAY."

299 and 399 radios. However, the Model EE-8A field telephone was more commonly used by the code talkers for communications transmission. Earlier models were contained in leather cases that were later replaced with more weather-resistant treated canvas cases.[14]

MESSAGES   The Comanche Code Talkers sent messages in everyday standard English as well as in coded Comanche. Communications in Comanche were normally sent only when a message required absolute security. There were two general types of messages sent by the code talkers, offensive and defensive. During maneuvers, both forms were practiced in field exercises. Defensive messages consisted primarily of reports of contacts with opposing forces, and their strengths and positions. Offensive messages generally focused on orders for movements, missions, resupply, and reports on one's own troops, equipment, and status.[15]

How messages were sent depended on the situation involved. The code talkers were usually available to the divisional, regimental, or artillery battalion commander. Only in rare instances did code talkers perform at the company level. Although necessary for security, normal procedure for sending messages in English was slow and time-consuming. At the regimental level, the regimental commander often wrote the message on a pad of paper, then gave it to a member of the message center, who in turn brought it to an operator to send. Thus, the normal channels in sending a message involved: (1) the officer who wrote the message, (2) receipt and coding or encoding by a member of the message center, (3) delivery to and transmission by an operator, (4) reception by the receiving operator, (5) relay to the message center, which would decode it, and (6) delivery of the message by the receiving message center to a receiving officer. If the message was urgent, the officer often wrote it out and delivered it in person. In every instance, however, officers wanted messages quickly, and this is where the code talkers contributed significantly. This slow process of multiple persons involved in encoding, sending, receiving, and decoding messages was exactly what the army was able to supersede by using the Comanche Code Talkers.

A code talker could quickly translate a written message mentally from English into coded Comanche and then transmit it verbally to another Comanche Code Talker on the other end, who could immediately receive and translate the message back into English for the appropriate recipient, thereby eliminating the time needed for tedious handwritten encoding and decoding. Sending messages for the code talkers was essentially no different than talking on the phone with a special list of coded words. Communication was accelerated and efficient, involved fewer channels, and while easy for the Comanche-speaking code talkers, was secure from enemy translation upon interception.[16]

COMBAT MESSAGES   In combat, messages sent by the code talkers were generally of a defensive nature, reporting on enemy troop locations, troop movements, types and strengths (numbers and resistance) of troops, and types and strengths of enemy weaponry (tanks, airplanes, machine guns, mortars, etc.). However, Allied or enemy troops and positions were also reported. Messages were also used to call for reserve troops, to request supplies, to request or direct artillery, and for summoning assistance by tanks. Occasionally, messages were used to pinpoint artillery and to call in air strikes. The quantity and content of messages varied greatly depending upon the circumstances and needs of the unit to which a code talker was assigned. Thus, some code talkers frequently sent requests for things such as air strikes, which others rarely did.[17]

In each case, the objective was to convey information in a form that was indecipherable by the enemy, thereby preventing the Germans from gaining military intelligence of either (1) the Allies' knowledge about Axis troops, or (2) information about Allied forces. Messages reporting the number and kind of prisoners captured, and the quantity and type of troops the Allies would be facing ahead, were frequently sent in Comanche, as the Allies did not want Germans to know they possessed information concerning the types and strengths of opposing troops.

Reports of enemy movements were also commonly sent in Comanche. Late in the war, when the German forces were nearly depleted, the Germans had been forced to conscript many older men. Upon realizing the deficiency of the German resistance, one code talker informed the command post of the opposition's depleted forces, which let them accelerate their advance, as it was known that minimal resistance lay ahead. Near the Siegfried Line, Forrest Kassanavoid once reported in code that the Germans they were encountering were so low on fuel that they were presently forced to use horse-drawn instead of motorized artillery. Not wanting the Germans to know that the Allies knew of their dilemma, the Americans sent the message in Comanche, again giving the Allied command secure valuable information on the German defenses.[18]

Another example of the defensive use of the code follows. Near the Siegfried Line, a small American detachment of men in the Fourth Division became distanced from their main lines. Surrounded by a significantly larger unit of German forces, they realized that they would be easily overrun if the Germans discovered their position. With little time

"ʉTEKWAPA NAKA: I HEAR WHAT YOU SAY."

to spare, the group needed desperately to call for reinforcements without letting the Germans know of their position and, more importantly, their situation. Efforts were made to see whether a code talker was in the unit. Elgin Red Elk happened to be in the unit and was instructed by his commanding officer to report the situation to the division in Comanche. The use of the Comanche language, avoiding German interception of the communications, allowed for the rapid arrival of reinforcements, which saved this group from heavy casualties and/or complete extermination or capture. As Forrest Kassanavoid recalled, "It was in these defensive positions where you used it quite a bit. . . . All critical information, something they felt was really top secret, was in Comanche." [19] It was in crucial situations that communications in Comanche were employed, and, reflecting one of the group's primary motivations for enlisting, the desire to make a unique linguistic contribution in communications, that their bilingual ability was most valued.

Although the coded messages were used frequently and for various purposes, the vast majority of coded communications focused upon a select number of military subjects. All of the code talkers stated that the three main things most frequently talked about in their coded communications were artillery, tanks, and machine guns. According to the code talkers these three items were the most serious instruments encountered on a regular basis during their participation in the European campaigns.

FREQUENCY   While the Comanche Code Talkers regularly sent communications messages, the frequency with which they used coded Comanche varied according to the levels of resistance encountered in particular areas, and thus the need for secure communications. As regular wire and radio systems were used for communications, messages in Comanche were transmitted only when commanders thought it was essential for security purposes. Battalion commanders often sent messages in standard English, which the code talkers transmitted in English. Forrest Kassanavoid stated that although he did not use code talking every day, he sent coded Comanche messages at least once a week, which became less frequent as the war progressed and the German forces weakened. Toward the end of the war, messages in Comanche were sent only once every couple of weeks or sometimes monthly, as the German resistance and need for such high-security communications declined. However, other code talkers in areas with more activity reported sending coded messages in Comanche much more frequently.

In combat, voice military message traffic was always kept as brief as possible for several defensive purposes. As Forrest Kassanavoid described:

Messages were always short, real short, they never went into details. I would say no more than three lines. I mean if you had a three line message you had a long message. They were all short, real short messages. . . . A message might say "Demand for repaired mine sweepers behind."[20]

Roderick Red Elk similarly commented, "Whenever we sent a message it was short, sweet, and to the point."[21] Upon successfully receiving a coded message in Comanche, the receiving operators often briefly acknowledged the message by replying, "Utekwapa naka: I hear what you say," a standard noncoded Comanche sentence.[22]

There were several reasons of a defensive nature for maintaining the brevity in voice message traffic. First, any lengthy radio transmission facilitates enemy directional finding, which could result in immediate shelling of the communicator's location. Second, German interceptors could learn to identify a particular headquarters unit by the accent of an operator's voice. Third, military radio frequencies were always extremely congested, and thus air time was in short supply. Fourth, there were literally thousands of radios in a single division. Thus, specific frequencies had to be allocated to several different uses, and only radio discipline made it possible to use the limited frequency allocations effectively. Fifth, for security purposes, the frequency assigned to a specific organization or unit was often changed, sometimes several times per day. A special section in the communication security elements of each major headquarters had the sole mission of assigning frequencies and call signs for each radio under its command. These assignments were printed in a highly classified signal operations instruction (SOI) manual, which only covered a period of a few days. Every few days, a revised edition was delivered by a messenger. The SOI included a special section by which communicators could authenticate each other before exchanging information. Sixth, if an SOI was thought to have been compromised, a new one was immediately issued to all authorized holders. Seventh, an infantry rifle company might be in several radio nets.[23] Since a rifle company could not carry that many radios, the communicator was kept busy changing frequencies depending upon who wanted to speak with whom at any given moment.[24] For example, a single infantry company might be linked to the following radio communications nets: (1) a company command net to platoons, (2) a battalion command net which linked the battalion headquarters and all the companies, (3) an artillery support net, (4) a reconnaissance element net, and (5) an air-ground liaison net, for directing or requesting air support.[25]

Although code talkers worked individually in some instances, they

131

also frequently worked in pairs. According to one code talker, the two code talkers working in a pair near the front lines were kept separate until a message was ready to send, in order to reduce the chances that both members of a team might be killed by one incoming shell. Because incoming artillery, bombing, and strafing frequently occurred from the front lines back to any of the active divisions, the chance of getting hit was always a reality. When a message was ready to send, the two were called together to the telephone to send a transmission. All messages were given to the Comanches in English. They in turn mentally translated them into coded Comanche without writing them down and relayed them verbally to the receiving operator. After each message was sent and received, the code talkers wrote it into English, initialed the message, and sent it back to the message center for logging. All messages were logged, recording who sent them, to whom they were sent, and the officers involved. Personnel from the message center could report the number of the message and the time sent, but not the content of the messages. A master register containing the complete content of all messages and a duplicate register were kept separate. The number of individuals who knew the content of the messages was limited to those involved in the channels of sending and receiving messages, which was made smaller through the use of the code talkers, who eliminated many of the channels used in regular army coded communications.[26]

Troubleshooting: "It's my time in the barrel."

After wire communication had been established between any of the different command levels in the division, much of the code talkers' time was spent checking lines, an activity known as "troubleshooting." Because of the constant barrage of German artillery shelling and mortar fire, wire lines were frequently broken and knocked out. An eight-man wire crew was in charge of checking and repairing all wire communication links. Troubleshooting involved monitoring and checking the lines for breaks between two communication points, and repairing them. Troubleshooting at night was the most difficult because of the lack of visibility, and because neither flashlights nor any type of vehicle could be used, as both would convey one's position to the enemy. Overall, troubleshooting was not regarded as difficult unless heavy shelling was being received in the immediate area. However, the code talkers were frequently under heavy shelling while laying and repairing communications lines. Forrest Kassanavoid recalled one instance when, in attempting to lay a line along a street in a small town, they received such heavy shelling that, before advancing, they had to seek cover until it ceased.

Depending upon how close they were to the front, laying line was also when the code talkers were most likely to come under small-arms fire.[27]

Carrying a field phone, one or two code talkers checked each line on foot by walking along and tracing the wire through their hands. Each operator looked for the appropriate colored identification tag containing a written circuit identification code name which identified the line they were checking or using. Periodically, a short wire attached to the bottom of the field phone would be clamped onto the line with a pair of needle-like clamps. The team would then crank its generator, which would ring the bell on the phone at the other end, just as a regular telephone rings at the receiving end, to see if an operator was on the other end. If an operator on each end of the line could be reached, then no break existed in the line, and the team could proceed to check another line. If only one operator was reached, then a break existed between the two links, such as between a regiment and the division, or a company and the battalion. Operators checking lines from each end sometimes met up between the two locations. As code talkers checking lines periodically called in, they could also be recalled to their assigned headquarters for sending and receiving messages, or instructed to check other communications lines.

Lines were often concentrated at crossroads, the shortest and quickest course for establishing communications by laying wires and for transportation traffic. Because crossroads facilitated communications links as well as the movement of troops and supplies, they were frequently the focus of artillery shelling and thus the most frequent location where lines were broken. The sounds of incoming shells told how close an individual shell was to one's position. When a repair had to be made, one code talker sometimes stood guard while the other conducted the repair. Team members regularly had to go out for line checks and repairs in open, isolated areas subject to frequent shelling. Members described troubleshooting and making repairs in such locations with the expression "It's my time in the barrel."

Tracing wires often led to tapping into a wrong line, as numerous U.S. and German lines often ran alongside of each other, making it difficult to identify specific wires in the rain, mud, and darkness. In their stateside training, the code talkers had been trained to splice wires in the dark in special blindfolded exercises. Frequently another Allied or even enemy unit was picked up by connecting into the wrong wire, and, having traced the wrong wire, they disconnected it and the whole procedure had to be repeated. German lines were frequently tapped into by mistake and, when the error was recognized, were often quickly disconnected to prevent the Germans from pinpointing their location with communications equipment which indicated a speaker's position. The Allied wire

133

sections had electrical devices called Wheatstone Bridges which measured the resistance of a short-circuited wire circuit. Comparing this measured resistance with the full-circuit resistance (measured when the circuit was installed) could indicate where a "short" was. Measurement of a shorted circuit could tell the distance to the short when the characteristics of the wire were known. Although an operator on either side could be pinpointed, members stated that they were rarely pinpointed for individual shelling, as neither the Allied nor Axis forces wanted to waste artillery fire in attempting to knock out a single operator out checking a line.[28]

The code talkers knew that both sides were constantly tapping into one another's communications lines. Forrest Kassanavoid recalled accidentally tapping into German lines frequently, but being unable to speak German, he could not understand what they were saying. When Germans realized that their lines had been tapped into, they usually disconnected them immediately. Because the Germans were retreating and on the defensive throughout most of the European theater, their abandoned but intact communication lines were not cut by the advancing Allies. As these lines were not connected to any other German forces behind the Allied lines, there was no need to cut them. The Allies left intact old lines which could be used for their own communications, and, by not cutting them, did not give their position away to the Germans.[29]

In addition to these problems, the European climate during the winter of 1944–1945 created other difficulties for the code talkers. The extremely damp, cold, rainy, and muddy conditions they encountered made finding wire lines difficult. When identification tags could not be found, operators simply tapped into lines and listened to see who was on the other end. Lines were progressively tapped into until an operator located the one he needed. Lines were often buried in the mud and had to be pulled up, cleaned of mud, and dried off before connecting a field phone to check a line's connections, often shocking the checker. The lack of rubber gloves added to the problem, as only standard issue cotton gloves were regularly provided and used during the war. When repairing a line one could also be electrically shocked by a surge of electricity in the line or when someone else placed a call on the line. Forrest Kassanavoid stated that although he was shocked often, it was not enough to hurt him seriously. Yet, it was often enough to prevent any further work on a line.[30]

Having gained a brief understanding of the code talkers' organization and duties, we now turn to their combat service in the European theater of World War II.

c·h·a·p·t·e·r · f·i·v·e

FIGHTING PO'SATAIBOO': CRAZY WHITE MAN

*Fear, I found out, is not knowing what you
are dealing with. If you know what you are
dealing with you're not as fearful. Anyway,
I got through the night all right.*

RODERICK RED ELK,
"COMANCHE CODE-TALKERS" (1992), P. 7

D-DAY (OPERATION OVERLORD): THE NORMANDY INVASION

For the Comanche Code Talkers, D-Day, Disembarkation Day, was the culmination of their nearly three and a half years of training. One of the primary reasons the Comanches had enlisted was to use their native language as a communications tool for the army. The remaining thirteen Comanche Code Talkers were well prepared and had come to Europe to fight Taawohonuu ("Our Enemy," the Germans) and Po'sataiboo' (Crazy White Man), their name for Adolph Hitler. The following accounts are those which were best remembered and which the remaining code talkers considered to be the most significant of their combat service. With accounts from only four of thirteen code talkers who saw active combat, the following in no way reflects the entire experiences of the Comanche Code Talkers or the Fourth Division's campaign. This is only a brief account of their service and the Fourth Division's activities, highlighting the personal experiences and perspectives provided by the remaining code talkers. For more extensive accounts of the combat narrative and campaign of the Fourth Infantry Division, refer to Fourth Infantry Division Association (1987, 1994) and to Appendices D, E, and F.

Operation Overlord, the Allied landing on Normandy Beach and Germany's "Atlantic Wall," had been planned for June 5, but due to rough weather had been postponed until the following day, June 6, 1944. On

136   H-hour, 6:00 A.M., some seven thousand ships transporting 250,000 troops of American, British, Canadian, Free French, Polish, Norwegian, and other nationalities began their assault on five strategic beachheads. Employing five landings of divisional strength, the idea was to establish a strong and mutually supportive landing base along the Normandy coastline from which to capture the Cotentin Peninsula and advance into the interior of France. With the Soviet Union pushing west toward Germany, and Allied forces advancing north from Italy, the establishment of a third front from Normandy would spread German forces thinner and create a vise with which to condense and squeeze the Germans.

The Fourth Infantry Division would spearhead one of the two American landings, at the beach designated Utah. After crossing the English Channel on the night of the 5th on large transport ships, the Allied forces dropped anchor off the coast of France around 2:00 A.M. on the morning of the 6th. From their vessels the troops could see the increasingly heavy German flak as members of the American Eighty-second and 101st Airborne Divisions were dropped inland. In rough seas and darkness, troops began to climb down landing nets into the bouncing LCVPs (landing craft, vehicle, and personnel) in preparation for the assault on the beach. At 6:10 A.M. Allied aerial bombing of the beaches began, followed by coastal shelling from Allied battleships, cruisers, and destroyers. By 6:30 A.M. final cover was provided by rocket-firing assault craft as the actual landing by U.S. troops began on the western end of the front.

At 7:25 A.M. the British, Canadian, and Free French Commandos (who had been trained in England) began their landing on the eastern end of the front. From the western to the eastern end of the beach front, the Allied troops landed in divisional strengths at the five individual beaches.[1] American forces landed on the Cotentin Peninsula at the beach code-named Utah (Fourth Infantry Division) and on the beach on the Calvados Coast code-named Omaha (Twenty-ninth and First Infantry Divisions). Composed of all volunteers, the U.S. Second and Fifth Ranger Battalions were assigned to capture the strategically placed and difficult to reach artillery battery at Pointe-du-Hoc located between Utah and Omaha Beaches. The U.S. Eighty-second and 101st Airborne Divisions were dropped on the Cotentin Peninsula behind Germans lines the night before to prevent any local German counterattacks against Utah Beach and to facilitate seizing the four exits from that beach that would enable the Fourth Division to rapidly move inland, cross a large adjacent area of low, swampy ground, and meet up with the airborne divisions. British and other troops landed on the beaches stretching westward from the mouth of the Orne River. These units included the British Fiftieth Infantry Division at Gold Beach on the west, the British Third Infantry Division, plus British and French commandos, at Sword Beach to the east, and the Canadian Third Infantry and Free French Commandos between them on Juno Beach. The British Sixth Airborne would protect the left flank by landing between the Orne and Dives Rivers.

As the troops arrived they encountered a wide array of defensive forms. Beach defenses included underwater mines, barbed wire, trenches, machine gun positions, 88-mm artillery, and automatic tankettes (carrying three-hundred-pound loads of TNT and designed to follow runways and crash into troops). Forts with 150-mm and 210-mm guns lay ahead. The degree of resistance varied dramatically. The stiffest resistance was encountered at Omaha Beach, requiring nearly half of a day to secure a solid position and resulting in some 2,200 casualties. At Utah Beach, resistance varied greatly, with some units receiving very stiff resistance with heavy losses while others met little resistance. For some who landed at Utah Beach, resistance was significantly less, due in part to the fortunate mistake that shifting currents resulted in some U.S. troops landing nearly one and a half to two kilometers from their designated position. Utah Beach was established on the coast two miles east of St. Martin de Varreville and six miles from Ste. Mere Eglise. Advance troops were able to begin securing a position on Utah Beach, thanks in part to the advance efforts of the U.S. Eighty-second and 101st Airborne Divisions, in less than one hour of heavy resistance, resulting in fewer than 200 casualties in the initial beach landing. Troops at Gold and Juno Beaches encountered the least resistance and were able to secure a position in less than two hours. At Sword Beach, British troops suffered from initially strong resistance and rising tides which pushed their landing crafts and troops forward into booby-trapped defenses.[2]

Utah Beach

Most of the Comanche Code Talkers landed at Utah Beach on June 6, 1944, in the successive waves of troop landings that began at 7:00 A.M. Due to recent flooding and changes in the ocean tide, the Fourth Division landed at Utah Beach about one hour before other Allied troops landed at Omaha Beach. A two-regiment front was employed, with two battalions each from the Eighth and Twenty-second Infantry Regiments. Troops from the Eighth Infantry Regiment were the first ashore and are reported to have been the first Allied unit to assault German forces on the Normandy beaches. The general commander of these landing forces was the assistant division commanding general, Brigadier General Theodore Roosevelt Jr., whose personal orderly was code talker Larry Saupitty.[3] Saupitty and the other code talkers assigned to the landing infantry regiments participated in the initial assault. The remaining code

138   talkers (assigned to the division artillery and division headquarters) arrived in landings throughout June 6, and on the following day.

Several factors facilitated an easier landing at Utah Beach than at Omaha Beach. First, the Germans were largely unable to effectively interfere with the Allied plans. German naval forces were not expecting any possible invasion for several days following severe storms, and without sufficient meteorological observation in the Atlantic, were unable to predict the break in the weather which came on June 6. In addition, no German naval patrols were encountered in crossing the channel, and only four German torpedo boats were briefly encountered late in the afternoon. E-boats at Cherbourg were discouraged by the rough seas and returned to their base, while U-boats in Brittany and the Bay of Biscay were too distant to reach the invasion fleet for several days. Although mines would normally have been the greatest German naval threat to the invasion, they had not been renewed in some minefield areas and were not placed in other areas that the Germans had planned to mine with their new "oyster" pressure mines. Thus the Allies were able to make their way to the French coast largely through the channels the Germans had kept open for themselves and which had been mapped for the Allies by ULTRA intelligence. Despite a valiant countereffort, the Luftwaffe was largely ineffective due to the small number of available fighters (Weigley 1981:93–95).

Second, the preliminary aerial bombings were conducted by the medium-range bombers of the Ninth Air Force. Brigadier General Samuel E. Anderson of the IX Bomber Command received permission to bomb visually under the overcast, which allowed the German forces to be hit much more effectively than they were at Omaha. Third, troops of the U.S. Eighty-second and 101st Airborne Divisions had landed inland on each side of the beach, thereby engaging the Germans. No paratroopers were used at Omaha Beach. In addition, some of the German troops assigned to cover the beach had been pulled back to counter the airborne troops, thus facilitating an easier landing at Utah Beach. The achievements of the Eighty-second and 101st Airborne Divisions on D-Day came at a very high cost, however, resulting in 1,259 killed, wounded, and missing (Weigley 1981:93). Although this was later declared a tactical mistake, their efforts were the primary reason the landing at Utah was secured later that day (Ambrose 1994:293, 577). Fourth, the beach and the elevation of the terrain behind Utah Beach were less steep than at Omaha. Fifth, and most importantly, the Germans were divided on where they expected an Allied landing to occur. Most expected an Allied landing to occur at Calais. At Arromanches, only General Erich Marcks anticipated that the western portion of the Calvados Coast would be a promising place for the Allies to land (Ambrose 1994:177). To increase the difficulty in a potential landing, the Germans had intentionally flooded much of the low farmland areas just behind the beach up to a width of 2,000 yards. As only a few roads and causeways crossed this area, once past the beaches, these were the routes on which the American forces would concentrate their efforts. Because of the flooding just inshore and then again at the base of the Cotentin Peninsula, German defenses were not as strong as farther east, and the defenders were more casual. In approaching the original designated location for landing at Utah, U.S. forces encountered still-choppy seas that quickly swamped two control vessels, and they consequently came ashore one and a half to two kilometers south of where they were supposed to be. This diversion produced fortunate results, as the defenses here were weaker than at the originally prescribed landing place. The landing of a significant segment of the American troops at this location resulted in less resistance. Nevertheless, the establishment of American forces on portions of Utah Beach was still costly in numbers of casualties and has recently received significant public exposure through the movie *Saving Private Ryan*, released in July of 1998.

Two German units happened to be on patrol near the Omaha Beach bluffs and engaged the Allied forces landing there. The strongest opposition came from the German Army's 352d Division, a strategically placed unit which was the only enemy division that Allied intelligence had not identified before D-Day. Major problems arose when the Third Battalion of the Twenty-second Infantry, which landed in the initial assault wave and was followed by the rest of the Twenty-second and the Twelfth in the subsequent waves, turned north to clear the originally intended beaches. It quickly met heavy resistance and could not initially take the German guns shelling the landings from a nearby ridge line. Before noon, the American infantry had secured the causeways leading across the inundations, and Major General Maxwell D. Taylor's 101st Airborne Division had already gained control of the western ends of four others. One causeway proved undefended and was not mined. The use of the airborne invasion tactics proved very beneficial by confusing German forces as to the exact concentrations and intentions of American forces in the area and by diverting part of the Germans' 352d Division away from Omaha Beach during the critical hours of the Allied landings there (Weigley 1981:91–93). The assault waves of the Fourth Division quickly grasped a sufficient foothold to allow demolition teams to clear paths for follow-up waves of troops by midmorning (Weigley 1981:91). Table 5.1, adapted from Gawne (1998), illustrates the assault waves of the Fourth Infantry Division at Utah Beach.

One of the principal missions of the Fourth was to meet up with and reinforce the Eighty-second and 101st Airborne Divisions, which had

TABLE 5.1. *Utah Beach—Fourth Infantry Division Assault Waves*

Co. F	Co. E	Co. C	Co. B.
Co. B 70th Tank Bn		Co. A 70th Tank Bn	
	Beach Obstacle Demolition Party		
Co. G		Co. A	
Co. H (support)		Co. D (support)	
2d Bn 8th Infantry		1st Bn 8th Infantry	
	Co. C 70th Tank Bn		
237th Engineer Battalion		299th Engineer Battalion	
3d Bn 8th Infantry Regt		3d Bn 22d Infantry Regt	
2d Bn 22d Infantry Regt		1st Bn 22d Infantry Regt	
	12th Infantry Regiment		

SOURCE: Adapted from Gawne (1998).

been dropped west of the inundated area and around Ste. Mere Eglise. As leading elements of the Fourth Division, members of the Eighth Regiment of the Fourth Infantry Division were also the first troops to meet up with scattered numbers of these airborne divisions six miles inland at Ste. Mere Eglise. Succeeding troops advanced farther inland, then flanked to the north as part of an operation that would eventually seal off the entire Cotentin Peninsula and its remaining German coastal defenses.

As Weigley describes the German defenses, "Allied aerial assault on Normandy's highways and rails left them altogether incapable of the kind of movement necessary to apply reinforcements in the critical first hours of the invasion" (1981:95). Although none of the Allied landings had reached the lines drawn on the NEPTUNE planners' maps as D-Day objectives, the forces at Utah advanced farther on the first day than those at Omaha.

Then assigned to the Fourth Infantry Division Headquarters, Forrest Kassanavoid came ashore in one of the later waves of troops. As he recalled:

we . . . went into Normandy on the first day of the invasion, but not until around noon. We were lucky we landed on Utah Beach, because we didn't meet near the resistance they did on Omaha.[4]

Some of the Americans at Utah Beach advanced a considerable distance before any serious resistance was met. As some of the code talkers described, in some areas "they practically walked to shore."

The first message received in Comanche by the code talkers at the division command was from Brigadier General Theodore Roosevelt Jr., reporting that he had landed safely. As Forrest Kassanavoid described:

> One of the boys, Larry Saupitty, was the driver–radio operator–orderly for Brigadier General Theodore Roosevelt Jr., who was the Assistant Division Commander. Well when they made the landing at Utah, General Roosevelt was the field commander of the forces that landed on Utah and he sent a message back to the command ship and he didn't want the Germans to know that they had landed at the wrong space because they landed about 2,000 yards away from where their initial point was supposed to be. And he didn't want the Germans to know that, so he sent a message back and he had Larry send a message back to the command ship in Comanche telling them that . . . the landing was good, but it was in the wrong place. So his message read like this, "Tsaaku nunnuwee. We made a good landing. Atahtu nunnuwee. We landed at the wrong place." And that was the message he sent and this was Larry Saupitty, a code talker . . . sending the message for Brigadier General Theodore Roosevelt Jr. . . . As far as we know, that was the first [combat] message that was sent in code, as a code, by a [Comanche] code talker.[5]

Realizing its location, the Fourth was faced with two options: try to shift all forces to the original assigned destination more than a mile to the north, or proceed where it had landed and continue inland across the causeways directly opposite its present position. It was here that General Theodore Roosevelt Jr. is reported to have said, "We'll start the war from right here." According to Ambrose (1994:279) it was Colonel James Van Fleet (commander of the Eighth Regiment, Fourth Infantry Division), and not Roosevelt, who made the decision to continue inland. However, Comanche Larry Saupitty, who was the driver–radio operator–orderly for General Roosevelt and was with him during the landing at Utah Beach, reported to his fellow code talkers that Roosevelt did make the decision, stating, "This is as good a place as any to start the war. We'll start right here." After two verbal requests to accompany the leading assault elements in the Normandy invasion were denied, a third written request by Roosevelt was approved. Landing with the first wave of the assault forces, Roosevelt repeatedly led groups from the beach and over the seawall, and established them inland. "His valor, courage, and **141**

142 presence in the very front of the attack and his complete unconcern at being under heavy fire inspired the troops to heights of enthusiasm and self-sacrifice. Although the enemy had the beach under constant direct fire, Brig. Gen. Roosevelt moved from one locality to another, rallying men around him, and directed and personally led them against the enemy. Under his seasoned, precise, calm, and unfaltering leadership, assault troops reduced beach strong points and rapidly moved inland with minimum casualties. He thus contributed substantially to the successful establishment of the beachhead in France" (Fourth Infantry Division Association 1987:39). Roosevelt, who died of a heart attack later in the campaign, was posthumously awarded the Medal of Honor. Because the Allied forces at Utah Beach landed at the wrong location and were thus without the precisely planned support they would have received at the correct location, coded messages probably helped save lives in this landing. One of the code talkers stated that had the Germans known of their mistaken landing they could have easily inflicted severe casualties and/ or possibly overrun them.

Other units landing at Utah encountered much stiffer resistance, as reflected in a later coded Comanche message from one regiment, "We're off to the right . . . from the designated area. The fighting is fierce. We need help." The receiving code talker responded, "Keep on going, you're doing well. You'll get reinforcements as soon as they come in."[6] One member recalled that his unit did not use any code talking in the initial D-Day invasion. "There wasn't really any need for any code talking. They know you're there and they know where you're at, and you know where they're at. So you just try to get through there and establish yourself."[7]

Pockets of resistance were found in some areas of Utah Beach. As the late Haddon Codynah, one of the first code talkers in his division to hit the beach, recalled in 1987:

Of course they was already fighting up there on the beach. Ah damn, it was a mess up there then. . . . We was trying to get on the land and get away from that water. We was just glad to get off that water, to get on the land, you know. From there the only thing we thought about was what we had to do, what we was trained for, to find our Regimental Headquarters, to find them and then provide communications back. Wherever they went, we had to stay with them.

I was scared many times later, but I was never scared half as much as while I was on that beach. I thought I would never get off.[8]

When the Fourth Division landed on Utah Beach, many of the regular infantrymen had no idea if the landing was the real thing or just another invasion exercise, because the American troops had been making realistic practice landings for several months in England. American troops had been making two to three realistic "dry run" landings per month on the eastern English coastline, which had been built up to look like the Normandy coast. The army would load troops and equipment onto ships and head into the English Channel at night. The following morning, the troops would land on an English beach with mock gunfire, explosions, incoming artillery, machine guns firing over their heads, and various charges being set off around them. Mock casualties and prisoners made the practice landings look even more realistic. In addition, the Allied troops frequently saw German U-boats attacking English ships near the English coast. Despite the artillery, gunfire, and even bodies lying around on the beach, many still thought D-Day was just another realistic mock landing. Forrest Kassanavoid stated, "Every time we'd go out, they'd say, 'this is the real thing.' We never knew which was the real thing."[9] As the troops began to see their own troops dodging real bullets, their fellow soldiers getting wounded and killed, and especially captured German troops being brought in by Allied soldiers, they soon realized that this landing was for real.[10]

One of the first duties of signal corps members, upon reaching a secure position above the beach, was to string wire for communications lines. Whenever possible, lines were strung on existing telephone poles so that tanks and other heavy traffic would not destroy the lines by driving over them. Often this involved climbing twenty-foot-high poles to string the lines. Roderick Red Elk recalled his impression of the Normandy landing:

When the real thing came along, we thought it was just another dry run. Maybe that's the way the Army works—they keep you confused and you don't know the real thing from the simulated thing. Anyway, we hit the beach on D-Day, plus one. Everything was going fine until we hit the beach. The track vehicles started coming in and they were chewing our lines up. There was one lonesome pole sitting out there, and part of what was left of a tree. But they couldn't get nobody to climb that tree because there was artillery shells coming in. I was still under the opinion that they were making it look realistic—I thought they were setting the charges off pretty close. I never did realize that it was the real thing, so I said, "Give me that wire, I'll go tie it in." So I put the climbers on and shimmy up that tree and tied it, then put a pike pole on the other side. While

143

FIGHTING PO'SATAIBOO': CRAZY WHITE MAN

I was up there (in the tree) I looked at the sand dunes of the beach and I saw five or six Germans holding their hands over their heads and one GI bringing them back. That's when I realized that this must be the real thing. Needless to say, I came down that pole [tree] in a hurry. (1992:3–4)

I was thinking "this is really realistic." When I saw the Germans being taken prisoner I thought this must be the real thing.[11]

I hollered down at those guys, I said, "This is it boys, this is it."[12]

Forrest Kassanavoid also remembered thinking the initial invasion was a practice landing. "When we heard, there was so much excitement that we really didn't give much thought to it [what it entailed]. When the actual invasion started, I thought it was just another dry run."[13] Another code talker also thought it was a dry run, and being of relatively short stature, stated that he was most concerned about being let off from the landing craft in deep water while wearing a full field pack.[14] Ambrose (1994:268–269, 535) reports several instances in which Anglo soldiers failed to realize that the landing at Utah Beach was the beginning of the actual Allied invasion until they actually saw casualties and encountered Germans. As soon as they landed, the code talkers began laying wire from their location to the Fourth Division.

As Ambrose describes, Hitler's Atlantic Wall, after four years of building, was useless once penetrated:

At Utah, the Atlantic Wall had held up the U.S. 4th division for less than an hour. At Omaha, it had held up the U.S. 29th and 1st divisions for less than one day. At Gold, Juno, and Sword, it had held up the British 50th, the Canadian 3rd, and the British 3rd divisions for about an hour. As there was absolutely no depth to the Atlantic Wall, once it had been penetrated, even if only by a kilometer, it was useless. Worse than useless, because the Wehrmacht troops manning the Atlantic Wall east and west of the invasion area were immobile, incapable of rushing to the sound of the guns. (1994:577)

Overall, the casualties at Utah were light in comparison with the attack the Fourth had suffered during training at Slapton Sands and to other landing sites on D-Day. The Eighth and Twenty-second Regiments suffered only 12 men killed and 106 wounded, while the Twelfth Regiment had a total of 69 casualties. Nearly all casualties were caused by sea and land mines. Overall, the speed and success of the landing at Utah Beach were astonishing. In less than fifteen hours, more than 20,000 troops and 1,700 motorized vehicles had been put ashore (Ambrose 1994:292).

Shortly after the Fourth Division advanced beyond the beachhead, it came upon the remains of the battleground of the Eighty-second and 101st Airborne Divisions, finding the bodies of numerous Germans on the ground, while many of the American paratroopers remained hanging in the trees or lay on the nearby ground where they had fought and died. As Haddon Codynah, whose unit encountered groups of the fallen airborne, recalled in 1987:

> About one or two o'clock that morning, before there were any of us went into the land, they had that 101st Airborne and [the] 82nd, that landed over there in the darkness ahead of us. While they were fighting those Germans, well that give us a chance to come in that morning. And then that daylight come, then and everything began to push in. And they started pushing them [Germans] back then. They got rid of some of those big pill boxes [fortified semisubterranean concrete bunkers] along the beaches up there. [We] got rid of them and got past that and then it wasn't so bad then. But them ole boys that was fightin' up there in the dark where they landed on those gliders, and the further we went inland, well we ran into some of those boys. Some of those boys was still hangin' on the trees that got shot up before they even got to the ground.[15]

As the Fourth Division continued inland, the code talkers continued to lay telephone wire in all conditions. Critical to their survival and construction of communications lines was the ability to judge the proximity of incoming artillery rounds according to the sound they made, which determined whether one needed to take cover quickly or not at all. Every time the infantry received resistance, the movements of the communications lines halted until the opposing force was cleaned out or pushed back. Having started at six o'clock in the morning, the troops were weary by midnight and had prepared to bed down for the night. Roderick Red Elk recalled:

> Everybody was tired and weary, and it still hadn't soaked into me that it was the real thing—even after seeing those Germans. We decided to call it quits for the night. We pulled off in a field— they've got hedge rows around them in France—and had just laid down, getting ready to go to sleep when we heard a couple of shells coming in. So we had to get out our shovels and start digging our holes. We got a pretty good night's sleep. (1992:4)

146　Having gone all day, the troops were supposed to dig a hole for the night, but some did not. Finally, two or three German shells came in. As Roderick Red Elk stated, "You ever see those gophers dig? You ought to have seen us dig. In a little bit we had that hole dug."[16]

As their units began to run low on telephone wire, Red Elk and three others were sent back to recover wire they had previously laid:

> The night we were laying the wire, before we quit it was dark. I told those guys they must have really bombed through there because we were hitting bumpy roads and had to really hold on. The next morning when we went back to pick up the wire we got to where I thought the bumpy road was[,] we were running over dead animals and dead soldiers. Enemy soldiers, not Americans. That was what we were running over. That's when I realized that we were really into it (the war), after I saw them. And you know what happens when a two and a half ton truck runs over a body? It's not a very good sight. (Red Elk 1992:4)

Finishing their assignment, they continued onward, following the infantry and maintaining their communications lines for them as they advanced.

Once established on land, the Fourth Infantry Division's goal was to advance toward Cherbourg to secure the essential seaport located there as a means to land supplies and troops for future advances. As Charles Chibitty described:

> Utah Beach that's where we were. . . . That peninsula that stuck out to the port town of Cherbourg, that's where we were trying to get to, to get to that town. The British and the Canadians they came in and held the counteroffensives off at Caan, while the rest of us turned right and went to the port town of Cherbourg, so that we took that place and they would have places where they could unload stuff, at that port town. (Hidden Path 2000)

Advancing toward Cherbourg, the troops prepared to stop. Roderick Red Elk and others were preparing to find a foxhole for the night, one of the many left by retreating Germans, near a hedgerow. Crossing a field to approach the hedgerow, they heard a barrage of artillery gunfire and the whistling sound of incoming shells. Making a direct approach toward the hedgerow, Red Elk saw the outline of the nearest hole and dove into a "slit trench" of several feet in length. Laying his gun across his abdomen, he remained flat on his back and drifted off to sleep. The next morning Red Elk was awakened by the chirping of several birds near the foxhole. Opening his eyes, he awoke to find a German soldier sitting up, eyes open, gun pointed across his body, looking at him from the other end of the trench. Afraid to move, lest the German see that he was alive and shoot him, Red Elk remained still, watching the German, who was watching him. Finally, Red Elk made a move by wheeling his gun around and pointing it at him, but the German did not respond. Red Elk got up and went over to check him, when he discovered that the German soldier was already dead. Taking the German's gun and closing his eyes, Red Elk left the foxhole and rejoined his unit as they prepared to move out for the day. He later told his fellow troops of how he had spent a peaceful night's sleep with a German guarding him all night![17]

The Hedgerows

The American forces continued to advance. With the airborne troops at Ste. Mere Eglise and the two-front landing from the Normandy beachhead, the local German forces, who had lost Cherbourg Harbor (on June 27), were caught in between. After two weeks the Allies captured the Cotentin Peninsula. Already intense, the fight for the Normandy area was further complicated by the local hedgerow country, or *bocage*, west of Carentan. Normandy farmers worked small plots, often only five to ten acres in size, each of which was divided by an entangling maze of hedgerows. About every hundred yards, fields were fenced off by high ridges of dirt pushed up as boundaries. These embankments were approximately six feet high by six feet wide, and had thick hedges and trees planted along the tops. The earthen structures and heavy hedges with their deep root systems formed effective fences for livestock enclosures. Few types of terrain could lend themselves so well to the needs of an infantry-based defensive position. The hedgerows provided excellent defensive cover for the Germans, while tremendously slowing the Allied advances. As one historian noted, "Frenchmen built them, Germans used them. Americans had to take them" (Vintage Video n.d.). The hedgerows were essentially a built-in obstacle course which the Germans used to their advantage. There were only two ways to advance, over the top or through small gates. The hedgerows were nearly impenetrable for infantry to go over, and although each field contained a small gate at one corner to allow a farmer to take livestock and equipment in and out, exits were easily covered by German machine-gun fire. The result was a slow, costly, and bitter form of fighting to the advantage of the defender. During the first day of hedgerow fighting the Fourth Division advanced only four hundred yards. Seven days later, a total of four miles had been gained (Fourth Infantry Division Association 1987:28). As Haddon Codynah described the hedgerow fighting, "The Germans dig holes and were just sitting and waiting for you to come."[18] With the large wet areas directly inland from Utah Beach and only four exit roads, the Germans also used dikes and dams to flood these portions of the French countryside, further slowing Allied progress. With no room to maneuver, the Allies could not use their armored vehicles to full advantage, and units moved a few yards at a time in fierce hedgerow-to-hedgerow fighting. Numerous air bombardments, planned to knock out the German hedgerow defenses, were prevented by weather conditions. Eventually, engineers and ordnance staffs mounted ramming rods on tanks that allowed them to plow through the hedgerows, yet this method still remained too slow to facilitate the American advance. After landing on D-Day, the Fourth Division pushed forward for twenty-six days until reaching its objective and was then relieved by the 101st Airborne Division. During the Normandy campaign Fourth Signal Company casualties were extremely high. More than five thousand Fourth Division soldiers lost their lives during the month-long operation.

The St. Lô Breakthrough

A beachhead had been established at Utah, and the capture of Cherbourg ensured a port through which advancing inland troops could be supplied. Up to this time the fighting had been slow, in difficult terrain, and costly. The cost of advancing had been high, and to prevent becoming bogged down in a war of attrition, the Allies had to deal a major blow to the German Army to send it retreating backwards while simultaneously allowing the Allied forces to capitalize on a rapid forward advance that would make optimal use of the tremendous forces amassed on the Cotentin Peninsula. An aerial assault, followed by a ground advance by the VII Corps with the Fourth Division in the center, the Ninth on the right, and the Thirtieth on the left, was planned to punch a hole in the German defenses and allow the newly arrived and waiting U.S. Third Army to pour through. In the meantime the Germans had reorganized at St. Lô, and this small town became the focal point that the Allies had to take in order to "break out" of the coastal hedgerow country. The Fourth had participated in clearing the Cotentin Peninsula in preparation for Patton's Third Army to build up and break through at St. Lô. The town of St. Lô was heavily bombed as the Allied and German forces took and retook the town, before it finally fell to the Allies.

In preparation for the breakthrough at St. Lô, Allied forces used heavy saturation bombing to prepare their advances. Ground forces, located between five hundred and a thousand yards from the closest portion of the target, placed yellow-orange markers to mark their positions for the first wave of bombers, then fell back to take cover. Beginning at 9:40 A.M.

dive bombers began the attack, followed by heavy bombers. Some three thousand planes participated in this assault. The last planes in each series of bombers then dropped white phosphorus markers to mark the position for the next wave of bombers. Charles Chibitty recalled how, after laying communications lines in preparation for the St. Lô breakthrough, they had fallen back and dug foxholes. Common to large-scale warfare, offensive mistakes sometimes occur, resulting in the loss of one's own troops through "friendly fire." With Chibitty's regiment slightly ahead of the others, the wind shifted, blowing the smoke and the white phosphorus dust back into Allied lines and inhibiting visibility. As a result several Allied bombers began to bomb their own troops by mistake, killing nearly a thousand American troops. Charles Chibitty survived the aerial assault (Hidden Path 2000).[19] As Haddon Codynah recalled after the saturation bombing, "There wasn't a living thing left out there."[20] Despite suffering many casualties, four assault companies advanced at 11:00 and met stiff resistance from the remaining German defenders. By the end of the day the drive began to increase in speed, and 2.5 kilometers had been gained by midnight. The Fourth Division pulled the attack forward, advancing farther than other units, and sometimes engaged in a running fight with columns of fleeing German troops.

While General George Patton was organizing his newly assigned units, and following the saturation bombings by B-17s and B-24s, armored units broke through west of St. Lô on July 25, 1944, allowing the Allied forces access to the open countryside, where the use of tanks could be maximized. Led by the infantry, tank units were sent up to clear out any resistance they met along the way. It was the taking of St. Lô that literally opened the gates to France, allowing the Allied forces to race across the open interior French countryside and forcing the Germans to retreat at a rapid pace. The Twenty-second Regiment received a Presidential Citation for its role in opening up the German lines. Patton's units were later instrumental in the breakout at Avranches on August 1 and in later advances. During August 6th and 7th German tank and infantry forces moved toward the See River and Avranches in an attempt to bisect the American forces to stop the supply lines to the First and Third Armies and thus compel them to stop. Intense fighting developed against the Thirtieth Infantry Division at Mortain. A combat team of the Fourth Infantry was called in to aid the Thirtieth in regaining its position at Mortain and to aid in rescuing the "Lost Battalion" of the Thirtieth, which had been surrounded by German forces. After completely defeating the German counteroffensive, this combat team was finally relieved on August 13th.

Roderick Red Elk and Melvin Permansu were assigned to the regiment that Patton picked to initiate the offensive advance, and helped **149** provide the communications for this regiment during the breakout through France. According to Red Elk, it was during Patton's breakout from St. Lô that he first used the code. As Patton pushed farther into the open French countryside, Red Elk and Permansu continued to report their position back to headquarters. Six or seven days after breaking through, Red Elk and others began to get messages from the division headquarters instructing Patton to halt until other Allied units caught up with him, but, as Red Elk stated, "He just ignored them. . . . Patton told us to ignore them too."[21]

After a few days of this rapid advance, the troops stopped to rest, and while smoking and talking, heard a tank start up and take off. A radio operator discovered that a German tank had penetrated their column, had run over two jeeps, and was approaching their position. Other units could not shoot at it without shooting directly toward other American troops. An officer directed them to radio back not to shoot, that his infantry would take care of the situation. As the tank approached, bazookas were readied by infantry members, who were instructed not to shoot until the tank passed by to prevent injuring other American units. As soon as the tank passed the unit, two bazookas made direct hits into the tank, causing it to explode.

The Allied troops continued to advance at a rapid pace. Patton's rapid advance often placed him forty to fifty miles ahead of the other Allied columns, with pockets of resistance on all sides. Yet his tactical maneuvering and rapid advance precluded any German forces from stopping him. During military advancements at this speed, anything can happen, and troops often found themselves running on reserve rations and gasoline supplies, without maps, and extremely low on ammunition (Fourth Infantry Division Association 1987:31). By the end of August, Patton was already beyond reach of his resupply elements. Eventually, Red Elk recalled, they got so far out that they were out of communications range with the division. The only way Patton could be stopped was to cut off his supply of petrol, forcing his tanks to halt. As Red Elk recalled, "We moved so fast that we didn't have time to string any wire. . . . It's history now, but people knew that the only way they could stop Patton was to cut off his field supply. They just wouldn't give him any more gasoline." Although remembering Patton for being mean-tempered, "cussing like a sailor," and wearing his two famous ivory-handled pistols, Red Elk described Patton with admiration, "He was a true general and he knew what he was doing."[22]

During their advance across France, the front was very fluid, and pockets of resistance could be encountered at almost any time. Near Paris, Charles Chibitty was near the front line behind a number of infantry when two German tanks advanced on them, killing several of the

American troops with machine gun fire. As the remaining soldiers took cover and prepared countermeasures, some French women and several children were caught in the middle. The soldiers shouted to them to get down, but they could not understand English and were apparently frozen in fear. Chibitty and others finally had to run and push them to the ground to keep them from being killed.[23]

After Patton was forced to halt to enable the other American forces to catch up to him, the code talkers were reassigned to their regular units, which advanced toward Paris. As the Allied forces continued their offensive push across France, the Comanche Code Talkers were instrumental in relaying messages about the location of enemy troops as the Allies pushed the German forces back to liberate Paris. Following the St. Lô breakthrough, and on to Paris, American movements were fast-moving, and radio again was the main form of communication. American forces were bivouacked in a large park five to six miles outside Paris. Because the French wanted to keep the city intact, and perhaps to mollify French pride, many of the American troops were ordered to wait just outside of the city while members of the fighting Free-French (also known as the FFL, or Forces Francaise de Liberation) entered and cleared out the remaining German snipers. The order gave the remaining troops five days to rest and recover, before advancing. Elements of the Fourth Division and the Second French Armored Division were ordered to take Paris. After advancing against sporadic small-arms fire, these forces reached the center of the city and liberated Paris by noon on August 25, 1944. Elements of the Fourth were the first American unit to participate in the liberation of Paris. As Forrest Kassanavoid recalled, "It was one big party when Paris was liberated."[24] However, when Paris was declared an open city, some American units were not allowed to go into or through the city. While the Fourth Division's Twelfth Regiment went directly through Paris, the other two regiments were ordered to proceed around each side of the city. Roderick Red Elk, whose regiment was not allowed to enter Paris, jokingly reflected:

My only regret was not getting too acquainted with all the French women. They declared Paris as an open city and wouldn't let us in there. Here we are sitting about five kilometers from supposedly where all the beautiful women hang out and we can't go in. That would be torture, wouldn't it?[25]

The Siegfried Line and the Dragon's Teeth

After leaving Paris, the Fourth Division advanced to the northeast. During this time a special task force (TF Taylor) operated northeast of **151**

152   St. Quentin, keeping in communication by Signal Corps 399 radios. Protected by two light tanks, a relay station was established south of St. Quentin, France, to ensure communication with the division command post at Urvillers. The Fourth Division entered Germany on September 11, 1944, by which time a complete wire system had been established and had become the main agency of communication. Throughout this period of combat, the message center platoon operated continuously, providing the division with twenty-four-hour-a-day service. Cryptographic crews were assigned to the most important radio stations to facilitate the coding and decoding of messages, while motor messengers operated constantly, often under significant enemy fire. On September 12, the Fourth Signal Company was commended by the commanding general for outstanding and meritorious services rendered to the division since D-Day.[26] In addition the Belgian Maquis, the Belgian resistance forces, provided essential information on German activities, and Belgian scouts served as guides with most reconnaissance vehicles.

As the Allies reached the German border, they were halted between September 15 and October 4 of 1944, when they encountered the Siegfried Line. This defensive structure was a long line of large pyramid-shaped concrete fixtures which stretched for miles along the German border. The Germans placed clusters of these pyramid-shaped concrete fixtures, two to four feet in height, in rows six or more wide. These structures were designed to prevent any vehicles from crossing through the area into Germany. With only a few feet between each clustered row of concrete pilings, the upright pyramids went on for miles along the German border and looked like menacing rows of teeth. In addition, reinforced concrete pillboxes six feet in thickness and nearly impervious to grenades were distributed throughout the area to further strengthen the defensive line. The Siegfried Line was popularly known among American troops as the Dragon's Teeth (a slang term for any antitank obstacles resembling upward-pointing teeth), because of the intense defensive combination of concrete pyramids, bunkers, antitank trenches, and hardened machine gun and artillery positions.

The stalled advance resulted in a period of readjustment and waiting. While this was the first stable front since D-Day, the conditions were miserable, due to German artillery, and as the weather changed to frequent rain, damp, foggy days and very muddy conditions ensued. Intense patrolling was undertaken, sometimes resulting in company-level battles. Here the Germans made a strong attempt to prevent the Allies from entering Germany. Most of the code talkers stated that along with D-Day, St. Lô, the Huertgen Forest, and the Battle of the Bulge, breaking through the Siegfried Line was one of the more difficult campaigns.

German troops were so well fortified in their pillboxes that hand grenades, explosive charges, and flamethrowers had to be used to capture most of them.

Indeed, Choctaw Code Talker Lieutenant Schlicht Billy was the first American to capture a pillbox on the Siegfried Line near Nieder-Wurzback, Germany, receiving a Silver Star for his actions.[27] Commanding officer Major Jack Treadwell published an account of how the event unfolded on March 17, 1945, when Billy's platoon encountered a seasoned Nazi division backed up by the Twenty-ninth Panzer Division (Treadwell 1957). Having already lost thirty to forty men killed and wounded, and finding his platoon unable to advance in conventional fashion, Billy took three or four men and crawled toward a German pillbox. Reaching the fortification, they succeeded in killing four Germans and entered the structure. However, in doing so, they were observed by flanking pillboxes and were quickly immobilized inside with intense machine gun and rifle fire. Billy reported his predicament to Treadwell: "I'm in this pillbox and I can't get out. I can't get out and I can't get the rest of my platoon up!" Realizing that Billy had just "opened" the door to the Siegfried Line, Treadwell directed efforts toward maintaining and strengthening the position.

Losing ten men, five wounded, and their radio, Treadwell and others finally reached Billy and his companions in the pillbox. Although they were unable to move, the pillbox was supplied with twenty-five sleeping bunks, and rations and water for months. Despite repeated attempts throughout the day, that night, and on the following morning to break out and capture the next pillbox to their right, the Americans remained immobilized. Lieutenant Billy was wounded and later evacuated on the night of the 17th. The remainder of Fox Company moved up to reinforce them. At 9:00 A.M. the next morning, Treadwell decided to take the offensive himself and raced across the open grassy field some eight hundred yards toward the pillbox to his left. Although immediately drawing intense machine gun, rifle, and mortar fire, Treadwell was able to drop down into the trench behind the three-room pillbox—and to his surprise found the back door wide open. Using his machine gun and a grenade, Treadwell sprayed the room with machine gun fire, then threw in a grenade, killing all of the Germans in the first room except two, whom he took as prisoners.[28]

Impervious to his offensive, the remaining troops had been in separate rooms with the adjoining steel doors shut. Although they were perfectly safe, the remaining Germans surrendered, thinking that their position had been totally overrun. Taking his prisoners back to his unit at the first pillbox, Treadwell set off toward the resistant pillbox to their right and, as he described, repeated his performance literally, dropping down in the trench behind each pillbox, spraying the central open room with machine gun fire, which killed or wounded most of the Germans, and then taking the rest prisoner. Knocking out the Germans' communications lines in the second pillbox facilitated the relative ease with which he captured the successive pillboxes. As Treadwell described, the pillbox occupants having no communications with their commanding officer and then experiencing a sudden burst of gunfire into their open unit, led each unit individually and successively to believe the area had been overrun. By going over open terrain from one pillbox to the next, Treadwell avoided the Germans in the connecting trenches, and they never knew what was happening until it was too late. After Billy's capture of the first pillbox, Treadwell captured a total of six additional pillboxes in ten minutes, for which he was awarded the Congressional Medal of Honor. This breach in the Siegfried defenses was so thoroughly exploited that eventually the whole division poured through the gap. Major Treadwell commended Billy's service: "He was a Choctaw Indian from Oklahoma, had been commissioned on the battlefield, and was a courageous and resourceful fighting man in whom I had the utmost confidence."[29]

The Huertgen Forest

The next major engagement for the Fourth Division was in the dense Huertgen Forest, south of the Aachen-Duren highway, near the Belgian-German border. The goal of this campaign was to seize the main road from Huertgen to Duren, allowing a major route into Germany. This region was considered so vital to the defense of the Roer dams, Duren, and the Cologne Plains that four German divisions and other miscellaneous units were willingly sacrificed to stop one American division. The Fourth Division operated in the forest from November 7 to December 6, 1944. The Germans' strength was greatly underestimated in this campaign. All of the remaining code talkers agreed that this was without a doubt the toughest fight of their experiences. In particular, the intensity of the German artillery in the heavily wooded Huertgen Forest was cited by all as the worst part of the war for them personally. The Huertgen Forest was a thick forest of pines and firs ranging up to 150 feet in height. In many areas the forest was so thick that visibility was limited to ten yards. Within the forest, a vast maze of natural steep ridges and deep ravines provided excellent positions for German defense lines. Possessing full knowledge of the ground, the Germans used all terrain features to their maximum potential, with extensive minefields and rows of concertina wire supported by great numbers of machine gun positions. Every few hundred yards to the east lay another defensive line. This series of defensive positions posed a formidable line of resistance (Fourth Infantry Division Association 1987:31).

In the thick forested area, the German shelling was especially devastating, as it produced endless shrapnel in the form of metal fragments as well as wooden splinters. As described by the code talkers, members frequently had to resort to constructing defensive structures of logs and sandbags over their foxholes or by digging receding tunnels back into the sides of their foxholes to escape the constant shelling. Especially dangerous were the butterfly or air burst bombs, a small type of antipersonnel bomb which exploded above the ground and scattered a lethal barrage of metal shrapnel resembling butterflies in flight. These artillery-fired devices could be detonated by impact or set with fuses to explode just prior to impacting the ground. In the Huertgen Forest the metal shrapnel from these devices also produced a similar mass of flying wooden splinters as it ripped through the heavy vegetation. The code talkers stated that so many air burst bombs were deployed that the tops of the trees were often completely absent in large areas of the Huertgen Forest. Several of the code talkers were among the large numbers of troops wounded by these air burst explosions. Forrest Kassanavoid described what he considered to be the most serious part of his service in Europe:

I think it was in the Huertgen Forest. . . . I remember we were over there and we got shelled and what they would do, that forest over there is so thick, you know it's a real wooded area and it was dangerous for us because a lot of these artillery shells that would hit, would knock these limbs off, and you could never tell whether you was going to get hit with one of those things. And of course, that was a hell of a fight over there in the Huertgen Forest. You know they had a rough time getting through there and I think we were there for damn near six weeks in there, and I think it was one of the worst combat experiences we had was in that Huertgen Forest in Germany. Of course at that time, see the Huertgen is right near the German border and we were just getting into Germany, and those Germans, they were going to do everything . . . that they can to push us out of their country. . . . That's why they put up such stiff resistance, and that's why we had it so rough there in that area there where we were fighting.

It was thick with trees and the Germans would use tree burst artillery shells. The splinters off the trees could kill you. It was

155

like a meat grinder. They'd send in troops and they'd just get chewed up.[30]

Charles Chibitty described some of his experiences in the dense, cold, and dark Huertgen Forest:

> Then they sent us to that Huertgen Forest. It started snowing [at] that time. But when me and that other Indian boy laid that line to the infantry, [the] road wasn't very wide, with a lot of pine trees. I seen those bodies laying there, both sides, both American and German. And when we got to the infantry we couldn't come back because it was dark and we had to stay there. Of course we had our telephone on that line too you know. And then boy it started snowing, really big flakes coming down and it really piled up quick. Sometime, morning time, I heard a grader coming through there. They had to keep that road open. And I often wondered, what happened to all those bodies that was laying there, and they're still finding dog tags over there, the same place where we was. Cause it wasn't half a mile ahead of us where the fighting was. Once in a while we had to get in battle, but we fall back because they didn't want us to get killed. Our job was to send messages, just like those Navajos. (Hidden Path 2000)

In addition to hard fighting and constant rain and snow in the Huertgen Forest, wire and messenger personnel encountered great difficulty in keeping communications open for the engagement. Enemy artillery constantly knocked telephone lines out, forcing the wire patrols, including the code talkers, to spend a large amount of time checking lines and troubleshooting. During World War II, many Allied and enemy communicators frequently resorted to taunting, jeering, attempting to confuse or impersonate, and even swearing at their enemy counterparts. One night Roderick Red Elk was out troubleshooting lines and had tapped into a line that was quiet. Hearing no one on the line, Roderick Red Elk was just about to say something in Comanche, when he heard a German operator ask, "*Was ist los?*" (What is wrong?) Having acquired a working knowledge of some German, Roderick replied back in German with a few "choice" words for his inquiring adversary. Taken off guard, the German immediately got quiet, and Red Elk quickly removed his clip from the line, breaking communications.[31] When he had found his unit's lines and checked them, he rang both directions to tell them that the line was in service again. About that time, the regiment toward the front called back to him to tell him that a German tank was approaching. The operator stated that the tank driver was "firing at random," didn't know what he was doing, and looked "like he was crazy." As he sat there finishing his tape jobs (wrapping a wire splice with rubber and then friction tape) and staking them down, Red Elk heard a shot way off. As he described:

> I heard a shot way off—BOOM. A little while later I heard another—BOOM. You've heard that old expression about tornadoes and how they sound—how they roar—like a boxcar coming through the air? Well, that's the way this thing sounded. The guy in the tank was shooting armor piercing shells, and that shell was coming through the top of the trees and clipping the limbs off. You see, armor piercing shells are called A.P. It wouldn't explode until it pierced something solid. It's meant to pierce the tank before it explodes. So the trees and branches weren't nothing—it was just going right through them. That put the fear in me, hearing that sound and not knowing what it was. Fear, I found out, is not knowing what you are dealing with. If you know what you are dealing with you're not as fearful. Anyway I got through the night all right. (Red Elk 1992:7)

Messages were again used to prevent German interception of vitally crucial combat information. As the Allies approached a potentially dangerous area of terrain in the Huertgen Forest through which they would have to pass, Forrest Kassanavoid sent back one coded message to the division command that they were approaching a narrow clearing in a heavily wooded area. Transmitting the message in Comanche prevented the Germans from knowing the exact situation the American troops faced and thus concentrating their artillery fire on the narrow pass, which would have resulted in greater American casualties.[32]

Battalion command posts were frequently targeted for shelling and knocked out. Artillery shelling and strafing remained ever-present dangers regardless of one's position in the lines. In addition to these threats, soldiers also fought the cold and wet weather, a lack of sleep, fatigue, hunger, and myriad other problems. Ernest Stahlberg described some of these hazards:

> Simmons and I and others were always in precarious positions. We were bombed at night and strafed while traveling in convoys. . . .
> In our off time we slept to make up for lost sleep. Also we tried to replace wet clothing, especially socks and underwear. After that we wrote our letters to home. As mail orderlies we always had letters to distribute.[33]

158   The construction or maintenance of a complete road net within the division zone was a major task complicated by intense shelling, deep mud, and countless mines, sometimes buried four deep or in groups of several hundred, which had to be removed from roads, firebreaks, and forest lanes. After nineteen days of intense and costly fighting, the Fourth Division broke through the German defenses. The intensity of the Huertgen Forest campaign was reflected by the status of the Fourth Division, which was pulled in at full strength but left at half strength, suffering 50 percent wounded or killed by the time the battle was over— a casualty rate that far surpassed even that of D-Day. Companies that were brought up to near full strength with reinforcements often found themselves with only half strength two days later. Often objectives were taken and counterattacks repelled by small companies of twenty-five to forty men. After advancing beyond the forest, much of which lay in the form of "twisted masses of shrapnel-torn stumps and broken trees," the Huertgen-Duren road was secured (Fourth Infantry Division Association 1987:32).

The Battle of the Bulge

After being pulled out of the Huertgen Forest, the Fourth Division was sent to Luxembourg City for rest, the first it had received since D-Day, and to await badly needed replacements and supplies. Some motorized equipment and tanks were partially disassembled awaiting new parts. This break also gave the Fourth Signal Company time to dress up lines formerly used by the Eighty-third Infantry Division. When the Fourth arrived on December 6, a heavy snow covered the ground. On December 16th, the Germans made a major counteroffensive, breaking through toward Bastogne and capturing significant concentrations of American troops. The German goal was to capture Luxembourg, a hub of Allied activities, headquarters of the Twelfth Army Group, and the home of Radio Luxembourg, while splitting the American First Army and leaving the troops in Luxembourg cut off and without a supply route. In addition, their drive toward Antwerp and the nearby seaports in Belgium, if successful, would also capture this important Allied supply route. Despite fatigue, low numbers, and disappearing supplies, the Fourth was ordered not to retreat. While fuel and ammunition were plentiful, food was in increasingly short supply. As the Germans continued toward Bastogne, the American troops in Luxembourg remained on guard, with a dwindling food supply (Red Elk 1992:7–9). This also forced the wire and radio personnel to return to combat teams to operate division wire and radio sets.

Despite its condition, the Fourth mustered all of the reserves it had. An assorted crew of two battalions of infantry; a company of cooks, military police, and medics; two battalions of engineers; reconnaissance troops; and any other miscellaneous troops in the area were placed on the front line to meet the advance of the reinforced 212th Volksgrenadier Division. Many men were lost in the bitter fighting in the snow or forced out of active service due to complications from trench foot. By December 26th, the Fourth halted the left shoulder of the German thrust into the American lines, saving the city of Luxembourg, and the tremendous quantities of supplies and road nets in the surrounding area. Even more important, the Fourth Division represented the barrier behind which the Allied forces to the south were able to reorganize and counterattack the German penetration into the Bulge, which shifted farther to the north after Luxembourg was secured (Fourth Infantry Division Association 1987:33–34).

Although out of necessity rather than for recreation, Roderick Red Elk had the opportunity to go deer hunting while near Luxembourg. One day Red Elk and another soldier were out in the nearby woods, when both happened to look up and see a deer, followed by others. Both men aimed and, as luck would have it, shot the same deer. They dressed the deer and left it hanging to drain the blood from the carcass. Nearly a mile from camp, they proceeded back to the mess hall in their camp. Locating the sergeant, they asked him if he knew how to cook a deer, to which he replied, "You get me one, and I can cook anything." Red Elk responded, "Well, if you can call somebody up and get us transportation I'll go to get you one." Not believing him, the sergeant reluctantly called the motor pool, and the motor pool sergeant sent over a three-quarter-ton truck. The two men proceeded to retrieve the deer, and brought it to the kitchen. As they dragged it out, Red Elk jokingly told him, "Here it is sergeant, get after it." In the meantime, while they were gone, the sergeant had called the company commander, and when they returned he was standing there waiting on them. Thinking they were in trouble, they found out that they were received with appreciation and that they were "kings for a day." While enlisted men and officers normally ate at different locations within the mess hall, Red Elk and his companion were seated at the head table. As they ate, the company commander asked them if they thought they could get more deer, to which they said they could. Asking them what they would need, Red Elk requested a detail of ten men, a jeep with a .30-caliber machine gun mounted on it, and a three-quarter-ton truck; these were promptly provided (Red Elk 1992:7–9).

The following day the group went back out into a long, narrow, and **159**

160   thickly wooded area about a quarter mile wide. Red Elk instructed the men, "You get on that side and come up through there banging the trees, hollering and whistling, and when you hear me start shooting, you just hit the ground." Red Elk and his friend remained sitting in the back of the jeep, camouflaged with the .30-caliber machine gun. Finally they heard the men conducting the drive and the approaching deer. Debating as to who would do the shooting, the men flipped a coin, and Red Elk won. He told his friend to stand back and count how many they got and to be ready to locate them and finish them off. Red Elk stated that he was unsure about how the .30-caliber would work, as it contained different types of shells: tracers which would burn a hole through whatever they hit, armor piercing shells which might go right through the deer, and others which exploded on impact. Containing a varied assortment of shell types, the .30-caliber provided more than adequate firepower for bringing down a deer. As six deer came running toward them, Red Elk began raking them with the .30-caliber machine gun. As he began shooting, several tracer bullets could be seen, and the jeep was shaking tremendously. Not knowing if he had hit any of them, he and his partner went to see. Finding four deer dead, they quickly dispatched a fifth, which had been wounded in the hip. After the shooting stopped, the other men in the detail brought their truck and loaded the deer. While doing this the men heard a noise, which proved to be the sixth deer, which had been wounded but had continued for another one hundred yards. With six deer, the men had enough food to feed the entire company and returned to camp. Everyone had deer steaks for two or three days, and Red Elk and his friend were promptly commended for their efforts (Red Elk 1992:7–9).

During late December of 1944 and January of 1945, the shortage of available wire became critical, and recovery of used wire was prioritized. Heavy snowfall and the icy condition of the wire made recovery even more difficult than normal; however, at no time during this period were operations seriously affected by the shortage. In January of 1945, the Fourth participated in an attack on the shoulder of the Bulge area, crossing the Sauer River and driving German troops progressively backward. Following a period of relief, the Fourth Division moved northward from Luxembourg, passed through Bastogne, and prepared an offensive attack on the Our River. Once again the division passed through southeastern Belgium, revisiting the area of the Battle of the Bulge and passing through the exact area of Bleialf, Schnee Eifel, and Brandscheid originally captured by the Fourth four months earlier. The Fourth Signal Company recovered equipment abandoned or partly destroyed by the 106th Division when it was previously forced out of the Bulge.[34]

Individual Combat Experiences

The combat experiences of individual code talkers varied greatly depending upon where they were assigned, the actions in which their individual units were involved, the intensity of the fighting, and how the fluidity of the front lines ebbed and flowed. Because the Comanche Code Talkers were scattered in two-man teams throughout the Fourth Division and were rarely in close contact with the others, their experiences sometimes differed significantly. Because offensive and defensive positions sometimes changed so quickly, it was often difficult to know exactly where the front line was. As one code talker expressed, "Often you never knew where the front line was or where you were." The most constant threat was always shelling. Some code talkers found themselves close enough to the front line and German troops to be under direct fire from small-arms fire, while others were rarely so close. All of the code talkers stated that, unquestionably, artillery was their most constant threat. Because both the regiments and the division were always within range of artillery fire, the code talkers, along with all other soldiers, were always within the range of artillery fire, which produced many close calls. The code talkers were often under shelling while attempting to lay and check wires between the division and individual regiments. One day, along the front lines of the Siegfried Line, mortar fire began to hit close to Charles Chibitty and the other members of his unit. Deciding to seek cover in a nearby bombed-out house, the men fell back. Chibitty turned to look back and saw his friend, a Private Mullins from New Jersey, still sitting where they had been. Calling to him, he received no response. Under fire, Chibitty maneuvered to get to him and carried him inside the house. Mullins took two deep breaths and then died; he had been pierced through the heart by a small piece of shrapnel.[35]

Occasionally members came under small-arms fire, especially during bivouac encampments and in the hedgerow country of France. Although armed like any regular infantryman, the code talkers were prevented from participating in actual combat in some instances. As Haddon Codynah explained, "We couldn't grab a gun and start shooting. We had to stay with our radios and get the messages through."[36] Despite maintaining communication primarily between the divisional and regimental levels, code talkers sometimes found themselves near the front lines and in close proximity to German troops. As one code talker recalled:

At times I had to use my machine gun, once in a while, but we could always fall back out, you know. I opened it up on a bunch of Germans. . . . I just raised hell and the driver turned around and

161

took off. . . . Sometimes we ended up on the front lines and in areas with many Germans. . . . We were like medics. . . . We don't get that combat pay, but we were in and out of the front line all the time.[37]

Sniper fire was another frequent problem for everyone, and especially for the code talkers while attempting to lay communications lines. Roderick Red Elk recalled how his unit was once under intense fire from two snipers. After several men in their unit were hit, they managed to kill both of the snipers. Although later wounded in the Korean War, Red Elk made it through World War II without being wounded. "I had a lot of close calls. I was either lucky or somebody was watching over me," he stated.[38]

Members agreed that the .88-caliber artillery was the most accurate and dangerous weapon that they encountered. As Roderick Red Elk described, "It was so accurate they could place it in your pocket if they wanted to."[39] Haddon Codynah recalled his closest call during the breakthrough at St. Lô and the destructive power of an .88-caliber artillery shell which lodged in the opposite wall of a concrete building, but did not explode.

I guess that was my closest call. We were holed up in a little concrete building. A German 88 shell—those things were wicked— went through a room right next to us without exploding. It took the leg off a major who was standing outside.[40]

In another incident, a German Tiger tank, one of the last sent against them, was blown up and halted right near their communications outpost. Codynah was among the troops who took the tank crew as prisoners. In searching the tank's interior for weapons, Codynah found, instead, an officer's sword and a regimental flag, which he brought home with him.[41]

None of the code talkers was ever captured or killed in action. Several were wounded in action and were awarded the Purple Heart, including Robert Holder, Forrest Kassanavoid, Perry Noyabad, Larry Saupitty, and Willie Yackeschi.

While laying wire from the division to a regiment during the Huertgen Forest campaign, Charles Chibitty and Willie Yackeschi were pinned down by mortar fire, when Yackeschi was raked across the back with shrapnel. Yackeschi was taken to the rear on a stretcher and loaded onto a vehicle for transportation to a field hospital. But not wanting to leave his unit, he jumped off the truck as it slowed down to cross a shallow ditch and returned to the other Comanches in the Twenty-second Regiment. Charles Chibitty described the incident:

But Willie, he's the one that always said they haven't got a bullet that could hit me. And he got put in with me . . . at St. Vith, before we went to the Huertgen Forest. That's where we got pinned down by mortar. That terrain from the road, it wasn't very deep, it was kind of sloped a little bit. We laid as flat as we could, but one shrapnel hit him across the back in Old Germany, and he jumped up and run. Boy we was hollering at him but he wouldn't even listen. They said medics had him, they finally got him and they had put those clamps on that big cut you know and had him laying down on his belly and another wounded guy on the other side. A few miles down when that terrain is rough you know, when they slowed down, he jumped off and came back where we was. Boy we told him he was crazy as hell. He should have stayed, he could have had a clean bed and good food. But they kept him around division headquarters, kind of in the aid station, kind of doing odd jobs because he just got, he looked like someone just got a knife about a foot long and scratched him across his back. (Hidden Path 2000)

Not long after landing on D-Day, Larry Saupitty was seriously wounded by two different shells. He was first hit by wood splinters after an .88 shell hit and splintered a tree above his foxhole in the French hedgerow country. He was also later hit by an air burst bomb. Pierced through his lung, head, and arm, he lay wounded an hour and a half before being found and was flown to an English hospital for a lengthy recovery. By the time he fully recovered from his wounds and was able to rejoin the Fourth Division, the war was almost over. Saupitty's cousin and fellow code talker Charles Chibitty described his wounds (Hidden Path 2000):

But Larry is the one that really got the worst one, Larry Saupitty. Not too long after D-Day he was radio man for Brigadier General Roosevelt. Then he had dug a hole underneath, close to a tree. At night that 88 came in and hit that tree and bursted on top of him. He said he was hit on the head, and one here (points to hand), and then one on his leg—those little shrapnels. But the one that was burning he said was the one that hit him in the chest. He hollered and hollered. What he was afraid of mostly he said was bleeding to death you know. But they finally found him. But they told me up in the front, they said, "Your little brother got hit," he was my first cousin, "go back and see him." . . . But they already flew him to England when I got back there.[42]

Perry Noyabad and Forrest Kassanavoid were both wounded by shrapnel from air burst bombs dropped during air raids, for which they re-

164 ceived the Purple Heart. Kassanavoid was wounded during a nighttime air raid, when one of the men in Kassanavoid's area left a light on in a tent, giving German aircraft a more than adequate target to focus on. Lightly wounded in the back, Kassanavoid stated that he did not feel the pain until after the attack was over. "In the excitement you don't feel the pain. . . . I was concentrating on getting that light out," he said. Robert Holder, Forrest Kassanavoid, and Roderick Red Elk each received a Bronze Star for valorous action in combat. Charles Chibitty received a Bronze Star Medal with V decoration. Perry Noyabad is reported to have received multiple Bronze Stars and a Silver Star. The code talkers also received the World War II Victory Medal; the European Theater of Operations, Europe–African–Middle Eastern Campaign Medal; American Defense Ribbon; and, to the amusement of the remaining code talkers, "most" received the Good Conduct Medal. They also received five campaign stars, one for each campaign they participated in.[43]

Despite the superhuman attributes and stereotypes associated with the Indian Scout Syndrome (Holm 1996:98–99, 173, 150) and the constant appellations of "Chief" bestowed by Anglo soldiers upon natives, members reported several cases of fear and how they dealt with it. As one code talker described:

> But I was scared as Hell too. One time I was so damned scared that I didn't want to move but I had to. Anybody say that they never been scared is either crazy as Hell or something. We was laying this line to the infantry, winter time, we was dirty. Right towards the end of the war new recruits came in there, all clean you know. Oh that little mortar, not the big mortar, the small mortar, that's how close we were, boy they started coming in. I was sitting in there in a ditch, with that big ole wire with us, telephone wire, and this man he recognized me as an Indian. There was a whole bunch of us, I don't know how many, tossed down in there. He said, "Hey Chief," he said, "Are you afraid?" You know just like that. So I turned around and I tell him, "You God-damn right I'm afraid," I said. "Any SOB not afraid is crazy as hell." That's what I said you know. I didn't know who he was or anything. And that ole boy he said something in the scripture, in the Bible. He says something about . . . If I get up there and it's my time, I'll be gone. But if not I'll be back. Kind of made me feel silly when he said that. But I guess that was probably the truth.[44]

As the American forces advanced across Europe, the response of the French, the Belgians, and the people of Luxembourg to the American troops was joyous. One code talker remembered the French running up to them and shouting, "Vive l'Amérique." However, as the Allies began to enter Germany, many of them found out that the Germans were afraid of them. As one code talker described it, German propaganda had instilled in their minds a belief that all American soldiers were "killers and gangsters." As the Allied forces pushed farther into German-held territory, they began to liberate some of the numerous concentration and death camps abandoned by the retreating Germans in late April and early May of 1945. Some elements of the Fourth Division encountered some of these camps near Munich, Germany. Dachau, a major Jewish concentration camp located just northeast of Munich, was liberated on April 29th of 1945. Munich was captured the following day. As most of the major Jewish concentration camps had "satellite" labor camps nearby, the Fourth Division most likely encountered some of these, when they passed just south of Munich. While they had heard of some of the activities within these camps, some of the code talkers stated that they were not prepared for what they saw. Roderick Red Elk described the camps simply as "Human hog pens . . . set up for slave labor." Like members of all the Allied forces, several of the code talkers gave their K-rations and cigarettes to the Holocaust victims they encountered until medical personnel and adequate food supplies reached the victims. Red Elk described an encounter he experienced in trying to help a survivor of one of the German concentration camps:

They had been scared so long that they couldn't believe it, that they was liberated. They were just in doubt. You walk up and hand them a cigarette and they just couldn't believe it. They thought just any minute that they was gonna get hit in the head. I offered an old lady one time, she may not have been old, but she looked old, one of those little chocolate bars that came in those rations. I offered her one and she wouldn't take it. I guess she was afraid I was going to poison her, so I opened it and broke a piece off and put it in my mouth and then I gave it to her and then she took it and ate it. I don't know what she was, what nationality she was. I tried to talk to her but I couldn't get nothing across to her. What little German I knew I tried to talk to her. Boy it was terrible.[45]

Charles Chibitty described meeting up with a group of recently liberated Jewish concentration camp prisoners:

Toward April and May we went around Munich and we missed that Holocaust at Munich, about fifteen, twenty miles. That's where they had those gas chambers and stuff. And that morning, when we got into those pine trees, daylight, there was about fifteen of those guys come out and I don't know how in the hell they was walking. They was so damned skinny, they was just bones. We couldn't talk to them because I was with a recon [unit], you know those guys that go in front. But me and that other Indian boy gave them all the K-rations, corned beef hash and everything we had you know, because we knew we could get some more, and what cigarettes we had. I didn't smoke, I did smoke sometimes when things got pretty hot because it calms me down. (Hidden Path 2000)

Making the Best of the Situation

Despite the day-to-day dangers during the war, humorous moments were derived from unexpected circumstances, and practical jokes did occur. The ability of Native Americans to find humor in dangerous situations is a common but sparsely documented phenomenon (Paul 1973; Holm 1992) that is common among soldiers of all backgrounds. Furthermore, the degree of psychological healing from combat among Native American veterans often has been shown to be higher than that among Anglos. That many Native American tribes provide greater community and popular support of their troops, and hold veterans in higher and more culturally based forms of esteem than is commonly found among Anglos (Holm 1992, 1996), undoubtedly helps. Plains Indian military and veteran societies have continued honoring and recognizing veterans in their respective, culturally distinct manners. These groups and their associated rituals have been highly successful in helping Native American veterans in their transition and adjustment to postwar life (Meadows 1995; Holm 1996).

As is common among veterans of many ethnicities, the Comanche Code Talkers loved to reminisce and tell humorous stories about dangerous situations and other fellow members of their unit. One humorous incident occurred during a temporary reprieve in the fighting. In early May, near the end of the war, Charles Chibitty met up with his older brother Mead Chibitty, who, although not a code talker, was serving in another infantry unit and spoke Comanche fluently. To play a joke on the other code talkers stationed at the message center at division headquarters, the two decided to let Mead get on Charles's telephone, call in to the command post, and pretend to be a German who could speak Comanche. Eager to get in on the action, Mead Chibitty called into the command post and said in Comanche, "I hear you're good. I'm your enemy. Go ahead and talk. I understand your Comanche language good." The receiving code talker was Willie Yackeschi, who was Charles's partner. Upon receiving the message, Yackeschi was temporarily caught off guard and thrown into a panic. He reported to the others at the message center, "Hey they got a German soldier on the other end of the phone and boy he can really speak good Comanche." The Comanches were all shook up at division headquarters. Yackeschi repeatedly asked, "Una haka?" [Who are you?] "Woho nʉ," [I'm your enemy] Chibitty replied. "Who are you?" Yackeschi kept inquiring, thinking someone had learned their language and broken their code. Mead continued in Comanche, "Go ahead and talk your Comanche language, I'm going to write it down." After egging him on for a while in Comanche, Mead finally told him in Comanche who he was. All the Comanches got a good laugh out of his having fooled his friend into believing he was a German fluent in the Comanche code.[46]

Members of the code talkers continually found humor in their daily experiences. Many of the members recalled many humorous incidents involving one of their fellow code talkers, a man they recall as "being about 220 pounds," who "loved to drink, fight, and never backed down from any dare or challenge." One code talker related the antics of another of his fellow code talkers. Always ready to accept a dare, he was talked by his fellow code talkers into intentionally cutting in on a dancing couple during a social event during their training. When the dancing man declined, the code talker who cut in on the couple responded to him with a remark that resulted in a fistfight. As some of the other code talkers appeared they saw that their fellow Comanche was easily having his way with the other soldier, having him pinned to the wall with his left hand over the man's face. Knowing the MPs were near, the other members pleaded with their friend to leave before they arrived and he got in trouble. Still holding the man, the code talker turned and replied, "OK, but I want to hit him just one more time." Forgetting his hand was over the man's face, he completed his last right-handed punch directly into his own left hand with such force that he broke it. Hurrying him from the scene of the fight, the other code talkers got a good laugh out of this.[47]

While advancing through Europe, Perry Noyabad, the son of a minister, once went up into a church steeple to pinpoint an enemy position. When he came down, the others teased him that they finally got him to go to church.[48] Forrest Kassanavoid recalled the following humorous incident concerning his close friend Perry Noyabad, who was often his code talking partner:

I think the most humorous thing that I ever seen happen was . . . during a raid at night, when we got raided on. We moved into this area. We moved off the line and we were kind of like in a, we was pulled back off the line and we were, everybody was digging their slit trenches, you know, for the night. You always had to dig a slit trench, you know for protection, you always got into the habit. You seldom slept, you know, above the ground, you always slept in that slit trench. So this one night my friend Perry dug a real shallow slit trench he did, not really enough to cover him up you know. He said, "Oh Hell, we never get raided this far back," he said. So that night we got an air raid and damn he didn't know what to do. Well there was this company that had been in this area before us and when they pulled out they just barely covered their garbage. Well that same pit was so deep that our cooks, because we had got a hot meal that evening, our cooks had gone ahead and thrown their garbage in there and they threw all their tin cans in there because we got a hot meal that night. So that night whenever we got that raid, well Perry remembered that that garbage pit was over there, so he ran and he jumped in that thing and I guess when he jumped in there, them damn cans cut his hands up. So damn, he come out of there and he was bleeding and so he went over to the aid station and they doctored him up you know, they wiped off his hands, he had blood, and you know they bandaged him up and everything and they give him a Purple Heart. And he told them, "I don't need that, I jumped in that garbage and I got cut up." And that guy said, "Aw Hell, take it. You got wounded didn't you." And I thought that was the damnedest incident that I remember. This guy jumping in that garbage pit and getting all cut up and they give him a Purple Heart for it. . . . He had been wounded I think a couple of times before and already had a couple of Purple Hearts. They just gave him another one.

He was the same guy. . . . Well he was quite a soldier. You know he got a Purple Heart and two or three Bronze Stars over there. So after the war this was a kind of incident that happened after the war. We were coming home, and Perry never did stay out of the stockade long enough. They'd always throw him in for getting drunk or something you know or getting company punishment or something. But he never could, during the war, wartime, all you had to do was go one year on good behavior and they'd give you a Good Conduct Medal. Well Perry never could get one. But he had Bronze Stars, he had Purple Hearts, I think he might even have had a French Decoration, I don't know. But he was kind of concerned because he said his dad was going to get after him, he was gonna get on his case because he didn't have a Good Conduct Medal. . . . To me that was really a funny incident. A man with all these decorations but didn't have a Good Conduct Medal. He always got company punishment or something and that's how come he couldn't qualify for a Good Conduct Medal.[49]

Moments of humor such as these provided brief relief from the everyday reality of warfare and reflect the Comanches' ability to persevere in adverse conditions. As Forrest Kassanavoid optimistically surmised:

> We brought home a lot of Purple Hearts and Bronze Stars, but no one was killed. . . . There was some joy in the fact that we served this country of ours. Not everything in the war was always so sad.[50]

Occasionally a few of the code talkers were able to get together and visit during periods between campaigns when their units had pulled back. After the Battle of the Bulge, most of the code talkers were temporarily reassigned to the division headquarters.

THE FINAL PUSH TO V-E DAY

After holding ground during the Battle of the Bulge and crossing into the Rhineland, the Fourth spent the last two weeks of February awaiting supplies at the Prum River. On March 1, its advance continued toward the Kyll River. Nine days of intense fighting against the German Fifteenth Parachute Regiment ensued before Adenau was captured. This regiment was "composed largely of extremely fanatical young men who fiercely resisted our advance. The quality of their resistance can best be explained by saying that they did not quit until they were killed. Even when confronted with overwhelming odds and when completely cut off from retreat, these men would not give up" (Fourth Infantry Division Association 1987:35).

On March 29th, the division crossed the Rhine River at Worms and began a fast-paced pursuit through Germany through the month of April, capturing several towns and important bridges on the Loisach and Isar Rivers. While some nearly intact German units occasionally made a stand and a fierce fight, many began to prefer fleeing or surrendering by this time. During much of April blown bridges and roadblocks presented greater difficulties than enemy troops. The Fourth Division crossed the Danube River on April 25th and began advancing over ten miles per day. By the time the division arrived on the southern outskirts of Munich the number of German prisoners captured had increased almost twofold each day. In the five weeks since crossing the Rhine, some 50,000 German prisoners were taken by the Fourth Division. During this time the Fourth Division overran many enemy signal installations, capturing German switchboards and wire cables that they used to supplement their own equipment. By May 1, 1945, the Fourth Division was at Wolfrathausen, in southern Bavaria. It soon was moved to the vicinity of Neumarkt, where communications between new and old command

170   posts were maintained by SR399 radios over an airline distance of 100 miles, by the use of a directional antenna. Later, 150-mile transmissions were successfully made. By V-E Day the Fourth Signal Company had reached Amberg, directly east of Nuremberg.[51]

By the time Germany surrendered on May 8, 1945, the Fourth Division had battled deep into the territory of the Third Reich, advancing to the Isar River in southern Germany. Some elements of the Fourth had reached Bad Tolz, only six miles from the Austrian border. From June 6, 1944, to May 8, 1945, the wire platoon of the Fourth Signal Company had laid over fifteen thousand miles of wire.[52] During its service in Europe, the Fourth Division was in actual contact with the enemy a total of 299 out of a possible 335 days. At one point, units of the division were on the line for almost 200 consecutive days without a break. Members of the Fourth Division and the Comanche Code Talkers participated in five major campaigns—Normandy, Northern France, Rhineland, Ardennes-Alsace, and Central Europe—and thus wear five stars on the European–African–Middle Eastern campaign ribbon. Those who landed with the assault elements of the division in the Normandy campaign also wear the Bronze Service Arrowhead on their theater ribbon. Although casualty estimates for the Fourth Division's service in World War II vary, its service and sacrifice were tremendous. Stanton (1984:82) reports that the Fourth Division had 4,097 men killed in action, 17,371 wounded in action, and 757 who died of wounds. More recent casualty statistics from the Fourth Infantry Division Association (1994:60) may be found in Table 5.2. Appendices C, D, and E provide concise accounts of the organization, movements, and combat narrative of the Fourth Division during its training and service in World War II. Appendix F provides a concise account of the organization, training, and combat service of the Fourth Signal Company during the war.[53]

Few divisions were as highly decorated as the Fourth Infantry Division in the Second World War, with numerous individual decorations being earned. Four members received the nation's highest military decoration, the Medal of Honor (Brigadier General Theodore Roosevelt Jr., Lieutenant Colonel George L. Mabry Jr., 1st Lt. Bernard J. Ray, SSgt. Marcario Garcia). Additional awards included: 1 Distinguished Service Medal (General Barton), 1,200 Silver Stars, 6,553 Bronze Stars, 100 Air Medals, 77 Distinguished Service Crosses, 25 Soldier Medals, 15 Legion of Merit Awards (Fourth Infantry Division Association 1987:37, 1994:60).

Numerous Presidential Distinguished Unit Citations were also garnered by elements of the Fourth Division. All three of the division's infantry regiments received citations for their bravery and accomplish-

TABLE 5.2. *Fourth Division Casualties in World War II*

Regiment	Killed in Action	Wounded
8th Regiment	1,276	5,248
12th Regiment	1,431	5,123
22d Regiment	1,653	6,053
Totals	4,360	16,424

SOURCE: Fourth Infantry Division Association 1994:60.

ments in nearly three hundred days of combat: the Eighth earned one citation for its service on the Normandy beaches, the Twelfth earned one citation for its service at Luxembourg, and the Twenty-second earned three citations for its service in the Huertgen Forest, and at St. Gillis–Marigny and Carentan. The Twenty-ninth Field Artillery earned one Presidential Unit Citation at the Normandy beaches, the Forty-second Field Artillery earned one citation at Luxembourg, and the Forty-fourth Field Artillery earned two citations for its service on the Normandy beaches and at St. Lô. The Fourth Engineers earned one Unit Citation for service in the Huertgen Forest, while the Seventieth Tank Battalion earned two Unit Citations for action in the Cotentin Peninsula and the Huertgen Forest. In addition, the Fourth Division earned the Belgium Fourragere for action in the St. Hubert–St. Vith region and for its achievements in the Battle of the Ardennes in the Echternach, Luxembourg area (Fourth Infantry Division Association 1994:60).

In late May 1945, the Fourth Signal Company was moved to Ansbach, where it established an extensive division wire net. The Fourth Division was immediately alerted for shipment to the Pacific. In June the company was moved to Memmelsdorf, Germany, a small town north of Bamberg, to begin preparations for redeployment to the Pacific. Here the unit was screened using the point system. Points were awarded for the number of months in service, time in combat, individual medals, and a number of other criteria. Approximately two thousand men having 85 or more points were transferred to the Ninety-ninth Signal Company, while low-point men were reciprocally transferred into the Fourth Division. At the time of Germany's surrender, Roderick and Elgin Red Elk, Perry Noyabad, and Melvin Permansu each had accumulated enough points to be discharged from service; however, because they were not being sent on to the Pacific campaign, they remained in Germany and were not discharged until October 1945 in Nuremberg. Haddon Codynah was **171**

172 discharged with more than the required 85 points in June 1945.[54] On June 22nd, the company began a motor movement to Camp Old Gold near Le Havre, France, arriving there on June 25. On July 3rd, the company boarded the U.S.S. *Excelsior* for the trip home. Arriving at Hampton Roads, Virginia, on July 12, the company was immediately sent to Camp Patrick Henry, Virginia, and divided into groups for shipment to the designated reception station nearest their homes for a thirty-day furlough.[55] The remaining Comanche Code Talkers were stateside on a thirty-day rest-and-recuperation leave at the camp closest to their home awaiting reassignment to the Pacific theater, when Japan surrendered in August 1945. All were discharged in the fall of 1945 in Oklahoma. The Comanches' military service as code talkers was complete.

c·h·a·p·t·e·r · s·i·x

"NʉMʉREKWA'ETʉʉ: COMANCHE SPEAKERS!"

After the war, the code talkers returned to their respective communities, resuming their lives and beginning new careers. Because the group never formed a proper name for themselves in the Comanche language, they simply became informally known within the army as the "Comanche Code Talkers." Elder Comanches at home simply referred to them with the expression "Nʉmʉrekwa'etʉʉ: Comanche Speakers."[1]

POSTWAR EXPERIENCES

As was typical of the return of warriors in many prereservation Plains Indian groups, Indian communities throughout the United States have continued to hold large-scale homecoming celebrations for veterans returning from World War I, World War II, Korea, Vietnam, and Operation Desert Storm. Beginning with service as cavalry scouts and formalizing at the end of World War I, the Comanche, as have many Native Americans, have blended traditional tribal martial customs with United States armed forces service. The result has been an ongoing and distinct form of Native American military syncretism. The widespread practices of religious ceremonies held for outgoing veterans and religious bundles and sacraments worn by soldiers overseas, and the revitalization of postwar celebrations and homecoming ceremonies, all led to a widespread increase of, and strengthened belief in, native cultural and religious activities (Meadows 1995, 1999). At the end of World War II, Southern Plains Indian communities honored military veterans through traditional martial celebrations featuring scalp, victory, round, and honor dances. Many of the initial victory celebrations and dances were held at local train depots, where great numbers turned out to meet their returning veterans.

174   Dances were frequently held on the spot, with veterans in their uniforms and tribal members in everyday street clothing. Several Comanche veterans, including some of the code talkers, brought home war trophies such as captured flags and banners, some of which were thrown down onto the ground and danced upon by tribal elders. Forrest Kassanavoid showed the author a Nazi flag he captured after Cherbourg fell. When he stepped off the train at Lawton, Oklahoma, his father took the flag and placed it on the sidewalk, where his relatives sang and performed a victory dance on it. Charles Chibitty recovered a Nazi flag from a building in May of 1945, and Haddon Codynah brought home a Nazi flag and sword from a captured tank. While the powwow, social dances, and fancy war dancing continued to grow into the 1940s, all of the older Comanche men's warrior societies, and some of the traditional forms of honoring veterans, became inactive by the end of World War II.

   Many Comanche servicemen had Native American Church meetings or Christian church services held for them by tribal elders before going overseas in service. Many carried specially blessed peyote buttons in buckskin bags worn around their necks, which had been blessed to ensure their protection. From the Comanches' perspective, these medicines had been effective for the code talkers, as all returned home alive. Elders had instructed the young servicemen to use the sacrament during their service for courage or when they felt bad. Several Plains Indian veterans I interviewed, including some of the Comanche Code Talkers, consumed portions of the sacrament while praying during the war. After his cousin and fellow code talker had been severely wounded, one code talker stated that he consumed some of the sacrament he carried and prayed while inside a foxhole, which made him feel better. Native American Church services were held again for many veterans in thanksgiving for their return. Forrest Kassanavoid had one such meeting sponsored for him by his father near Cache, Oklahoma. In later years Haddon Codynah served as a Native American Church (NAC) priest, or "roadman," conducting services throughout his life.

   Forrest Kassanavoid explained why Native American Church meetings were so commonly held for returning veterans:

> I would say that the main reason that they did that was because it was just, you know back in the old days they used to have these dances that they had when the warriors came back. And by that time [1945], they weren't having that many dances, but the Native American Church was still . . . a lot stronger than it is today and so I think more or less because of the joy of the family members coming home they had these meetings you know.[2]

For those Comanches from Christian-oriented families, special Christian church services were again held. Charles Chibitty had a prayer meeting sponsored for him upon his return.

However, despite their service record and the generally equal treatment they received from fellow non-Indian soldiers, some Indian veterans discovered continued discrimination from Anglo society upon returning home. Indians in Arizona and New Mexico, including returning veterans, were still denied the right to vote after the war. In addition, restrictions inhibiting Indians from legally drinking alcoholic beverages were seen as highly discriminatory. The passage of an 1802 law authorizing the president to regulate the selling of alcoholic beverages among tribes resulted in a situation where Indians were denied access to liquor both on and off the reservation. However, this law was also only enforced in and around Indian communities and reservations. Widespread non-Indian stereotypes about Indian alcoholism and about many Indian servicemen being drunkards only exacerbated the problem. For many Indian servicemen drinking alcoholic beverages with their fellow non-Indian soldiers had been an acceptable activity (legally by the U.S. military, and socially by Indians and non-Indians alike) at military post exchanges, and had become an important symbol of equality (Bernstein 1991:136). With no formal Indian veterans organizations existing at the end of the war and the double standard concerning the consumption of alcohol, many Native American veterans joined Anglo Veterans of Foreign Wars (VFW) and American Legion posts following the war. As one elder Comanche veteran told me, "Many veterans joined simply to have a place to drink a cold beer without getting arrested. They didn't hassle you in the veterans' clubs, you weren't discriminated against."[3] Forrest Kassanavoid described this policy as it affected the postwar Comanche community in southwest Oklahoma:

They had an old law, an old federal law which said that they could not sell alcohol beverages to Indian people who lived west of the Indian Meridian . . . so this law says Indian people living west of the Indian Meridian cannot buy publicly any kind of alcohol beverages. So therefore if you were a veteran . . . you couldn't just go to a grocery store or any kind of store and buy you a six-pack of beer, because you lived west of the Indian Meridian. And you couldn't go into a bar and get a drink, but if you were a member of the American Legion, V.F.W., or any kind of veterans organization that had a bar inside that building, as long as you had a membership card saying that you were a member of that organization, they never did question you. 'Cause as far as they were concerned you were a vet-

176   eran and you're a legionnaire. You're a veteran and you're a member
of the V.F.W. and everyone you know, they just didn't discriminate
against anyone. But this other way you know, publicly they discriminated against you because you were Indian and lived west of the
Meridian. But on the east side it was different, they didn't come
under that law. So what they did, they all joined the American
Legion or the V.F.W. so they could go and have a bottle of beer when
they got off. All they had to do was just walk in the club and order
it and that was it.[4]

Although membership in Anglo veterans clubs was not totally satisfactory in a cultural sense (American Legion and VFW posts were rarely active in Indian affairs), and this dissatisfaction in part led to the later
revival of older, more traditional cultural forms among many tribes in
the 1950s through the 1970s (Meadows 1999:391–397), participation in
these clubs was an important postwar activity in which Indian veterans
established a greater degree of civil rights and equality than was found
among the general American populace. Not until 1948 were Indians in
Arizona and New Mexico granted suffrage, and not until 1953 did Congress repeal the discriminatory liquor laws and grant Indians the same
status as non-Indians with respect to alcohol in off-reservation locales.

Education and Careers

After returning home and being honored individually or in groups with
other veterans, the code talkers gradually resumed their daily lives and
continued or started their educational and occupational pursuits. Three
of the members pursued college educations. Using the G.I. Bill, Forrest
Kassanavoid enrolled at Cameron College in Lawton, Oklahoma, in the
spring of 1946. He finished in 1947 and became the first Indian to graduate at Cameron College under the G.I. Bill. Kassanavoid then attended
Oklahoma A&M College (now Oklahoma State University) at Stillwater,
Oklahoma, from 1947 to 1948, where he graduated, and later attended
Wichita State University. After being discharged from the army following World War II, Kassanavoid also served two enlistments, for a total of
six years, in the Oklahoma National Guard as a staff sergeant. Kassanavoid next worked for four years for a private military supplier for the
U.S. government at the Fort Sill Indian School, on the Ft. Sill military
post. He then worked as an administrative services assistant for the U.S.
Postal Service in the finance office at a U.S. postal accounting center for
twenty-eight years. He retired from the postal data center in Minneapo-
lis, Minnesota, in 1981. He later worked for several years in the Johnson
O'Malley Program at Indiahoma, Oklahoma. Johnson O'Malley is a fed-

eral government program established to assist Indians in getting an education. The Indian Parent Committee of Indiahoma, Oklahoma, sponsors Comanche-language classes and applied for a grant to help teach the Comanche language. Kassanavoid periodically taught Comanche-language classes until his death in 1996. Kassanavoid was an Eagle Scout and a member of the Comanche Reformed Church and the Post Oak Mennonite Brethren Church.[5]

Previously having attended Oklahoma A&M College, Wellington Mihecoby also used the G.I. Bill to complete his college education. Returning as a junior, Mihecoby received a degree in Agricultural Education and worked for the Bureau of Indian Affairs, teaching at the Navajo Indian school in Farmington, New Mexico. Larry Saupitty enrolled as an art major at the University of Oklahoma, but died shortly thereafter from health problems associated with the wounds he received in the war. He was the first of the Comanche Code Talkers to die.[6]

Some of the code talkers continued careers in the military. Melvin Permansu remained in the army, retiring after twenty years of service. Haddon Codynah also retired from a career in the army, then continued to use his skills as a communications operator in working with a telephone company. Simmons Parker remained in the army for a period before serving as a clerk for the army at the nearby Ft. Sill army post. Clifford Otitivo also worked as a civilian employee for the army at Ft. Sill.[7]

Other members of the group entered into various arenas of private business. After serving in the army from 1940 to 1945, Roderick Red Elk reenlisted in January of 1946 and, after serving in the Korean War, was discharged in December of 1951 after receiving a severe shrapnel wound to his leg. Red Elk owned and operated a cafe for a number of years in Lawton, Oklahoma, and later worked as a beverage distributor for Charles Dickens Budweiser Distribution Co. until his retirement. Red Elk was an originator of and a consultant for the Comanche Language Preservation Project and secured several grants for this group. He was a gourd dancer, an avid hand game player, and a member of the Comanche Indian Veterans Association, the Walters Service Club, and the Lawton, Oklahoma, VFW post. Red Elk, who was a horse racing jockey in his youth, with several first-place finishes in Oklahoma, was also a member of the Quarter Horse Association.[8]

Elgin Red Elk returned to farm and work with racehorses, and inherited a large oil lease. Perry Noyabad owned and operated a tavern in Cyril, Oklahoma. Other members of the group relocated to larger urban areas for jobs during the large-scale Native American Relocation Programs following the war. Robert Holder moved to Oklahoma City and later Sapulpa, Oklahoma. Albert Nahquaddy Jr. was involved in the Oklahoma City–area building trades as a house painter. Charles Chi-

178   bitty moved to Tulsa, Oklahoma, where he pursued a career in a glass company. Chibitty was responsible for installing many of the beautiful stained glass windows in churches and other buildings throughout the Southern Plains region. A well-known dancer, Chibitty was featured in a statewide billboard advertisement promoting Oklahoma tourism in the early 1990s. As a lifetime member of the Tulsa, Oklahoma, VFW, Chibitty served as the chief of staff in the 1994 Tulsa Veterans' Day Parade. Anthony Tabbytite moved to California where he pursued a career in the dry cleaning business. Morris Sunrise received disability funds from the Veterans Administration for injuries sustained in service.[9]

Cultural Pursuits

At the end of World War II, many of the earlier public Comanche cultural activities, especially traditional military societies and veterans' dances, were inactive. Where scalp and victory dances with veterans' songs had once been performed to honor returning veterans, Native American Church and Christian church meetings prevailed at the end of World War II. As occurred throughout numerous Native American communities, the return of significant numbers of veterans necessitated the honoring of these individuals according to traditional tribal customs, through song and dance. The honoring and receptions held for incoming veterans fostered the postwar revival of earlier veteran traditions and military dance societies. While military societies were not initially revived, the high frequency of send-offs and homecoming celebrations resulted in an immediate and dramatic increase of social-oriented powwows containing traditional and diffused forms of dancing and singing that continued through the 1950s (Meadows 1999).

As powwows and honor dances increased after the Korean War, more and more Comanches began to participate. Following the end of the Korean War traditional military societies began to be revived throughout Southern Plains Indian communities, a development which continues to the present (Meadows 1999). Between 1970 and 1976, three traditional Comanche men's societies were revived, the Comanche War Dance Society in 1970, the Comanche Little Ponies in 1972, and the Tuhwi (Black Knives) Society in 1976. Other groups were also formed during the 1970s, including the Comanche Gourd Clan, the CIVA (Comanche Indian Veterans Association), and numerous powwow and descendants' clubs (Meadows 1999). Familiar with singing and dancing since their youth, several of the code talkers began actively participating in the revival of numerous Comanche men's societies and dance organizations. The CIVA became very active in honoring Comanche veterans and in providing charitable aid to Comanches in need. Roderick Red Elk, a member of the CIVA, explained some of the functions of the Comanche Indian Veterans Association:

> Everywhere you go, you honor them [veterans]. We've got a lot of veterans in our tribe that are highly decorated and they don't get any recognition at all. So we as a veterans' organization, we have an annual celebration that we try to recognize them that way, make them special guests or whatever.[10]

Forrest Kassanavoid served as one of four head men in the Comanche War Dance Society from its revival in 1970 until 1994, and was also inducted into the Comanche Gourd Clan. Charles Chibitty was a prominent fancy war dancer and has also participated in Tuhwi Society ceremonials. Haddon Codynah, Roderick Red Elk, Ed Nahquaddy, and Ralph Wahnee all partook in gourd dances as members of the CIVA. Kassanavoid and Nahquaddy frequently participated in powwows in the straight dance category.[11]

Several factors precluded the Comanches, despite their active participation in community life, from forming a code talker organization as the Navajo Code Talkers did. Foremost, with only seventeen Comanche Code Talkers, there were really not enough to form a club. This number was further reduced, as three members (Codynah, Permansu, and Parker) continued immediate postwar careers in the military service. Five members of the group (Holder, Chibitty, Mihecoby, Nahquaddy, and Tabbytite) had relocated to other towns outside of the Comanche communities, and one (Saupitty) died shortly after the war. Thus, only eight of the seventeen members remained in the immediate Comanche community on a full-time basis in the years immediately following the war.

As Forrest Kassanavoid recalled:

> You know . . . after we came back for a long time, we never did [really get together], we were more or less individuals and did not see too much of each other. . . . After we started dancing, that's when we started . . . becoming closer together. That's when we started associating with each other more often. I don't know why that was, I guess we were just, I guess just 'cause there was just really nothing there to hold us together you know, like in a social life or anything. I think that's the reason why. No clubs or organizations [existed]. But then after these organizations started and we seen different ones were in there and different people started dancing, that's when we really started getting closer together.[12]

RECOGNITION

One might wonder how the Comanche Code Talkers, having made such a uniquely valuable contribution in the war effort, were recognized for their efforts. Though there were occasional, brief recognitions at Comanche tribal dances and gatherings, the code talkers were never formally recognized by the United States military or government until over forty-four years after the war. Although the Comanches were not instructed to remain silent about their code system and service as code talkers as the Navajo were, government concerns that Native American codes would be needed in future conflicts combined with the Comanches' small number and modesty to keep their story largely a secret beyond the Comanche community until 1989.

Because the code talkers were fluent in both Comanche and English, they did not have to write home for help in creating any of the coded terms. Although one code talker stated that a picture and article about the group appeared in the local newspaper after they were recruited, many Comanches did not know the full extent of their linguistic contribution and service in the war until they returned home. All of the code talkers recalled the large tribewide homecoming held in the summer of 1946 for all World War II veterans south of Walters, Oklahoma, on the allotment of Herbert Homovich (an uncle of code talker Roderick Red Elk). Sponsored by the Walters Service Club, the three-day celebration and powwow contained recognition and dances. With subsequent celebrations held for Korean War veterans, the annual "Walters Powwow," better known as the Comanche Homecoming, evolved into the first postwar annual Comanche tribal gathering.[13] One code talker stated that although he wasn't sure how the other veterans felt at such recognitions, he noted that some of the other Comanche veterans seemed to support the praise of the code talkers.[14] This tradition of honoring all veterans continues in the form of the annual Comanche Homecoming held every July at Walters, Oklahoma, and at Comanche public gatherings and dances held on Memorial Day and Veterans Day. Code talkers indicate that, following these events, they were occasionally recognized at tribal gatherings with the singing of honor songs and praise, such as at the Comanche Homecoming in July of 1983.

The United States government and the Pentagon itself maintained measures not to publicly recognize or promote knowledge of the Comanche and Navajo Code Talker units for more than two decades after the end of World War II. The achievements of the code talkers were kept secret by the military, which believed their service might be needed again in future conflicts. Some Native American communications operators, including the Navajo, served in the Korean and Vietnam Wars (Belleranti 1983:42), before the codes were declassified by the government. This was done in 1968, lifting former military restrictions and, in 1969, allowing public recognition of the Navajo contributions (Hafford 1989: 45; Escue 1991:20; Watson 1993:42).

For years the story of the Fourth Division Comanche Code Talkers remained untold, while newspapers were full of accounts of the exploits of the marines' Navajo Code Talkers in the Pacific. When asked why the story of the Comanche Code Talkers and the Fourth Signal Company had not been told, 1983 Comanche Homecoming chairman Raymond Nauni Jr. stated, "It goes back to the old Comanches. They told nothing to outsiders. It just wasn't done. That is a custom we need to change. I hope there is a big crowd at the powwow to honor our veterans. They deserve it."[15] Some of the code talkers I visited with stated that they never really talked about their role as code talkers much after returning, and they had not been that interested in pressing for recognition of their role in the war.

This modesty relates to traditional Plains concepts of publicly speaking about one's self. In the past, Comanche warriors generally only spoke of their martial accomplishments while at military society meetings providing a standard format for coup recitations, when challenged concerning their bravery and truthfulness, or when asked to for a specific purpose. Among the Comanche as well as the neighboring Kiowa and Naishan Apache, contemporary veterans are often reluctant to publicly recite their own accomplishments, except when asked to do so for a specific purpose such as a naming ceremony or military society rituals. More commonly, when a highly decorated veteran is called into the center of the arena another veteran or relative will publicly speak about the honored veteran's accomplishments. Many highly decorated Native American veterans I visited with were extremely modest about their service. Thus their small size, culturally based modesty regarding military service, and lack of postwar documentation kept the Comanche Code Talkers little known outside of their tribal community.

Knights of the Order of National Merit

Unfortunately, many veterans of various backgrounds and from various wars have gone unrecognized. With a total of 432 Congressional Medals of Honor awarded for World War II and 1.2 million African Americans serving in the war, only recently were the first seven African Americans posthumously honored with the Congressional Medal of Honor. Because the statute of limitations imposed a 1952 cutoff date for giving the award to World War II veterans, Congress had to pass a waiver of the statute to enable these awards to be given.[16] Thousands of Anglo-Americans

181

working on the military intelligence effort known as "Ultra" against the Germans (not to be confused with the Ultra program in the Pacific) were unrecognized until 1974, when a participant broke the law to reveal the secret program.[17]

In relation to their proportionally higher enlistment ratio, Native Americans have not received adequate recognition for their military service. Despite the valuable contribution made by the Choctaws in World War I and the Comanches in World War II, neither have ever been formally recognized for their service. Many Choctaws and Comanches, including some of the code talkers, felt that their unique service deserved some type of recognition in light of the enormous attention given to the Navajo. Finally, in 1989, both tribes were formally honored by the French government. By 1986, the French government had begun a program to honor Allied soldiers from both world wars. To commemorate the seventieth anniversary of America's entry in the First World War on April 6, 1917, France announced that it wanted to honor fifty Americans with the French National Order of Merit for their service in the two world wars. These awards were presented on April 6, and later on April 17, 1987, in Paris. The French consul in Houston, Gerard Dumont, asked Dr. C. Alton Brown, France's honorary consul in Oklahoma, to recommend noteworthy Oklahomans who had served in either war for the French National Order of Merit. As Gerard Dumont stated, "Theirs was a very original contribution to the Allied war effort, and I thought it would be very interesting to get recognition in France."[18]

Along with Dr. Brown, Mike Wright of Scientific Social Research, a Norman, Oklahoma–based consulting company, was active in the effort to gain recognition for the Native American code talkers from Oklahoma who had helped France to regain its own country in both world wars. Mr. Wright, who became interested in the code talkers, conducted the preliminary historical research to determine the role the code talkers performed in World Wars I and II. Initially, four Oklahoma Indian nations were determined to have served in native language communications in the two wars, the Choctaw in both wars, the Comanche (later discovered to have served as code talkers in both wars), and the Kiowa and Pawnee in World War II. Recognizing that fifty such awards were insufficient to include the total number of Native American code talkers, and because it was impractical to enter the dozens of code talkers' names into competition for the fifty medals, Dumont and Wright suggested that individual tribes be recognized. As Mr. Dumont explained, "The idea would be that by honoring the tribes, it would be possible to honor the code talkers within those tribes." This idea was then presented to the French government with the recommendation to recognize the Comanche and Choctaw Code Talkers for their service. Oklahomans then decided to hold their own ceremony at the Oklahoma State Capitol if any of the Oklahoma Indian nations were so honored. The response of the French government finally led to a special awards ceremony for the Choctaw and Comanche Nations in Oklahoma City. It is largely through the efforts of Dr. Brown and Mr. Wright that the French government was induced to formally honor the code talkers for their efforts.[19]

On November 3, 1989, the French government and the State of Oklahoma jointly honored the surviving Comanche Code Talkers from World War II, and posthumously honored the Choctaw Code Talkers from World War I, at a ceremony held at 3:00 P.M. in front of the Oklahoma State Capitol Building in Oklahoma City. Attending the ceremony were numerous dignitaries, including Comanche Tribal Chairman Kenneth Saupitty; Choctaw Tribal Chairman Hollis Roberts; the French Consul General for Oklahoma and Texas, Bernard Guillet; Oklahoma Governor Henry Bellmon; U.S. Senator David Boren; the Governor General of France Overseas Territories and Prime Minister of France under President Charles De Gaulle, the Honorable Pierre Messmer; and others. The Choctaw flag was carried by Schlicht Billy, the last surviving Choctaw Code Talker to use his native language in World War II. The Comanche flag was carried by the three surviving Comanche Code Talkers (Chibitty, Kassanavoid, and Red Elk), escorted by the Comanche Indian Veterans Association. The Comanche Nation Singers sang the Comanche Flag Song.

The Chevalier de l'Ordre National du Merite (Knight of the Order of National Merit) was presented to Choctaw Tribal Chief Hollis Roberts and to Comanche Chairman Kenneth Saupitty, representing the Choctaw and Comanche Nations, in honor of the code talkers' contribution to France in World Wars I and II. This recognition was bestowed in the form of a medal, certificate, and plaque to each tribal nation. The Choctaw and Comanche tribal flags were folded by Native American veterans in military fashion to which the medals were pinned on each respective flag by the Honorable Pierre Messmer. The French government then presented each surviving Comanche Code Talker with a certificate and a medal formally awarding the Chevalier de l'Ordre National du Merite. This award is the highest honor France can bestow on citizens of another nation. The afternoon program reads, "The award recognizes the achievement of the Indian Nations in preserving their tribal identities and languages." French Army Major Jacques de Vasselot, the French liaison officer at Ft. Sill, said he had never heard of Native American code talkers until coming to Oklahoma. Aware of their roles in both wars, he stated, "It is important to remember who helped us to be free."[20]

Finally, after so many years, the Comanche and Choctaw Nations **183**

184   were formally recognized, both for their military service and for their cultural and linguistic perseverance. As Mike Wright stated in his address at this presentation:

> We in Oklahoma are frequently reminded that our state was once called Indian Territory. On this occasion I think it is appropriate to bear in mind that for many centuries this entire hemisphere was Indian Territory, and so it remained until the people who discovered the continent before Columbus lost it to conquest. But now, today, we honor the Indian tribes because in the face of this unfriendly circumstance, they were able to preserve enough of their tribal identities and languages to be available in moments of crisis with their rare skills, to rescue the beneficiaries of this conquest. In doing so, they gave new meaning to the word gracious.[21]

The presentation of awards was made jointly by the French representatives and Oklahoma state officials.[22] Following the lengthy exchange of gifts and bestowal of awards, the program was concluded with several cultural presentations by the Comanche and Choctaw Nations. Woogie Watchetaker, a respected traditional Comanche healer, held a prayer and blessing. Forrest Kassanavoid invited Major General Foster to join them on the stage with the other dignitaries. Watchetaker blessed all of the honorees at this time. Noted Comanche artist, the late Doc Tate Nevaquaya, gave a beautiful flute performance. Lincie Battiest of the Choctaw Nation and Eddy and Donnita Sovo of the Comanche Nation performed the Lord's Prayer in sign language. The Choctaws then performed round, intertribal, ruffle, and Indian two-step dances. Introduced and narrated by Ed Yellowfish, the Comanche Tuhwi (Black Knives) Society performed Comanche victory, scalp, war, buffalo, and Tuhwi Society dances and veterans' songs to honor the code talkers.[23]

The Choctaw Nation had gone some seventy-one years without any formal recognition of its service by the State of Oklahoma or the United States. Recognition would finally be given by the French government. As Choctaw Tribal Chief Hollis Roberts reflected, "Although the French and Choctaw Governments have made efforts to show their appreciation to these men and their families, the U.S. Government has yet to present any visible recognition, in spite of documents from military archives. . . . This is something you probably won't read in history books, it's a shame a foreign government had to be the one to step in and honor our Native American Code-Talkers" (Twin Territories 1991). The Comanche Code Talkers had gone nearly forty-five years without any formal recognition. As Forrest Kassanavoid reflected:

It was over forty years before anything actually happened you know. Up to that time we were . . . just members of the tribe and no special status or no special recognition or anything. And then after the French Government came over here and did that little ceremony up there at Oklahoma City, that's when they began to get the tribe and tribal members and organizations began to become more aware of the fact that there were still some code talkers around, and that's when they really got into it. But prior to that period . . . occasionally at a dance they might call us out, but it was not that often.[24]

The honoring of the Choctaw and Comanche Code Talkers in 1989 significantly turned the tide of public knowledge concerning the groups, their contributions, and how they would be viewed in the years to come. This increased awareness affected the response both within code talkers' respective tribes and by non-Indians. After 1989, the code talkers began to receive the recognition that was long overdue, including frequent requests from various news media, military organizations, and cultural centers to tell their story. Following the 1989 awards ceremony, Kassanavoid and his wife Marian were guests of his old unit (now the 124th Signal Company) at a week-long reunion at Ft. Carson, Colorado, in 1989. As word of their service spread, so did their recognition by various groups and administrations.

In September of 1992, Forrest Kassanavoid and Ed Nahquaddy traveled to St. Louis, where they spoke about the Comanche Code Talkers at the Missouri Botanical Gardens. During their visit, the surviving Comanche Code Talkers were awarded a U.S. Defense Department Certificate of Appreciation, from the Office of the Secretary of Defense, signed by Dick Cheney. The certificate states:

Office of the Secretary of Defense
Awards this
Certificate of Appreciation
to

_____

For distinguished service as a member of the Comanche Code Talkers. In that capacity you helped secure one of history's greatest victories by the forces of freedom over tyranny and oppression. Your courage and contribution during World War II merit a special place in military history. You have the distinction of serving not one but two nations—the United States of America and the Comanche nation—with honor, courage, and valor. In a very real sense, thousands of fellow service members owe their lives to you. Your distinguished service reflects great credit upon yourself and the Department of Defense.[25]

Similarly, as Deputy Defense Secretary Donald Atwood stated at the recognition of the Navajo Code Talkers exhibit at the Pentagon, "Every person and every group of people bring something special to our nation in time of crisis. It's those times that bring out the best in all Americans" (Wigginton 1992). Truly, the Comanche Code Talkers contributed uniquely and significantly in the Second World War.

Following the 1989 Oklahoma City presentation, the Comanche Code Talkers also began to receive frequent public honors from various dance and veterans' organizations within the Comanche tribe. Family members of the code talkers have expressed to me that they are extremely proud of their relatives' contributions. While all veterans are frequently honored in Native American public gatherings, Comanches frequently and specifically express that they are proud of the code talkers because of the unique way in which they used their linguistic skills. The Comanche tribe recognized the code talkers at the First Comanche Nation Fair, held at Eagle Park, on the Ft. Sill military base, west of Lawton, Oklahoma, on Saturday, September 25, 1992. During the afternoon program, the surviving code talkers were called forward and praised for their service. In addition to celebrating their heritage of military service and honoring the code talkers for their contributions, the Comanche tribe dedicated a new Army helicopter, appropriately named "Comanche."[26] In 1992, the Department of Defense also dedicated a display focusing on Native American code talkers (King 1992).

In June 1993, the remaining Comanche Code Talkers and Major General (Ret.) Hugh F. Foster Jr. were guests at a sovereignty symposium in Tulsa, Oklahoma, which contained an exhibit on the code talkers containing several World War II photographs. In September of 1993 the code talkers were honored by Heritage America at Ft. Sill, Oklahoma, for their contributions to the victories of the World War II Allies. To commemorate the fiftieth anniversary of the D-Day landing, CBS became interested in interviewing veterans of the D-Day invasion. The CBS officials located the code talkers through the previous veterans gatherings they had attended in St. Louis and at Cahokia Mounds in Illinois (Norrish 1994), and reporters contacted the remaining code talkers in December of 1993. Later that month, Forrest Kassanavoid and Charles Chibitty were both interviewed by CBS for *D-Day*, a documentary which aired on Thursday, May 26, 1994. To the members' surprise, the CBS reporters were more interested in their recruitment, training, and education than with how the code talkers actually functioned in combat. Hosted by Dan Rather and General Norman Schwartzkopf, the special featured interviews commemorating the fiftieth anniversary of the D-Day landing, including a brief excerpt recounting the role the Comanche Code Talkers performed.[27] Each code talker was also presented with an individual plaque at the annual Comanche Homecoming in Walters, Oklahoma, in 1994. In the fall of 1994, the artillery center at Ft. Sill, in Lawton, Oklahoma, also recognized each of the remaining Comanche Code Talkers with individual plaques commemorating their service. Charles Chibitty and Roderick Red Elk were both honored at Tinker Air Force Base in Oklahoma City on May 8, 1995, for their wartime contributions as code talkers. In 1995, the National Security Agency (NSA) at Ft. George G. Meade, Maryland, organized a display featuring the activities of the Comanche, Navajo, and Choctaw Code Talkers in World Wars I and II.

Since the 1989 reunion, Major General Foster has kept in touch with the surviving Comanche Code Talkers, having traveled several times to the Comanche community in Oklahoma to attend the now-annual Comanche Nation Fair and other cultural events at which the code talkers and he are regularly honored. On April 28, 1994, at the spring dance of the Comanche War Dance Society, Forrest Kassanavoid formally adopted Foster as a member of his family, giving him the name Poo-ee-whee-tek-wha Eks-ah-bahnna (Puhihwitekwa ekasahpana'), or "Telephone Soldier" (lit., "Metal Talk Red Sash," combining the terms for telephone and talking and the old Comanche name for military officers who wore red waist sashes).[28] This was indeed an appropriate name for Foster, reflecting his military rank and role with the group. Major General Foster is the only surviving non–Native American to have had actual experience in the creation of a Native American military linguistic code. Major General Foster reflected on his association and work with the code talkers: "They were a remarkably cheerful, good-natured group, mostly retiring, and not great conversationalists. Loyal to the hilt, dependable, and hard working. I truly enjoyed working with them."[29]

Some of the Comanches made and maintained lifetime friendships with some of their non-Indian fellow soldiers. Assigned combat partner and lifetime friend of Simmons Parker, Ernest Stahlberg recalls, "I [had] never met any Indian before. There was no problems as a whole. Some were good friends with non-Indians, others merely accepted them as fellow soldiers. There was never any hostile attitudes that I was aware of. . . . My relations with the Indians was always pleasant. I found they were the same as people as the rest of us—meaning non-Indians. . . . I have only pleasant memories of my time in the Signal Corps and my re-

188   lationship with all the Indians." Stahlberg reminisced about their correspondence, "Even after we were discharged Simmons [Parker] and I kept in touch now and then, until he died. His grandmother made baby moccasins for my daughter. . . . My daughter still has them now. When he died his wife sent me a photo of him. Prior to that time, she sent me a photo of their first child." Similarly, John Eckert, who was closest with Simmons Parker and Larry Saupitty, maintained correspondence with Simmons Parker until the time of Mr. Parker's death. Mr. Eckert recalled that he had pictures of all of Parker's children.[30]

On September 20, 1996, Forrest Kassanavoid passed away. Exactly one year later a feast–giveaway–memorial dance was held for him in Lawton, Oklahoma. Forrest was very active in Native American and non-Indian dance circles. As a result, Native Americans and non-Indians came from all over the United States to attend the memorial. A posthumous award was presented to Mrs. Marian Kassanavoid by Carney Saupitty Jr. and Carol Cizik. As Mr. Saupitty read:

> This is a Comanche proclamation whereas the Comanche Nation recognizes that it is appropriate to bestow special acknowledgment upon Mr. Forrest Kassanavoid posthumously. And whereas Forrest Kassanavoid participated in several campaigns across Europe, earning the Purple Heart, the European–African–Middle Eastern Campaign Medal with five Bronze Stars, American Defense Ribbon, and Good Conduct Medal. And whereas Forrest Kassanavoid served in the United States Army during World War II as a Comanche Code Talker, and as one of the Comanche Code Talkers, he helped to perfect the code in the Comanche language that was never cracked by the Axis Powers. And whereas Forrest Kassanavoid believed in the preservation of the Comanche language and taught a class in his hometown of Indiahoma, which was open to all people. And whereas the Comanche Nation believes that Forrest Kassanavoid represented his family, the Comanche Nation, and all Indian People as a positive role model and served with dignity and distinction. And whereas Forrest Kassanavoid is truly deserving of this posthumous recognition for his efforts and accomplishments throughout his life, now therefore, I, Carney Saupitty Jr., speaking for Keith Yackyonney, chairman of the Comanche Nation, do hereby proclaim and designate September 20, 1997, as Forrest Kassanavoid Day, in honor and memory of Mr. Forrest Kassanavoid. Thank you.[31]

Following a series of lulus (ululations, voiced tremolos performed by women to show honor and appreciation during dances, giveaways, etc.) in his honor, Carol Cizik added:

As the vice chairman of the Comanche Nation and in behalf of the Comanche tribe, I declare this as Forrest Kassanavoid Day, and this day will be known, from this day forward, among all the Comanche Nation as Forrest Kassanavoid Day.[32]

Speaking of Mr. Kassanavoid, Maynard Hinman (Ponca) stated, "He was a Comanche Indian first, and everything else was secondary. He was a Comanche Indian and he was proud of it. . . . In a time when everyone says an Indian can't do it, he did it all."[33] Nothing could have been more true. Five days after Forrest Kassanavoid's memorial dance, Mr. Roderick Red Elk passed away on September 25, 1997.[34]

In March of 1998, Mrs. Elizabeth B. Pollard of Anadarko, Oklahoma, drafted and began soliciting signatures for a petition to the Congress of the United States on behalf of Native American code talkers of both World Wars I and II. Because these code talkers have never formally been recognized by the United States government and because France bestowed its highest honor on the remaining Choctaw and Comanche Code Talkers in 1989, this petition seeks to have these servicemen honored in a similar manner by awarding them the Congressional Medal of Honor.[35]

More recently, Charles Chibitty, the last remaining Comanche Code Talker who saw combat action, received the Knowlton Award from the U.S. Army. The presentation was held on November 30, 1999, at the Pentagon's Hall of Heroes in Washington, D.C. Established in 1995, the Knowlton Award recognizes people for outstanding military intelligence work and is named for Revolutionary War veteran Lieutenant Colonel Thomas Knowlton. Interest in the Comanche Code Talkers continues to increase. On November 9, 2001, the Comanche Indian Veterans Association (CIVA) and the Oklahoma Bar Association honored the Comanche Code Talkers at the U.S. Attorney's Office in Oklahoma City. Included in the program were an excerpt from a recent television documentary recounting the story of the Comanche Code Talkers, and the flying of the Comanche Nation flag alongside the Oklahoma state flag and United States flag at the U.S. Attorney's Office. Charles Chibitty, the last surviving Comanche Code Talker, continues to receive frequent requests for interviews and to speak publicly on the group's experiences.[36]

THE CONTINUED IMPORTANCE
OF NATIVE AMERICAN CODE TALKING

The increasing recognition of the importance of Native American code talking continued well after the end of World War II. This trend is demonstrated by: (1) postwar military instructions for code talkers not to discuss their service or code talking, (2) the maintenance of these re-

190 strictions for the Navajo until 1968, and (3) continuation of the United
States military discourse concerning the code talkers (largely pertaining
to the Navajo) after the war. A series of military communications from
the Department of Defense Armed Forces Security Agency and the Army
Security Agency at the Pentagon in the fall of 1950 indicate that the
growing knowledge of the Navajo Code Talkers was sufficient to make
their continued use a possibility. These documents emphasize the potential further use of Navajo Code Talkers, but also mention the possibility of using other native populations. However, these data also clearly
point to the continued concern of the armed forces with available numbers and bilingual fluency, and that "native language code talkers" were
sufficient primarily for tactical or battlefield situations.

DEPARTMENT OF DEFENSE
ARMED FORCES SECURITY AGENCY
Washington 25, D.C.

In reply refer to
AFSA-ooK/ef
Serial:0678
Oct 19 1950

SUBJECT: Utilization of American Indians as Communica-
tion Linguists
TO: Chief, Army Security Agency
The Pentagon
Washington, 25, D.C.

Reference: ASA (GAS-23) ltr to DIRAFSA dtd 4 Oct 1950
1. Receipt of the reference is acknowledged.

2. The following specific answers are given to the questions
in paragraph 1 of the reference:

a. What degree of security is afforded by the use of American Indians as native language "code talkers"?

The degree of security afforded is sufficient for communication up to and including CONFIDENTIAL. Reliability of
communications would be problematical unless the "code
talkers" were thoroughly trained.

b. Would the security of Indian language "code talking" be
sufficient to allow its use within or between units for
battlefield or other communications where COMINT value
to an aggressor would diminish rapidly and only short term
communication security is necessary?

Yes. Indian language "code talking" is adequate for short term security.

c. Would AFSA recommend the use of American Indians as native language "code talkers" as a means of regular secure communications?

No: only under special circumstances as in the case of the Navajo "code talkers." For security of regular communications dependence should be placed on literal ciphers or on ciphony equipments now under development.

3. The article on Navajo Code Talkers is correct as far as it goes but it leaves out certain details which make it misleading in its implications. At the beginning communications were unsatisfactory because of deficiencies in the Navajo vocabulary. The Marine Corps was unable to make as extensive use of the Navajo "code talkers" as had been desired because the 420 quota referred to in the article exhausted the able-bodied English speaking males in the tribe. The Marine Corps was forced to stop recruiting Navajo and to limit their use as "code talkers." The Aleuts, for example, were recommended to the Navy in World War II but were not used. It is possible that other small American tribes could be used in a similar manner, but the same limitations would exist. In the planning stages, as contrasted to the tactical stages of an operation, written communications are superior to voice communications and excellent literal cipher systems are currently available.

4. It may be concluded that it is feasible and practicable to use American Indians as communication linguists, as in the case of the Navajo "code talkers," provided:

a. This is done locally or at least on a small scale.

b. This is done intelligently.

c. This has the enthusiastic support of everyone concerned.

d. This is limited to tactical or battlefield communications.

e. Their loyalty can be guaranteed.

S.P. COLLINS
Colonel, Signal Corps
Deputy Director, AFSA.[37]

192   These same concerns are further emphasized in a second document which further indicates that while the use of native language code talkers for tactical or battlefield situations was deemed acceptable, their use was not considered appropriate for higher levels of military communications.

G-2-ASA SUBJECT: Utilization of American Indians

THRU: ACofs, G-2   FROM: ACofs, G-2-ASA   DATE 24 OCT 1950
TO: ACofs, G-3   COMMENT NO. 2
                                               Maj. ------147 Ext 46

1. With the number of Indian languages or dialects used by American Indians (approximately 1500) it would be impractical to attempt to determine, without detailed study, testing, and analysis, the particular language or languages that are the most difficult to translate, which are the least known, and which could be expected to offer the greatest degree of security for communication transmissions.

2. Indian language communication transmissions would be more difficult and more time consuming for an enemy to translate than English, voice or CW, clear text transmissions, hence, they afford more security than English, voice or CW, clear text transmissions.

3. The degree of security afforded by American Indians when used as native language "code talkers" is sufficient for communications up to and including CONFIDENTIAL.

4. The security of American Indian language "code talking" would be sufficient to allow its use within or between units for battlefield or other communications where the COMINT value to an enemy would diminish rapidly and only short term communication security is necessary.

5. The use of American Indians as communication linguists for the transmission of messages within or between small tactical units, similar to "Marauder," and between such units and a friendly command post, is considered both feasible and practicable.

6. Certain provisos to the use of American Indians as communication linguists are necessary and any use must be dependent thereon. These provisos are:

a. Use must be executed locally or at least on a small scale.

b. Uses must be executed intelligently.

c. Use must have the enthusiastic support of everyone concerned.

d. Use must be limited to tactical or battlefield communication.

7. Training for Indians to be used as native language communication linguist:

a. In the event it is decided to use Indian language "code talkers" by the Department of the Army, it is recommended that the Marine Corps be contacted for their experience in the training of Navajo for such duties.

b. The Army Security Agency, while not responsible for training of this nature, has on file a letter from a Mr. Alban Rogers, 418 Park Avenue, Swarthmore, Pa., dated 17 October 1948, in which Mr. Rogers states that he trained a few Navajo Indians in Australia, during World War II for use in transmission of messages; that the Navajo he trained were intelligible to each other but not to anyone else who might know the language. Mr. Rogers further expressed his willingness to cooperate and to make a study, prepared by him since the war, available to the proper authority.

c. Training requirements for Indians to be used as native language "code talkers" should be rigid and comprehensive, particularly insofar as their proposed duties are concerned. Indian "code talking" must be fast, secure, and reliable. Training should include:

(1) Practice, over land lines and radio, in the translation of English text military messages into the Indian language and back into English.

(2) Determination, by the Indians, and the use of new words and phrases in the Indian language necessary for military use to include a complete military vocabulary.

(3) Practice in transmitting exclusively in the Indian language. No mixture of English and Indian language could be permitted from a COMINT and COMSEC point of view.

8. A deterrent to the use of American Indians as native language "code talkers" is the small number of able bodied Indians available for military service who have the required educational background and who speak both the Indian and English languages. The responsibilities of the Indians, so

used, makes mandatory the establishment of fairly high standards of education, physical stamina, Indian and English language fluency, aptitude, loyalty, and adaptability to the role of "code talker."

9. ASA cryptosystems, because of the highly classified matter transmitted, must be secure for extended periods of time. In view of the CONFIDENTIAL limitation of American Indian "code talkers" it is not feasible to consider such use of American Indians by the Army Security Agency.

10. Subject to the above, the Army Security Agency has no objections to the use of American Indians as "code talkers" for battlefield transmission of communications.

FOR THE ASSISTANT CHIEF OF STAFF, G-2:
1 incl.
Security Check—P.A. Bonney   [AG ASA Stamp illegible].[38]

One communication sent from the Indian Association of America to President Harry Truman in 1950 proposed the postwar organization of military reserve training units composed of Indians who were World War II veterans and fluent speakers of their respective tribal languages. The plan was reportedly proposed to the office of the Joint Chiefs of Staff and the Department of Defense and was then under favorable consideration.[39] Nevertheless, the importance of Native American code talkers is reflected in the recognition of their potential throughout the upper echelons of the Department of Defense in the immediate post–World War II era.

COMPARISON AND CONTRAST

In order to place the context and significance of the Comanche Code Talkers' experiences and contributions in perspective, comparison with the experiences of other Native American code talkers is needed. Members of several tribes used their indigenous languages for communications transmissions as an impromptu de facto or Type 2 Native American code. That is, many officers had Native Americans send communications transmissions in their everyday language on a "use them if you have them" basis. However, the Comanche and Navajo were used most extensively in the most formally developed Type 1 Native American code talker programs during the Second World War. Accordingly, they offer the best opportunity for comparison. Furthermore, not until this work have sufficient data on another Native American code talking unit been compiled to allow comparison with the extensive Navajo literature. Thus, this work allows the first comparison between two Native American code talking programs.

Our exploration of the major elements of the Comanche Code Talkers' development and enlistment factors (defense of land and people, cultural background, boarding school experiences, employment) leaves an important question. How do the experiences of the Comanche Code Talkers compare with those of the more numerous and well-known Navajo Code Talkers? I offer a brief comparison and contrast between the major aspects of the Comanches' background, training, and combat experiences as code talkers and those of the Navajo. While the Comanche data have already been presented, subsequent citations in this section are presented primarily for demonstrating the Navajo data.

The experiences of the two groups, enrolled in two completely unrelated programs in independent branches of the U.S. armed forces, will be demonstrated to have been relatively similar in terms of actual code formation and use. However, significant differences existed regarding boarding school background, ease in adjusting to basic training, unit size due to armed forces policy, actual combat conditions, and postwar recognition.

Background

Both the Comanches and Navajo experienced lengthy periods of tremendous biological and cultural genocide at the hands of the American government and people. Yet despite this record of past treatment, both volunteered to defend their land and people and set aside any bitterness to use their native languages and risk their lives in defense of the United States government, the same government which had forcibly and brutally placed their grandparents on reservations.

As perceived by the soldiers themselves, the European and Pacific theaters of war were significantly different. Numerous World War II veterans that I have interviewed emphasized the differences between the two theaters of the war. Some Native American World War II veterans, including some of the Comanche Code Talkers, described the European theater as "a more mechanized war." The European theater demanded a more offense-oriented procedure for the Allies and a defensive effort by the Axis; once out of the French hedgerow country, movements were often frequent and rapid, and involved long distances. Distances between engagements in the Pacific theater were often great; however, each ground operation was more compressed than in Europe. The Pacific theater of action involved a slower, more intense type of warfare, including more thickly vegetated terrain, trench warfare, repeated advancements

196 and withdrawals, "Banzai attacks" (McClain 1994:70–71), and even Kamikazes. In addition, veterans commented on another major difference between German and Japanese soldiers. While Germans would surrender under certain circumstances, Japanese troops generally would not and often fought to the very last man, which often forced U.S. troops to eradicate all remaining resistance in order to take and secure an area. Yet even after they gained control of an area, remaining isolated pockets of Japanese troops would surprise U.S. army and marine units by attacking them from their rear.

Code Talker Formation

Both code talking programs were formed for the same reasons and communications needs: speed, accuracy, security in transmission, and security in having a nonwritten code form based on a unique linguistic system. Thus, speed and security in communications, combined with the susceptibility to wire and phone tapping and radio monitoring by enemy forces, formed the basis for both the Comanche and Navajo Code Talking programs. In forming code terms both groups turned to their own respective cultural and environmental backgrounds, using native ideologies to form code terms for modern military items. American forces thus held an advantage over both German and Japanese where it was often most critical, as front line units could exchange communications with their top commanders in less time than with standard written codes and without fear of their messages being deciphered. Had the Japanese thought to employ in a similar fashion the language of the native Ainu, which differs significantly from Japanese, the war might have been very different.

Enlistment and Training

This work has shown that the underlying factors involved in Native American entrance into military service, or the process of militarization for Native Americans, differed significantly from that for non–Native Americans and are much more complex than most scholars have realized. The Comanches' traditional cultural emphasis of a martial ethos and protection of homeland, their boarding school experiences, their opportunity and desire to make a unique military contribution with their language, and the desire to remain together as a distinct ethnic unit constituted a unique set of cultural factors leading to enlistment, most of which affected other Native Americans as well. These factors also enabled their experiences in basic training to be relatively easy and this training to be shorter than that for most non-Indian recruits. All but one of the Comanches had been through government-run Indian boarding schools, and most of them benefited from the example of their parents' prior boarding school experiences. Based on the members' descriptions of their own experiences and compared to their parents' generation, the code talkers seem to have had little difficulty in adjusting to the boarding school format.[40] In contrast, the Navajos' general lack of off-reservation experience, familiarity with relative freedom on their reservation, lack of knowledge of the English language, and general reluctance to send their children to boarding schools differed significantly. These factors resulted in an initially traumatic experience in adjusting to boarding school–style military commands and rigid training schedules, and their instructors' frustrations with their extreme patience, resistance to agitation, and nonaggressive nature. These aspects of basic training were initially difficult for some Navajo (Paul 1973; Escue 1991; McClain 1994:40). Only 102 of the 420 Navajo Code Talkers had attended federal high schools (Paul 1973:105–113). Many potential Navajo Code Talker recruits were deferred due to an insufficient knowledge of English. Those Navajo who attended boarding schools also underwent forced assimilationist attempts to prevent them speaking their language (Kawano 1990:xv; McClain 1994:51). Yet they quickly adapted to their new environment (Paul 1973:14–22; Kawano 1990:6; McClain 1994). The Comanches' experiences in Indian boarding schools had already accustomed them to speaking fluent English and familiarized them with many of the basic military procedures concerning marching, schedules, punctuality, and following orders. Although Comanche and Navajo both underwent systematic language suppression in government boarding schools, its ineffectiveness proved to be a boon, as the armed forces soon came recruiting fluent speakers. By the early 1940s, bilingual Native Americans were valued by at least some military personnel.

The Comanche and Navajo familiarity with endurance, the hardships encountered in everyday life on reservations and in Indian communities, and a traditional ideology which taught individuals not to complain about minor discomforts, gave them an already well-developed outlook regarding training endurance and perseverance. This outlook was highly praised by military officers and admired by fellow Anglo soldiers, who often marveled at their physical endurance and skills (Paul 1973:79; Bernstein 1991:44). Instances of recruits eating bananas and drinking water to gain weight in order to enlist are documented among the Navajo (Kawano 1990:63, 91) and Comanche. Aside from stereotypical expectations, typified by the appellation of all Indians as "Chief," Comanche Code Talkers and other Indian veterans indicate that malicious race friction was virtually unknown between Indians and whites in the military. Similar findings are recorded for the Navajo (McClain 1994: **197**

198   43). Unlike the treatment given to Afro-Americans, non–federally recognized Native Americans (individuals whose tribal group lacks a formal treaty, the basis of federal recognition, with the United States
government), and mixed Afro–Native Americans, federally recognized
Native American servicemen were enlisted as Indians and were judged
by their military peers largely by their performance and not by the color
of their skin (Paul 1973:18, 94).[41] Like non-Indian soldiers, Comanche
and Navajo Code Talkers frequently lost rank for minor demerits they
earned (McClain 1994:42–43). Throughout the rigors of basic training
and the horrors of combat many humorous incidents occurred for both
the Comanches and Navajo (Paul 1973:18, 62–63, 70–72, 94; Kawano
1990:36, 50; McClain 1994:132), and cultural performances of Indian
song and dance by both the Comanches and Navajo were popular among
Anglo soldiers and local civilians (Paul 1973:20). Members of both code
talker programs were similarly trained as basic communications operators in all basic forms of communications procedures, including semaphore, Morse code, radio and telephone, message writing, wire laying,
pole climbing, and equipment repair (Paul 1973; Tully 1995).

Exposure

One of the greatest differences between the two groups was in the attempts by the different branches of the armed forces to keep the code
talker projects secret. During 1942–1943, the Comanches received significant exposure in East Coast newspapers in connection with their exhibitions of boxing and Indian dancing and singing. Although the Comanche Code Talker project was not expanded due to army policy, of
which some factors remain unclear, the significant media exposure may
have influenced the army not to expand it further. Conversely, great efforts were made to keep the Navajo project secret (Paul 1973; McClain
1994:77, 91–98), and information concerning the Navajo service as code
talkers was not formally released until 1968. Whereas nearly everyone
in the Fourth Division knew of the Comanche Code Talkers from their
media coverage and recreational activities, fellow soldiers were not allowed near the Comanches during their code training and thus had
no in-depth knowledge of what they were doing. In contrast, the Navajo
code talkers were a highly secret marine program (Kawano 1990:12).
This secrecy and their physical appearance often resulted in their being
mistaken in identity (Paul 1973:85–91; Kawano 1990:11, 42, 54, 72;
Tully 1995; McClain 1994) and in language (Paul 1973:32, 52, 72; Mc-
Clain 1994) as Japanese. Whereas Navajo Code Talkers were frequently
confused with Japanese and full-time Anglo bodyguards were assigned
to them for protection, the Native Americans in the European theater

were generally so distinct from Germans and Italians that there was no concern for security measures.[42] On at least seven different instances, Navajo Code Talkers were nearly killed by U.S. servicemen unable to differentiate them from Japanese because of their physical appearance, and even the Japanese confused the Navajo as Japanese, later believing they must be Alaskan natives (Paul 1973:85–91).[43]

Service

The major differences between the Navajo and Comanche Code Talkers are found in the overall differences between the European and Pacific theaters of World War II, the Navajo Code Talkers' numerically greater role in front line fighting, and in some of the types of messages that were sent. In addition to transmitting sensitive military communications, the Navajo Code Talkers were used to report enemy troop locations, direct troop movements, and call in air strikes and artillery bombardments. Aside from the Navajos' greater role in aerial messages, the communications service performed by the two groups differed little qualitatively. Code talkers normally worked in teams of two (Paul 1973; Escue 1991:20), and both Comanche and Navajo Code Talkers sent messages in standard English as well as in their coded native languages. Messages of similar content of both an offensive and a defensive nature were commonly sent in code, and both sets of code talkers provided radio, telephone, and hand-delivered communications using their coded languages (McClain 1994:115). One major difference was that once higher-echelon officers in the South Pacific became familiar with the Navajo and their effectiveness, the Navajo only answered to the message center chief and officers of "two Stars and up" (McClain 1994:117). While the Navajo had a formally coded alphabet, impromptu spelling allowed the Comanche to transmit proper names in identical form when necessary. Although all were assigned communications personnel, members of both tribes served in a number of positions which included service as code talkers and message center personnel, and other duties as regular troops. Troubleshooting lines was a common part of Comanche and Navajo Code Talker service. The frequency of coded transmissions was in direct relation to the ability of enemy forces to intercept vital messages, to the enemy's ability to react to intercepted communications, and to the proximity, size, and strength of resistance of local enemy forces at a given time. Members of both code talker groups occasionally had fun telling off or swearing at, in English or German, enemy operators attempting to tap into their lines (Escue 1991:18). While commanding officers in the Pacific were at first reluctant to use Navajo Code Talkers, even after they had performed effectively (Paul 1973; Escue 1991; **199**

200   McClain 1994:89), the surviving Comanche Code Talkers indicated that there was no observable reluctance by officers to use them for communications.[44] Numerous lives were saved by both code talking units, and members of both sets of code talkers performed valiantly and were highly decorated for their service. Numerous Comanche and Navajo Code Talkers were wounded. While no Comanche Code Talkers were killed in action, eleven confirmed Navajo made the supreme sacrifice for their nations, one by "friendly fire" (Paul 1973:54–57, 64–66; Kawano 1990:10; McClain 1994:105).[45] Although the type of combat and terrain differed significantly and the Navajo were more subject to intense close-quarters combat, the Comanches were never immune from bombing, strafing, artillery shelling—the ways in which most of the Comanches were wounded—and periodic small-arms and sniper fire.

In addition to the natural longing for home, family, and friends, many Indian veterans of World War II that I have spoken with described feelings of loneliness and a degree of isolation from being the only Indian in their unit. Franco (1999:165–166) reports similar findings among isolated native servicemen and servicewomen, and several cases of strong intratribal and intertribal bonds that quickly developed between Indians in the same unit or in neighboring units. Because they served in part as an all-Indian communications unit, the Comanches do not appear to have encountered these feelings to the same degree as other, more isolated, native servicemen. Indeed, several of the code talkers stated that the ability to enlist and serve together as a unit was a principal motivation in their enlistments. Although data on the Navajo attitudes toward this are lacking, their situation was similar in that they were in close proximity to fellow Navajo a considerable portion of the time.

Belief

Members of numerous Native American groups held sacred and social ceremonies before, during, and after their military service in World War II. Before going overseas and during their time in service, both Comanche and Navajo servicemen maintained their traditional belief systems. Comanches had Native American Church and Christian church meetings prior to going overseas and carried blessed peyote bundles on their person during the war, while other area meetings were held in their home communities for their benefit while they were overseas. Navajo underwent Blessing Way ceremonies prior to leaving to ask for protection. The Navajo also had meetings held in their behalf by community members at home, and underwent ritual preparation with sacred corn pollen among themselves, as before the invasion of Iwo Jima. Some carried bags of sacred corn pollen while in combat (Paul 1973:104; Escue

1991:18; Tully 1995). Peyote among the Comanche, corn pollen among the Navajo, and prayers by both in their native languages were used similarly by members in combat for ensuring protection in dangerous situations and to ensure safe passage (Paul 1973:81–82, 106). Several Navajo in the First Marine Division held a ceremonial dance before leaving for Okinawa and after its capture (Paul 1973:91; Escue 1991:19). While in service, members of both tribes retained their tribal identity through the continuation of language, religion, and sociocultural interaction.

Postwar Return

Upon returning, Comanches were briefly honored with Native American Church meetings, Christian church meetings, powwows, and victory dances. Returning Navajo underwent Enemy Way ceremonies for ritual religious and spiritual cleansing of the body and mind but otherwise received no formal homecoming (McClain 1994:226). The Navajo Enemy Way ceremony is a traditional curative ceremony held after Navajo raids and battles with other Indians and non-Indians. A three-day ceremony, the rite employs a diagnostician (to identify the problem), a male herbalist (to prescribe appropriate herbs), and a traditional doctor (to perform the purification ceremony). The rite is designed to purify individuals who have met various types of non-Navajo peoples, some of whom might be evil, to blot out memories of what happened, and to help them return to normal life. As with other Navajo healing ceremonies, this is achieved through ritual to restore *hozho*—in other words, to bring them back into harmony with all that is around them. If no curative ceremony is held, it is believed that individuals will eventually suffer mentally and physically (Paul 1973:104–105). McClain (1994: 226–227) notes how the pressures of not being able to discuss their experiences created social and psychological readjustment problems for some Navajo, and how these were eased through traditional curing ceremonies. While the Comanche Native American Church and Christian church prayer meetings are more associated with protection and thanksgiving for a safe return than with ritual cleansing, they function similarly, facilitating a traditional community-oriented religious and psychologically based adjustment back to normal community life. Subsequent honoring ceremonies were important for expressing appreciation for veterans' service and their status as veterans.

Post-1968 Recognition

Primarily due to their greater number (420 Navajo serving in the Third, Fourth, and Fifth Marine Divisions), the Navajo Code Talkers have received greater attention and recognition than other, smaller groups of Native American code talkers or communications operators. The Navajo were first recognized in 1969 at the Fourth Marine Division Association Reunion in Chicago, where they received special medals commemorating their service. Soon after, recognition included Certificates of Appreciation from the President of the United States in December 1971 (Kawano 1990: 12–13). On July 9–10, 1971, sixty-five Navajo Code Talkers convened for a two-day code talker reunion, sponsored by the Navajo Nation and the U.S. Marine Corps at the Navajo Tribal Museum in Window Rock, Arizona, to organize the Navajo Code Talkers Association.[46] The group held its first meeting on Veterans Day of that same year, where demonstrations of code talking were conducted (Paul 1973: 146). The association meets once a month in Gallup, New Mexico, and sponsors a scholarship program. Through the efforts of then Arizona Senator Dennis DeConcini, August 14, 1982 (the thirty-seventh anniversary of the Japanese surrender, V-J Day, or Victory in Japan) was declared National Navajo Code Talker Day by President Reagan, and the Navajo Code Talkers were honored with a Certificate of Recognition (Belleranti 1983:76; Escue 1991:20; Tully 1995). The Gallup, New Mexico, Chamber of Commerce houses a collection of historic photos, posters, trophies, radios, and other related Navajo items. In addition, the city of Phoenix, Arizona, erected the first permanent tribute to the Navajo Code Talkers, in the form of a fourteen-foot-high sculpture by Doug Hyde of a young Indian boy carrying a flute (Hirshfelder and deMontano 1993:232–234). In recognition of the Navajo Code Talkers' contributions the Marine Corps recruited an all-Navajo platoon in observance of the thirty-ninth anniversary of the original twenty-nine code talkers. Many of the members of this platoon were relatives of the original Navajo Code Talkers (Durrett 1998:106). There are presently over two hundred surviving Navajo Code Talkers (Kawano 1990:xv). The Choctaws and Comanches were not formally recognized until November 3, 1989. Presently, Charles Chibitty is the only surviving Comanche Code Talker who saw combat action. At present there are only three remaining Hopi Code Talkers. There are no surviving Choctaw Code Talkers. Throughout the postwar years Comanche and Navajo Code Talkers have participated in local, regional, and national public ceremonies, celebrations, parades, and veterans functions.

When asked why the Navajo have received more attention than any of the other tribes with code talkers, all of the Comanche Code Talkers cited the larger size of the Navajo group. This response reflects the army's skepticism about Native American code talkers and its policy during World War II not to adopt additional or further expand existing Native American code talker units. Several Native American populations contained more than adequate numbers of fluent speakers who could have served as code talkers. This issue of army policy is of great comparative and scholarly significance, as the expanded utilization of these additional and available Native American linguistic resources would have unquestionably aided the war effort in both theaters of action, based on the results with Choctaw, Comanche, Navajo, and other native code talkers. The issue of size constitutes one of the major differences between the Comanches and Navajos. Forrest Kassanavoid jokingly stated, "They must have had a better publicity agent than us."[47] Roderick Red Elk reflected on the difference in the size of the groups:

I think the main reason is they were bigger in numbers. Like four or five hundred [420] of them, where there was sixteen, seventeen of us. And they got more exposure being from Arizona and New Mexico than us poor old Okies down here [we] didn't get no exposure at all. That's the only way I can see it. Their language, to them, is just as sacred as ours is to us.[48]

As part of the Native Americans in Defense of Our Nation Exhibit, the Navajo, Comanche, and others were honored by the Pentagon in 1992 with an exhibit documenting the history of Native American code talking, to highlight the service and experiences of these groups. The exhibit was part of a larger permanent exhibit honoring American Indians, including the Comanches (DiNicolo n.d.:6–7; Wigginton 1992). At the unveiling of the exhibit, Navajo President Peterson Zah recalled:

I remember several years ago when I came to the Vietnam memorial and saw the statue dedicated to American warriors. There was a white soldier. There was a Chicano. There was a black service person. I went away thinking there needs to be one other person. That's the American Indian, because of all the ethnic groups in this country there are none who have volunteered more to defend our nation than the American Indian. (Wigginton 1992)

Indeed, estimates of the percentage of Native American participation in relation to their total population exceeded that of any other American ethnic group represented in World War II, including Anglo-Americans (Collier 1942:29), and this ratio was higher also for some categories of the number of wounded and killed (Bernstein 1991:55, 61; Haynie 1984:7; Hale 1992; Wigginton 1992).

While already found in children's books, recently the story of the Navajo Code Talkers has been expanded to children's toys. In February 2000, Hasbro toy company released the first "Navajo Code Talker" ac-

204 tion figure as the twenty-second member of its classic G.I. Joe action figures. When the action figure's arm is lifted, the figure says seven phrases in Navajo, followed by English translations. Messages include "request air support" and "attack by machine gun." The figure comes with a short history of the Navajo Code Talkers. World War II Navajo Code Talker Sam Billison provided the voice and phrases for the toy, which were accelerated, in comparison to his normal voice, in the toy version. Hasbro agreed to donate $5,000.00 to the Navajo Code Talkers Association and to provide each of the surviving Navajo Code Talkers with one of the action figures. As Sam Billison emphasized, "This will let people know about the code talkers. I think it's really going to put us on the map."[49]

Code talkers of both tribes returned home to assume leadership in their tribal communities and government, and to contribute to the cultural continuity of their people. Following the war, many of the Navajo Code Talkers became a force for social, economic, and political change as well as cultural retention. Having seen the outside world, the returning veterans were better prepared to deal with it. Many sought equality and education, in part through use of the G.I. Bill. While some returned to jobs at home, in various trades or the BIA, others moved to larger urban locales and pursued careers there. Many Navajo Code Talkers became leaders in tribal government, businessmen, and educators who fought to improve Navajo civil rights and the economy (Paul 1973:113; Begay 1981:93; Tully 1995; McClain 1994:228–229).

Likewise, some of the Comanche Code Talkers returned to pursue college educations or successful business careers. Generally, the Comanche Code Talkers did not actively pursue any roles in tribal government. Perhaps more importantly, however, and despite the group's limited size, many of the Comanche Code Talkers were involved in the revival and strengthening of traditional Comanche dance and warrior societies in the 1970s and in the continuation of the Native American Church (Meadows 1995). Some code talkers realized the need to ensure the survival of their language and later taught classes in their native language. Navajo Code Talker Teddy Draper returned to teach the Navajo language to children on the Navajo Reservation (Durrett 1998:112). Roderick Red Elk was one of the originators of the Comanche Language Preservation Project, serving as a consultant and helping to secure grants for the project. Forrest Kassanavoid taught Comanche language classes in his hometown of Indiahoma, Oklahoma, for several years.

In sum, the major differences between the Comanche and Navajo Code Talkers were unit size, the circumstances surrounding their public exposure during training and during service overseas, and the distinct differences between the European and Pacific theaters of combat. Con cerning training, code formation and content, the role of codes in communications uses, and the general range of postwar educational, economic, and cultural activities, the experiences of the two code talking groups were generally similar. In comparing the overall postwar activities of the Comanche and Navajo Code Talkers, many similarities are also found.

REFLECTIONS: "WE'D PROBABLY DO IT AGAIN IF WE HAVE TO, EVEN AT OUR AGE."

What were the meaning, importance, and significance of the Comanches' role and contributions as code talkers? What did being a code talker represent to the members themselves? How did they view themselves and their experiences? As a case study, the Comanche Code Talkers demonstrate several things: the value of native languages and bilingualism; tenacity in maintaining language, culture, and ethnic identity in the face of encapsulation within a larger encompassing and assimilationist socioeconomic system; and the use of syncretism to maintain traditional cultural values and practices while adjusting to changing circumstances. Because of the complexity of warfare there is no way to accurately estimate the full extent of the code talkers' role in the European and Pacific theaters of both world wars. From the veterans' own accounts and those of their commanding officers, Choctaw, Comanche, Navajo, and other Native American code talkers contributed usefully and uniquely in the war effort. Because the Comanche code was a unique communications tool that was used in several dangerous situations and was not broken, the Comanche Code Talkers undoubtedly saved lives during World War II, and, had the program been expanded, it is logical to assert that their contribution would only have increased.

Service as a code talker gave members a sense of pride in themselves, and in knowing that they—not only as individuals, but also as Comanches through their traditional culture—could contribute to the larger American war effort. As Comanches, U.S. citizens, and members of the United States Army, they were proudly bilingual. As such, they set an example of excellence for their fellow servicemen and their tribe.

Despite their valuable communications skills, the Comanche Code Talkers remain very modest about their contributions in the war. One code talker stated that he and the others never thought of themselves as anything special and didn't brag of their wartime experiences. Other Comanches have frequently stated that the members themselves have never sought the frequent attention they are now receiving. After returning from service, the members simply picked up their lives. Aside from serving as code talkers, the Comanches were no different than any other soldier, as they pulled the same regular duties as other non-Indian soldiers while waiting to transmit messages in English or coded Comanche and lay wire for transmission lines. Members stated that they were just "plain enlisted men." According to the members' own accounts, some obtained the rank of private first class or corporal, but often lost their rank from getting "busted down" for drinking, fighting, rowdiness, and other typical soldier "fun" after getting together on the weekend to celebrate each other's promotions. However, despite always finding time for fun, the code talkers never let their off-duty activities interfere with their assigned duties.[50]

The meaning of the Comanche Code Talkers' experiences—what they thought of themselves and their service—is best conveyed by the views of the surviving members that I interviewed. The following statements collected during my fieldwork allow the members to elaborate on their service—in their own words. As Forrest Kassanavoid explained:

> We never thought of ourselves as specialists. . . . We never thought of ourselves as special just because we were code talkers. We were regular soldiers, with one other duty assigned to us. We pulled KP and guard duty just like everyone else, and as far as we know, we weren't protected in any special way. We do know none of us was captured, and as far as we've heard, they never broke our code.[51]

Likewise, Roderick Red Elk pointed out that no leader was ever chosen from the group, "We just did it as a group."[52] Forrest Kassanavoid reflected on the importance of the Comanche code and his role as a code talker:

> I think it [the code] gave the Army a means of communications that they would not have otherwise had and just what impact it had, you know of course some of the messages they sent might have been sent [without using the code], but they could have been, you know, decoded by the Germans. Because right there at the first I think that they were in such a rush to get some of those messages through that they might have been easily intercepted. And I think the impact that the code talkers had was the fact that they had this code that they used which . . . the enemy couldn't break. That was really an advantage that the Army had. . . . It definitely saved some lives.

> I think that some of the messages they sent, I think they served their purpose, I think that the contribution was there. I don't know

how much it helped to win that war or how confident those people who had been in communications, the people who were in higher command thought, but that's what I think.

The modesty of the code talkers is further reflected, as Kassanavoid continued:

All those years that you know I had served as a member of the armed services, and when I came home from the war, it never dawned on me . . . that I was a code talker. And I think when it began to really strike me was when those fellows I had served with began to die and I began to realize that there's not many of us left and then all at once after about forty some years, damn near fifty years, they began to have activities you know. Like they'd have maybe a recognition ceremony of the code talkers and that's when I began to realize what a really great honor and privilege it was for a person to have served as a Comanche Code Talker. But it took all those years to really have an effect on me.[53]

When asked what had been his most significant experience as a code talker, another member of the group replied:

Well, that I did something that the army wanted, and that was the language, we could send messages on. What little we did that, like Roderick and I here, we had done something for our country, where the Germans couldn't understand what we was talking [about]. And I always tell him and the other boys, my only regret was that it took fifteen to twenty years before they recognized the Navajo. It took about twenty-nine years before they recognized us on that "What's My Line" deal they had on television, they brought the Comanche Code Talkers up. After that many years, some of our comrades and cousins, and second and third cousins are not here to enjoy the recognition we're getting these days.[54]

This code talker continued:

After all of it was over with, they finally honored us at the state capitol. But to know that I at least done something for the country, what little I did. Because there were thousands and thousands of soldiers that got killed you know. If what little we did saved some of those lives, then I'm proud I was part of it you know.

Like I always say, the only regret that I have is that my comrades, my cousins, and others that was with us, is not here to enjoy things like this [our videotaped studio interview] that is happening to us after all of these years. That's what I want to say.[55]

The remaining code talkers spoke of how using their native language during the war gave them a sense of pride in service to not only the American people, but to the Comanche people and tribe as well. The Navajo express similar sentiments concerning the pride they have felt in using their language as code talkers. As Navajo Code Talker Harold Foster stated, "I was happy and proud to be able to use my language in the service of my country" (McClain 1994:93). Similarly, Thomas Begay expressed, "I thought that using our language was a good idea. . . . Using the Navajo language as a disguise was very clever" (McClain 1994:93).

Finally, I asked each of the surviving combat-active Comanche Code Talkers, "What would you most like future generations of Comanches to remember about the Comanche Code Talkers?"

Roderick Red Elk replied:

I guess the contribution that we had made might go down in the history books. And I would strongly advise the rest of the Comanche people if they don't know their language, relearn it and how to speak it. Because that's a gift that was given to us and we need to retain that language and the only way I can see it, how to do that, would be to teach some of the younger ones the language, so we can retain our language, keep it ongoing.[56]

Forrest Kassanavoid responded:

I think what I would like for them to refer to or to think of most was the landing they made on D-Day on Utah Beach. That the code talkers all, they landed there. Because you know that was the greatest single, probably battle that they fought in during World War II. That the code talkers were at the landing at Utah Beach at Normandy.[57]

Finally, another of the code talkers stated:

That we did something, to use our language as the Navajo [did] when they went to the Pacific against the Japs and we against the Krauts. We did something, and we have, like he and I [pointing to

Roderick Red Elk] could talk our tribe [tribal language] fluently, sit down and speak to others and don't use no English. And that I was glad that I could do that for the country. Even though they didn't recognize us for so long, and they finally did, and the country of France honored us with medals. It's known as, when you translate it, it's "Knights of the National Merit Medal of Honor," which is good.

And we'd probably do it again if we have to, even at our age![58]

CONCLUSION

The topic of Indian code talkers has long had great human interest appeal. It is, in itself, a compelling story. During the research for this manuscript I saw a tremendous growth of interest in this topic, especially concerning the less-publicized non-Navajo groups that are little known and even less documented. As word of this manuscript spread I frequently received phone calls, letters, e-mails, and requests to speak on the subject from both home and abroad (cf. Saville 2001). Unfortunately, government and other attempts to formally honor and recognize the Choctaw, Comanche, and many other groups have come largely too late. By the time of the 1989 ceremony at the Oklahoma State Capitol, there were no surviving World War I Choctaw Code Talkers and only three Comanche Code Talkers who saw combat. Charles Chibitty is the last Comanche Code Talker. Over the past few years he often lamented in public statements that, while he appreciated the awards and recognition, they came too late for the others, and that now, he had to "Enjoy it by himself." In December of 2000, President Clinton approved legislation to award the original twenty-nine Navajo Code Talkers with Congressional Gold Medals—the highest civilian award Congress can bestow. Four of the five living members of the original twenty-nine were able to attend the awards ceremony in the Washington, D.C., Capitol Rotunda on July 26, 2001 (Marine Corps League 2001:51). The remaining Navajo Code Talkers were awarded Congressional Silver Medals in the fall of 2001. The Navajo also recognized their tribal code talkers at the 2002 Winter Olympics in Salt Lake City, Utah. In January of 2001 efforts to recognize the remaining three Hopi Code Talkers gained national attention.[59] In turn, Congresswoman Kay Granger of Texas has introduced a congressional bill (H.R. 3512) to honor the Comanche Code Talkers with Gold Congressional Medals of Honor. Recently the author was contacted by the Library of Congress to collaborate in compiling a

210   list of all known Native American code talkers. In light of the various overwhelming forms of dominance imposed through the processes of forced encapsulation and acculturation, cultures like the Comanches' deserve credit for their resiliency, which enabled the maintenance of their linguistic integrity. The obscurity of the Comanche language to Axis intelligence provided a small but valuable contribution to the Allied war effort.

The rising interest in Native American code talking has resulted in an increase of public claims of World War II code talking by many less well-known (i.e., non-Choctaw, -Comanche, and -Navajo) tribes. Most of these claims appear to be by small, informally based groups that performed some degree of Type 2 code talking. In turn, some members of Type 1 code talking groups and their tribes have expressed displeasure and resentment toward these recent claims. Primarily these sentiments are based on two factors: (1) the fact that they have never heard of these smaller, sometimes impromptu groups of code talkers, and (2) that Type 1 code talkers tend not to view Type 2 code talking as a true form of code talking because it did not involve formally devised codes and training.

As with other smaller and lesser known Native American code talking units, the significance of the Comanche Code Talkers' role in World War II should not be measured by the length of their messages or by the frequency at which they were sent, but by the Comanches' ability and willingness to provide a limited but ingenious contribution to the United States armed forces in a crucially vital period. Native Americans enlisted in great numbers for a complex combination of reasons that were primarily culturally appropriate to them but quite different from what mainstream America perceived: (1) traditional cultural factors (warrior-based themes), (2) acculturative factors (boarding schools), (3) contemporary economic factors (employment), and (4) patriotism for the defense of their own lands and peoples and the United States. Two additional motivations existed for code talkers, the desire to (1) "stick together" with their relatives and fellow Comanches as specialized native units and (2) provide a specialized military communications skill through the use of their native languages. The Comanche Code Talkers' ability to provide a unique linguistic contribution in a time of need was one of the major reasons for their voluntary enlistment.

The United States should be thankful that its attempts at forced assimilation to the then largely Anglo-Saxon Protestant cultural model, including forms of punishment now considered illegal and in violation of human civil rights, failed. Despite the obvious benefits of multilingualism for knowledge, travel, and international business, many Americans remain opposed to any sanctioned bilingualism in the American education system. In attempting to dissuade "non-progressive" states proposing to pass "English only" legislation overturning Title V, now Title XI (the Indian Education Act); and Title VII (the Bilingual Education Act), Lydia Whirlwind Soldier points out the service of the Navajo Code Talkers and the contemporary practicality of bilingualism:

> My point in all of this is that these men, in spite of their experiences with persecution and oppression, continue to set an example of excellence for their people. They were truly, proudly bilingual. They embraced American society and carried their language and heritage with them. They demonstrated that Native American culture is relevant in today's society. . . .

> The Navajo Code Talkers inspired many with their quiet determination to preserve their language and culture and still remain patriotic to our country. There's a lesson to be learned here. We, as Americans, must learn to appreciate the diversity and bilingualism that exists within our society instead of promoting discrimination with "English only" legislation for our schools. Languages are an integral part of our identity. We must allow people, especially our children, to have pride in their identity and exercise their right to make their own choices. Bilingualism helped save our country during World War II. . . . Monolingual people have no reason to be threatened by bilingualism. (1995:65)

We are all lucky that government attempts to forcibly replace Indian languages with English did not fully succeed. Indeed, many Americans owe their lives and those of their immediate ancestors to members of the Assiniboine, Chippewa (Ojibwa), Choctaw, Comanche, Creek, Hopi, Kiowa, Menominee, Navajo, Oneida, Pawnee, Sac and Fox, Seminole, Sioux, and other Native American peoples who spoke their language in coded or de facto noncoded form in behalf of the United States armed forces. The National Cryptologic Museum at the National Security Agency in Maryland currently houses an exhibit recognizing Comanches, Choctaws, Kiowas, Winnebagos, Seminoles, Navajos, Hopi, and Cherokees as code talkers during World War II.

Just how many lives were saved by the service of these veterans and their ingenious use of their native languages will never be fully known. Many individuals in units containing code talkers or in adjoining units never even knew of their presence and the advantages which their languages and codes gave to the cause. There is more than adequate evidence that the Navajo Code Talkers saved many lives and shortened the **211**

212 conflict in the Pacific theater of the war (Paul 1973; McClain 1994:68, 175, 221–222). The staffing of Navajo Code Talkers in ComAirSoPac (Commander Air South Pacific) circuits reduced pilot fatality rates from 53 percent to less than 7 percent (McClain 1994:118). The speed of Navajo Code Talker messages accelerated standard code machine transmissions from four hours to two and one-half minutes (McClain 1994: 67–68, 153). As the marines consolidated their shoreline positions during the first forty-eight hours of the invasion of Iwo Jima, over eight hundred messages were sent without error by six Navajo radio nets operating around the clock. When the marines raised the American flag on Mount Suribachi, Navajo Code Talkers relayed the message in their code, "sheep-uncle-ram-ice-bear-ant-cat-horse-itch." In endorsing the continued use of the Navajo Code Talkers after securing Okinawa, Colonel H. G. Newhart considered the Navajo code essential and the only choice for secure communications transmission, as "security was assured" and it was the "only secure means of delivering classified traffic on these circuits within a reasonable time" (McClain 1994:201–202).

Was the Comanche Code secure? No Comanche messages are known to have ever been broken by the German forces. Did the Comanche Code Talkers save lives? In comparing humint and sigint military intelligence between the Civil War and World War II, historian and World War II veteran Peter Maslowski points out:

> Without military intelligence, humint or sigint, the Civil War might well have lasted about four years. . . . That is, military intelligence made no fundamental difference in the war; however, so little sophisticated, detailed work has been done on the subject that this cannot be stated with certainty. The same cannot be said about World War II, when military intelligence clearly had a profound impact. Without the Allies' sigint superiority, the war would have been longer, American and British casualties would have been far greater, and the postwar world would undoubtedly have been different. (1995:81–82)

Because military operations in World War II relied so heavily on sigint (signal intelligence) communications, the Comanche and other Native American groups contributed by providing small units with hidden and/or coded native languages. This represents an advantage on any scale, and the Comanche accounts of when and in what situations the code was used make it clearly apparent that some lives were saved through the use of this form of communications. Whether code requiring formal training (Type 1) or informal noncoded (Type 2) forms were used, the use of Native American languages as a military tactic was consciously and intentionally devised and deployed to render American military communications secure and thereby served as an aid in saving lives.

The Choctaw, Comanche, Navajo, and other Native American code talkers served in the United States' wars voluntarily and gave their respective nations an honored position in the Anglo world that is only recently beginning to gain the full recognition that it deserves. However, it should not be necessary for Native Americans to go to war, or to have to form an ethnic military unit, for Western non-native peoples to understand and respect these Native American groups. The postwar actions of many Native American code talkers and other servicemen have promoted and increased such understandings. Many made use of the skills they had learned in the military, the educational opportunities offered to them under the G.I. Bill, and business investments which demonstrated their ability to compete in the outside, non-Indian world. Most have resided both in and out of their native communities, adjusting to and accepting many Anglo ways but always remembering, celebrating, cherishing, and living within the vast diversity of their own rich traditional heritage.

Long overlooked, the Comanche Code Talkers played a small, yet important and unique role in contributing to the Allied effort in the European theater of World War II. Everyone who contributed in World War II is important, and each has a valid and important story to tell. Although increasing, the relatively small size of the Native American population compared to the U.S. total throughout the twentieth century (about 0.8 percent in 1990, Utter 1993:17) has led to Native Americans being overlooked in terms of military recognition. Proportionally, however, Native American contributions in the wars of this century are very significant but relatively unknown outside of native communities and a few scholars. The Comanche Code Talkers' role was relatively small and but one of many relatively unknown contributions. What makes their contribution significant is not their numbers, but the unique historical circumstances of their bilingual and bicultural background and how they were willing to use this in defense of their own people and the United States. The impact of Native American code talkers is indeed another example of an accommodationist irony, perhaps an undeserved blessing that numerous Indian nations graciously bestowed upon the United States government and armed forces.

The Comanche Code Talkers have left a rich legacy for the Comanche Nation that will be handed down through future generations. Presently, there are fewer than two hundred fluent speakers of the Comanche language. However, tribal members, in conjunction with the Comanche Tribal Culture and Language Preservation Committee, are working to reverse this trend. The Comanche Nation currently has several lan-

213

214   guage classes and an immersion program in which young tribal mothers are placed with fluent speakers. In addition, the Comanches are the
first tribe outside of Alaska and Hawaii to embark on a CD-ROM language program.[60] I hope the day will come when there are once again
many Comanche speakers. Perhaps the old Comanches said it best with
the brief expression they used to refer to the Comanche Code Talkers,
"Numurekwa'etuu: They Spoke Comanche," or "Comanche Speakers"!

a·p·p·e·n·d·i·x · a

MEMBERS OF COMPANY E,
142D INFANTRY, THIRTY-SIXTH DIVISION,
WORLD WAR I (FROM *DAILY OKLAHOMAN*,
NOVEMBER 18, 1917)

(in alphabetical order by tribe and last name)

1. *Arapaho*—Bret Risingbear.
2. *Caddo*—Francis Johnson, Sam Kahoosky.
3. *Cherokee*—George Adair, Joseph L. Bark, James Beaver, Sam Beaver, Gee D. Butler, Jesse H. Carey, James Chisholm, Alexander R. Chuculate, William Chum-Wa-Looky, James C. Cochran, Willie Cochran, Joseph Crittenden, Jack Davis, John F. Davis, Boot Dillis, John Doublehead, Lerow Downing, George Eagle, Fred E. Falling, Maynard Farr, Jesse Fixon, James Fogg, Martin Foreman, Newton M. Foster, Anderson Gonzalis, Napoleon Grayson, James Grigsby, Burney Gritts, John B. Gritts, Jack Hair, Lubbin Hopotubbee, William N. Johnson, Richard Keener, George Keys, Louis Kingfisher, Sampson Leach, Tom Leach, Benjamin Littlejohn, Henry Locuse, John Lucas, John H. McCracken, Davis McPherson, George E. Mankiller, Henry C. Martin, Frank Miller, Thomas Muscrat, George O'Field, Alford H. Potts, Floyd L. Pride, Wyly Proctor, Jess Rodgers, William Runway, Emmett Ryan, Jess Scraper, Walter Scuggins, Richard Sellers, David Shell, Charles T. Silk, Juney Smith, Stoke Smith, Robert Spade, John C. Triplett, Gid Vann, Richard Waters, Chewey Watt, Isaac Wayne, Sunday White, Frank Youn.
4. *Cheyenne*—Herbert Whiteshield.
5. *Chickasaw*—Abel B. Brown, Cubby Colbert, Humphry Colbert, Buster Davis, Perry P. Duckworth, Thomas Hitcher, Simeon James, Felix James, Johnson Jimmie, Watson John, Edmond Lewis, Dotson Lilley, *Pete Maytubby*, Joe Perry, Intolubby H. Underwood.
6. *Choctaw* (code talkers in italics)—Charley Jackson (cook), Cor-

poral Oscar T. Loman, Allington T. Nelson (mechanic), Corporal Cole Nelson, Corporal Leo M. Thomas, *First Sergeant Columbus E. Veach.*

Privates: Chester A. Ainsworth, Sidney Ameahtubbee, Culliston Anna, Jesse J. Atkinson, John W. Battiest, Samuel S. Beames, Tandy Beck, Dawson Billy, *Mitchell Bobb*, Dave Bohanan, Stacy Bohannon, Luke Bond, Elias Brown, Nicholas E. Brown, Martin Charles, James E. Cole, Silas Columbus, John Cooper, Simeon Cusher, George E. Davenport, Joseph H. Davenport, Jonas Durant, *James Edwards*, Stetson Eleomonotubbi, Edward Fobb, Alexander W. Folsom, Grover C. Folsom, *Tobias W. Frazier*, Robert Fulton, *Benjamin W. Hampton*, Kennedy Hardy, Wylie B. Harrison, Nelson Homer, Eastman Hoparkentubbee, Willis Hudson, Bennie James, Charles James, Grant Johnico, Daniel Johnson, Jimmie Johnson, Noel Johnson, Grayson Jones, Morris Jones, Edward Larney, James Lewis, Jeff F. Lewis, *Solomon B. Lewis (Louis)*, William Lewis, Sam Loman, Frank Lucas Eugene Lyles, Oscar R. McClure, Alex McCoy, Sam McCoy, Edgar McGee, Silas G. McGee, Jackson J. McKinney, Kelly Y. Melley, Vance Moore, Leo B. Nelson, Henry Newsom, Hodges T. Peter, Thornton J. Porter, John Rasha, Rufus T. Risner, Amos Simon, Robert Sockey, *Robert Taylor*, Daniel Terrell, Wilson Thomas, Ellis Thompson, Jefferson Thompson, Adolphus S. Tubby, Peter Wall, Arch Wallace, John Wallace, Jacob Walley, Curley White, Eli Williams, Cabin Wilson, Willie Wilson.

7. *Creek*—John Berryhill, Moses Birdcreek, Tiger McIntosh, Silas Scott, Ben Simmons, Jimmie Sullivan, Thomas Solomon.

8. *Delaware*—William T. Everett, Ray Longbone, John W. Parker, Irving L. Smith, William B. Smith.

9. *Osage*—George Bacon-Rind, Charley Choteau, William McKinley, Neal C. Panther, Oakly A. Pappan, James Watsins, Joseph Watson.

10. *Peoria*—Asa Forman.

11. *Ponca*—Kenneth Headman, Richard Hinman.

12. *Quapaw*—Levi Goodeagle, Jess Quapaw.

13. *Seminole*—Nemo Cheparney, Thompson Deer, Taylor Hardridge, Sumpsy Harjoe, Harry Jones, Walter Wise.

14. *Shawnee*—Charles T. Baker, Sam Daugherty.

a·p·p·e·n·d·i·x · b

WORLD WAR I CHOCTAW CODE TALKERS (BIOGRAPHICAL DATA COURTESY OF JUDY ALLEN, CHOCTAW NATION OF OKLAHOMA, *BISHINIK* NEWSPAPER)

SOLOMON BOND LOUIS (SOMETIMES MISSPELLED LEWIS)

Choctaw Roll #1755, full-blood Choctaw.
  Born April 27, 1898, at Hoochatown, Indian Territory. Died April 22, 1972.
  Member of 142d Infantry, Company E, Thirty-sixth Division.

ALBERT BILLY

Born October 8, 1885, at Howe, Indian Territory, full-blood Choctaw.
  Member of 142d Infantry, Thirty-sixth Division, family believes in Company E.

MITCHELL BOBB

Born 1895, full-blood Choctaw.
  Member of 142d Infantry, Company E, Thirty-sixth Division.

JAMES (JIMPSON M.) EDWARDS

Choctaw Roll #2739, born October 23, 1898, Golden, Indian Territory.
  Member of 142d Infantry, Company E, Thirty-sixth Division.

VICTOR BROWN

Born 1896, Goodwater, Indian Territory. Died 1966.
  Member of 143d Infantry, Thirty-sixth Division.

BEN CARTERBY

Born 1892, full-blood Choctaw.
Member of 142d Infantry, Company E, Thirty-sixth Division.

JOSEPH OKLAHOMBI

Born May 1, 1894, Bokchito, Indian Territory. Died April 1, 1960.
Member of 143d Infantry, Headquarters Company, Thirty-sixth Division.

WALTER VEACH

Born May 18, 1884. Died October 1966.
Member of 142d Infantry, Company E, Thirty-sixth Division.

CALVIN WILSON

First name misspelled as "Cabin" on Choctaw Roll Books and military records.
Born September 25, 1895, Eagletown (sometimes mistakenly reported as Goodwater), Indian Territory.
Member of 142d Infantry, Company E, Thirty-sixth Division.

ROBERT TAYLOR

Born 1895, Bokchito, Indian Territory.
Member of 142d Infantry, Company E, Thirty-sixth Division.

PETE MAYTUBBY

Member of 142d Infantry, Company E, Thirty-sixth Division.

BENJAMIN W. HAMPTON

Choctaw Roll #10617, born Bennington, Indian Territory.

JEFF NELSON

Member of 142d Infantry, Company E, Thirty-sixth Division.

TOBIAS FRAZIER

Born 1892, full-blood Choctaw.
Member of 142d Infantry, Company E, Thirty-sixth Division.

BENJAMIN COLBERT

Unit unknown.

ORGANIZATION OF THE FOURTH INFANTRY DIVISION, 1941–1945 (STANTON 1984:81–82)

1. TYPICAL ORGANIZATION (1941)

Eighth Infantry Regiment (Motorized)
Twelfth Infantry Regiment (Motorized)*
Twenty-second Infantry Regiment (Motorized)
Headquarters and Headquarters Battery Division Artillery
Twentieth Field Artillery Battalion (155 mm)
Twenty-ninth Field Artillery Battalion (105 mm)
Forty-second Field Artillery Battalion (105 mm)
Forty-fourth Field Artillery Battalion (105 mm)
Headquarters, Fourth Motorized Division
Headquarters and Military Police Company
Fourth Engineer Battalion
Fourth Medical Battalion
Fourth Quartermaster Battalion
Fourth Reconnaissance Troop
Fourth Signal Company

*Assigned October 24, 1941

2. TYPICAL ORGANIZATION (1944–1945)

Eighth Infantry Regiment (Motorized)
Twelfth Infantry Regiment (Motorized)
Twenty-second Infantry Regiment (Motorized)
Headquarters and Headquarters Battery Division Artillery
Twentieth Field Artillery Battalion (155 mm)
Twenty-ninth Field Artillery Battalion (105 mm)

220
Forty-second Field Artillery Battalion (105 mm)
Forty-fourth Field Artillery Battalion (105 mm)
Fourth Reconnaissance Troop (Mechanized)
Fourth Engineer Combat Battalion
Fourth Medical Battalion
Fourth Counter Intelligence Corps Detachment
Headquarters Special Troops
Headquarters Company, Fourth Infantry Division
Military Police Platoon
704th Ordnance Maintenance Company
Fourth Quartermaster Company
Fourth Signal Company

Seventieth Tank Destroyer Battalion	(attached 6/9/1944–3/23/1945, 3/23–27/1945, and 4/6–5/9/1945)
610th Tank Destroyer Battalion	(attached 1/25–3/10/1945, 3/17–5/8/1945)
776th Tank Destroyer Battalion	(attached 4/9–4/18/1945)
801st Tank Destroyer Battalion	(attached 6/13–10/15/1944, 10/30–11/8/1944)
802nd Tank Destroyer Battalion	(attached 12/9/1944–1/27/1945)
803rd Tank Destroyer Battalion	(attached 11/9–12/25/1944)
893rd Tank Destroyer Battalion	(attached 8/23–9/29/1944)
377th AAA Auto Weapons Battalion	(attached 6/14/1944–3/23/1945, 3/23–27/1945, and 4/6–5/9/1945)

3. OVERSEAS WARTIME ASSIGNMENTS

VII Corps—2/2/1944
VIII Corps—7/16/1944
VII Corps—7/19/1944
V Corps—8/22/1944
VII Corps—11/8/1944
VIII Corps—12/7/1944
III Corps—12/20/1944
XII Corps—12/21/1944

VIII Corps—1/27/1945
Twelfth Army Group—3/10/1945
VI Corps—3/20/1945
XXI Corps—3/25/1945
Seventh Army—4/8/1945
Third Army—5/2/1945
III Corps—5/6/1945

4. LOCATION OF THE FOURTH INFANTRY DIVISION, 1941–1945

The Fourth Infantry Division was activated as the Fourth Division at Ft. Benning, Georgia, on June 1, 1940. It was reorganized as the Fourth Division (Motorized) on August 1, 1940, and as the Fourth Motorized

Division on June 11, 1941. The division was moved to Dry Prong, Louisiana, on August 1, 1941, for the IV Corps Louisiana Maneuvers and returned to Ft. Benning, Georgia, on August 27, 1941. The division was next moved to Ft. Jackson, South Carolina, on October 30, 1941, for the First Army Carolina Maneuvers and arrived back at Ft. Benning, Georgia, on December 3, 1941. The Fourth arrived at Camp Gordon, Georgia, on December 29, 1941, and proceeded to the Carolina Maneuver Area on July 7, 1942. The Fourth returned to Camp Gordon, Georgia, on August 31, 1942, and moved to Ft. Dix, New Jersey, on April 12, 1943, where it was redesignated as the Fourth Infantry Division on August 3, 1943. It was next sent to Camp Gordon Johnston, Florida, on September 19, 1943, for the III Corps Carrabelle Maneuvers. The Fourth arrived at Ft. Jackson, South Carolina, on December 1, 1943, and was then staged at Camp Kilmer, New Jersey, from January 4, 1944, until it departed from the New York P/E (Point of Embarkation) on January 18, 1944. It arrived in England on January 26, 1944, where it remained until it participated in the assault on Normandy, France, on June 6, 1944. The Fourth Division crossed into Belgium on September 6, 1944, into Germany on September 11, and then went to Luxembourg on December 12, 1944, and returned to Belgium on January 28, 1945, and to Germany on February 7, 1945. It returned to France on March 10, 1945, and reentered Germany on March 29, 1945. The Fourth returned to the New York P/E on July 10, 1945, and moved to Camp Buckner, North Carolina, on July 13, 1945, where it was deactivated on March 12, 1946.

a·p·p·e·n·d·i·x · d

COMBAT NARRATIVE OF THE FOURTH INFANTRY DIVISION (STANTON 1984:82)

Reinforced by the 359th Infantry of the Ninetieth Infantry Division, the Fourth Division assaulted Utah Beach, France, on June 6, 1944, with the Eighth Infantry leading against light resistance. The Eighth Infantry relieved the isolated Eighty-second Airborne Division at Ste. Mere Eglise and countered several German attacks on June 7, 1944. The following day, the division began its drive on the Cotentin Peninsula toward Cherbourg, and with naval gunfire support, the Twenty-second Infantry took Azeville fort and Ozeville on June 9. The division reached the Germans' main defenses at Cherbourg by June 21 and, on the following day, began its assault with the Twelfth Infantry augmented by tank support. On June 25 the division breached the fortressed city and garrisoned it until relieved by the 101st Airborne Division at the end of the month. The division then proceeded south to participate in the general offensive in France.

On July 6, the division advanced offensively toward Periers and participated in the COBRA breakout on July 25. The division continued south, and after taking St. Polis following a furious battle on August 5, countered German attacks at Avranches and committed the Twenty-second Infantry in the Le Teilleu area. Elements of the division then entered Paris with French army units on August 25. On September 1, riding on tanks of the Fifth Armored Division's CCA, the division pushed to Chauny and assembled near Mezieres, moving forward from the Meuse River on September 6. On the 14th the division penetrated the West Wall in the Schnee Eifel, but the Twelfth Infantry was stopped after small gains over the next few days, despite costly attacks. The Eighth and Twenty-second Infantry also failed to take Brandscheid, and the offensive halted on September 17, in the face of German counterattacks.

Making slow progress through October, the division moved into the Zweitfall area, where it relieved the Twenty-eighth Infantry Division on November 6. Fighting in the Huertgen Forest, the Twelfth Infantry was subjected to a strong German counterattack on November 10, which cut off regimental elements until the 15th of November. The Eighth and Twenty-second Infantry had a gap wedged between them in forest fighting, which stopped the offensive on the 19th. During five costly days of combat in the Huertgen Forest, the division had gained only 1½ miles. Attacks were renewed on November 22, and the Twelfth Infantry finally closed the gap on November 28. After severe fighting, the Twenty-second Infantry took Grossahau by frontal assault the following day. The Eighth Infantry reached the edge of the Huertgen Forest on the 30th, but failed in further advances. On December 3, the division was relieved by the Eighty-third Infantry Division and moved to Luxembourg.

While in Luxembourg, the division was subjected to the fury of the German Ardennes Counteroffensive on December 16, 1944. Despite heavy losses and the loss of several isolated components, it managed to hold its lines at Dickweiler and Osweiler. Reinforced by tanks, the Twelfth Infantry made several unsuccessful efforts to rescue trapped elements near Echternach. On December 22, 1944, the division renewed attacks there which finally took the town on December 27.

On January 17, 1945, the Eighty-seventh Division took over the division's zone along the Sauer from Echternach to Wasserbilling, releasing the Fourth Division to seize the heights overlooking the Our and to cross the river at Bettendorf on January 22. The Fourth Division resumed the offensive on January 29, and advanced into Germany on February 1, breaching the outer defenses of the West Wall along the Schnee Eifel River near Brandscheid on February 4. On the 9th, the division crossed the Pruem River with the Eighth Infantry, storming the town itself on February 12. The division then went on the defensive on February 11, defending the river from Olzheim to Watzerath against counterattacks. On February 28, the division crossed the river in force, but the Twelfth Infantry was only able to make negligible gains. On March 4, Gondel sheim was finally taken, and the division raced out of the Pruem bridgehead behind the Eleventh Armored Division to the Kyll on March 6. The Eighth Infantry reached the Honerath area by March 8, and on the 30th, the division completed crossing the Rhine and, following behind the Twelfth Armored Division, was ferried across the Main at Ochenfuhrt on April 2. The Twelfth and Twenty-second Infantries fought a determined opposing German force up the wooded slopes in the Koenigshofen area, and the general offensive was resumed on April 10. The drive toward Rothenburg started on April 11 against strong German defenses. The city was finally taken by the Twelfth Infantry on April 17, as the Eighth reached Ansbach the same day.

The division then moved north toward the Danube, where forward elements crossed it on April 25. The Eighth Infantry established a bridgehead across the Lech at Schwabstadl on April 27, and by the end of the month, the Twelfth and Twenty-second Infantries had reached the Isar River bridges at Miesbach. The division was relieved by the 101st Airborne Division in that sector on May 2, 1945. On May 4, it moved to Neumarkt, where it began occupation duties under the Third Army on May 8, 1945.

a·p·p·e·n·d·i·x · e

FOURTH INFANTRY DIVISION CAMPAIGN (JUNE 6, 1944, TO MAY 8, 1945)

1944

June

6	Omaha Beach
6	Blosville
6	Audoville–La Hubert
7	Ste. Mere Eglise
7	Bondienville
7	Saussetour
8	Beuzeville-au-Plain
8	Joganville
9	St. Flexel
9	Fresville
10	La Bisson
10	Montebourg
20	Anneville
20	Valognes
20	La Tardiverie
21	Saussemesnil
23	Bois du Coudray
23	Hau des Blonds
24	Hau Cauchon
25	Rufosses
26	Tourlaville
28	Cherbourg
30	Orglandes

July

1	Gourbesville
4	Appeville
5	Carentan
7	Meautis
7	Le Bus
9	Les Ormeaux
10	Raffoville
11	Sainteny
21	Le Have
21	Le Hommet d'Athrenay
24	Amigny
25	St. Lô
28	Marigny
29	La Vanterie
30	Le Chess-Doriere

August

1	La Mancelliere
2	Villedieu-les-Pocles
3	Le Bourigny
4	St. Pois
4	St. Laurent de Cuves
5	Brecay
6	Le Mesnil Gilbert
8	Chevreville
12	Desertines
17	Carrouges
24	Nozav
25	Paris
26	Savigny-sur-Orge
26	Bois de Vincennes
28	Villevause
29	Chelles
29	Montgo
30	Rozieres
31	Vivieres
31	Brassoir

September

2	Itancourt
2	Grugies
5	Vireux
6	Houdremont, Belgium
7	Reinne
7	Lubin
7	Haut-Fays
8	Redu
9	Laveselle
10	Hamroulle
10	Fraiture
11	Ste. Marie
12	St. Vith
12	Galhoussen
13	Alferstag
13	Utzenich, Germany
14	Radscheid
15	Schlausenbach
15	Siegfried Line (until Oct. 4)

October

4	Holzheim, Belgium
4	Hunningen

November

Huertgen Forest, Germany

7–22	Zweifall
29	Schevenhutte

December

8	Junglinster, Luxembourg
12	Senningen
26	Wecker
27	Sandweiler
28	Consdorf

1945

January

1   Hemstal
8   Betzdorf, Germany
17   Meispeit, Luxembourg
19   Ermsdorf
21   Gilsdorf
27   Moinet, Belgium
28   Burg, Reuland
29   Oudler
31   Lommersweiler

February

1   Elcherath, Germany
2   Alferstag, Belgium
4   Ameischeid
5   Halenfeld, Germany
5   Schwieler
8   Buchet
9   Schnee Eifel

March

2   Prum
3   Willerath
5   Wallersheim
6   Muilenborn
10   Honerath
12   Weinsheim
13   Varrene de Portieux, France
14   Gerbersvillers
20   Ohlungen
21   Dauendorf
26   Ellerstam, Germany
27   Bad Durkheim
30   Bonsweiler
30   Erlenbach
31   Guttersbach
31   Amorbach
31   Konigheim

April

1	Hardenheim
1	Reichenburg
3	Gaubuttelbrum
3	Ochsenfurt
6	Erlach
7	Bernsfelden
13	Marktstett
13	Bieberehren
14	Freudenbach
16	Adelshofen
17	Binzwangen
18	Kirnberg
19	Schillingsfurst
19	Weissenkirchberg
20	Breitenau
21	Bergbronn
22	Stocken
22	Wasseralfingen
23	Westhausen
24	Oggenhausen
24	Enbat
25	Gundelfingen
25	Lauingen
26	Weisingen
26	Landensberg
27	Welden
27	Agawang
27	Grossaitingen
28	Strassberg
29	Winkl
29	Tirkenfeld
30	Moorenweiss
30	Ober Pfaffenhofen
30	Perche

May

1	Wolfratshausen
1	Bairawies
1	Gauting
2	Finsterweld

230 3   Schonegg
     5   Sulzbach
     5   Rosenburg
     8   Burglenfeld

1. Fourth Infantry Division Battle Stars: Normandy, Northern France, Rhineland, Ardennes (Belgium Bulge), Central Europe.

2. Highlights
     Utah Beach—June 6, 1944
     Breakthrough at St. Lô—July 25, 1944
     Helped relieve the "Lost Battalion," Thirtieth Infantry Division at Mortain—August 11, 1944
     First through the Siegfried Line—September 14, 1944
     First infantry division in Germany—September 11, 1944
     Battle of Huertgen Forest—November and December 1944
     Saved City of Luxembourg—December 1944

a·p·p·e·n·d·i·x · f

FOURTH SIGNAL COMPANY ACTIVITIES, 1940–1945 (UNITED STATES ARMY, 4TH INFANTRY DIVISION 1946:95)

COMMANDERS 1940–1945

1st Lt. John Williamson	June 6, 1940–June 21, 1940
Captain T. J. Tully	June 21, 1940–October 1, 1940
Captain Guy E. Parker	October 1, 1940–February 12, 1941
Captain A. E. McCrary	February 12, 1941–September 9, 1941
1st Lt. Mark L. Thompson	September 9, 1941–February 11, 1942
Captain S. W. Crisman	February 11, 1942–September 6, 1943
1st Lt. Philip Bragar	September 6, 1943–August 10, 1944
Captain W. F. Dunaway	August 10, 1944–February 13, 1945
Captain T. M. Zurhorst	February 13, 1945+

The Fourth Signal Company was organized on June 1, 1940, at Ft. Benning, Georgia, as the signal company of the Fourth Division. Enlisted cadre for the organization was transferred from the Second Signal Company, Ft. Sam Houston, Texas. The enlisted personnel for the company were recruited primarily from Pennsylvania, Maryland, Virginia, and Tennessee.

In January 1941 the company was assigned sixteen [actually seventeen] Comanche Indians, recruited from Oklahoma. It was planned to use these Indians as voice radio operators to transmit and receive messages in their own "unwritten language." While seldom so employed, they represented a valuable auxiliary security element.

In February 1941 the organization received its first selectees. An additional five hundred men were assigned to a Provisional Signal Training Battalion, staffed by personnel from the company. This provisional battalion trained the men in wire, message center, and radio procedure for the communication detachments and sections in the regiments, battalions, and companies of the division.

On January 18, 1944, the company embarked on the U.S.A.T. *George Washington*, and landed in Liverpool, England, on January 29, 1944, from which place it moved to its billets at Tiverton, Devon. The company engaged in the specialized training essential for the forthcoming invasion of the continent.

In the period June 1–3, 1944, the company loaded aboard ships for the invasion of France and, on the 6th and 7th of June, landed on Utah Beach, Normandy. From D-Day on, at least one, and sometimes three, means of communication were in continuous operation. The company furnished wire and radio teams to each of the infantry regiments of the division, and these men were highly commended for their performance of duties. In the battle for Cherbourg, wire was used as the main agency of communication. During the Normandy campaign the signal company casualties were extremely high.

After the St. Lô breakthrough and on to Paris the situation was fast moving, and radio again was the main agency of communication. The division entered Paris on August 25, 1944, and the pursuit was continued to the northeast. During this latter move, a special task force (TF Taylor), operating northeast of St. Quentin, was kept in communication by use of a Signal Corps Radio 399. A relay station, protected by two light tanks, was also established to ensure communication with the division command post at Urvillers, south of St. Quentin, France. The division entered Germany on September 11, 1944, at which time a complete wire system was established, which became the main agency of communication.

Throughout this period of combat, the message center platoon was operating continuously, giving the division twenty-four-hour-a-day service. Cryptographic crews were assigned to the most important radio station in order to facilitate the coding and decoding of messages. Motor messengers operated constantly, often in the face of hazardous enemy fire.

On September 12, 1944, the Fourth Signal Company was commended by the commanding general for outstanding and meritorious services rendered to the division during the period from June 6, 1944, to September 1944.

From November 7 to December 6, 1944, the division was operating in the Huertgen Forest, and due to the hard fighting and consistent rain and snow, wire and messenger personnel had an extremely difficult task keeping communications open. Enemy artillery frequently "knocked out" telephone lines, and they had to be checked constantly by wire patrols. The company moved to Luxembourg City on December 6, 1944, where the wire section "dressed up" lines formerly used by the 83rd Infantry Division. This was intended as a rest area, being the first relief the division had had since June 6, 1944. However, the counteroffensive on the 16th of December made it necessary that the wire and radio personnel return to the combat teams to operate division wire and radio sets.

During the latter part of December 1944 and the month of January 1945, the shortage of wire became critical, and the recovery of used wire was emphasized. Recovery was made extremely difficult because of snowfall, which was very heavy, and the icy condition of the wire; however, at no time were operations seriously hampered by the lack of field wire.

In February 1945, the division was fighting in the Schnee Eifel, an area originally captured by the Fourth Division in September 1944. The Fourth Signal Company recovered equipment, abandoned or partially destroyed by the 106th Division when it was forced out of the Bulge in December.

During the latter part of April, on the drive to the Danube River and beyond, many enemy signal installations were overrun. Captured German switchboards and wire cables were used to some extent to supplement our equipment.

On May 1, 1945, the company was located in Wolfratshausen, in southern Bavaria. Several days later the movement began to a new area in the vicinity of Neumarkt, Germany. Communication began between the new CP and the old CP and was maintained by SCR 399s with voice communication established over an airline distance of 100 miles by employment of a directional antenna. Later, 150-mile transmissions were made successfully. More than 15,000 miles of wire had been laid by the wire platoon from June 6, 1944, to May 8, 1945.

V-E Day found the company located in Amberg, Germany, directly east of Nurnburg. In the latter part of May 1945, the company moved to Ansbach, Germany, and established an extensive division wire net.

In June, the company moved to Memmelsdorf, Germany, a small town directly north of Bamberg, to begin preparations for redeployment to the Pacific. Here the unit was screened, and men having 85 or more points were transferred to the 99th Signal Company, while low-point men of that organization were transferred into the Fourth Signal Company. On June 22, the company began a motor movement to Camp Old Gold, near Le Havre, France, and arrived there June 25, 1945. On July 3 the organization boarded the U.S.S. *Excelsior* for the trip home. Upon its arrival at Hampton Roads, Virginia, on July 12, 1945, the company

233

234   was immediately sent to Camp Patrick Henry, Virginia, and divided into groups for shipment to the reception stations nearest their homes for a thirty-day recuperation furlough.

After the furloughs the men reported to the company's new station at Camp Butner, North Carolina.

a·p·p·e·n·d·i·x · g

GLOSSARY OF COMANCHE CODE TERMS

Approximately 250 Comanche code terms were devised for use in World War II. Unfortunately, no complete list of them exists. As Major General Foster stated to me, "My small pocket notebook is long gone in the sands of North Africa." Below is a list of some of the code terms. All code terms were compiled from my interviews with Forrest Kassanavoid, Roderick Red Elk, and Charles Chibitty, and from correspondence with Major General Foster. After nearly fifty years, some terms were no longer remembered.

I am indebted to Jean O. Charney, who enthusiastically provided orthographical standardization for all terms. For a more thorough understanding of Comanche grammar and orthography, refer to Charney's (1993) *A Grammar of Comanche*.

CODE TALKERS

Comanche Code Talkers—Nʉmʉrekwa'etʉʉ—"Comanche speakers," from Nʉmʉnʉʉ (Comanches), tekwa (speak), and -'etʉʉ (plural nominalizing suffix).

AIRCRAFT

airplane—pʉnnʉtsa yʉtsʉ'etʉ—"flies by itself," from pʉnnʉ (reflexive/possessive prefix), tsa (topic marker), yʉtsʉ (fly, singular subject), and -'etʉ (nominalizing suffix). Also pʉnnʉtsa yori'etʉ—"Something that flies itself," from pʉnnʉ (reflexive/possessive prefix), tsa (topic marker), yori (fly, plural subject), and -'etʉ (nominalizing suffix).

bomber—hutsuu no'avakatʉ or no'avakatʉ hutsuu—"pregnant bird," from hutsuu (bird), no'ava or no'af (pregnant), and katʉ (have, verbal ending). Term for any type of bomber.

fighter plane—(1) pʉnnʉtsa yʉtsʉ nahru'etʉ—"they fight flies by itself," from pʉnnʉ (reflexive/possessive prefix), tsa (topic marker), yʉtsʉ (fly, singular subject), nahru (fight), and -'etʉ (nominalizing suffix). (2) pʉnnʉtsa yʉtsʉ' noo'atʉ—"they fight flies by itself," from pʉnnʉ (reflexive/possessive prefix), tsa (topic marker), yʉtsʉ (fly, singular subject), nua (travel), and -tʉ (noun or verb suffix).

transport plane—pʉnnʉtsa yʉtsʉ tʉnoo'etʉ—"flies by itself cargo,"—from pʉnnʉ (reflexive/possessive prefix), tsa (topic marker), yʉtsʉ (fly, singular subject), tunoo (freight, pack), and -'etʉ (nominalizing suffix).

GUNS AND BAYONETS

bayonet—tawo'i' nahuu'—"gun knife," from tawo'i' (gun) and nahuu' or nahoo' (knife).

gun—tawo'i' or rawo'i'—"gun," any type of gun, pistol, rifle, etc.

.30-caliber machine gun—tʉtsahkʉna' tawo'i'—"sewing machine gun," from tʉtsahkʉna' (sewing machine) and tawo'i' (gun). So named because sound of machine gun resembled the rat-a-tat-tat sound of a manually pumped treadle or Singer sewing machine.

.50-caliber machine gun—piatʉtsahkʉna' tawo'i'—"big sewing machine gun," from pia (big), tʉtsahkʉna' (sewing machine), and tawo'i' (gun).

bazooka—ekasahpana' piatawo'i'—"soldier's big gun," from ekasahpana' (soldier's), pia (big), and tawo'i' or rawo'i' (gun).

ARTILLERY AND EXPLOSIONS

artillery—piata'wo'i'—"big gun," from pia (big) and ta'wo'i' or ra'wo'i' (gun). Same term for all artillery field pieces, howitzers, cannons, etc.

flamethrower—no term, rarely used in Europe, more in Pacific.

grenade—tʉepʉhtsatʉ—"small explosion," from tʉe (little, small), pʉhtsa (to burst), and -tʉ (noun or verb suffix).

howitzers—piata'wo'i'—"big gun," from pia (big) and ta'wo'i' (gun). The 155- or 240-caliber artillery.

105 howitzer—tʉtaatʉ piata'wo'i'—"small big gun, small gun-cannon," from tʉtaatʉ (small), pia (big), and ta'wo'i' (gun). The 105-caliber howitzer artillery.

55 howitzer—wahatʉ mo'ovetʉ piata'wo'i'—literally "two fives or double five big gun," from wahatʉ (two), mo'ovetʉ (five), pia (big), and ta'wo'i' (gun). The 55 howitzer or Long Tom. Fifty-five would be mo'ovetʉ sʉma ma mo'ovetʉ.

88 howitzer—namewatsʉkwitʉ namewatsʉkwitʉ piata'wo'i'—"eight, eight, big gun." The 88-caliber howitzer artillery.

landmine—pʉhtsa'etʉ—"goes off by itself," from pʉhtsa (to burst) and -'etʉ (nominalizing suffix). Also sometimes described as "it's under the ground—it will kill you."

mine sweepers—tatʉ'eti ura'etʉ—"finds it," from tatʉ'eti (blows up—per Forrest Kassanavoid), ura (find something), and -'etʉ (nominalizing suffix).

mortars—nakohtoo ta'wo'i'—"stove gun," from nakohtoo (stove) and ta'wo'i' (gun).

shells or bullets—navaaka—"bullets, lead," literally "its arrow," from na (reflexive pronoun) and vaaka (arrow). Term for any rifle or artillery shells or bullets.

AUTOMOBILE AND TRANSPORTATION ROUTES

automobile—pʉnnʉtsa nuhki'etʉ—"runs to and fro by itself," from pʉnnʉ (reflexive/possessive prefix), -tsa (topic marker), nuhki (run off, run away), and -'etʉ (nominalizing suffix). Named in opposition to a wagon or buggy that is horse drawn.

car—navukuwaa—"without a horse," from na (reflexive prefix), puku (horse), and waa (without).

cargo truck—Piatʉnoo'—"big freight/cargo [hauler]," the two and a half ton truck, from pia (big), tʉnoo (freight, a pack, cargo carrier), and (') (nominalizing suffix).

jeep—tʉenavukuwaa—"little car," from tʉe (little) and navukuwaa "without a horse," from na (reflexive prefix), puku (horse), and waa (without). Given by Forrest Kassanavoid as "small could run either way [automobile]"—jeep or smaller German vehicles, from tʉe (small) and navu ([could run] either way), in reference to ability of vehicles to go forwards and in reverse.

mountain—toya, a regular term.

big road—piavoi, piapu'e, or piavu'e—"big road/trail," from pia (big) and road.

BOATS

boat—pawovipukʉ—"boat," from pa (water), wovi (wood), and puku (horse); the regular Comanche term for any boat.

large boat—piapawovipukʉ—"large boat," from pia (big) and pa (water), wovi (wood), and puku (horse); the regular Comanche term for any large boat.

backpack radio—muyake'—"radio."

radio—(1) tᵾnaki—"listen!" or "listening," from tᵾnaki ("Listen! Be quiet and listen! etc.) (2) watsitekwapᵾ—"hiding talking," from watsi (to hide), tekwa (talk, singular subject), and -pᵾ (noun suffix).

telephone—puhihwi tekwapᵾ—"metal talking," from puhihwi (metal or money) and tekwapᵾ (talking). This is the regular Comanche word for the telephone.

telephone exchange—puhihwi tekwapᵾ kahni—"metal talking house," from puhihwi (metal or money), tekwapᵾ (talking), and kahni (house).

wire—tᵾhtᵾma—"fence enclosed," from tᵾh (indefinite object prefix) and tᵾma (enclosure or fenced in). A regular non-coded Comanche term. (Also known as soni wᵾhtᵾma?, wire or bailing wire.)

switchboard—term unavailable.

telegraph—see telephone.

PERSONNEL AND INFANTRY

officer—ekasahpana' paraiboo'—"soldier-chief," from ekasahpana' (soldier) and paraiboo' (chief or leader).

rank—ekasahpana' nakohpoo—"soldier branded," from ekasahpana' (soldier) and nakohpoo (brand).

General—tatsinuupi paraiboo'—"star chief," from tatsinuupi (star) and paraiboo' (chief or leader).

Brigadier General—sᵾmᵾ tatsinuupi nakohpooᵾ—"one-star branded" or "branded with one star," from sᵾmᵾ (one), tatsinuupi (star), and nakohpoona (branded).

Two-Star General—waha tatsinuupi nakohpoona—"two-star branded" or "branded with two stars," from waha (two), tatsinuupi (star), and nakohpoona (branded).

Three-Star General—pahi tatsinuupi nakohpoona—"three-star branded" or "branded with three stars," from pahi (three), tatsinuupi (star), and nakohpoona (branded).

Four-Star General—hayarokweetᵾ tatsinuupi nakohpoona—"four star branded" or "branded with four stars," from hayarokweetᵾ (four), tatsinuupi (star), and nakohpoona (branded).

Colonel—piahuutsu'—"big bird," from pia (big), and huutsu (bird).

Lieutenant Colonel—tosapuhihwitᵾ—"silver metal/money," from tosa (white/silver), puhiwhi (metal, money,) and -tᵾ (noun, or verb, suffix).

Major—ekapuhihwitᵾ—"red metal," from eka (red), puhihwi (metal, money), and -tᵾ (noun, or verb, suffix).

Captain—waha nakohpoo—"two brands," from waha (two) and nakohpoo (brand).

Lieutenant—s̶u̶m̶u̶ nakohpoo—"one brand," from s̶u̶m̶u̶ (one) and na-kohpoo (brand).

Sergeant—pahi nahkohpoo—"three brands," from pahi (three) and na-kohpoo (brand).

Corporal—waha navoon̲a—"two marks," from waha (two) and navoon̲a (marked).

Private First Class—s̶u̶m̶u̶ navoon̲a—"one mark," from s̶u̶m̶u̶ (one) and navoon̲a (marked).

Private—no official code term used for this rank, probably ek̲asah-pana'—"soldiers"—was used.

branded—nakohpoor̶u̶—"branded." (Note: Officers are "branded," en-listed personnel are "marked.")

star—tatsinuup̲i—"star."

enemy—wohon̶u̶u̶—"enemies," from woho (enemy) and -n̶u̶u̶ (noun suffix, plural).

Germans—Taawohon̶u̶u̶—"our enemy."

Adolf Hitler—Po'sa taiboo'—"Crazy White Man," from po'sa (crazy) and taiboo' (non-Indian).

artillery soldiers—piata'wo'i' ek̲asahpana'—"big gun soldiers," from pia (big), ta'wo'i' (gun), and ek̲asahpana' (soldiers).

infantry soldiers—ta'wo'i' ek̲asahpana'—"gun soldiers," from ta'wo'i' (gun or rifle) and ek̲asahpana' (soldiers).

soldiers—ek̲asahpana'—"soldiers." According to Forrest Kassanavoid the term literally means "red stomachs high up," from ekap̲i (red), sah-pa'ana' (stomach, side of), and pa'at̶u̶ (high up). In former times, all U.S. military officers wore red waist sashes, so Comanches developed the term for army cavalry officers located around nearby Ft. Sill, Oklahoma, and it came to be applied to all Anglo soldiers. At least three pronuncia-tions exist for "soldier": (1) ek̲asahpana', (2) ekasahpana, and (3) ek̶u̶sah-pana' (Robinson and Armagost 1990:16, 220).

paratroopers—pohpit̶u̶u̶ ek̲asahpana'—"jump soldier," from pohpi or pohbi (jump), -t̶u̶ (suffix, probably plural verb), and ek̲asahpana' (sol-diers). Distinguished in code as (1) friendly soldiers jump (haitsi'i eksah-pana' pohbit̶u̶) or (2) enemy soldiers jump (wohho eksahpana' pohbit̶u̶).

STRUCTURES

command post—Paraiboo'-puhk-cute-nah, from Paraiboo' (chief, boss) and puhk-cute-nah (located). Exact etymology unavailable.

hospital—nat̶u̶su'u̲ kahni—"medicine house," from nat̶u̶su'u̲ (medi-cine) and kahni (house).

house—kahni; any type of house, dwelling.

239

240 *railroad*—kunawaikina pu'e—"fire wagon road," from kuna (fire), wai-kina (wagon), and pu'e (road).

railroad station—kunawaikina pu'e kahni—"fire wagon road house," from kuna (fire), waikina (wagon), pu'e (road), and kahni (house).

road—po'e or pu'e—"road" or "trail."

overpass—pu'e ʉpa'a havitʉ—"road lying over you," from: pu'e (road), ʉ (you), pa'a (over, above), havi (lie, singular object), -tʉ (nominalizing suffix).

underpass—pu'e ʉtuhkatʉ—"road lying beneath you," from pu'e (road), ʉ (you), tuhka (under), and -tʉ (nominalizing suffix).

tunnel—Sik-week-nee (dug out). Exact etymology unknown. Also known as kahnitaikʉ.

SUPPLY POINTS

ammo dump—navaaka utsa—"bullet place," from navaaka (bullet lead), utsa (possibly -u, that), and -tsa (topic marker).

POL point—navaa utsa. See ammo dump.

ration point—tʉhka utsa—"food place," from tʉhka (food), utsa (possibly -u, that), and -tsa (topic marker).

TANKS

tank—wakaree'e—"turtle."

a·p·p·e·n·d·i·x · h

KNOWN NATIVE AMERICAN CODE TALKERS OF WORLD WARS I AND II (TRIBES, GROUP SIZE, FORM OF CODE TALKING, AND MILITARY UNITS)

Tribe	Type of Code Talking	Unit
	World War I	
Cherokee	2	Probably 36th Div.
Cheyenne	2	Presently unknown
Choctaw (15)	1	Co. E, 142d Inf. Reg., 36th Div. 143d Inf. Reg., 36th Div.
Comanche	2	Presently unknown
Osage	2	Probably 36th Div.
Yankton Sioux	2	Presently unknown
	World War II	
Assiniboine	2	Co. B, 163d Inf. Div.
Cherokee	2	Presently unknown
Chippewa/Oneida (17)	2*	32d Inf. Div.
Choctaw	2	K. Co., 180th Inf. Reg., 45th Inf. Div.
Comanche (17)	1	4th Sig. Co., 4th Inf. Div.
Hopi (11)	1	U.S. Army, 223d Batt.
Kiowa	2	689th Fld. Art. Batt., XX Corps
Menominee	2	Presently unknown
Muscogee/Creek and Seminole	2	a. 195th Fld. Art. Batt. b. Aleutian campaign
Navajo (420)	1	U.S. Marine Corps 3rd, 4th, 5th Marine Divisions

242

Pawnee	2	Presently unknown
Sac and Fox (19)	2*	18th Iowa Inf.
Sioux (Lakota and Dakota dialects)	2	a. 302d Rec. Team, 1st Cav. Div.
		b. 32d Fld. Art. Batt., 19th Reg. Combat Team

Type 1—Formally developed special coded-encoded vocabularies in Native American languages.
Type 2—Informal use of everyday noncoded Native American languages.

Based on available information, groups designated as Type 2 code talkers most likely used largely noncoded or minimally coded forms of their native languages for military communications.

*Because the Chippewa-Oneida and Sac and Fox were specifically recruited for communications work, some code formation may have occurred but is presently unknown.

n·o·t·e·s

1: THE ORIGINS OF NATIVE AMERICAN CODE TALKING

1. This compilation is by no means complete. In chronological order, these include both books (Paul 1973; Bixler 1981, 1992; Kawano 1990; Aaseng 1992; McClain 1994; Greenberg and Greenberg 1997) and smaller articles (*Marine Corps Chevron* 1943; Marder 1945; *New York Times* 1945; Langille 1948; Simmons 1971; Navajo Tribal Museum 1972; Langerquist and Johnston 1975; Begay et al. 1977; Begay 1981; McCoy 1981; Belleranti 1983, 1984; Link 1986; Armstrong 1989; Hafford 1989; Davis 1990; Jere 1990; Escue 1991; Nabokov 1991:341–343; King 1992; Donovan 1992; *Sea Services Weekly* 1992; Crosswind 1992; Watson 1993; Rawls 1996:7–9). Archival sources include: BF n.d.; ND n.d.; DDIOHP 1970–1971; MCOHP 1971; HQMC 1982; and NHCOA. Recent children's books on the Navajo Code Talkers include Hunter (1996), Jones (1997), and Daily (1997). Two films focusing on the Navajo Code Talkers have been produced (NAPBC 1986; Tully 1995). Numerous articles on Navajo Code Talker appearances, awards, and recognitions continue to appear in various southwestern United States newspapers (*Scottsdale Daily Progress* 1981; *Sunday Oklahoman* 1992; *Arizona Republic* 1992). In addition, numerous information pages and briefs can be found on the Internet.

2. *Indian Record* 1970. See also Holm (1996) and Britten (1997:59) for discussion of the accuracy of these estimates.

3. U.S. Department of the Interior, Bureau of Indian Affairs, ARCIA, 60th Congress, 1st Session, (Washington, D.C.: U.S. Government Printing Office, 1918).

4. *Indian's Friend*, January 1918; Bureau of Indian Affairs, ARCIA, 1918–1920, (Washington D.C.: U.S. Government Printing Office, 1920), pp. 8–10. See also Haynie 1984:7; Holm 1985:151; Bernstein 1991:22; Parman 1994:60, Britten 1997:58–60, 73, 84.

5. Mike Wright, Scientific Social Research, to Dr. C. Alton Brown, Honorary French Consul, March 3, 1987; Mike Wright, Scientific Social Research, to Per-

244 sons Involved in Code-Talker Research, February 18, 1987; Judy Allen, Choctaw Nation of Oklahoma, *Bishinik* Drawer 1210. First Lieutenant John R. Eddy, Report on the American Indian Soldier (Spring 1919), Historical Section, General Headquarters, Records of the American Expeditionary Forces, Records Group 120, National Archives, MRB, NARA. Biographical materials on the Choctaw Code Talkers: Miscellaneous discharge papers of Victor Brown, Solomon Louis, James Edwards, and Benjamin Hampton, courtesy of Judy Allen. Individual discharge papers and copies of military pay rosters confirm the presence of these Choctaws in Company D, 141st Infantry, Company E, 142d Infantry, and the Headquarters Company of the 143d Infantry.

    6. *Daily Oklahoman,* November 18, 1917. Although this article is entitled "Fifteen Tribes Represented in Indian Company," members of only fourteen actual Native American populations were present. The "Fifteenth" was a Corporal J. Sullivan, an Anglo member of the so-called "Irish Tribe" which belonged to the unit. Corporal Sullivan served under Choctaw Captain Veach and was being transferred to the headquarters of Brigadier General Roy Hoffman at the time of this article.

    7. Kahn (1967:550) states that the Choctaws were in Company D, 141st Infantry; however, the letter of A. W. Bloor (Colonel 142d Infantry Commanding) specifically states the 142d in two instances. See First Lieutenant John R. Eddy, Report on the American Indian Soldier (Spring 1919), Historical Section, General Headquarters, Records of the AEF, Records Group 120, NARA; White (1976); White (1979:20); *Bishinik* (1986a).

    8. According to Imon (1977:86–87), Choctaw Indian–language communicators were said to have been used to transmit orders for a preemptive attack against the "Prussian Guards Division" during the St. Mihiel offensive on October 7th and 8th of 1918. However, the Thirty-sixth Infantry Division was not engaged at St. Mihiel, as Oklahomans in the 357th and 358th Infantry Regiments of the Ninetieth Division undertook this assault (Franks 1984:33–35, 120–121). Imon is most likely referring to the attack by the Thirty-sixth Division's 142d Regiment down the northern slope of Mont Blanc toward and along the sunken road to Saint-Etienne-a-Arnes (Franks 1984:118–119). Bloor's report (First Lieutenant John R. Eddy, Report on the American Indian Soldier [Spring 1919], Historical Section, General Headquarters, Records of the American Expeditionary Forces, Records Group 120, National Archives) indicates that the first action in which the Choctaws were employed as code talkers was on October 26th and 27th of 1918 at Forest Ferme; however, it is possible they were first employed on October 7th and 8th in the attack on Mont Blanc. There appears to be additional confusion in the Imon (1977:87) statement that the unit was under the command of a Colonel Brewer, which may be a confusion with Colonel Bloor. "Indian-language Communication in World War I," August 8, 1986, unpublished document in possession of the author, courtesy of Judy Allen and the Choctaw Nation. See also *New York Sun,* February 2, 1938; Levine (1921); *New York American,* November 13, 1921.

    9. *New York Sun,* February 2, 1938.

    10. This information was obtained by Len Green from Solomon Louis (often misspelled as Lewis) in 1979. Louis, the last surviving World War I Choctaw

Code Talker, died in 1982 or 1983. Tobias Frazier claims to have originated the idea to use the Choctaws as code talkers. *Bishinik* 1987b. See also *New York Sun*, February 2, 1938.

11. A 1921 *New York American* article (written by a former lieutenant in the American Expeditionary Force) states that the code talkers came from Company E, 142d Infantry and that the leader of the Indian team was Chief George Baconrind, not Solomon Louis. "Indian-language Communication in World War I," August 8, 1986, unpublished document in possession of the author, courtesy of Judy Allen and the Choctaw Nation. Imon (1977:87) states that Solomon Louis was requested by commanding officers to select a number of Choctaws as communications operators. *New York Sun*, February 2, 1938.

12. *Daily Oklahoman*, November 18, 1917.

13. First Lieutenant John R. Eddy, Report on the American Indian Soldier (Spring 1919), Historical Section, General Headquarters, Records of the American Expeditionary Forces, Records Group 120, National Archives, MRB, NARA.

14. Presumably this refers to Captain Johnston and Lieutenant C. Veach. The latter was transferred to the Forty-second Division after the Armistice (White 1979:20). Captain Walter Veach, a Choctaw, who was already serving in and commanding Company H of the Oklahoma National Guard prior to the American entrance into World War I and who may be the Lieutenant C. Veach cited by White, was requested in 1917 to form an all-Indian company composed of all Oklahoma natives. *Durant Daily Democrat*, October 17 or 18, 1966.

15. P.C. most likely refers to the French "Poste de Commandement," as C.P. is now commonly used by the American armed forces to represent Command Post. Hugh F. Foster Jr. to the author, March 3, 1996.

16. First Lieutenant John R. Eddy, Report on the American Indian Soldier (Spring 1919), Historical Section, General Headquarters, Records of the American Expeditionary Forces, Records Group 120, NARA, MRB. Bloor's report received much attention in the press (White 1979:20). This January 23, 1919, correspondence was also reprinted in the Choctaw tribal publication *Bishinik* (1986a) in July 1986. According to National Archives personnel, this is the only published account concerning the Choctaw Code Talkers in the First World War. Peterson 1986.

17. J. W. Wright, Colonel, Infantry, Army War College, Washington D.C., to Col. S. P. Collins, Acting Chief, Signal Security Branch, A.S.F., Arlington, Virginia, September 29, 1943, NARA. Peterson 1986.

18. McCoy (1981:68) states that the Choctaw transmitted "uncoded messages" in World War I; however, White (1979:17–18) demonstrates that some specialized "coded" vocabulary was developed and provides examples of such terms. A. W. Bloor to Commanding General 36th Division, January 23, 1919, "Correspondence. Reports and Other Records Relating to American Indians Serving with the AEF, 1917–1919," RG 120, NARA, MRB. See also *American Indian Magazine* 1919.

19. *Lawton Constitution*, October 3, 1989. United States Army discharge papers and additional records courtesy of Judy Allen and the Choctaw Nation of Oklahoma. Copies in possession of the author.

20. Franks (1984:29–30) provides a valuable assessment of the Choctaw Code

245

Talkers' effectiveness in the successful capture of Forest Ferme in October 1918, the task assigned to the Thirty-sixth Division (U.S.) after the French Seventy-third Division had been "brutally repulsed" in an effort to take the German position there. Although he does not cite Bloor's 1919 memorandum, Franks's information is consistent with it, in that the Third Battalion of the 142d Infantry was to be the assault unit for an attack scheduled for October 17, 1918. The mission which the Choctaw Code Talkers helped to prepare was a complete success, with no counterattack materializing. See also Barnes (1922).

21. *Fort Worth Star Telegram*, January 19 and June 11, 1919; *New York Times*, September 19, 1945.

22. While his account clearly contains a highly inaccurate imitation of what spoken Choctaw sounded like to Germans unfamiliar with the language, the point is well made. Captain Levine was formerly of the Air Service, American Expeditionary Forces and author of "Circuits of Victory," which tells of the code system used by the army in World War I.

23. United States Army discharge papers of Joseph Oklahombi, Benjamin Hampton, Solomon Louis, Tobias Frazier, and Victor Brown, courtesy of Judy Allen and the Choctaw Nation of Oklahoma. Copies in possession of the author.

24. Unknown—3, courtesy of Judy Allen and the Choctaw Nation of Oklahoma. Copy in possession of the author.

25. *Bishinik* 1987b.

26. "Choctaw Stopped War Wire Tappers," *New York Sun*, February 2, 1938; Plunkett 1987; "Choctaw Code Talkers: Native Language Turns the Tide of Battle," newspaper article (Unknown—4), Tuskahoma, Oklahoma, ca. 1987. Articles courtesy of Judy Allen and the Choctaw Nation of Oklahoma. Copies in possession of the author. It is interesting, even ironic, to note that Oklahombi's ancestral surname translates as "Man or People Killer." The suffix -hombi, or "killer of," is a common suffix in Choctaw names and has correlates in several southeastern tribal naming systems.

27. Plunkett (1987); "Choctaw Code Talkers: Native Language Turns the Tide of Battle," newspaper article (Unknown—4), Tuskahoma, Oklahoma, ca. 1987. Articles courtesy of Judy Allen and the Choctaw Nation of Oklahoma. Copies in possession of the author. "Choctaw Stopped War Wire Tappers," *New York Sun*, February 2, 1938.

28. In addition, a total of four Croix de Guerre and several other Church War Cross awards for gallantry were awarded to members of the 142d Infantry Regiment of the Thirty-sixth (Bucholz et al. 1996:2). Although a special report on American Indians as soldiers was written in 1919, in which the Thirty-sixth Division figured prominently, it was based only on "divisions . . . within easy reach of Chaumont" and did not include the Ninetieth Division, which had a comparable number of Native American servicemen. However, intradivisional assessments of Native American soldiers and their combat service with the Ninetieth Division were very positive (NARA, Study of American Indians; White 1996: 193–194).

29. Plunkett (1987); "Choctaw Code Talkers: Native Language Turns the Tide of Battle," newspaper article (Unknown—4), Tuskahoma, Oklahoma, ca. 1987. Articles courtesy of Judy Allen and the Choctaw Nation of Oklahoma. Copies in

possession of the author. "Choctaw Stopped War Wire Tappers," *New York Sun,* February 2, 1938:30.

30. When the Navajo Nation honored its code talkers from World War II, President Reagan issued a proclamation pointing out that other Indian tribes had used their native languages for the good of the United States in previous wars. The Choctaw Nation was the first tribe listed in that proclamation (*Bishinik* 1986a).

31. Of the eight original Choctaw Code Talkers, one was from Bryan County, one from Choctaw County, and six were from McCurtain County, Oklahoma (*Bishinik* 1986b).

32. Code Talkers Decoration Ceremony, Oklahoma State Capitol, November 3, 1989, program in the author's possession; *Bishinik* 1986a; Twin Territories 1991; *Bishinik* 1994a:3.

33. The following list includes all known Comanche veterans of World War I: Calvin Atchavit (Medal of Honor Winner), Toacesy Bluehorse, Edward H. Clark, Gilbert Conwoop, Dewey Maddox, James Maddox, Alfred Mahseet, Carl Mahseet, Lee Mahseet, Sam Mullins, Albert Nahquaddy Sr., Hugh Otipoby, John Mack Pahdopony, James Pekah, Private Sam Saupitty, Samuel Tabbytosevit, James Tahkofper, Cleveland Tahpay, Mickey Tahdooahnippah, Sam Tahmahkera, Norton Tahquechi, Private William C. Tarcypokeadooah, Pfc. Bert Taunah, Lawrence Tomah Sr., Corporal Thomas Tip Ah Parker, Phillip Lookingglass, John Wahkahquah, Jacob Wahkinney, Thomas Wermy. Comanche Veterans Memorial, Comanche Tribal Complex, Lawton, Oklahoma; author's field notes. Britten (1997:91) reports Hezekiah Chebatah and Owen Yackeyonney as members of Company G, Thirteenth Infantry.

34. *Indian Sign* (ca. 1940).

35. "Comanches Again Called for Service," *New York Times,* December 13, 1940. Professor Becker may have been related to Herwanna Becker Barnard, who wrote her Master's thesis on Comanche mythology and folklore in 1941 at the University of Oklahoma.

36. Haddon Codynah to Joe Todd, April 8, 1987.

37. Albert Nahquaddy Jr. to the author, July 24, 1996. Mr. Nahquaddy stated that an officer overheard his father and another Comanche conversing in Comanche to sight in an artillery gun, and that this resulted in the use of the Comanche language for military communications by several other Comanches in World War I.

38. *American Indian Magazine* 1919.

39. Author's field notes.

40. ARCIA 1919:16.

2: NATIVE AMERICAN VETERANS AND CODE TALKERS IN WORLD WAR II

1. W. Preston Corderman, Colonel Signal Corps, to Colonel McCormack, September 8, 1943, Declassified Document Authority NND963016, RNSA. My thanks to Judy Allen for photocopies of the original documents from the NSA archives cited for this chapter.

247

248

2. J. W. Wright, Colonel Infantry, Army War College, Washington, D.C., to Col. S. P. Collins, Acting Chief, Signal, Security Branch A.S.F., Arlington, Virginia, September 29, 1943, RNSA.

3. Carter W. Clarke, Colonel, General Staff, Assistant Officer, G-2, February 21, 1944, "Subject: Indians—Use of in Communications Work," RNSA.

4. Carl I. Wheat, Wheat and May Attorneys at Law, to Colonel William Friedman, March 10, 1944, June 30, 1944; William Friedman to Carl Wheat, SPSIS-3, March 14, 1944; extract from report, Signal Officer, South Pacific Area, March 31, 1944, "Crypto: The Use of Indians for Radio Transmission Security Purposes," William Friedman, Director of Communications Research, Headquarters, Army Service Forces, Office of the Chief Signal Officer, Washington, D.C., to Carl I. Wheat, May 1, 1944, July 26, 1944; J. M. Marzolf, Major, Air Corps, Chief, Cryptographic Branch, Communications Control Division, Office of the Air Communications Officer, to Chief Signal Officer, War Department, Washington, D.C., July 12, 1944, NND963016, RNSA.

5. Carl I. Wheat, Wheat and May Attorneys at Law, to Colonel William Friedman, March 10, 1944, NND963016, RNSA.

6. Ibid.

7. The Use of Navajo Indians for Radio Transmission Security Purposes, SRH-120:100–103, MRB. See McClain (1994:124–125) for more complete excerpts of this meeting.

8. Charles E. Henshall, 1st Lt., SPSIS-4, 17 June 1944, Ext. 307, SRH-120: 105, MRB.

9. Armstrong (1989:54–55) states that the navy was testing the use of Navajo and other Native Americans as potential code talkers in January of 1944 under the direction of Admiral Aubrey Fitch, Commander Aircraft South Pacific Force. The army had already trained the Comanche unit by late September of 1941, and the marines had already trained the first contingents of Navajo Code Talkers in June of 1942 and had employed them in combat beginning with the invasion of Guadalcanal in the fall of 1942.

10. Utilization of American Indians as Communications Linguists, National Archives, MRB, pp. 008–016, Washington, D.C., October 24, 1950.

11. Department of Defense Armed Forces Security Agency, National Archives, MRB, pp. 045a–045b, Washington, D.C., October 19, 1950.

12. Aubrey W. Fitch, Admiral, U.S. Navy, Commander Aircraft, South Pacific Force, to Commanding General, South Pacific, January 15, 1994, Serial 046, "Subject: Indians—Use in Communications Work," National Archives, RNSA.

13. Extract from report, Signal Officer, South Pacific Area, March 31, 1944, "Crypto," NND963016, RNSA.

14. William Friedman, Director of Communications Research, Headquarters, Army Service Forces, Office of the Chief Signal Officer, Washington, D.C., to Carl I. Wheat, May 1, 1944, NND963016, RNSA.

15. Carl I. Wheat, Wheat and May Attorneys at Law, to Colonel William Friedman, June 30, 1944, NND963016, RNSA.

16. J. M. Marzolf, Major, Air Corps, Chief, Cryptographic Branch, Communications Control Division, Office of the Air Communications Officer, to Chief

Signal Officer, War Department, Washington, D.C., July 12, 1944, NND963016, RNSA.

17. William Friedman, Director of Communications Research, Headquarters, Army Service Forces, Office of the Chief Signal Officer, Washington, D.C., to Carl I. Wheat, July 26, 1944, NND963016, RNSA.

18. Personal communication to the author, January 1997.

19. "Marine Corps Response to Wheat and May Letter. The Use of Navajo Indians for Radio Transmission Security Purposes," SRH 120 Document, MRB, Lt. Col. Smith, U.S.M.C. (Arlington Annex—Room 2126), April 15, 1944, 1300–1430 hours. See also McClain (1994:264–266).

20. Tom Kavanagh, personal communications to the author, June 6, 1996, March 19, 2001. Wagner worked around the Indiahoma area and Post Oak Mission in 1932. Wagner is also sometimes listed as Gustav (Kavanagh 2001).

21. *Cannoneer* 1992:9A. This account undoubtedly refers to the 1934 Santa Fe Laboratory of Anthropology Fieldschool. Led by Ralph Linton, five graduate students (two of whom were from Columbia University) conducted a summer fieldschool on Comanche ethnography. Linton was advised by Wagner, and the field party also worked out of Post Oak Mission and around the Indiahoma area with several of the same consultants Wagner had worked with. Although Wagner was later suspected of being a spy, he was never arrested. Tom Kavanagh (n.d.a:2–5), personal communication to the author, March 19, 2001.

22. Author's field notes. These observations are obtained from over nine years' work on the Kiowa language with noted Kiowa tribal linguist and historian Parker P. McKenzie, the inventor of the written Kiowa language, who was one of Harrington's two consultants in the early 1920s. Cf. Meadows and McKenzie (2001).

23. The last Choctaw Code Talker, Schlicht Billy, passed away January 19, 1994 (*Bishinik* 1994b:3–4). I was unable to interview Mr. Billy before his death to determine the extent of the Choctaws' training and performance as code talkers in World War II. An interview with Mr. Billy (*McAlester News—Capital and Democrat*, November 15, 1989) does not mention any special code training, and states that "Billy said he and other Choctaws used the language unformally [informally?] in radio communication over small walkie-talkies during the European campaign of World War II." Furthermore, the Code Talkers Dedication Ceremony held at the Oklahoma State Capitol on November 3, 1989, recognized only the Choctaw Code Talkers from World War I and the Comanches from World War II. Mr. Billy served as the flag bearer for the Choctaw Nation flag in this ceremony; however, no recognition of any World War II Choctaws was included in the program. Thus, as there is no mention of any training or code terms in the literature on the Choctaw Code Talkers, it appears that the Choctaws in World War II used only the regular Choctaw language, and not a specially coded Choctaw language, in sending messages. Mike Wright, Scientific Social Research, to Dr. C. Alton Brown, Honorary French Consul, March 3, 1987. Mr. Billy was awarded the Silver Star for his heroism and the wounds he received in single-handedly capturing the first German pillbox in the heavily fortified Siegfried Line (*Bishinik* 1992b:4, 1994a; Treadwell 1957:66). Author's field notes, 1999.

250

24. *Arizona Republic*, January 6, 2000.

25. *New York Times*, February 16, 1941, August 31, 1941; *Indians at Work* 194113. See also Bernstein 1991:46, Townsend 2000:144.

26. *Bishinik* 1987a:10 and *McAlester News* 1989 provide the best accounts of the Choctaws in World War II.

27. The Third Field Artillery Battalion at the time was assigned to the Second Cavalry Division commanded by Captain George Ruhlen. It was the last horse artillery unit in the U.S. Army. It became an armored artillery battalion in July 1942. Rodgers n.d.; Renee Jones n.d.; Time-Life (1993:116–117).

28. Avis Little Eagle, *Indian Country Today*, June 8, 1994. Author's field notes, 1999.

29. John Tsatoke to Mike Wright, March 23, 1987. Mr. Tsatoke states, "I have information about the Code Talkers that is of interest to you. I and a number of my Kiowa tribesmen were involved in this Project. . . . We didn't have a special unit set up for this. . . . We would talk over the radio at various times when needed and sometimes among ourselves." Mike Wright to Mr. Gerard Dumont, Consulat General de France, March 26, 1987. Forty-fifth Infantry Division Museum, Oklahoma City, Oklahoma.

30. Murray Marder, *New York Times*, September 15, 1945.

3: "GET HIM BACK ON THAT SCALE AND WEIGH HIM AGAIN!"

1. John Collier, "Memoranda on Proposed Plan for Recruiting Indian Signal Corps Personnel," October 4, 1940, Accession Number 53A-367, Box 475, Federal Records Center, Suitland, Maryland; "Comanches Again Called for Army Code Service," *New York Times*, December 13, 1940; "Indians' Code Upsets Foe: They Speed Dialect Messages by Radio in War Games," *New York Times*, August 31, 1941. See also Bernstein (1991:46). Forrest Kassanavoid to the author, July 12, 1993. Unfortunately, I have been unable to uncover further information of the exact mechanics of this selection process.

2. "Indians' Code Upsets Foe: They Speed Dialect Messages by Radio in War Games," *New York Times*, August 31, 1941.

3. Review of the Fourth Infantry Division's assignments in Stanton (1984: 81), combined with the service accounts of the surviving Comanche Code Talkers, Forrest Kassanavoid, Roderick Red Elk, Charles Chibitty, and Major General (Ret.) Hugh F. Foster, clearly indicates the existence and completion of the army's Comanche code talking training program prior to the initial idea or formation of the marines' Navajo program, as indicated by Paul (1973:8–11).

4. "Comanches Again Called for Army Code Service," *New York Times*, December 13, 1940:16.

5. Author's field notes. According to one member of the unit, the first group of Comanches was recruited by an army colonel, while the second group was recruited through the Bureau of Indian Affairs Agency at Anadarko, Oklahoma, and then sent to the army recruiting station in Oklahoma City. In an interview with Joe Todd of the Oklahoma Historical Society (May 25, 1988), Karty maintains that he first devised a plan to form an all-Indian army, then, that being too

big, modified his plans to that of an all-Indian platoon, then scaled both down to an all-Comanche Indian unit, which he eventually devised to serve as communications operators using their native language in the Army Signal Corps. Although Karty acknowledges that he began to organize and recruit members under the supervision of Anadarko Agency Superintendent (McCowen) and an army officer who came two days after the superintendent had talked to him, he maintains the idea was his own (Bill Karty to Joe Todd, May 25, 1988). Mr. Karty also stated to me in 1990 that the idea was initially his own. One unsupported source (Jones n.d.) even attributes the initial idea of forming an all-Comanche code talking unit to Karty's wife, who then prompted Karty to move the idea through the bureaucracy. In another source, Karty himself is quoted as crediting his wife Evelyn with the idea for recruiting code talkers (Daily Oklahoman, May 30, 1988). Indeed, similar animosity is recorded by Bixler (1981:86–87) concerning Navajo Carl Gorman's confrontation of Philip Johnston, who was invited to be a guest speaker at the First Navajo Code Talkers' Reunion on July 9 and 10, 1971, at Window Rock, Arizona. Johnston, an Anglo, did devise the idea to use the Navajos as code talkers. He was instrumental in presenting the idea to the military and in later recruiting some of the Navajos and contributing some, but by no means all, of the Navajo code lists and terms.

6. "Comanches Again Called for Service," New York Times, December 13, 1940. Haddon Codynah to Joe Todd, April 8, 1987. According to Hale (1992:415), who interviewed Karty over the telephone, Karty, then director of the CCC camp at Fort Cobb, came up with the idea of using the Comanche language as a part of the military's communications and presented the idea to W. B. McCowen, the superintendent of the Bureau of American Indian Affairs at Anadarko, Oklahoma. McCowen agreed and presented the plan to military officials, who authorized the development of using Native American languages in the Signal Corps. Another source states that Karty was contacted by somebody in the War Department. However, Codynah's account, supported through interviews with other code talkers, and the fact that Codynah was also working in the CCC-ID, and was most likely able to monitor the development of the recruitment process, lend support to his account. Some of the remaining code talkers have repeatedly and vehemently stated that Karty was only involved in the recruitment of some of the first group of Comanches into service, and in driving them to the recruitment station in Oklahoma City. Karty, who remained at Ft. Cobb, Oklahoma, did not serve in World War II, but did later serve in the American Occupation Forces in Japan (Daily Oklahoman, May 30, 1988). There is also a considerable amount of verbal and nonverbal tension concerning Karty's repeated appearances at public honorings and recognitions of the code talkers, in which he insists on publicly recounting his version of his role in the code talkers' development. The author witnessed one such incident at the Comanche Nation Fair in 1992. As one code talker stated, "He is always trying to steal the show and take credit for what he didn't do." Author's field notes. The recent video on the Comanche Code Talkers (Hidden Path 2000) credits Karty with the idea, but provides no discussion of the subject.

7. Haddon Codynah to Joe Todd, April 8, 1987.

252

8. Haddon Codynah to Joe Todd, April 8, 1987; see also *Lawton Constitution*, July 9, 1983.

9. Contrary to Hale's (1992:415) assertion, the remaining code talkers indicate that Karty's role was limited to recruiting some, but not all, of the seventeen men, and in helping to transport one group of them to the recruiting station in Oklahoma City. Although Karty later served overseas during the American occupation of Japan, he states that he did not serve in the military during World War II and had no role in the code talker training at Ft. Benning, Georgia, and that the code was formed after the code talkers entered service. Bill Karty to Joe Todd, May 25, 1988; author's field notes.

10. Albert Nahquaddy to the author, July 24, 1996.

11. Author's field notes, February 7, 1995.

12. Forrest Kassanavoid to the author, November 22, 1994, April 25, 1995, January 29, 1996; Roderick Red Elk to the author, January 10, 1995, August 4, 1995; author's field notes, February 7, 1995, August 4, 1995.

13. Forrest Kassanavoid to the author, January 29, 1996.

14. *Cannoneer* 1992:9A.

15. Forrest Kassanavoid, Roderick Red Elk, Charles Chibitty to the author (miscellaneous interviews); *Lawton Constitution*, July 9, 1983. Roderick and Elgin Red Elk were cousins, as were Charles Chibitty and Larry Saupitty. In addition, Morris Sunrise was a classificatory uncle to Charles Chibitty. Nahquaddy was related to eleven of the other sixteen members. Family names were translated by Forrest Kassanavoid, Roderick Red Elk, Charles Chibitty, Albert Nahquaddy Jr., and other members' relatives.

16. Comanche Veterans Memorial, Comanche Tribal Complex, Lawton, Oklahoma.

17. Haddon Codynah to Joe Todd, April 8, 1987.

18. Roderick Red Elk to the author, January 10, 1995.

19. *Lawton Constitution*, September 8, 1992.

20. Author's field notes, February 7, 1995.

21. Forrest Kassanavoid to the author, April 25, 1995.

22. *Cotton Electric Current*, April 18, 1994:13.

23. Albert Nahquaddy Jr. to the author, July 24, 1996.

24. Roderick Red Elk to the author, January 10, 1995, August 4, 1995. Author's field notes, August 4, 1995.

25. *Lawton Constitution*, July 9, 1983.

26. Thomas Holm, personal communication to the author, November 1996.

27. Forrest Kassanavoid to the author, April 25, 1995.

28. Forrest Kassanavoid to the author, April 25, 1995; see also *Lawton Constitution*, September 8, 1992.

29. Forrest Kassanavoid to the author, January 29, 1996.

30. Author's field notes, February 7, 1995.

31. Vintage Video n.d.; Ivy Green: History 2000; 4th Infantry 2000.

32. Vintage Video n.d.; NIM-FB n.d.

33. *Lawton Constitution*, September 8, 1992.

34. Roderick Red Elk to the author, August 4, 1995.

35. Roderick Red Elk to the author, August 4, 1995; author's field notes, August 4, 1995.

36. Author's field notes, August 4, 1995.

37. Forrest Kassanavoid to the author, April 25, 1995, January 11, 1996.

38. Author's field notes, February 7, 1995.

39. Unknown—1 1942. Copy of news clipping in possession of the author.

40. Forrest Kassanavoid to the author, January 11, 1996.

41. Unknown—1 1942; Forrest Kassanavoid to the author, January 11, 1996.

42. *Lawton Constitution*, September 8, 1992; Roderick Red Elk to the author, August 4, 1995.

43. John Eckert to the author, telephone conversation, March 4, 2000.

44. Forrest Kassanavoid to the author, November 22, 1994; Roderick Red Elk to the author, August 4, 1995; author's field notes, August 4, 1995.

45. Author's field notes, August 4, 1995.

46. Author's field notes, February 7, 1995.

47. Major General (Ret.) Hugh F. Foster to the author, February 7, 1995, February 5, 2001.

48. Ibid.

49. Ibid.

50. Ibid.

51. Hugh Foster to the author March 5, 1996, February 5, 2001.

52. Forrest Kassanavoid to the author; author's field notes.

53. Hugh Foster to the author, February 7, 1995. Foster later stated that the total was closer to 250 terms. The exact number will probably never be known.

54. Author's field notes, February 7, 1995, August 4, 1995; Forrest Kassanavoid to the author, February 18, 1994, and November 22, 1994, April 25, 1995, January 11, 1996; Roderick Red Elk to the author, January 10, 1995, August 4, 1995; author's field notes.

55. Roderick Red Elk to the author, January 10, 1995.

56. A review of the interviews of remaining code talkers reveals different accounts, suggesting that in designating the size of artillery or manual firearms, an operator might: (1) specify the actual number (such as 105 or 88) or (2) might simply list the numbers involved (such as eight, eight).

57. Roderick Red Elk to the author, January 10, 1995. Charles Chibitty remembered another individual making the analogy between a bomber full of bombs and catching catfish full of eggs (Hidden Path 2000).

58. Forrest Kassanavoid to the author, November 22, 1994.

59. Ibid.

60. *Lawton Constitution*, July 9, 1983; Hugh F. Foster to Towana Spivey, May 16, 1991, Ft. Sill Museum Archives.

61. Forrest Kassanavoid to the author, January 11, 1996; *Lawton Constitution*, October 3, 1989.

62. Forrest Kassanavoid to the author, January 11, 1996.

63. Author's field notes, August 4, 1995.

64. Author's field notes, February 7, 1995, August 4, 1995. For an audio exam-

254 ple of this system of spelling for proper names and how the code was used, see Charles Chibitty in Hidden Path Productions (2000).

65. Author's field notes, February 7, 1995; Forrest Kassanavoid to the author, April 25, 1995.

66. Author's field notes.

67. Haddon Codynah to Joe Todd, April 8, 1987.

68. Author's field notes, August 4, 1995.

69. Major General (Ret.) Hugh F. Foster to the author, February 7, 1995. In the early 1990s, Foster wrote a sample of the original terms he remembered in a World War II–era notebook similar to the original, which was placed in the National Security Agency archives at Ft. Meade, Maryland.

70. Roderick Red Elk to the author, January 10, 1995.

71. *Sunday Enquirer* (Columbus, Georgia), ca. 1941–1942. Copy of article in author's possession.

72. 4th Division Motorized 1942, copy of article in author's possession.

73. Roderick Red Elk to Joe Todd, June 21, 1988. Roderick Red Elk to the author, August 4, 1995; author's field notes, August 4, 1995.

74. Ernest Stahlberg, letter to the author, March 9, 2000.

75. Forrest Kassanavoid to the author, April 25, 1995; author's field notes, August 4, 1995. See also Red Elk (1992:1).

76. Author's field notes.

77. Roderick Red Elk to the author, August 4, 1995; author's field notes, August 4, 1995. Forrest Kassanavoid to the author, April 25, 1995. Albert Nahquaddy Jr. to the author, July 24, 1996.

78. Roderick Red Elk to the author, August 4, 1995; author's field notes, August 4, 1995. Forrest Kassanavoid to the author, April 25, 1995. Although some of these weight categories do not match up with the exact weight categories of the time, they are listed as given by the members.

79. Author's field notes; Unknown—1 (1942), copy of news clipping in possession of the author. Author's field notes, August 4, 1995.

80. Unknown—2 (1942), copy of article in author's possession. The "29th Infantry" probably refers to the Twenty-ninth Field Artillery Battalion, assigned to the Fourth Infantry Division during 1941–1945 (Stanton 1984:81).

81. Ibid.

82. Author's field notes, August 4, 1995.

83. Forrest Kassanavoid to the author, January 11, 1996.

84. Roderick Red Elk to Joe Todd, June 21, 1988.

85. In military terminology a "Camp" was the designation for a temporary location. Some time after World War II, it was redesignated a permanent installation and renamed Ft. Gordon. Hugh Foster to the author March 5, 1996, February 5, 2001. Albert Nahquaddy Jr. to the author, July 24, 1996.

86. Hugh F. Foster to the author, February 7, 1995; Hugh F. Foster to Towana Spivey, May 16, 1991, Ft. Sill Museum Archives.

87. Forrest Kassanavoid to the author, January 11, 1996.

88. *Lawton Constitution*, July 9, 1983.

89. Forrest Kassanavoid to the author, January 11, 1996.

90. Ibid.

91. Out of respect for the privacy of the three discharged members, I have chosen not to elaborate any further on the circumstances of their discharges.

92. NIM-FB n.d.

93. Haddon Codynah to Joe Todd, April 8, 1987.

94. Roderick Red Elk to Joe Todd, June 21, 1988.

4: "ᵾTEKWAPA NAKA: I HEAR WHAT YOU SAY."

1. This chapter provides only a brief discussion of the military and signals communication organization of the U.S. Army and the Fourth Division during this period. This material is intended only to describe the general context in which the code talkers served and is not a comprehensive account of military communications. Hugh Foster to the author, February 7, 1995. I am greatly indebted to Major General (Ret.) Hugh F. Foster for helping me with the material to develop this brief synopsis of military organization and communications structure.

2. Hugh Foster to the author, February 7, 1995. See also Hoegh and Doyle (1946:412–418) for a detailed description of the composition of Army infantry divisions.

3. Hugh Foster to the author, February 7, 1995.

4. Author's field notes. The reserve infantry regiment was there to be used when needed, and it is used more often than not. The artillery battalion was almost always used to some extent. Hugh F. Foster to the author, March 3, 1996.

5. In combat, the divisional headquarters is usually divided into three echelons: (1) division advance: command group and small staff group (operations and intelligence); (2) division main: deputy command group, principal staffs, etc.; and (3) division rear: administration (adjunct, personnel, finance, etc.). Hugh Foster to the author, March 3, 1996.

6. Roderick Red Elk to the author, January 10, 1995; Forrest Kassanavoid to the author, July 12, 1993, November 22, 1994.

7. Forrest Kassanavoid to the author, November 22, 1994.

8. Ernest Stahlberg, letter to the author, March 9, 2000.

9. Hugh Foster to the author, March 3, 1996.

10. Hugh Foster to the author, February 7, 1995.

11. Forrest Kassanavoid to the author, April 25, 1995.

12. Forrest Kassanavoid to the author, November 22, 1994.

13. Forrest Kassanavoid to the author, November 22, 1994, April 25, 1995.

14. Major General (Ret.) Hugh Foster to Towana Spivey, May 16, 1991, Ft. Sill Museum Archives; author's field notes, August 4, 1995.

15. Hugh Foster to the author, April 12, 1995. Written military message traffic is encoded into five-character code groups and transmitted by radiotype or landline teletype. Thus, the preceding sentence could be transmitted as ABNSX QKLPI AMNIT ORVEB WMSFT, etc. Spaces in the original message were transmitted as characters to conceal word lengths. The letter "A" in the original message would be transmitted as various other letters at various times. Numeric digits were spelled out to prevent transmission or decoding errors. Most signal corps units prepared and reproduced pages and pages of random five-letter groups. **255**

256 They were given to the teletype and radio operators to transmit and receive during training. In combat, the amount of radio traffic between specific headquarters could be a clue to impending activity. It was therefore often desirable to maintain a steady flow of traffic, much of which was spurious. Thus, these pages of five-letter random letter groups were inserted into maneuver training traffic when deemed appropriate, or just to keep the communicators busy if communications traffic was otherwise light.

16. Author's field notes.

17. Ibid.

18. Forrest Kassanavoid to the author, April 25, 1995. Although the Germans used great numbers of horses throughout the war, both in North Africa and various parts of Europe, by this time it was realized that they were running low on transportation and fuel.

19. Forrest Kassanavoid to the author, April 25, 1995; *Cannoneer* 1992:9A.

20. Forrest Kassanavoid to the author, April 25, 1995.

21. Roderick Red Elk, *Lawton Constitution*, October 3, 1989.

22. Author's field notes.

23. Hugh Foster to the author, April 12, 1995.

24. Ibid.

25. Hugh Foster to the author, February 7, 1995. Because messages were sent to the division, the code talkers played little role in air strikes. If an air strike were to be called, the air liaison officer (usually a man who had completed twenty-five missions but did not wish to return stateside) at the division had to send a message on to the air corps tactical command, at which level there were no code talkers involved.

26. Author's field notes.

27. Forrest Kassanavoid to the author, November 22, 1994, April 25, 1995; author's field notes.

28. Author's field notes.

29. Forrest Kassanavoid to the author, April 25, 1995.

30. Forrest Kassanavoid to the author, November 22, 1994.

5: FIGHTING PO'SATAIBOO': CRAZY WHITE MAN

1. Greystone Communications 1994.

2. Ibid.

3. As Forrest Kassanavoid recalled, Roosevelt stated, "There's not a bullet that'll kill a Roosevelt." About Roosevelt's death, Kassanavoid added, "He died of a heart attack shortly after the invasion of Normandy." *Lawton Constitution*, October 3, 1989.

4. *Cotton Electric Current*, April 18, 1994.

5. Forrest Kassanavoid to the author, July 23, 1996. Kassanavoid also related this incident in another interview (*Cannoneer* 1992:9A), "During the Normandy Invasion, a unit made a landing at Utah Beach, and afterwards they realized they landed at the wrong spot. They wanted to let the command know they were not where they were supposed to be, but they didn't want the Germans to know it. The message we sent was 'pia atah tuku tane way,' or in English 'right beach,

wrong place'—the wrong landing actually turned out to their advantage." See also *Bugle Bulge* (1994:26).

6. Author's field notes, February 7, 1995, August 4, 1995.

7. Author's field notes.

8. Haddon Codynah to Joe Todd, April 8, 1987; *Lawton Constitution*, July 9, 1983.

9. Forrest Kassanavoid to the author, November 22, 1994.

10. Bryant (1993a:20).

11. *Lawton Constitution*, October 3, 1989.

12. Bryant (1993a:21).

13. *Lawton Constitution*, May 26, 1994.

14. Author's field notes, August 4, 1995.

15. Haddon Codynah to Joe Todd, April 8, 1987.

16. Roderick Red Elk to the author, August 4, 1995.

17. Roderick Red Elk to the author, January 10, 1995.

18. Haddon Codynah to Joe Todd, April 8, 1987.

19. Author's field notes, February 7, 1995; Haddon Codynah to Joe Todd, April 8, 1987. According to one code talker who survived the bombing, nearly a thousand U.S. troops were killed and wounded by Allied bombing in this location.

20. Haddon Codynah to Joe Todd, April 8, 1987.

21. Roderick Red Elk to Joe Todd, June 21, 1988.

22. Roderick Red Elk to the author, January 10, 1995. See also Red Elk (1992:6).

23. Author's field notes.

24. Forrest Kassanavoid to the author, November 22, 1994; NIM-FB n.d.

25. Roderick Red Elk to the author, August 4, 1995.

26. NIM-FB n.d.

27. *McAlester News—Capital and Democrat*, November 15, 1989. In addition to several commendations and awards, Schlicht Billy was wounded four times, and received the European–African–Middle Eastern Theater Medal with a cluster of five Bronze Stars, and was a 2d lieutenant at the time he was discharged (Schlicht Billy—Transcript of Military Record, courtesy of Judy Allen; *Bishinik* 1987a, 1987b). See also Treadwell (1957:66) for his account of Billy's capturing of the first German pillbox on the Siegfried Line.

28. Treadwell 1957:66.

29. Ibid.

30. Forrest Kassanavoid to the author, January 11, 1996; *Lawton Constitution*, October 3, 1989.

31. Roderick Red Elk to the author, January 10, 1995.

32. Forrest Kassanavoid to the author, April 25, 1995, January 11, 1996.

33. Ernest Stahlberg, letter to the author, March 9, 2000.

34. NIM-FB n.d.

35. Author's field notes, February 7, 1995. Hidden Path (2000).

36. *Lawton Constitution*, July 9, 1983.

37. Author's field notes, February 7, 1995.

38. Roderick Red Elk to the author, January 10, 1995.

39. Roderick Red Elk to the author, July 23, 1996.

40. Haddon Codynah to Joe Todd, April 8, 1987; Haddon Codynah to Sharrock (*Lawton Constitution* 1983)—this article contained a picture of Codynah with the German sword and banner he captured.

41. Ibid.

42. Author's field notes, February 7, 1995, August 4, 1995; Forrest Kassanavoid to the author, November 22, 1994.

43. *Lawton Constitution*, October 3, 1989. Because military regulations prohibit acquisition of a serviceman's career record except by immediate relatives, I was unable to acquire a complete list of the awards earned by the code talkers.

44. Author's field notes.

45. Roderick Red Elk to Joe Todd, June 21, 1988.

46. Author's field notes, August 4, 1995; Forrest Kassanavoid to the author, April 25, 1995. Another account of the story stated that the transmission went, "Sah-kuh-nah nah-qhay" (I hear you're good). "A wau-hau-nuh" (I'm your enemy). "Sah-nah num-i-nah-quay" (I speak good Comanche fluently). A colonel finally cut into their conversation and asked who they were. After telling the colonel who they were and that they were just "Talking in Indian," the officer responded that the last portion of their exchange was "not in Indian" but was satisfied as to the harmlessness of the activities. Hidden Path 2000.

47. Author's field notes.

48. Forrest Kassanavoid to the author, April 25, 1995.

49. Forrest Kassanavoid to the author, January 11, 1996.

50. Forrest Kassanavoid to the author, November 22, 1994, April 25, 1995; *Daily Oklahoman*, August 18, 1992.

51. NIM-FB n.d.

52. NIM-FB n.d.

53. For a more in-depth account of the entire European Theater of combat, refer to MacDonald (1969) or Weigley (1981).

54. *Lawton Constitution*, July 9, 1983; Roderick Red Elk to the author, July 23, 1996.

55. NIM-FB n.d. The Fourth Signal Company later became the 124th Signal Battalion when the army reorganized after World War II.

6: "NUMUREKWA'ETUU: COMANCHE SPEAKERS!"

1. Author's field notes.

2. Forrest Kassanavoid to the author, January 11, 1996.

3. Author's field notes.

4. Forrest Kassanavoid to the author, April 25, 1995.

5. Forrest Kassanavoid to the author, January 11, 1996; *Lawton Constitution* 1996.

6. Forrest Kassanavoid to the author, January 11, 1996, January 29, 1996.

7. Forrest Kassanavoid to the author, January 11, 1996; Roderick Red Elk to the author, July 23, 1996.

8. Roderick Red Elk to the author, August 4, 1995; *Lawton Constitution*, September 26, 1997.

9. Forrest Kassanavoid to the author, January 11, 1996; author's field notes, February 7, 1995. Tabbytite reportedly has not maintained contact with the other members of the group since the end of the war.

10. Roderick Red Elk to the author, August 4, 1995.

11. Forrest Kassanavoid to the author, January 11, 1996.

12. Ibid.

13. Roderick Red Elk to the author, August 4, 1995. More recently, the Comanche Nation Fair, first held in 1992, has regularly included public honorings of the surviving Comanche Code Talkers.

14. Roderick Red Elk to the author, January 10, 1995.

15. *Lawton Constitution*, July 9, 1983.

16. *Daily Oklahoman*, January 14, 1997.

17. Personal communication to the author. One military historian reports that historians today still know very little about "Ultra" because, as the British government has told the scholarly community, it will never open some of the records relating to this intelligence group.

18. Renee Jones n.d.; *Lawton Morning Press*, February 12, 1987:A1; *Daily Oklahoman* (1987a, 1987b), April 6, 1987; *Tulsa Tribune*, March 18, 1989; C. Alton Brown to Mike Wright, February 9, 1987; Press Release—Scientific Social Research, Norman, Oklahoma, February 9, 1987.

19. Ibid.

20. Recently, the surviving code talkers have expressed dissatisfaction because the staff at the Comanche Tribal Complex has been unable to account for the plaque's location. *Lawton Constitution*, October 3, 1989; program, audio- and videotape of Code Talkers Decoration Ceremony, Oklahoma State Capitol, November 3, 1989, Oral History Collections, Oklahoma Historical Society, Oklahoma City. Copy of program and audio- and videotapes in possession of the author. Twin Territories 1991; *Daily Oklahoman*, November 5, 1989.

21. Mike Wright, November 3, 1989; program, audio- and videotape of Code Talkers Decoration Ceremony, Oklahoma State Capitol, November 3, 1989, Oral History Collections, Oklahoma Historical Society, Oklahoma City. Copy of program and audio- and videotapes in possession of the author.

22. Author's field notes. To the disappointment of many, only a brief background was provided concerning the actual Choctaw and Comanche Code Talkers, and the surviving Comanche Code Talkers were not given the opportunity to speak at the ceremony. Several Indians and non-Indians in attendance made comments to this effect.

23. Program, audio- and videotape of Code Talkers Decoration Ceremony, Oklahoma State Capitol, November 3, 1989, Oral History Collections, Oklahoma Historical Society, Oklahoma City. Copy of program and audio- and videotapes in possession of the author.

24. Forrest Kassanavoid to the author, January 11, 1996.

25. Certificates courtesy of Charles Chibitty and Forrest Kassanavoid, copies in possession of the author.

26. Author's field notes. The Kiowa Black Legs Society previously named an army OH-58D helicopter "Kiowa Warrior," at the Kiowa Black Legs Fall Society Dance in October of 1990 (Meadows 1991:117).

260

27. *Lawton Constitution*, May 26, 1994:3a; *Cotton Electric Current*, April 18, 1994:13.

28. Hugh F. Foster to the author, January 23, 1995, February 24, 1996.

29. Hugh Foster to the author, February 7, 1995.

30. Ernest Stahlberg, letter to the author, January 29, 2000. John Eckert to the author, telephone call, March 4, 2000.

31. *Forrest Kassanavoid Memorial Dance*, video recording, September 20, 1997. Copy in author's possession. The five Bronze Stars refer to campaign stars for each major campaign the code talkers were in during World War II.

32. Ibid.

33. Ibid.

34. *Lawton Constitution*, September 26, 1997.

35. Petition to the Congress of the United States on Behalf of the Native American Code Talkers of World War I and World War II. Drafted by Elizabeth B. Pollard, copy in possession of the author. To assist her in preparing this petition, I furnished Mrs. Pollard with portions of this manuscript to define the two types of Native American Code Talkers and to demonstrate the distribution of tribes involved during both world wars. This information and the current status of the petition may be obtained at the following Web sites, http://aises.uthscsa.edu/discussion/1998/0062.html, or by sending an e-mail request to lpollard@smokesig.com.

36. *Daily Oklahoman*, December 1, 1999; *Anadarko Daily News*, November 27, 2001; Hidden Path 2000; Adare 2002.

37. Department of Defense Armed Forces Security Agency, National Archives, MRB, Washington, D.C., October 19, 1950, pp. 045a–045b.

38. NARA, MRB, Washington, D.C., October 26, 1950, pp. 005a–005b.

39. Letter from Indian Association of America to President Harry Truman, National Archives, Military Reference Branch, Washington, D.C., September 15, 1950, p. 073; Utilization of American Indians as Communications Linguists, NARA, MRB, Washington, D.C., pp. 008–016, October 24, 1950.

40. Author's field notes.

41. Ibid.

42. Ibid.

43. Paul (1973:85–91) records at least seven such cases, while Kawano (1990: 11, 42, 54, 72) records three such instances, involving Eugene R. Crawford, David Jordan, and Roy Notah.

44. Author's field notes.

45. Daily Oklahoman, August 18, 1992.

46. Sixty-nine Navajo Code Talkers attended this meeting (McClain 1994: 233).

47. Forrest Kassanavoid to the author, January 11, 1996.

48. Roderick Red Elk to the author, August 4, 1995.

49. *Anadarko Daily News*, March 2, 2000.

50. Forrest Kassanavoid to the author, November 22, 1994, April 25, 1995, January 11, 1996; Roderick Red Elk to the author, January 10 and August 4, 1995; author's field notes, February 7 and August 4, 1995.

51. *Lawton Constitution*, September 8, 1992; *Cannoneer* 1992:9A.

52. Roderick Red Elk to Joe Todd, June 21, 1988.

53. Forrest Kassanavoid to the author, January 11, 1996, April 25, 1995.

54. Author's field notes, August 4, 1995.

55. Author's field notes, February 7, 1995; Meadows (1995).

56. Roderick Red Elk to the author, August 4, 1995.

57. Forrest Kassanavoid to the author, July 23, 1996.

58. Author's field notes, August 4, 1995; *Anadarko Daily News*, July 25, 2001.

59. *Arizona Republic*, January 6, 2001.

60. "Language Preservation: Saving Comanche on the computer," *Anadarko Daily News*, May 6–7, 2000.

b·i·b·l·i·o·g·r·a·p·h·y

Aaseng, Nathan. 1992. *Navajo Code Talkers*. New York: Walker Publishing Co.

Adair, John. 1947. "The Navajo and Pueblo Veteran: A Force for Cultural Change." *American Indian* (4): 5–11.

———. 1948. "A Study of Cultural Resistance: The Veterans of World War II at Zuni Pueblo." Ph.D. diss., Department of Anthropology, University of New Mexico.

Adair, John, and Evon Vogt. 1949. "Navajo and Zuni Veterans: A Study of Contrasting Modes of Culture Change." *American Anthropologist* 51 (4): 547–562.

Adare, Sierra S. 2002. "The Last Comanche Code Talker." *World War II*, January, pp. 58–64.

Ambrose, Stephen E. 1994. *D-Day June 6, 1944: The Climactic Battle of World War II*. New York: Simon and Schuster.

ARCIA *(Annual Report of the Commissioner of Indian Affairs)*. 1918–1920. U.S. Department of the Interior, Bureau of Indian Affairs. Washington, D.C.: U.S. Government Printing Office, 1920.

Armstrong, Richard N. 1989. "For the U.S. Marines in the Pacific, Navajo 'code-Talkers' Were a Secret Communications Weapon." *World War II Magazine* 3 (6): 10, 54–60.

Barnes, C. H. 1922. *History of the 142nd Infantry of the Thirty-sixth Division*. Blackwell Job Publishing Co.

Begay, David. 1981. "The Navajo Code Talkers." *Four Winds* 2 (3): 62–64, 90–93.

Begay, Keats, et al. 1977. *Navajos and World War II*. Tsaile, Ariz.: Navajo Community College Press.

Belleranti, Shirley W. 1983. "Code Talkers." *Westways Magazine*, May, pp. 40–42, 76.

———. 1984. "The Code That Couldn't Be Cracked." *Retired Officer*, November, pp. 33–35.

Bernstein, Alison R. 1991. *American Indians and World War II: Toward a New Era in Indian Affairs*. Norman: University of Oklahoma Press.

264 Bixler, Margaret T. 1981. "The Navajo Code Talkers of World War II: A Background Study in Acculturation." Master's thesis. University of New Haven, Connecticut.

———. 1992. *Winds of Freedom: The Story of the Navajo Code Talkers of World War II.* Darien, Conn.: Two Bytes Publishing Company.

Britten, Thomas A. 1997. *American Indians in World War I: At War and at Home.* Albuquerque: University of New Mexico Press.

Bruce, Norman. 1973. *Secret Warfare: The Battle of Codes and Ciphers.* Washington, D.C.: Acropolis.

Bryant, Troy. 1993a. "Comanches Used Their Language to Help Confuse WWII Enemies." *Purple Heart Magazine,* March–April, pp. 20–22.

———. 1993b. "Navajo Marines Also Baffled Enemy in WWII." *Purple Heart Magazine,* March–April, pp. 21, 23.

Chafe, Wallace L. 1962. "Estimates Regarding the Present Speakers of North American Indian Languages." *International Journal of American Linguistics* 1 (28): 162–171.

———. 1965. "Corrected Estimates Regarding Speakers of North American Indian Languages." *International Journal of American Linguistics* 31 (4): 345–346.

Charney, Jean O. 1993. *A Grammar of Comanche.* Lincoln: University of Nebraska Press.

Chastaine, Capt. Ben H. 1920. *Story of the 36th: The Experiences of the 36th Division in the World War.* Oklahoma City: Harlow Publishing Company.

Collier, John. 1942. "The Indian in a Wartime Nation." *Annals of the American Academy of Political and Social Science* 223 (September): 29–35.

Conn, Gen. Stetson, ed. 1963. *United States Army in World War II: The History of the European Theater of Operations.* 9 vols. Prepared under the direction of Hugh M. Cole and Charles B. MacDonald. Washington, D.C.: Office of the Chief of Military History.

Daily, Robert. 1997. *The Code Talkers: American Indians in World War II.* New York: Franklin Watts Publishing Company.

Davis, Goode, Jr. 1990. "Proud Tradition of the Marines' Navajo Code Talkers: They Fought with Words—Words No Japanese Could Fathom." *Marine Corps League* 46 (1): 16–26.

Dempsey, James. 1983. "The Indians and World War One." *Alberta History* 31 (3): 1–8.

DiNicolo, Capt. G. M. n.d. "Pentagon Opens Native American Exhibit." World War II dispatch, Operations Directorate.

Dunlay, Thomas W. 1982. *Wolves for the Blue Soldiers: Indian Scouts and Auxiliaries with the United States Army, 1860–90.* Lincoln: University of Nebraska Press.

Durret, Deanne. 1998. *Unsung Heroes of World War II: The Story of the Navajo Code Talkers.* New York: Facts on File.

Escue, Lynn. 1991. "Coded Contributions: Navajo Talkers and the Pacific War." *History Today* 41 (July): 13–20.

Fourth Infantry Division Association. 1987. *4th Infantry "Ivy" Division Steadfast and Loyal.* Paducah, Ky.: Turner Publishing Co.

———. 1994. *Fourth Infantry Division Steadfast and Loyal, Vol. II.* Paducah, Ky.: Turner Publishing Co.

Franco, Jere' Bishop. 1999. *Crossing the Pond: The Native American Effort in World War II.* Vol. 7, War and the Southwest Series. Denton, Tex.: University of North Texas Press.

Franks, Kenny A. 1984. *Citizen Soldiers: Oklahoma's National Guard.* Norman: University of Oklahoma Press.

Gawne, Jonathan. 1998. *Spearheading D-Day: American Special Units of the Normandy Invasion.* Paris, France: Histoire and Collections.

Goddard, Ives. 1978. "Eastern Algonquian Languages." In *Handbook of North American Indians 15 (Northeast),* ed. Bruce G. Trigger, pp. 70–77. Washington, D.C.: Smithsonian Institution.

Greenberg, Henry, and Georgia Greenberg. 1996. *Power of a Navajo. Carl Gorman: The Man and His Life.* Santa Fe, N.Mex.: Clear Light Publishers.

Hafford, William E. 1989. "The Navajo Code Talkers." *Arizona Highways,* February, pp. 36–45.

Hale, Duane K. 1982. "Forgotten Heroes: American Indians in World War I." *Four Winds* 3 (2): 38–41.

———. 1992. "Uncle Sam's Warriors: American Indians in World War II." *Chronicles of Oklahoma* 69 (4): 408–429.

Harrington, John P. 1928. *Vocabulary of the Kiowa Language.* Smithsonian Institution, Bureau of American Ethnology, Bulletin 84. Washington, D.C.: United States Government Printing Office.

Haynie, Nancy Anne. 1984. *Native Americans and the Military: Today and Yesterday.* Fort McPherson, Ga.: U.S. Army Forces Command Public Affairs, Command Information Branch.

Hirshfelder, Arlene, and Martha Kreipe deMontano. 1993. *The Native American Almanac: A Portrait of Native America Today.* Englewood Cliffs, N.J.: Prentice Hall Press.

Hoegh, Leo A., and Howard J. Doyle. 1946. *Timberwolf Tracks: The History of the 104th Infantry Division 1942–1945.* Washington, D.C.: Infantry Journal Press.

Hollow, Robert C., and Douglas R. Parks. 1980. "Studies in Plains Linguistics: A Review." In *Anthropology on the Great Plains,* ed. W. Raymond Wood and Margot Liberty, pp. 68–97. Lincoln: University of Nebraska Press.

Holm, Tom. 1978. "Indians and Progressives: From Vanishing Policy to the Indian New Deal." PhD. diss., University of Oklahoma, Norman.

———. 1985. "Fighting a White Man's War: The Extent and Legacy of American Indian Participation in World War II." In *The Plains Indians of the Twentieth Century,* ed. Peter Iverson, pp. 149–168. Norman: University of Oklahoma Press.

———. 1992. "Patriots and Pawns: State Use of American Indians in the Military and the Process of Nativization in the United States." In *The State of Native America,* ed. M. Annette Jaimes, pp. 345–370. Boston: South End Press.

———. 1996. *Strong Hearts, Wounded Souls: Native American Veterans of the Vietnam War.* Austin: University of Texas Press.

265

266 Hunter, Sara Hoagland. 1996. *The Unbreakable Code.* Flagstaff, Ariz.: Northland Publishing Co.

Imon, Frances. 1977. *Smoke Signals from Indian Territory,* vol. 2. Wolfe City, Tex.: Henington Publishing Company.

Iverson, Peter. 1990. *The Navajos.* Indians of North America Series, Frank W. Porter III, general editor. New York: Chelsea House Publishers.

Jere, Franco. 1990. *Patriotism on Trial: Native Americans in World War II.* Ann Arbor, Mich.: University Microfilms International.

Johnson, Broderick H., ed. 1977. *Navajos and World War II.* Tsaile, Ariz.: Navajo College Press.

Johnston, Philip. 1964. "Indian Jargon Won Our Battles." *Masterkey* 38 (October–December): 131–132.

Jones, Catharine. 1997. *Navajo Code Talkers: Native American Heroes.* Greensboro, N.C.: Tudor Publishers, Inc.

Kahn, David. 1967. *The Codebreakers: The Story of Secret Writing.* New York: MacMillan Co.

———. 1983. *Kahn on Codes: Secrets of the New Cryptography.* New York: MacMillan Co.

Kavanagh, Thomas W. 1996. *Comanche Political History: An Ethnohistorical Perspective 1706–1875.* Lincoln: University of Nebraska Press.

———. n.d. *A Comanche Sourcebook: Notes of the 1933 Sante Fe Laboratory of Anthropology Field Party.* Recorded by Waldo R. Wedel, E. Adamson Hoebel, and Gustav G. Carlson. Edited by Thomas W. Kavanagh.

Kawano, Kenji. 1990. *Warriors: Navajo Code Talkers.* Tucson, Ariz.: Northland Publishing Company.

LaBarre, Weston. n.d. "Autobiography of a Kiowa Indian." Manuscript, copy in the author's possession.

Langerquist, Syble, and Philip Johnston. 1975. *Philip Johnston and the Navajo Code Talkers.* Billings, Mont.: Montana Council for Indian Education.

Langille, Vernon. 1948. "Indian War Call." *Leatherneck* 31 (3): 37–40.

Link, Martin. 1986. *We Talked Navajo.* Gallup, N.Mex.: Indian Trader Newspaper.

McClain, Sally. 1994. *Navajo Weapon.* Boulder, Colo.: Books Beyond Borders.

McCoy, Ronald. 1981. "Navajo Code Talkers of World War II." *American West* 18 (6): 67–73, 75.

MacDonald, Charles B. 1969. *The Mighty Endeavor: American Armed Forces in the European Theater in World War II.* New York: Oxford University Press.

Marder, Mt. Sgt. Murray. 1945. "Navajo Code Talkers." *Marine Corps Gazette,* September, pp. 10–11.

Marshall, LTC Malcolm. 1994. *Proud Americans.* London: New Hampshire.

Maslowski, Peter. 1995. "Military Intelligence: Unmasking Those Fearsome Apparitions." In *War Comes Again: Comparative Vistas on the Civil War and World War II,* ed. Gabor Boritt, pp. 51–82. New York: Oxford University Press.

Meadows, William C. 1991. "Tonkonga: An Ethnohistory of the Kiowa Black Legs Society." Master's thesis, University of Oklahoma, Norman.

———. 1995. "Remaining Veterans: A Symbolic and Comparative Ethnohistory of Southern Plains Indian Military Societies." Ph.D. diss., University of Oklahoma, Norman.

———. 1999. *Kiowa, Apache, and Comanche Military Societies: Enduring Veterans, 1800 to the Present.* Austin: University of Texas Press.

Meadows, William C., and Parker P. McKenzie 2001. "The Parker P. McKenzie Kiowa Orthography: How Written Kiowa Came into Being." *Plains Anthropologist* 46 (177): 233–248.

Meriam, Lewis, et al. 1928. *The Problem of Indian Administration.* Institute for Government Research. Baltimore: Johns Hopkins Press.

Mikkanen, Arvo Q. 2001. "Comanche Code Talkers Finally Gain Recognition." *Anadarko Daily News,* November 7.

Moseley, Susan. 1988. "Choctaw Code-Talkers." *Oklahoma Today,* July–August, p. 13.

Nabokov, Peter. 1991 [1978]. *Native American Testimony: A Chronicle of Indian-White Relations from Prophecy to the Present, 1492–1992.* New York: Penguin Books.

Navajo Tribal Museum. 1972. *They Talked Navajo: The United States Marine Corps Navajo Code Talkers of World War II.* Window Rock, Ariz.: Navajo Tribal Museum.

Parks, Douglas R. 1988. "The Importance of Language Study for the Writing of Plains Indian History." In *New Directions in American Indian History,* ed. Collin G. Calloway, pp. 153–197. Norman: University of Oklahoma Press.

Parman, Donald L. 1994. *Indians and the American West in the Twentieth Century.* Bloomington: Indiana University Press.

Paul, Doris A. 1973. *The Navajo Code Talkers.* Pittsburgh: Dorrance Publishing Co.

Raines, Rebecca Robbins. 1996. *Getting the Message Through: A Branch History of the U.S. Army Signal Corps.* Washington, D.C.: Center of Military History, United States Army.

Rawls, James R. 1996. *Chief Red Fox Is Dead: A History of Native Americans since 1945.* New York: Harcourt Brace.

Red Elk, Roderick. 1991. "Comanche Code-Talkers." *Prairie Lore* 27 (1): 113–114, Book 86.

———. 1992. "Comanche Code-Talkers." *Prairie Lore* 28 (1): 1–10, Book 88.

Richardson, Rupert N. 1933. *The Comanche Barrier to South Plains Settlement.* Glendale, Calif.: Arthur H. Clark Co.

Ritzenthaler, Robert. 1943. "The Impact of War on an Indian Community." *American Anthropologist* 45: 325–326.

Robinson, Lila Wistrand, and James Armagost. 1990. *Comanche Dictionary and Grammar.* Summer Institute of Linguistics and the University of Texas at Arlington.

Shy, John. 1986. "First Battle in Retrospect." In *America's First Battles,* ed. Charles E. Heller, Lieutenant Colonel, United States Army Reserve, and William A. Stofft, Brigadier General, United States Army, pp. 327–352. Lawrence: University Press of Kansas.

Simmons, Isabel. 1971. "The Unbreakable Code." *Marine Corps Gazette* 55 (11): 59.

268   Stallings, Laurence. 1963. *The Doughboys: The Story of the AEF, 1917–1918.* New York: Harper and Row.

Stanton, Shelby L. 1984. *Order of Battle: U.S. Army, World War II.* Novato, Calif.: Presidio Press.

Stewart, James M. 1943. "The Navajo Indian at War." *Arizona Highways,* June, pp. 22–23.

Tate, Michael L. 1986. "From Scout to Doughboy: The National Debate over Integrating American Indians into the Military, 1891–1918." *Western Historical Quarterly* 17 (October): 417–437.

Terrett, Dulany. 1956. *The Signal Corps: The Emergency (to December 1941). (United States Army in World War II: The Technical Services).* Department of the Army, Office of the Chief of Military History, United States Army. Washington, D.C.: U.S. Government Printing Office.

Thompson, George Raynor, and Dixie R. Harris. 1966. *The Signal Corps: The Outcome (Mid 1943 through 1945). (United States Army in World War II: The Technical Services, vol. 3).* Department of the Army, Office of the Chief of Military History, United States Army. Washington, D.C.: U.S. Government Printing Office.

Thompson, George Raynor, Dixie R. Harris, Pauline M. Oakes, and Dulany Terrett. 1957. *The Signal Corps: The Test (December 1941 to July 1943). (United States Army in World War II: The Technical Services, vol. 2).* Department of the Army, Office of the Chief of Military History, United States Army. Washington, D.C.: U.S. Government Printing Office.

Thornton, Russell. 1987. *American Indian Holocaust and Survival: A Population History since 1492.* Norman: University of Oklahoma Press.

Time-Life Books. 1993. *The Way of the Warrior.* The American Indian Series. Alexandria, Va.: Time-Life Books.

Townsend, Kenneth W. 2000. *World War II and the American Indian.* Albuquerque: University of New Mexico Press.

Treadwell, Major Jack L. 1957. "The Platoon That Suckered the Siegfried Line." *Male* 7 (11): 14, 66–70.

United States Army, 4th Infantry Division. 1946. *4th Infantry Division.* Washington, D.C.: United States Army, 4th Infantry Division.

United States Department of Commerce. 1937. *Fifteenth Census of the United States: 1930. The Indian Population of the United States and Alaska.* Prepared under the supervision of Dr. Leon E. Truesdell, Chief Statistician for Population. Washington, D.C.: United States Government Printing Office.

United States Department of the Interior. 1939. *Statistical Supplement to the Annual Report of the Commissioner of Indian Affairs. For the Fiscal Year Ended June 30, 1939.* Tables II and III. Washington, D.C.: United States Government Printing Office.

———. 1940. *Annual Report of the Commissioner of Indian Affairs.* Washington, D.C.: United States Government Printing Office.

———. 1945. *Statistical Supplement to the Annual Report of the Commissioner of Indian Affairs. For the Fiscal Year Ended June 30, 1945.* Tables I and II. Washington, D.C.: United States Government Printing Office.

Utter, Jack. 1993. *American Indians: Answers to Today's Questions*. Lake Ann, Mich.: National Woodlands Publishing Company.

Van Der Rhoer, Edward. 1978. *Deadly Magic*. New York: Scribners.

Vogt, Evon. 1948. "Navajo Veterans: A Study of Acculturation." Ph.D. diss., Department of Anthropology, University of Chicago.

———. 1949. "Between Two Worlds: Case Study of a Navajo Veteran." *American Indian* 5 (1): 13–21.

———. 1951. *Navajo Veterans: A Study in Changing Values*. Papers of the Peabody Museum of American Archaeology and Ethnology (41).

Walker, Willard. 1980. "Incidental Intelligence on the Cryptographic Use of Muskogee Creek in World War II Tactical Operations by the United States Army." *International Journal of American Linguistics* 46 (2): 144–145.

———. 1983. "More on the Cryptographic Use of Native American Languages in Tactical Operations by United States Armed Forces." *International Journal of American Linguistics* 49 (1): 93–97.

Wallace, Ernest, and E. Adamson Hoebel. 1952. *The Comanches: Lords of the South Plains*. Norman: University of Oklahoma Press.

Watson, Bruce. 1993. "Navajo Code Talkers: A Few Good Men." *Smithsonian* 24 (5): 34–45.

Weigley, Russell F. 1981. *Eisenhower's Lieutenants: The Campaign of France and Germany, 1944–1945*. Bloomington: Indiana University Press.

Whirlwind Soldier, Lydia. 1995. "Bilingualism vs. Monolingualism in a Non-Progressive State." *Wicazo Sa Review* 11 (1): 64–65.

White, Lonnie J. 1978. "Major General Edwin St. John Grebel." *Military History of Texas and the Southwest* 14 (1): 7–20.

———. 1979. "Indian Soldiers of the 36th Division." *Military History of Texas and the Southwest* 15: 7–20.

———. 1996. *The 90th Division in World War I: The Texas-Oklahoma Draft Division in the Great War*. Manhattan, Kans.: Sunflower University Press.

White, Richard. 1982. *The Roots of Dependency: Subsistence, Environment, and Social Change among the Choctaws, Pawnees, and Navajos*. Lincoln: University of Nebraska Press.

White, W. Bruce. 1976. "The American Indian as Soldier, 1890–1919." *Canadian Review of American Studies* 7 (Spring): 15–25.

NEWSPAPER SOURCES

Anadarko Daily News. 2000a. "G.I. Joe to Honor War Code Talkers." March 2.

———. 2000b. "Language Preservation: Saving Comanche on the Computer." May 6–7.

———. 2001a. "Code Talkers Helped America Win Wars." November 27.

———. 2001b. "Code Talkers to Receive Medals for WWII Service." July 25.

Arizona Republic. 1992. "Pentagon Honors Navajos, Code Nobody Could Break." September 18.

———. 2001. "Forgotten Heroes. Non-Navajo Code Talkers Seeking Equal Recognition," by Mark Shaffer. January 6.

Cannoneer (military base newspaper, Ft. Sill, Oklahoma). 1992. "Comanche

270   Code Talkers Plan Weekend Reunion," story and photo by Jean Schucker. September 24.

Daily Oklahoman. 1917. "Fifteen Tribes Represented in Indian Company." November 18.

———. 1987a. "French Draw Attention To Indians' War Service." April 6.

———. 1987b. "Indian Nations among Nominees for French Honor," by Ellen Knickmeyer. April 6.

———. 1988. "Ceremony to Remember Comanche Code Talkers," by James Johnson. May 30.

———. 1989. "In Plain English: Thank You! Ceremony Honors Wartime Code Talkers." November 5.

———. 1992. "Comanche 'Code Talkers' Reminisce on War," Associated Press, St. Louis. August 18.

———. 1997. "Slain State Soldier Gets WWII Honor." January 14.

———. 1999. "Army Honors 'Code Talker,'" Associated Press, Washington, D.C., December 1.

Donovan, Bill. 1992. "Navajo Code Talkers Made History without Knowing It." *Arizona Republic*, August 14.

Durant Daily Democrat. 1979. "Durant in the Past." August 16.

———. 1966. "Ends with Death of Walter Veach." October 17 or 18.

Fort Worth Star Telegram. 1919. January 19 and June 11.

Lawton Constitution. 1983. "Comanche Unit Had Unique Role in World War II," by Tom Sharrock. July 9.

———. 1987. "'Code-Talking' Indians to be Honored by France." February 12.

———. 1989. "Comanches vs. the Nazis: Radio Messages Were Unbreakable Code, and Code Talker Saw Brutal Fighting," by Steve Metzer. October 3.

———. 1992. "Comanche Code Talkers Celebrate Service," by Kim McConnell. September 8.

———. 1994. "Comanche 'Code Talkers' Interviewed about D-Day Experiences," by Kim McConnell. May 26.

———. 1996. Obituary for Forrest Kassanavoid. September 22.

———. 1997. Obituary for Roderick Red Elk. September 26.

Lawton Morning Press. 1987. "French to Honor Sooner Indian 'Code Talkers.'" February 12.

Levine, Capt. Lincoln A. 1921. "Amazing Code Machine That Sent Messages Safely to U.S. Army in War Baffles Experts: Warfare Tricks That Puzzled Germans." *New York American*, November 13.

McAlester News—Capital and Democrat. 1989. "Choctaw Codetalker 'Just Doing Job' in Smashing Line," by James Beaty. November 15.

New York Sun. 1938. "Choctaw Stopped War Wire Tappers: Germans at St. Mihiel Finally Circumvented by Indians of the U.S. Forces." The Sun's Rays [column]. February 2.

New York Times. 1940. "Comanches Again Called for Army Code Services." December 13.

———. 1941a. "Indians' Code Upsets Foe: They Speed Dialect Messages by Radio in War Games." August 31.

———. 1941b. "Indians Volunteer for Defense Army. To Speak Another Dialect" (special to the *New York Times*, Omaha, Nebraska, February 15). February 16.

———. 1945. "Navajo Code Talk Kept Foe Guessing: Indians with Marines, Using Rare Native Tongue, Insured Secrecy of Messages," by T/Sgt. Murray Marder. September 19.

Plunkett, Barry. 1987. "Oklahoma's Greatest War Hero Also Choctaw Code Talker." Newspaper clipping, August, courtesy of Judy Allen and the Choctaw nation.

Saville, Guy. 2001. "Speaking in Code." *Independent on Sunday* (London, England). May 6.

Scottsdale Daily Progress. 1981. "Navajo WWII 'Code Talkers' Recalled," by Diana Balazs. April 21.

Sunday Ledger Enquirer. ca. 1941. "The Comanches Aren't Coming, They Have Come—And They're among the Best Men at Benning," by Cal Parker.

Sunday Oklahoman. 1992. "Navajos to Remember WWII Code That Baffled Japanese." August 23.

Tulsa Tribune. 1989. "Unsung Heroes. Indian Code-Talkers Due Honors for Wartime Efforts," by Diana Nelson Jones. March 18.

Tulsa World. 1989. "Comanche Language a Natural Code for Allies during War," by Steve Metzer. October 8, 1989.

Unknown—1. 1942. "Red Men Enjoy White Man's Play War: Oklahoma Indians Answer Army's 1942 Call with Whoop." July. Newspaper clipping from near Ft. Benning, Georgia.

Unknown—2. 1942. "4th Signal Boys Cop Major Bouts on Boxing Card." ca. July. Newspaper clipping from near Ft. Benning, Georgia.

Unknown—3. ca. 1966. "Choctaw Tongue Proved Too Tough for Germans." Newspaper clipping courtesy of Judy Allen and the Choctaw nation.

Unknown—4. ca. 1987. "Choctaw Code-Talkers: Native Language Turns the Tide of Battle." Newspaper clipping courtesy of Judy Allen and the Choctaw nation.

PAMPHLETS, PERIODICALS, AND SPECIAL BULLETINS

American Indian Magazine. 1919. "Played Joke on the Huns." Vol. 7, no. 2, p. 101.

Bishinik (the Choctaw tribal newspaper). 1986a. D.C. "Archives Acknowledge Choctaws as 1st 'Code-Talkers.'" July.

———. 1986b. "Germans Confused by Choctaw Code Talkers." August.

———. 1987a. "Choctaw Language Also Used in WWII for Military Communications." April.

———. 1987b. "Victor Brown 'Fooled the Germans' in France." April.

———. 1989. "Award Presented in Honor of Code-Talkers." November.

———. 1992a. "History of the Choctaw Code-Talkers." August.

———. 1992b. "Schlicht Billy Last Living Choctaw Code-Talker—Enlisted in WWII," by Margie Buckheister. August.

272   ———. 1994a. "Choctaw Men Were Very First Code-Talkers, Using Their Native Language for Secret Messages in WWI." June.

———. 1994b. "Services for WWII Choctaw Code-Talker, Schlicht Billy." January.

———. 1996. "Choctaw Code-Talkers Were Original Ones to Use Native Language in War: 'From Cursing to Code-Talking'" (paper originally written by John Calloway, November 1992). August.

Bucholz, Rodger, William Fields, and Ursula P. Roach. 1996. *20th Century Warriors: Native American Participation in the United States Military*. Prepared for the Department of Defense by CEHIP Inc., Washington, D.C. Washington, D.C.: Department of the Navy—Naval Historical Center, Washington Navy Yard.

Bugle Bulge. 1994. "Ever Heard of 'Code Talkers'?" February, p. 26.

Cotton Electric Current. 1994. "Comanche Indians 'Talking The Talk' Buffalo Germans during World War II." April 18, p. 13.

Crosswind. 1992. "Pentagon Praises American Indians." November 13.

4th Division Motorized. 1942. *4th Signal Grew with Division*, Ivy Leaf Anniversary Edition. Ft. Benning, Ga.

4th Infantry. 2000. Internet information—4thinfantry.org (http://4thinfantry .org/info.html).

HQMC (Head Quarters Marine Corps: Reference Section, History and Museums Division). 1982. "Navajo Code Talkers in World War II." May 14.

Indian Record. 1970. *The American Indian in the World War* (Special Issue: Indians in the Military). Office of Indian Affairs Bulletin 15, Bureau of Indian Affairs. November.

Indians at Work. 1941. Vol. 9, no. 2 (October).

Indian's Friend. 1918. January edition newsletter.

Indian Sign. ca. 1940. This source was a photocopied print from a microfilmed source which had identifying information cut off from the edge. On the basis of four adjacent columns of printed material, it appears to be a newspaper or periodical from the Oklahoma City area.

Ivy Green: History. 2000. "The Fourth Infantry Division: 'The Fighting Fourth'" (http://hood-ivygreen.army.mil/history/history.asp). July 28.

Jones, Renee. n.d. *Comanche Codetalking on D-Day*. Fort George G. Meade, Md.: National Security Agency.

King, Jodi A. 1992. "DOD Dedicates Code Talkers Display." *Pentagram* 24 (September): 3.

Little Eagle, Avis. 1994. "World War II Lakota Code Talkers Used Language to Outwit the Enemy." *Indian Country Today*, June 8.

Marine Corps Chevron. 1943. "Navajos Readying to Make Going Tough for 'Japanazis.'" January 23.

Marine Corps League. 2001. "Navajo Code Talkers Honored." Vol. 57, no. 4, p. 51.

Masterkey. 1941. "Indians as Code Talkers." Vol. 15, no. 6, p. 240.

NIM-FB (National Infantry Museum, Fort Benning, Georgia). n.d. Fourth Signal Company (miscellaneous documents), p. 95. Courtesy of National Infantry Museum, Fort Benning, Georgia.

Norrish, Dick. 1994. "Comanche Code Talkers Entertain Crowds at Heritage America." *Cahokian*, Winter, pp. 6–7. Cahokia Mounds Museum Society, Collinsville, Illinois.

Rodgers, Michael W. n.d. *Indian Code-Talkers of WWII*. Ft. Benning, Ga.: U.S. Army Signal Museum.

Sea Services Weekly. 1992. "DOD Hails Indian Code Talkers." November 27, pp. 9–10.

Senior Scholastic. 1953. "The First Americans Are Last." March 4, pp. 5–6.

Twin Territories. 1991. "History of the Choctaw Code-Talkers." Vol. 1, no. 8, p. 1.

Wigginton, F. Peter. 1992. *Pentagon Ceremony Hails Loyalty of American Indians*. Press pack, American Forces Information Service, Washington, D.C., November 16.

Wright, Mike. 1986. "Unsung Heroes: Indian Military 'Code Talkers.'" *Oklahoma Observer* 18 (20): 19.

ARCHIVAL SOURCES ON NATIVE AMERICAN SERVICEMEN AND CODE TALKERS

BF (Frank, Benis M.) n.d. "Navajo Code Talker in World War II." Memo. Marine Corps Museum.

DDIOHP (Doris Duke Indian Oral History Project, University of Utah). 1970–1971. Includes the following interviews and other materials: Martin Link, July 6 and July 19, 1971; Code Talkers' Reunion, July 7–9, 1971; Code Talkers' banquet, July 10, 1971; Sounds of the Reunion, July 9, 1971; Rapheal Yazzie, July 9, 1991; Phillip Johnston, November 6, 1970; Thomas H. Begay, July 14, 1971; James Nahkai Jr., July 15, 1971; Jimmy King, July 1971; Paul Blatchford, August 16, 1971; Mr. and Mrs. O. C. Haven, July 7, 1971; Wilfred Billey, July 9, 1971; Navajo Code Talkers, July 1971; Dan Akee, July 10, 1971; Rev. R. O. Hawthorne, July 9, 1971.

Duke University Indian Oral History Project. 1970–1971. Interviews with Dan Akee, Sidney Bedoni, Thomas Claw, Teddy Draper, Harold Y. Foster, Rev. R. O. Hawthorn, Samuel T. Holiday, Dennie Hosteen, William McCabe, James Nahkai Jr., Pete Sandoval, Samuel J. Smith Sr., George B. Soce, Frank Thompson, Ralph Yazzie.

MCOHP (Marine Corps Oral History Program). 1971. Marine Corps Historical Center, Washington, D.C. Oral interviews with former Navajo Code Talkers during the first reunion of Navajo Code Talkers of World War II at Window Rock, Arizona, July 9–10, 1971: John Benaly, Judge W. Dean Wilson (William Dean Yazzie), Paul Blatchford, Sidney Bedoni, Alex Williams Sr., Carl Gorman, Wilfred Billey, Jimmy King Sr.

MRB (Military Reference Branch). Record Group 120. Utilization of American Indians as Communications Linguists. Special Research History (SRH) #120, RG457 (declassified by National Security Agency). Letter from A. W. Bloor, Colonel 142nd Infantry to the Commanding General 36th Division (Attention Captain Spence), January 21, 1919.

NARA (National Archives and Records Administration). RG127. Entry 18. Office of the Commandant—General Correspondence (Jan. 1939–Jun. 1950): File #1535-75, folders 13–14, 17–20; file #2185-20, folder 4. Washington, D.C.

274 ———. Study of American Indians. Historical Section, GHQ, Records of the AEF, Records Group 120, National Archives.

ND ("Navajo Dictionary"). n.d. "Code of Navajo Marines in World War II." Declassified DOD DIR 5200.9. Marine Corps, Washington, D.C.

NHCOA (Naval Historical Center, Operational Archives). Washington, D.C. USMC Historical Division Chronological, Box 576, WWII Command File. "Navajo Dictionary." Revised June 15, 1945.

RNSA (Records of the National Security Agency). Central Security Service, Historic Cryptographic Collection, Pre–World War I through World War II. CBM152-34744. SSA Memorandum, "Use of American Indians as Communications Operators."

FILMS

In contrast to the documentation of the Navajos, there is no known film of the Comanche Code Talkers in training or action. Three film sources are known (Oklahoma Historical Society 1989, Meadows 1995a, Hidden Path 2000). Still photography in the collections of surviving code talkers and recent pictures in local museums exist.

Forrest Kassanavoid Memorial Dance. 1997. September 20, Lawton, Oklahoma. Copy in author's possession.

Greystone Communications Inc. 1994. *D-Day: The Total Story.* 3 vols. A&E (Arts and Entertainment) Video.

Hidden Path Productions. 2000. *Comanche Code Talkers. The Last Comanche Code Talker "Recollections of Charles Chibitty."* Mannford, Oklahoma.

Meadows, William C. 1995a. *Comanche Code Talkers of World War II.* Videotaped interview with Roderick Red Elk and Charles Chibitty, August 4, 1995. Hosted and produced by William C. Meadows. A copy of this interview was donated by the author to the Western History Collections, University of Oklahoma.

NAPBC (Native American Public Broadcasting Consortium). 1986. *Navajo Code Talkers.* Lincoln, Nebraska. Produced by Tom McCarthy and KENW-TV. 27:23.

Oklahoma Historical Society. 1989. *Code Talkers Decoration Ceremony.* State Capitol Building, Oklahoma City, Oklahoma. Oral History Collections, Oklahoma Historical Society, November 3.

Tully, Brendan W. 1995. *Navajo Code Talkers: The Epic Story.* Tully Entertainment. 55:00.

Vintage Video. n.d. *The 4th Inf. Division.* Produced by the Army Pictorial Center, United States Army. VH5476.

INTERVIEWS AND CORRESPONDENCE

Allen Judy. 1996. Telephone conversations with Judy Allen, editor of *Bishinik* newspaper, Choctaw Nation of Oklahoma. *Bishinik* newspaper, Drawer 1210.

Miscellaneous biographical materials and research notes on the Choctaw Code Talkers. Copies in author's possession.

Brown, C. Alton. 1987. Letter to Mike Wright, February 9, 1987. Copy courtesy of Mike Wright.

Chibitty, Charles. 1995. Interviews and phone conversations with the author, 1995–2001.

Codynah, Haddon. 1987. Interview with Joe Todd, April 8, 1987. Oklahoma Historical Society, Oklahoma City, Oklahoma. OHS tape numbers 87.16.a and 87.16.b.

Eckert, John. 2000. Norristown, Pennsylvania. Telephone conversation with the author, March 4, 2000; letter to the author March 12, 2000.

Foster, Hugh F., Jr., Major General U.S. Army (Retired). 1991. Interview with Towana Spivey at Ft. Sill Museum Archives, Lawton, Oklahoma, May 16.

———. 1995. Correspondence with the author, January 23, 1995, February 7, 1995, April 12, 1995, February 24, 1996, March 3, 1996, March 5, 1996.

———. 1996. Telephone conversations with the author, February 21, 1996, February 5, 2001.

Karty, William (Bill). 1988. Interview with Joe Todd, May 25. Oklahoma Historical Society, Oklahoma City, Oklahoma. OHS tape numbers 88.75.a and 88.75.b.

———. 1990. November. Conversation with the author. Norman, Oklahoma.

Kassanavoid, Forrest. 1993–1996. Interviews with the author, July 12, 1993, February 18, 1994, November 22, 1994, April 25, 1995, January 11, 1996, January 29, 1996, and July 23, 1996.

Kavanagh, Thomas W. 1996. Personal communication to the author, June 6.

———. 2001. E-mail to the author, March 19.

Nahquaddy, Albert (Edward), Jr. 1996. Interview with the author, July 24.

Peterson, Trudy Huskamp. 1986. Acting Assistant Archivist for the National Archives to James R. Jones, House of Representatives, Washington, D.C., September 11, 1986. National Archives and Records Administration, Washington, D.C.

Red Elk, Roderick. 1988. Interview with Joe Todd, June 21. Oklahoma Historical Society, Oklahoma City, Oklahoma. OHS tape numbers 88.90.a and 88.90.b.

———. 1995. Interviews with the author, January 10, 1995, August 4, 1995, July 23, 1996.

Stahlberg, Ernest. 2000. Hendersonville, North Carolina. Letters to the author, January 29, February 25, March 9.

Tsatoke, John. 1987. Letter to Mike Wright, March 23. Copy courtesy of Mike Wright.

Wright, Mike. 1987. Scientific Social Research to Dr. C. Alton Brown, Honorary French Consul, March 3. Scientific Social Research to Persons Involved in Code-Talker Research, February 18, March 28. Scientific Social Research to Mr. Gerard Dumond, Consulat General de France, March 26. Copies courtesy of Mike Wright.

i·n·d·e·x